REVIVALISM AND SEPARAT[
IN NEW ENGLAND, 1740–1800

Also by C. C. Goen

Broken Churches, Broken Nation: Denominational Schisms and the Coming of the American Civil War

REVIVALISM AND SEPARATISM IN NEW ENGLAND, 1740–1800

Strict Congregationalists and Separate Baptists in the Great Awakening

C. C. GOEN

With a New Introduction

The Frank S. and Elizabeth D. Brewer Prize Essay of the American Society of Church History

Wesleyan University Press
Middletown, Connecticut

LIBRARY OF CONGRESS CATALOGING-IN-PUBLICATION DATA

Goen, C. C.
 Revivalism and separatism in New England, 1740–1800: Strict Congregationalists and
Separate Baptists in the Great Awakening / by C. C. Goen: with a new preface by the author.
—1st Wesleyan ed.
  p.   cm.
 Reprint. Originally published: New Haven: Yale University Press, 1962.
 Bibliography: p.
 Includes index.
 ISBN 0-8195-5186-4
 ISBN 0-8195-6133-9 (pbk.):
 1. Great Awakening. 2. Dissenters, Religious—New England—History—18th century.
3. Congregational churches—New England—History—18th century. 4. Baptists—New
England—History—18th century. 5. New England—Church history. I. Title.
BR520.G6 1987
277.4'07—dc19   87-18350
                                                                             CIP

All inquiries and permissions requests should be addressed to the Publisher,
Wesleyan University Press, 110 Mt. Vernon Street, Middletown,
Connecticut 06457.

Distributed by Harper & Row Publishers, Keystone Industrial Park,
Scranton, Pennsylvania 18512.

Manufactured in the United States of America

Wesleyan Paperback, 1987

To Betty

CONTENTS

MAPS

INTRODUCTION TO
THE WESLEYAN EDITION

When this book first appeared twenty-five years ago, one reviewer greeted it with the exuberant exclamation, "Harken, Church History majors in quest of a thesis topic—Mr. Goen may well be your patron saint." He predicted that *Revivalism and Separatism* "should keep others . . . busy for some time to come" because it "has opened a well-stocked cache of new research possibilities." [1] Other scholars, somewhat more restrained, remarked in various ways that the book broke new ground in the exploration of eighteenth-century American religious history. Some thought it raised about as many questions as it answered. I was not unhappy about that and readily confessed that such a result had been part of my intention. Since no book, even less one that attempts to explore previously uncharted territory, either can or should attempt to answer all possible questions, the problem is to decide which questions to raise, which ones to try to answer, and which ones to leave for others. That dictated my choice of a panoptic perspective, as described in the first preface and defended in the second (1969). It still seems to me that the choice was correct, and I continue to uphold it. Judging from my correspondence over the years, I surmise that directly or indirectly *Revivalism and Separatism* has stimulated several studies that carried my tentative investigation further, with positive consequences for historical understanding.

A few years ago a new study of sectarian movements in eighteenth-century New England began by noting the growing recognition of the importance of sects to American history. The author commented,

> A new line of interpretation opened in 1962 with C. C. Goen's exploration of religious dissent as a function of revivalism. Since

1. Oscar Walter Roberts, review of *Revivalism and Separatism, Union Seminary Quarterly Review* 18 (1963): 177.

then, there has appeared a wide range of new studies investigating the political and intellectual dimensions of sectarian movements. A fair measure of the new historical awareness of sects is the prominent place they occupy in the general histories of American religion written by Sydney Ahlstrom, Winthrop Hudson, and Robert T. Handy.[2]

And so the book's influence goes on—sometimes in ways I could not foresee at the time I wrote it.

I was gratified, therefore, when the Wesleyan University Press proposed to reissue the work. For one thing, the book's renewed availability will ease the frustration of having to reply hopelessly to those who still ask my help in locating a copy for purchase. (I have never seen the volume in a used bookstore or listed in a used book catalog. The few people I know who have found a copy through a rare-book search service have told me that the price was fifty dollars or more.) On the other hand, I confess to harboring some ambivalence about seeing it reissued. The historiography of the Great Awakening in New England has advanced far beyond my original work, not only in the unearthing of more source materials but also in the intensity and method of analysis. By *intensity* I refer mainly to a growing list of local studies, many of them focused on a single town or parish, that allow the authors to test many of the generalizations offered in my panoramic overview. In addition, both local and regional studies have exploited methods of social history and psychobiography considerably more sophisticated than those I knew in 1960. Such methods have delivered some fascinating possibilities for analyzing revivalistic conversion, the phenomena of separatism, and the overall impact of the Great Awakening.

SOME EXAMPLES OF RECENT SCHOLARSHIP

Among the more interesting local studies of recent years is that of Mansfield, Connecticut. In 1968 I was pleasurably surprised to receive a letter bearing a return address on Separatist Road in Storrs, Connecticut. The writer, James H. Barnett, professor of sociology at the University of Connecticut, told me that he and his wife lived on a tract of land embracing the site of the old Mansfield Separate Church. Although nothing remained except a few stones of the building's founda-

2. Stephen A. Marini, *Radical Sects in Revolutionary New England* (Cambridge, MA: Harvard University Press, 1982), 3. Marini focused primarily on Freewill Baptists, Universalists, and Shakers, all of whom drew significant strength from groups described in *Revivalism and Separatism*.

tion, Professor and Mrs. Barnett decided to investigate the history of the church. A thorough search of local and state archives turned up no records of the church itself but did yield enough clues to enable the Barnetts to piece together a reasonably satisfying account. Their work took ten years and in 1978 bore fruit in *On the Trail of a Legend*, a brochure of seventy-six pages whose title suggests the difficulty of reaching firm factual results in this kind of enterprise.[3] The Barnetts discovered several errors that other authors, myself included, had carried forward from Isaac Backus and his contemporaries, and they tested several common generalizations that attempt to explain the rise and decline of separatism. A few were substantiated, a few questioned, others left in abeyance.

Revivalism and separatism in Norwich, also in eastern Connecticut, have been explored with considerable sophistication by J. M. Bumsted and Gerald F. Moran. Beginning with 1718 and working up through the Great Awakening, Moran studied the subjects of conversion and discovered that in the 1740s, conversion "did not represent a cross section of the town, but rather appealed to the economically and socially less established members of the community"—thus providing new evidence on a dimension of the revivals that is still under lively investigation.[4] Bumsted, whose dissertation on the ecclesiastical history of colonial southeastern Massachusetts well equipped him to understand the impact of the Great Awakening, discovered a complex of factors leading to the withdrawal of Norwich dissidents from the pastoral care of Benjamin Lord. Almost from the beginning of troubles, Bumsted wrote, "it becomes difficult to distinguish between opponents motivated predominantly by evangelical pietism and those motivated by other reasons. Those clearly identifiable as radical pietists, totally opposed to the parish system, constituted a minority of the adherents of the 'Separate' position." Bumsted's careful sorting—and the difficulties that it encountered—resulted from a close examination of local tax

3. James H. and Esther D. Barnett, *On the Trail of a Legend: The Separatist Movement in Mansfield, Connecticut, 1745–1769* (Mansfield, CT: Mansfield Historical Society, 1978). That the Barnetts, living on the very site, spent ten years "on the trail" without reaching decisive confirmation of all aspects of the "legend" is a cautionary tale in itself. Other would-be students of this movement, take heed!

4. Gerald F. Moran, "Conditions of Religious Conversion in the First Society of Norwich, Connecticut, 1718–1744," *Journal of Social History* 5 (1971–72): 338. For generalizations regarding the economic and social status of the subjects of the revival, see Edwin S. Gaustad, *The Great Awakening in New England* (New York: Harper & Row, 1957), 43–47; Goen, *Revivalism and Separatism*, 188–91; and Winthrop S. Hudson, *Religion in America*, 4th ed. (New York: Macmillan, 1987), 72–73.

rolls, land transactions, probate records, and other archival materials.[5]

New London, Connecticut, long known as the scene of riotous revivalism and insurgent separatism, has been the subject of several scholarly investigations. Most informative are the studies of Peter Onuf, who discovered the previously unknown records of the New London Separate Church in a mislabeled file box at the Connecticut State Library. On the basis of these and other local records, he was able to draw a "group portrait" of the Separates showing that they represented few of the old-line families of the town and that their pre-revival connections with the standing church were quite tenuous. On the average, they tended to be younger and poorer than long-time members of that church and to include more men and fewer heads of households.[6] Onuf later collaborated with Harry Stout in a new study of James Davenport, "prodigal of the Great Awakening" (discussed herein on pages 19–27), whom they reinterpreted as more than an aberrant fanatic. Seen in wider context, Davenport emerged as a sign of "a crisis in the ministerial profession, rapid social change, popular rebellion against established authority, lay congregationalism, and [various] economic and social factors," all of which portended "a frighteningly new cultural landscape." [7]

Probably the best-known (and most studied) separation, in Connecticut at least, occurred in Canterbury. John W. Jeffries has taken another look at the copious records with an eye to nonreligious factors in the schism. He discovered that the division was not along lines of wealth, age, sex, or geography, but between the old established families who dominated politics and others with about as much wealth but less political power. The separation was opposed mainly by those with traditionally close ties to the political and religious establishment, who had a natural interest in its continued dominance.[8]

5. John Michael Bumsted, "The Pilgrim's Progress: The Ecclesiastical History of the Old Colony, 1620–1775" (Ph.D. diss., Brown University, 1965); idem, "Revivalism and Separatism in New England: The First Society in Norwich, Connecticut, as a Case Study," *William and Mary Quarterly* 24 (1967): 606.

6. Peter S. Onuf, "New Light in New London: A Group Portrait of the Separatists," *William and Mary Quarterly* 37 (1980): 627–43. Additional "new light on New London" is supplied in Richard Warch's fine article, "The Shepherd's Tent: Education and Enthusiasm in the Great Awakening," *American Quarterly* 30 (1978): 177–98 (see p. 63 herein).

7. Harry S. Stout and Peter S. Onuf, "James Davenport and the Great Awakening in New London," *Journal of American History* 70 (1983–84): 558. Less insightful is Robert W. Brockway, "The Significance of James Davenport in the Great Awakening," *Journal of Religious Thought* 24 (1967–68): 86–94, which simply draws, with little evidence of new research, from Brockway's 1951 dissertation of the same title.

8. John W. Jeffries, "The Separation in the Canterbury Congregational Church:

William F. Willingham pursued demographic studies of Windham, Connecticut, and concluded that religious experience correlated closely with the social psychology of the community. His findings also confirmed the thesis of Philip Greven concerning how changes in family life conditioned patterns of religious experience.[9] J. M. Bumsted's close study of local records enabled him to construct a social profile of Norton, Massachusetts, in the time of the Great Awakening. Bumsted found that a shortage of available land and a series of crop failures had frustrated the younger men, making them susceptible to the leveling force of a new religious appeal. When their minister opposed the revival, this young, landless, and politically powerless class, most of whom had come into the parish church in recent years, separated from that church. Various others joined them, so that factions in the ensuing church struggle "cut across generations [and] socio-economic status." [10] Such conclusions partially contradict simplistic generalizations about age and class conflict; and although they provide more accurate close-up pictures, they leave us somewhere short of firm conclusions about the sociological determinants of separatism. The need for continued scholarly attention to specific towns and churches, therefore, is evident.

Biographical studies of lesser-known figures are likewise rewarding. In a recent article of sensitivity and insight, Leigh Eric Schmidt has rescued from oblivion and calumny Andrew Croswell, pastor of the Eleventh Congregational Church in Boston, a figure fully as fascinating and significant as James Davenport. Mark A. Noll has shed important new light on Ebenezer Devotion, pastor of the Third Parish in Windham from 1735 to 1771; and publication of the diary of Solomon Prentice has called new attention to another colorful character.[11]

Religion, Family, and Politics in a Connecticut Town," *New England Quarterly* 52 (1979): 522–49.

9. William Floyd Willingham, "Windham, Connecticut: Profile of a Revolutionary Community, 1755–1818" (Ph.D. diss., Northwestern University, 1972); idem, "The Conversion Experience During the Great Awakening in Windham, Connecticut," *Connecticut History* 21 (1980): 34–61; and idem, "Religious Conversion and the Second Society of Windham, Connecticut, 1723–1743: A Case Study," *Societas* 6 (1976): 109–19. Cf. Philip J. Greven, Jr., *The Protestant Temperament: Patterns of Child-Rearing, Religious Experience, and the Self in Early America* (New York: Knopf, 1977).

10. See J. M. Bumsted, "Religion, Finance, and Democracy in Massachusetts: The Town of Norton as a Case Study," *Journal of American History* 57 (1970–71): 817–31.

11. Leigh Eric Schmidt, " 'A Second and Glorious Reformation': The New Light Extremism of Andrew Croswell," *William and Mary Quarterly* 43 (1986): 214–44; Mark A. Noll, "Ebenezer Devotion: Religion and Society in Revolutionary Connecticut," *Church History* 45 (1976): 293–307; W. Ross Beales, Jr., ed., "Solomon Prentice's Narrative of the Great Awakening," *Proceedings of the Massachu-*

Regional and comparative studies enlarge the focus somewhat. James Patrick Walsh has examined the pure-church idea in eighteenth-century Connecticut, while Howard Frederic Vos has restudied the Great Awakening in the same colony; both studies attempt, in different ways, to set the revival and the resultant controversies more firmly in the social and political context of the times.[12] Elizabeth C. Nordbeck has produced a fine study of the Great Awakening in northern New England, fleshing out the New Light character of many churches and communities treated only sketchily or not at all in *Revivalism and Separatism*.[13] Remembering that eighteenth-century revivalism was a transatlantic affair, at least two scholars have offered useful comparative studies: John William Raimo focused on Boston and Bristol, while Michael J. Crawford looked more broadly at the origins of revivalism in England and America.[14]

For unexcelled (and probably unexcellable) scope, and in many respects depth, however, one must turn to the magisterial work by William G. McLoughlin, *New England Dissent, 1630–1833: The Baptists and the Separation of Church and State*.[15] In 1,348 pages McLoughlin tells in massive detail the story of every phase, down to the final abolition of compulsory religious taxation in Massachusetts in 1833, of New England's hard-fought battles for religious liberty. Since the Separates and Separate Baptists bore the brunt of that struggle in the crucial last half of the eighteenth century, McLoughlin devotes more pages to them than there are in the whole of *Revivalism and Separatism*. I have registered my reactions to this work in a review

setts *Historical Society* 83 (1971): 130–47. The unpublished diary of Stephen Williams of Longmeadow, MA (at the Longmeadow Public Library), has been fruitfully exploited by Mary Catherine Foster, "Hampshire County, Massachusetts, 1729–1754: A Covenant Society in Transition" (Ph.D. diss., University of Michigan, 1967); and Patricia J. Tracy, *Jonathan Edwards, Pastor: Religion and Society in Eighteenth-Century Northampton* (New York: Hill & Wang, 1980).

12. James Patrick Walsh, "The Pure Church in Eighteenth-Century Connecticut" (Ph.D. diss., Columbia University, 1967); and Howard Frederic Vos, "The Great Awakening in Connecticut" (Ph.D. diss., Northwestern University, 1967).

13. Elizabeth Currier Nordbeck, "The New England Diaspora: A Study of the Religious Culture of Maine and New Hampshire, 1613–1763" (Ph.D. diss., Harvard University, 1978). Nordbeck has summarized her dissertation in "Almost Awakened: The Great Revival in New Hampshire and Maine, 1727–1748," *Historical New Hampshire* 35 (1980): 23–58.

14. John William Raimo, "Spiritual Harvest: The Anglo-American Revival in Boston, Massachusetts, and Bristol, England, 1739–1742" (Ph.D. diss., University of Wisconsin, 1974); and Michael J. Crawford, "The Invention of the American Revival: The Beginnings of Anglo-American Religious Revivalism, 1690–1750" (Ph.D. diss., Boston University, 1978).

15. 2 vols. (Cambridge, MA: Harvard University Press, 1971).

published shortly after it appeared,[16] and here again I speak with appreciation of the diligence and detail that give it enduring value. In pursuit of his principal theme (there are many subthemes, too) McLoughlin centered primarily on those aspects of the Separate/ Separate Baptist movements bearing on the issue of religious liberty. But he did so on the basis of sustained digging in local archives and an admirable grasp of the wider context in which local events have larger meaning. This research allowed him to go much farther in sociological interpretation than I did in *Revivalism and Separatism*. In fact, McLoughlin's earlier review of my book was in large part a sustained polemic against my failure to exploit more fully the local records that could have given more substance to the section on "Non-Theological Factors in the Separate Movement" (pages 185–93 herein).[17] Although he criticized me severely then for "an excessively theological approach" ("ecclesiological" would be more accurate), he concluded in *New England Dissent* that the basic issue on which the separations turned actually was the freedom and purity of the church, "the question of reforming Christianity to conform to the original gospel and practice of Jesus and his disciplines [*sic*, disciples?]."[18] I take this as confirmation of my long-standing belief that people are often moved primarily by the force of religious convictions, which was the underlying presupposition of *Revivalism and Separatism*.

It is nevertheless quite evident that recent historical writing on the Great Awakening ranges far beyond the assumptions and categories of my work. Outstanding among the new interpretations is Richard L. Bushman's *From Puritan to Yankee: Character and the Social Order in Connecticut, 1690–1765*. Drawing on psychoanalytic theory, Bushman explained Puritan susceptibility to conversion in terms of guilt produced by resisting divinely ordained authority and yielding to the drives for wealth and power. Experiencing conflict between their prideful ambition and the long-inculcated duties of humility and submission to authority, people responded readily to the awakening preachers' condemnations of sin and offers of God's mercy. Inasmuch as "the Awakening affected people of all classes," Bushman concluded that "a psychological earthquake had reshaped the human landscape." As a result, those who found peace with God through an intensely personal experience tasted a new freedom to contest with earthly powers. "Far from instilling submission to the old authority," Bushman noted, "the revival planted the conviction that God's power was given to individuals, clearing the way for men to resist in good conscience when

16. *William and Mary Quarterly*, 28 (1971): 664–66.
17. *William and Mary Quarterly* 20 (1963): 284–89.
18. Pp. 343, 428.

the occasion arose." The occasions did arise—in the establishment's attempt to suppress the revival and, later, in the Stamp Act and all of England's other "intolerable acts" against the colonies—and in every case, the New Lights were in the forefront of resistance. Out of their experiences in the revival they began to create a new social order more conformable to their emerging new identity, and in the process they were transformed "from Puritan to Yankee." [19]

From a similar perspective, Cushing Strout investigated a neglected aspect of the revival in "Young People of the Awakening: The Dynamics of a Social Movement." (Almost all the contemporary accounts of the Awakening testify to its immense appeal to the young, and it is curious that this group has not been examined more intensively.) Strout found the same psychosocial dynamics among this group that Bushman had identified in the population at large, and he concluded that the revival undermined the respect for authority traditionally impressed upon the young, making possible for them a new group identity and a new politics.[20] I would add only that this transition took place most visibly among the Separates, who not only resisted the established powers but also institutionalized their dissent in free churches where they could actively take charge of their own affairs. Such movements carry the possibility of enormous political as well as religious consequences.

Gary Nash, whose impressive study of American cities in the last half of the eighteenth century sparkles with many fresh insights, confirmed the conclusions of both Bushman and Strout. Impressed by the large number of young, poor, and powerless attracted to the revival, Nash wrote, "For almost all the awakened, but especially for those from the lower echelons, the revival years involved an expansion of political consciousness and a new feeling of self-importance, as people partook of spontaneous meetings, assumed a new power in ecclesias-

19. Richard L. Bushman, *From Puritan to Yankee: Character and the Social Order in Connecticut, 1690–1765* (Cambridge, MA: Harvard University Press, 1967), pp. 185, 187, 227, and passim. Also helpful for understanding conversion in psychodynamic terms, although focused primarily on the seventeenth century, are Patricia Caldwell, *The Puritan Conversion Narrative: The Beginnings of American Expression* (New York: Cambridge University Press, 1983); and Charles Lloyd Cohen, *God's Caress: The Psychology of Puritan Religious Experience* (New York: Oxford University Press, 1986).

20. Cushing Strout, "Young People of the Great Awakening: The Dynamics of a Social Movement," in *Encounter with Erikson: Historical Interpretation and Religious Biography*, eds. Donald Capps, Walter H. Capps, and M. Gerald Bradford (Missoula, MT: Scholars Press, 1977), 183–216. See also Strout's "Fathers and Sons: Notes on 'New Light' and 'New Left' Young People as a Historical Comparison," *Psychohistorical Review* 6 (1977–78): 25–31.

tical affairs, and were encouraged repeatedly from the pulpit to adopt an attitude of skepticism toward dogma and authority." The leaders of the revival, Nash concluded, were preaching a truly radical message, one that would come to fruition only in the Revolution and the experiment in nation building that was to follow.[21]

Such interpretations do not explain everything about the Awakening and its aftermath, of course, but I find them exceptionally stimulating. I am somewhat chagrined that in 1960 I did not perceive some of the more radical implications of the materials I dealt with in writing this book. Now, after a larger quantity and variety of data have been examined more closely and some of their implications drawn out more imaginatively, perhaps the most that can be claimed for *Revivalism and Separatism* is that it stands as some kind of base line from which the newer interpretations have proceeded. That modest achievement, I believe, is ample justification for republishing it in the late 1980s.

POSSIBILITIES FOR FURTHER INVESTIGATION

Several issues remain unresolved. More local studies of the type described above are needed. Beyond further efforts to ascertain whether certain generalizations are still warranted, the scholarly agenda now includes a question as to the viability of the very term *Great Awakening*. The issue was raised by Jon Butler, who decried the label as nothing more than "interpretative fiction." Jousting with just about everybody in print, Butler argued that the Awakening was not "great and general" but merely a series of local or regional events, that it affected only half the colonies, that it was not uniquely American, and that it had little or no political influence—especially on the Revolution—and small effect even on church growth.[22] Butler probably won't carry many of those points, but he has raised some important issues nevertheless. I should think that after a sufficient number of careful local studies, the next significant step would be for some well-equipped scholar to essay a general history of the whole Awakening to assess more accurately its overall impact throughout the British colonies of North America. Two recent surveys are useful as introductions, but their brevity and lack of documentation leave major questions unanswered. Like the many source books that have appeared in the last two decades, they focus mainly on New England, giving sec-

21. Gary B. Nash, *The Urban Crucible: Social Change, Political Consciousness, and the Origins of the American Revolution* (Cambridge, MA: Harvard University Press, 1979), 215.

22. Jon Butler, "Enthusiasm Described and Decried: The Great Awakening as Interpretative Fiction," *Journal of American History* 69 (1982): 305–25.

ondary attention to the Middle Colonies, some to Virginia, and little or none to the rest of the country.[23]

Another question—hardly yet raised, much less explored—concerns the role of women in the Awakening. Several women converts are described in Jonathan Edwards's *Faithful Narrative* (1737), and in *Some Thoughts on the Revival* (1742) his most fully described exemplar of evangelical piety is a woman.[24] Rereading *Revivalism and Separatism* with consciousness newly raised by the feminist awakening, I found only one reference to women preaching—and that is not even indexed! (It's on page 130, where Ebenezer Frothingham, a Separate leader, defends women exhorters.) Andrew Croswell, the New Light preacher of Boston, also defended women preachers in *A Letter . . . to the Rev. Mr. Turell* (Boston, 1742), while Charles Chauncy often condemned those who permitted "WOMEN, yea, GIRLS to speak in the assemblies for religious worship." These references are evidence that women were active among the New Lights; and in spite of what social historians are uncovering about the predominance of young males, it is clear that the Awakening was not solely a man's movement. These unsilent women need to be dug out of the records and brought to historical visibility.

Another understudied dimension of the Awakening is its rhetoric. When I was engaged in my recent research on the slavery controversy in the antebellum churches, a professional rhetorician pointed out that preachers did a great deal by their sermons to create and sustain public attitudes, and that a technical analysis of their rhetorical strategy could deliver new insights for understanding the historical situation. Applying that wisdom to the eighteenth century, I suggest that not enough

23. J. M. Bumsted and John E. Van de Wetering, *What Must I Do to Be Saved? The Great Awakening in Colonial America* (Hinsdale, IL: Dryden Press, 1976); and Cedric B. Cowing, *The Great Awakening and the American Revolution: Colonial Thought in the 18th Century* (Chicago: Rand McNally, 1971). The former is a modest survey; the latter, notwithstanding its character as an essay in intellectual history, is the more broadly focused. The most comprehensive source book is Alan Heimert and Perry Miller, eds., *The Great Awakening: Documents Illustrating the Crisis and Its Consequences* (Indianapolis: Bobbs-Merrill, 1967); also useful are Richard L. Bushman, ed., *The Great Awakening: Documents on the Revival of Religion, 1740–1745* (New York: Atheneum, 1970); J. M. Bumsted, ed., *The Great Awakening: The Beginning of Evangelical Pietism in America* (Waltham, MA: Blaisdell, 1970); Douglas Sloan, ed., *The Great Awakening and American Education: A Documentary History* (New York: Teachers College, 1973); David S. Lovejoy, ed., *Religious Enthusiasm and the Great Awakening* (Englewood Cliffs, NJ: Prentice-Hall, 1969); and Darrett B. Rutman, ed., *The Great Awakening: Event and Exegesis* (New York: Wiley, 1970).

24. *The Great Awakening*, ed. C. C. Goen, vol. 4 of *The Works of Jonathan Edwards*, gen. ed. John E. Smith (New Haven: Yale University Press, 1972), 68–70, 331–41; the "exemplar" was his wife, Sarah.

has been done in rhetorical studies of the Great Awakening and the sectarian movements that emerged in its wake. Most students of the Awakening, if they consider sermons at all, treat them as theological treatises, literary texts, or political statements. Few analyze the sermons as rhetorical devices, instruments of a strategy of persuasion that would decisively influence the shaping of public oratory in America, political as well as religious.

An early clue to the possibilities of this line of investigation came from Perry Miller, who examined Jonathan Edwards's adaptation of Lockean psychology to the strategy of preaching in his essay on "Edwards, Locke, and the Rhetoric of Sensation," first published in 1950 and reprinted in the author's collection of essays, *Errand into the Wilderness*. Edward M. Collins, Jr., a speech scholar, pursued Miller's suggestion in "The Rhetoric of Sensation Challenges the Rhetoric of the Intellect," an article contrasting Edwards and James Davenport with Charles Chauncy. Another early study came from Eugene E. White, who in 1951 published a brief study of Whitefield, Tennent, and Davenport; he followed this work in 1972 with *Puritan Rhetoric: The Issue of Emotion in Religion*, a book that examined the major revivalists. Another rhetorician, Ernest G. Bormann, devoted two chapters in his *The Force of Fantasy* to preachers of the Awakening, giving most sustained attention (predictably) to Jonathan Edwards.

The only historian *qua* historian to explore rhetorical strategies and their effects in and after the Great Awakening, so far as I know, has been Harry S. Stout, whose essay on "Religion, Communications, and the Ideological Origins of the American Revolution" limned the possibilities of this angle of approach. Adapting to the itinerant evangelists Marshall McLuhan's dictum that "the medium is the message," Stout suggested that Whitefield and other preachers fashioned a new rhetorical strategy for communicating unfamiliar ideas in familiar terms. Itinerants spoke as one individual to others, on no authority besides their own experience, and thus convinced their hearers that the traditional authorities had lost their force. The result, whether intended or not, was to facilitate radical social change.[25] There are a few other

25. Perry Miller, *Errand into the Wilderness* (Cambridge, MA: Harvard University Press, 1956), 167–83; Edward M. Collins, Jr., "The Rhetoric of Sensation Challenges the Rhetoric of the Intellect," in *Preaching in American History: Selected Issues in the American Pulpit, 1630–1967*, ed. DeWitte Holland (Nashville: Abingdon, 1969), 98–117; Eugene E. White, "Decline of the Great Awakening in New England: 1741 to 1746," *New England Quarterly* 24 (1951): 35–52; idem, *Puritan Rhetoric: The Issue of Emotion in Religion* (Carbondale, IL: Southern Illinois University Press, 1972); Ernest G. Bormann, *The Force of Fantasy: Restoring the American Dream* (Carbondale, IL: Southern Illinois University Press, 1985). Harry S. Stout, "Religion, Communications, and the Ideological Origins of

rhetorical studies, many of them still buried in dissertations, and nearly all of them focusing only on the major figures. It seems to me that many opportunities remain for fruitful investigation of Awakening oratory from the perspective of speech communication scholars.

The issue about which students of eighteenth-century religious history still argue most is nationalism: to what extent, if any, did the Great Awakening contribute to colonial unity, the revolutionary temper, and "the rising glory of America"? (One of the early reviewers of this book puzzled over something I had not suggested at all, namely, "the paradox of a separatist movement [that] became a breeding ground for nationalism.") I have long been intrigued with H. Richard Niebuhr's comment that the Awakening was "our national conversion." He was not claiming that most Americans experienced evangelical conversion but that the revivals transcended local and particular allegiances, stimulating and reinforcing a rising national self-consciousness; in short, they began the process of creating among scattered and diverse people a common sense of nationhood. George Whitefield has been called, with some justification, "the first American," because in ranging throughout the colonies he made Georgians, Pennsylvanians, New Englanders, and all other provincials aware of common concerns and offered them resolution in a common experience. Through his wide-ranging ministry he became both the instrument and the symbol of an emerging intercolonial unity. The Awakening thus became, in the words of John Higham, "the moment in American history when [religious] ideology undertook the task of forging a new solidarity among individuals who had lost through immigration and competition any corporate identity." It seems plausible to add that it was especially the New Lights—and particularly those in New England—who shaped their religious experiences into a mechanism for launching a counterattack against an oppressive establishment, thereby learning a political strategy for feeding the fires of revolution.[26]

---

the American Revolution," *William and Mary Quarterly* 34 (1977): 519–41. In a larger study, *The New England Soul: Preaching and Religious Culture in Colonial New England* (New York: Oxford University Press, 1986), Stout combined rhetorical analysis with perceptive social history, but the breadth of this work precluded additional depth; the one chapter on the Great Awakening is too brief to provide the detailed investigation for which I am calling here.

26. See J. R. Vitelli, review of *Revivalism and Separatism*, in *Pennsylvania History* 30 (1963): 505–06; H. Richard Niebuhr, *The Kingdom of God in America* (New York: Harper & Brothers, 1937), 126; Alan Heimert, *The American Mind from the Great Awakening to the Revolution* (Cambridge, MA: Harvard University Press, 1966), 139–48; and John Higham, "Hanging Together: Divergent Unities in American History," *Journal of American History* 61 (1974): 11. Cf. also C. C. Goen, *Broken Churches, Broken Nation: Denominational Schisms and the*

The most unrestrained advocates of this thesis are Alan Heimert and William G. McLoughlin. The latter has been kind enough to write that my *Revivalism and Separatism* "is essential to understand the relation between religion and the Revolution," so I would find it difficult to argue with his claim that New Light resistance to the ecclesiastical establishment was easily transformed into nationalistic opposition to political tyranny. But even though many other scholars find significant linkage between the Awakening and the Revolution, it would be less than honest not to acknowledge that the thesis is far from universally accepted. Jon Butler has entered the strongest demurrer; and although his conclusion seems overstated, the arguments on which it is based should not be dismissed lightly.[27] *Revivalism and Separatism*, with its more intentionally ecclesiological focus, makes no explicit claims on the point and therefore contributes only some of the evidence that others adapt to their own purposes. I would argue, however, that precisely because the immediate effect of the Separate and Separate Baptist movements was to erode the traditional structure and authority of the geographical parish and justify the principles of voluntary association and local autonomy, their long-range impact was to reinforce the rising republicanism that became the ideology of the Revolution. In any event, we should keep the question open, awaiting a definitive comprehensive general study of the Awakening and its aftermath, which may clarify the issue but probably not settle it.

"THE WRITTEN LETTER REMAINS"

Benjamin Franklin once chided George Whitefield for rushing rashly into print with "Unguarded Expressions and even erroneous Opinions" that would become cause for later regret. "But," Franklin observed, "*litera scripta manet*"—a warning that no writer should take lightly.[28]

Coming of the American Civil War (Macon, GA: Mercer University Press, 1985), 19–22.

27. William G. McLoughlin, " 'Enthusiasm for Liberty': The Great Awakening as the Key to the Revolution," in Jack P. Greene and William G. McLoughlin, *Preachers and Politicians: Two Essays on the Origins of the American Revolution* (Worcester, MA: American Antiquarian Society, 1977), 50. See also Stout, "Religion, Communications, and the Ideological Origins"; John F. Berens, "Religion and Revolution Reconsidered: Recent Literature on Religion and Nationalism in Eighteenth-Century America," *Canadian Review of Studies in Nationalism* 6 (1979): 233–45; and Mark A. Noll, "The Church and the American Revolution: Historiographical Pitfalls, Problems, and Progress," *Fides et Historia* 8 (1975): 2–19. Butler, "Enthusiasm Described and Decried," has given in notes 1–5 a long list of other scholars who affirm significant connections between the Awakening and the Revolution.

28. *The Autobiography of Benjamin Franklin*, eds. Leonard W. Labaree et al. (New Haven: Yale University Press, 1964), 180.

Were I writing this book today, it probably would not turn out very differently. My appreciation for the newer historical methods does not persuade me that the original approach was totally wrong, any more than I think social and psychological history are totally right.[29] The true spirit of historical inquiry welcomes light from all sources, while remaining open to critical judgment as to which explanations are most plausible. True wisdom preserves a humility that refuses to absolutize any historical account—even one's own—as final and complete. We are all seedpickers, ever anxious to hear or tell some new thing, and that is what keeps the historical enterprise going.[30]

There are, nevertheless, some things in this book I would change, had I the opportunity and inclination to rewrite it today. I would want to incorporate the sharpened definition of evangelicalism and its three-staged pattern of conversion (pages 14–17 herein), which I worked out for my "Editor's Introduction" to Jonathan Edwards's writings on the Great Awakening.[31] Having read Edmund S. Morgan, *Visible Saints;* Robert G. Pope, *The Half-Way Covenant;* and Norman Pettit, *The Heart Prepared,* I could probably write more intelligently not only about the morphology of conversion but also about the Halfway Covenant and the Puritan doctrine of preparation (page 41 herein).[32] In describing the organization of the (Separate) Stonington Baptist Association in 1772 (pages 264–67) I completely missed an earlier body by this name, an oversight that McLoughlin soon brought to historians' attention.[33] I was dreadfully wrong in my ill-informed speculation about the last years of Nathan Cole (pages 142–43); after discovering his latter-day defense of his newly adopted Baptist beliefs, I rewrote for the present edition two paragraphs and a note (71) to conform with the evidence. Although I remain fairly content with how

29. I cordially identify with Jacques Barzun's rejoinder to the "new" history, *Clio and the Doctors: Psycho-History, Quanto-History, & History* (Chicago: University of Chicago Press, 1974). His plea for the formative role of history in the cultivation of minds, rather than for instruction in facts, suits my own temper quite well.

30. The allusion is to St. Paul's encounter with the Athenian philosophers, Acts 18:16–34. They ridiculed the apostle as a "seedpicker" (Greek, *spermologos*), one who gleans here and there from whatever sources present themselves.

31. *The Great Awakening,* ed. Goen, 1–4, 25–32.

32. Edmund S. Morgan, *Visible Saints: The History of a Puritan Idea* (New York: New York University Press, 1963); Robert G. Pope, *The Half-Way Covenant: Church Membership in Puritan New England* (Princeton: Princeton University Press, 1969); and Norman Pettit, *The Heart Prepared: Grace and Conversion in Puritan Spiritual Life* (New Haven: Yale University Press, 1966).

33. William G. McLoughlin, "The First Calvinistic Baptist Association in New England, 1754?–1767," *Church History* 36 (1967): 410–18, reprints all the known records of the early years of this early association.

I presented Isaac Backus (pages 215–24 and passim), had McLough-lin's critical edition of his diary been available in 1960, I would have enjoyed fleshing out these sections with more material directly from Backus himself.[34]

All of the quotations from Jonathan Edwards should be cited from what is available in the Yale edition of his works. Since it was not possible to copy-fit revised notes for this republication, the references are supplied herewith.[35]

As for the sexist language in previous editions, I can only plead the ignorance endemic in a pre-enlightened age. In the early 1960s few writers questioned the traditional assumption that masculine words could convey generic meaning, and I followed that assumption un-thinkingly with no conscious intention to exclude half the human race. Over the past dozen or so years, most literate people have become sensitive to the implications of gender usage. I had hoped that in this republication of *Revivalism and Separatism* I could replace all sexist terms with inclusive ones, but alas, the time and cost of making such corrections proved to be prohibitive. I trust that readers of today will forgive the offense and be assured that I do know better now.

The charts of the Appendix remain as problematical today as they were when I first compiled them. That is a long list of churches, and most of them were as individualistic as the people who constituted them. Their multifarious character made it almost impossible to de-velop a classification scheme that fits all churches or pleases all critics.

34. William G. McLoughlin, ed., *The Diary of Isaac Backus*, 3 vols. (Provi-dence: Brown University Press, 1979). McLoughlin has also edited *Isaac Backus on Church, State, and Calvinism: Pamphlets, 1754–1789* (Cambridge, MA: Har-vard University Press, 1968) and written a biography, *Isaac Backus and the American Pietistic Tradition* (Indianapolis: Little, Brown, 1967). Cf. also Stanley Grenz, *Isaac Backus—Puritan and Baptist: His Place in History, His Thought, and Their Implications for Modern Baptist Theology* (Macon, GA: Mercer Uni-versity Press, 1983), written almost entirely from presentist concerns.

35. The cross-references are as follows:

p. 13, n. 19, should read: *"The Faithful Narrative* (first published 1737), in *The Great Awakening,* ed. C. C. Goen, vol. 4 of *The Works of Jonathan Edwards,* gen. ed. John E. Smith (New Haven: Yale University Press, 1972), p. 160." (Note that "The Faithful Narrative" is now the preferred way of referring to what has been popularly called "The Narrative of Surprising Conversions.")

p. 14, n. 20, should read: "Ibid., p. 170. Samuel Hopkins. . . ."

p. 14, n. 21, should read: "Ibid., p. 163."

p. 14, n. 22, should read: "Ibid., p. 168."

p. 14, n. 23, should read: "Ibid., p. 151."

p. 18, n. 30, should read: *"Some Thoughts on the Revival of Religion in New England* (1742), in *The Great Awakening,* ed. Goen, p. 388. . . ."

p. 34, n. 72, should read: *"Some Thoughts on the Revival,* in *The Great Awakening,* ed. Goen, p. 499."

I have carefully considered the arguments of various correspondents who wanted to add or delete certain churches as dictated by their own researches, and I have decided to leave the list as it is. On page 305, if there were room, I would note under Mansfield that there were Separates also in the Second Parish, but they organized no church; that those who migrated in 1751 to Wantage, New Jersey, organized a Baptist church there in 1756; and that the Separates remaining in Mansfield disbanded in 1765.[36] To those who still wish to criticize the list, I would only urge that they read very carefully the directions for understanding it, on pages 300–01.

My final comment has to do with the promise made at the end of the original edition and reasserted in the "Preface to the 1969 Edition" to produce a book on revivalism in the southern colonies, a promise I now consider rash and ill advised. I did collect a fair quantity of materials for such a book, but too many other tasks demanding higher priority intervened. Now, to state the matter plainly, the project has grown so cold as to be for all practical purposes dead. Since other interests continue to clamor for attention, I doubt that it will revive, and therefore I have excised the promise from this edition. *Revivalism and Separatism in New England,* initially projected as volume 1 of a two-volume work, will have to stand alone—as it has been doing for twenty-five years. If it inspires a younger scholar to pursue the southern phase, that will be adequate consolation.[37]

Wesley Theological Seminary   C. C. Goen
Washington, DC
15 March 1987

36. For these and other details, see Barnett and Barnett, *On the Trail of a Legend.*

37. The field is not entirely vacant. On the Separate Baptists there is William L. Lumpkin, *Baptist Foundations in the South: Tracing Through the Separates the Influence of the Great Awakening, 1754–1787* (Nashville: Broadman Press, 1961). John B. Boles's study of *The Great Revival, 1787–1805: The Origins of the Southern Evangelical Mind* (Lexington, KY: University Press of Kentucky, 1972) admirably treats the later southern revivals, while Rhys Isaac, *The Transformation of Virginia, 1740–1790* (Chapel Hill: University of North Carolina Press, 1982), along with Isaac's other incisive writings and an unpublished Ph.D. dissertation by Ronald Wilson Long, "Religious Revivalism in the Carolinas and Georgia, 1740–1805" (University of Georgia, 1968), helps to fill in for the middle years.

PREFACE TO THE 1969 EDITION

Probably most authors can empathize with Ronald A. Knox, who described in the Preface to *Enthusiasm* how that monumental study had grown to be part of his very life. "Strange," he commented wistfully, "that a thing which is so much part of oneself should go out into the world, and lie in shop-windows, and be handled by reviewers."

Reviewers do handle a book, all right, as their reception of this volume attests. One complained that the story unfolded in "an unnecessarily repetitive fashion," while another observed that the writer "organized his material well in an arrangement that accents the lucidity of his presentation." One saw "a clear picture of revivalistic separatism in a whole geographical area," another "a panorama of dots . . . with the terrain in between largely an expanse of whiteness." One thought "the book suffers from an excessively theological approach"; another found its chief value in the "graphic reminder that the question of religious liberty, for that matter, the whole Church-State concern, is basically a theological problem." One discovered only "broad generalities," another "some rather involved and careful interpretation." One opined that "Goen could have made a significant contribution to our understanding of the Separates had he dealt with social, political, and economic attitudes"; another asserted that "the author has explored the sociocultural dimension . . . with great insight." And whereas a German scholar closed a lengthy review by saying, "Man legt die Arbeit sehr befriedigt aus der Hand," an American colleague simply sighed, "This is not an easy book to read." I can only wonder whether I have not sent into the world an elephant to be handled rather than a book to be read.

Possibly such diverse reaction was to be expected in view of the fact that I was exploring territory little charted by historians previously. Precisely because separatism in and after the Great Awakening had never been studied systematically, it seemed to me most desirable to focus with a wide-angle lens, even though that meant some loss of depth and detail in specific situations. I still think such a choice was justified, and my continuing correspondence bears out the prediction of one reviewer that the book would open up several new possibilities for theses and dissertations. To critics who were unhappy because I focused too broadly, or interpreted too theologically, or relied too much on printed sources, I can only reply that I apparently wrote a somewhat different book than their predilections might have led them to write—and this by intention. One might surmise that this essay spoke an early and provocative word on the subject concerning which a definitive statement must await a number of detailed studies still in process or yet to come.

While others continue to work the always-fertile soil of New England history, I am attempting to fulfill the promise of p. 299, n. 10. In 1960 I proposed to write the history of the Separate Baptists in the South, suspecting that they were the chief source of the romantic evangelicalism which has long characterized Baptist life in that region. In my first prospectus, Chapter I was devoted to the New England origins of the Separates. When I got into this, however, I found so much unworked material that Chapter I had to become Volume I, making it necessary to project a sequel on the Southern Separates. Unfortunately, the materials to support a study of religious dissent in the colonial South do not exist in nearly so orderly and well-preserved a state as they do for New England. My search for these fugitive and ephemeral sources is turning the second volume into a work of ten years or more —but it is slowly taking shape as *Revivalism in the Southern Colonies.* Seeing that most readers seized upon my promise with an eagerness I had not anticipated, I hope they will not take it amiss if I plead for patience.

Thanks are due Archon Books for their willingness to undertake this present edition. It is essentially the same as the first. Encouraged by Franklin H. Littell's heady comment that "this is history as it ought to be written," I have not felt impelled to revise any of my main judgments. Several errors of detail and ambiguities of expression, however, have been corrected. To students and colleagues who called most of these to my attention, I am duly grateful.

C. C. Goen

Washington, D.C.
March 31, 1969

PREFACE TO THE FIRST EDITION

The Great Awakening in New England brought not peace but a sword. Although genuine revival came to many churches throughout a wide region, there were numerous places where revivalism became an uncontrollable ferment, dismaying even its friends by the resultant "errors in doctrine" and "disorders in practice."

Efforts on the part of the standing order to subdue the new religious enthusiasm soon provoked a revolt. Out of the complex of issues that led to open rupture came almost one hundred separatist churches, marking a permanent shattering of the Congregational establishment in New England. A large proportion of these revivalistic separatists passed over into the Baptist fellowship, powerfully augmenting and revivifying this denomination, which had remained aloof from the Awakening, and eventually producing significant changes in it.

There are two ways in which an investigation of separatist phenomena might be conducted. One would be a thorough depth study of a small number of separatist churches presupposed to be typical, with generalizations based on the findings. The other would be to extend the scope of the study in an effort to determine insofar as possible the location, circumstances, and characteristics of every discoverable separatist congregation. In spite of the loss of depth in the latter method, I have chosen it: so little has been done in this area that a panoramic view of revivalistic separatism seems desirable.

This choice meant that it was not possible in every case to go to sources. There was indeed opportunity to consult various manuscript church records, as well as letters and journals of important participants in the separatist movement, and good use was made of them in the text. Some materials of this nature are printed, in whole or in part, in various historical collections. In many instances, however, there was no choice but to rely on records and manuscripts quoted liberally in the local church, town, and county histories which are so conveniently abundant for New England. Their availability broadened the scope of the investigation and made it possible to demonstrate that separatism was much more widespread than has been suspected previously. A major help also was the fact that many of the men who participated in the revivalist-separatist controversies were not at all backward about publishing their "true" sentiments and exposing their opponents' "errors." Timothy Cutler of Boston remarked that since Whitefield's coming (1740), "our presses are for ever teeming with books." These published pamphlets were immeasurably helpful in the present work.

This work began as a Yale dissertation and has passed through two subsequent revisions—one for the Brewer contest of the American Society of Church History, and one for publication by the Yale Press. Confronted with the impossibility of naming all those whose suggestions and assistance have been so helpful—even indispensable—I gratefully recall some who have aided most in my research and writing. I am especially indebted to the staff of the Yale libraries, not only for making available the rich resources of this institution but for securing from other archives many materials which ordinarily do not circulate. The curators at the Connecticut Historical Society at Hartford, Connecticut, the New London County Historical Society at New London, Connecticut, and the American Baptist Historical Society at Rochester, New York, also have been most helpful.

Personal debts to my mentors loom equally large, none more than that to Sydney Ahlstrom of Yale University, who has saved me from many inaccuracies of interpretation and infelicities of expression. Mrs. Ola Mae Martin faithfully typed the final copy of the manuscript, and Miss Mamie Goen cheerfully performed the tedious task of proofreading. Editors David Horne and Julee MacGowan of the Yale Press have gone far beyond the demands of duty to help produce an acceptable book in a pleasing format. To the founders of the Brewer Fund, the officers of the American Society of Church History who administer it, and the judges who conducted the 1960 contest, I am likewise grateful. Thanks are also due the Ford Foundation for a grant in aid of publication.

Choicest praise, however, must go to my wife, even though her role in the production of this work was entirely nontechnical. Surely some special reward is reserved for those patient women who not only endure bookwriting husbands but even encourage them!

C. C. G.

Wesley Theological Seminary
Washington, D.C.
August 15, 1961

1. THE CONGREGATIONAL CHURCHES OF NEW ENGLAND AND THE GREAT AWAKENING

New England's Way in Church and State

In 1676 the Connecticut magistrates wrote to the English Lords of Trade: "Our people, in this colony, are some of them strict Congregational men, others more large Congregational men, and some moderate Presbyterians." [1] The differences in polity preference that colored eighteenth-century revival controversies had roots reaching far back into the history of Puritan New England. In the Bay Colony a more strict congregational view had prevailed, while in Connecticut the "moderate Presbyterians" controlled the religious establishment. To understand the movement which forms the theme of this book, the documents of New England's church way—namely the Cambridge Platform of 1648 and the Saybrook Platform of 1708—must be briefly examined.

Massachusetts' Cambridge Platform asserts that "the matter of a visible church are *Saints* by calling" (III, 1).[2] Ordination is to be performed by the elders of the church, or, if the church has none, by brethren whom the church may choose; but in no case may a minister be ordained at large. "Church officers, are officers to one church, even that particular, over which the Holy Ghost hath made them overseers" (IX, 6). A testimony of religious experience is to be required of all who desire to be admitted to full communicant status, even though they may have been baptized in infancy as the children of believing parents. "Because holy things must not be given unto the unworthy, therefore it is requisit, that these as well as others, should come to their tryall & examination, & manifest their faith & repentance by an open profession thereof, before they are received to the Lords supper, & otherwise not to be admitted there unto" (XII, 7).

This calls for comment. A perennial problem of Calvinistic faith has been how to know the elect; although one can never be certain,

---

1. Leonard Bacon, "Historical Discourse," *Contributions to the Ecclesiastical History of Connecticut* (New Haven, 1861), p. 26.
2. Quotations from the Cambridge Platform are from Williston Walker, *Creeds and Platforms of Congregationalism* (New York, 1893), pp. 205–37.

three presumptive tests have been posited. With Calvin these were a correct profession of faith, an upright life, and participation in the sacraments. Among the Puritans, however, the third test became personal religious experience: one who could not testify to an inner experience of regeneration was not to be received at the Lord's Table.

Connecticut's Saybrook Platform was the product of "large Congregational men" and "moderate Presbyterians" who wanted a system of closer connection and control over the churches. Article II of this document provided:

> That the Churches which are Neighbouring each to other shall consociate for the mutuall affording to each other such assistance as may be requisite upon all occasions ecclesiasticall: And that the particular Pastors & Churches within the Respective Countys in this Government shall be one Consociation (or more if they judge meet) for the end aforesaid.[3]

The effect was to set up a semipresbyterian system linking together all the churches of a given district in an ecclesiastical judicatory. The consociations functioned as standing councils to assist the churches upon "all occasions ecclesiasticall," which would include ministerial ordinations, installations, and dismissals. From their actions there was no appeal, save that in particularly difficult cases a neighboring consociation might be called in for advice. To ensure that no vote violated the desires of the clergy, it was provided that no action should be binding which did not have a majority of ministers as well as a majority of the whole council. The authority of consociational decisions was upheld by Article VI, providing:

> That if any Pastor and Church doth obstinately refuse a due attendance and Conformity to the Determination of the Council that has Cognizance of the Case & Determines it as above, after due patience used they shall be Reputed guilty of Scandalous Contempt & dealt with as the Rule of Gods word In such Case doth provide, & the Sentence of Non-Communion shall be Declared against such Pastor & Church, and the Churches are to approve of the said Sentence by withdrawing from the Communion of the Pastor & Church which so refuseth to be healed.

The platform provided also for associations of ministers in each county; these were for consultation, licensing of candidates, recommendation of supplies and pastors, etc. Delegates from the county

3. Quotations from the Saybrook Platform are from Walker, pp. 502–05.

associations were to comprise a General Association for the whole colony.

The Connecticut General Assembly, long accustomed to asserting its role as "nursing father," imposed the Saybrook scheme by legislative decree. Independent thinkers in the colony thought such action highly arbitrary at several points: its pretension that the sixteen men at Saybrook voiced the unanimous consensus of all the ministers and churches, its exclusion from the benefits of establishment of any minister and church that should refuse conformity, its condescension to nonconformists who might reject the platform only at the cost of forfeiting their legal standing. Nor was its autocratic highhandedness lost on the churches of Connecticut. In the eastern part of the colony, which was still virtually frontier territory, reception was far from enthusiastic; the churches of New London County, with but two or three exceptions, renounced it altogether.[4] Norwich rejected it, even though its pastor, John Woodward, had been scribe of the Saybrook Synod. When he tried to impose the act by suppressing the clause allowing "sober dissent," the town's representatives exposed his duplicity—for which pains they were censured by the church and expelled from the legislature. But Woodward was dismissed, and the next pastor settled on the express condition that the church would not be subject to the obnoxious platform. New Haven County churches adopted a minimized interpretation of it, and wrote in their minutes that they considered themselves purely a "Congregational confederation of Congregational churches." But Fairfield County in the west placed an ultrapresbyterian construction on it, changing the "non-communion" in Article VI to "excommunication," and making the consociation a full-fledged church court.

The Saybrook Platform, as implemented by legislative decree, marked the parting of the ways of the Massachusetts and Connecticut churches, and led to the drawing of the latter into closer affinity with the Presbyterian churches of the Middle Colonies. More important for the present study, by agitating the arguments over ecclesiastical polity it set the stage for the controversies of a generation later and explained why they were much more acrimonious in Connecticut than elsewhere.

PRELUDE TO REVIVAL

Saints in short supply. Not all the children of the founders professed the piety of their parents. In New England, therefore, the passion for

4. S. Leroy Blake, *The Later History of the First Church of Christ, New London, Connecticut* (New London, 1900), p. 8.

purity in church and godly order in society was diluted, not only by subsequent settlers with small religious concern but also by the very offspring of the Puritans themselves. The insistence of the early Congregationalists upon a regenerated church membership has already been pointed out, as has the necessity of credible testimony of personal religious experience as prerequisite to full church membership. In the logic of their covenant theology it was presumed that the children of the saints were also included in the covenant of grace; this was the basis for baptizing them in infancy. But when the first generation gave way to one of lesser faith and looser life, the younger members, though baptized in infancy, could not honestly testify to a personal conversion experience; and their relation to the church was in considerable doubt. The burning question arose over the baptizing of *their* children. Since only the children of professing Christians were "in the covenant," strict adherence to original practice would leave these children unbaptized—presumably to grow up as heathen. Some of the more liberal ministers urged that such persons be admitted to church membership so that their children might receive baptism, but the majority held that to follow this procedure would undermine their fundamental tenet, the ideal of the pure church.

This question, already pressing in 1648, was sidestepped by the Cambridge Synod. But it had to be dealt with, and the ministerial convention of 1657 reached a compromise which was confirmed by a Massachusetts synod in 1662. Known as the Halfway Covenant, it admitted that persons baptized in infancy, even though not professing Christians, were connected somehow with the visible church and were capable of passing along to their children the same degree of membership that they themselves possessed. They were permitted to present their children for baptism, provided they themselves were of upright life and would "own the covenant" into which they had been born. They were not, however, to partake of the Lord's Supper or vote in church affairs; hence they were "halfway" members.[5] The ministers who adopted this dubious and illogical compromise were doubtless concerned chiefly to hold within the sphere of churchly influence those who could not qualify for full membership, rather than let them slip away altogether. But it soon opened a door into the church for those who had no "birthright claim," for all persons of reputable conduct came to be permitted to declare publicly their acceptance of covenant obligations in order to present their children for baptism. In actual

5. Although this had political implications through limitation of the franchise to church members, the reasons for change seem to have been entirely religious.

operation, the Halfway Covenant served not to lead men into full relationship with the church but to encourage them to remain content with their halfway status. The measure designed to protect experiential piety in the churches actually furthered its decline.

In spite of widespread resistance, the Halfway Covenant soon gained acceptance among almost all the Congregational churches in New England. As a result, before the end of the century every community had a small body of professing Christians who were the "church," a larger group of halfway members who were the "congregation," and the unconverted population who made up the territorial parish. Even these lines were vague and indefinite. When the new charter of 1691 wrested political control from the saints and threw the churches back on their own resources, they discovered that their only hope lay in a continuity of committed members. This impaled them on a further dilemma: halfway members had to come all the way or the churches would perish; but it is hypocrisy to profess a nonexistent experience, and it is sin to partake of the Lord's Supper unworthily.

The Gordian knot was cut by Solomon Stoddard of Northampton, Massachusetts. He held that the Lord's Supper was a converting ordinance, and was for all adult members of the community who were not scandalous in life. Emphasizing that none can know who is truly a saint, he asserted that a church must proceed only on the basis of what is visible, namely a man's acceptance of the creed and his willingness to seek sanctifying grace through worship and communion.

> He gave up distinguishing between the covenants, and henceforth baptized not merely the children of members, but all the children in town; he took into the communion not merely the professing adults, but all adults. At one fell swoop he cured the evils of the Half-Way Covenant by going beyond it; he uprooted the New England Way in Northampton, and identified the visible church no longer with the community of the saints, but with the town meeting—where he himself was dictator and lawgiver.[6]

Stoddard thus turned away from evident election as a basis for church membership and toward making the means of grace available through the church to the whole community. He was followed, in spite of

6. Perry Miller, "Solomon Stoddard, 1643–1729," *Harvard Theological Review,* 34 (1941), 298. The last phrase is literally true. His autocratic bearing and wide influence earned for him the title "Pope Stoddard."

anguished outcries from the eastern clergy, by most of the churches of the Connecticut Valley.[7]

Frontier revivals. Whatever else might be said of Stoddardeanism, it brought members into the churches. Stoddard himself experienced repeated harvests in his own church in 1679, 1683, 1696, 1712, and 1718. "In each of them . . . the greatest part of the young people in the town, appeared chiefly concerned for their salvation." [8] The same phenomenon occurred at sporadic intervals in some of the churches touched by Stoddard's influence. At Windham, Connecticut, in 1721 the church received eighty persons in six months; this was at a time when it was only two decades old and had slightly more than a hundred members.

Across the colony, in New Milford, the young people experienced an awakening of religious concern in 1727, when some sixty united with the church.[9] Jonathan Parsons became pastor at Lyme in 1731, and that summer a revival broke out among the young people; he encouraged them to come to the Lord's Supper, and in less than ten months fifty-two had joined the church. Jonathan Edwards' notes on his boyhood experiences mention several seasons "of remarkable awakening" in his father's parish at East Windsor. All these harvests occurred in churches that practiced the Halfway Covenant and were heavily swayed toward Stoddardeanism.

Testimonies during the Great Awakening, however, make it appear that most of the sporadic revivals were based on a concern for salvation by works, which taught men to help themselves to the means of grace institutionalized in the church. There was little conviction of the sinfulness of all human character and conduct, and no consequent casting of oneself on the mercy of God in faith alone. A striking change occurred in Jonathan Parsons. After Calvinistic preaching had "awakened" all New England, he was converted to those doctrines and confessed that in 1731 he had been too optimistic in counting his

7. Ibid., p. 303. Stoddard did teach the necessity for divine grace in salvation. But this was in the hands of God; man's concern was with the public praxis of the visible church.

8. Benjamin Trumbull, *A Complete History of Connecticut* (New Haven, 1818), 2, 135. Miller claims that Stoddard taught Jonathan Edwards, his grandson and successor, how to "manage" revivals and produce the conversion experience ("Stoddard," p. 320).

9. This revival was accompanied by "enthusiastic," or inner light, doctrines. An account of it is given by one who shared in it as a youth: *Memoirs of the Life of David Ferris, an Approved Minister of the Society of Friends . . . Written by Himself* (Philadelphia, 1855), pp. 20–25.

converts and too hasty in admitting them to the Lord's Supper. Also, he confessed that he himself had been trusting too much in his own self-righteousness and not enough in the sufficiency of Christ.

The revival of Westminster doctrines in the Connecticut Valley is attributable in the first instance to Jonathan Edwards (1703–58), who succeeded his grandfather Solomon Stoddard at Northampton in 1729. Convinced that the doctrine of human ability which underlay the gradual shift to Arminian principles was a dangerous heresy, he preached in 1734 a series of five sermons on justification by faith alone. These messages were broadsides of pure and uncompromised Reformed doctrine. That all men justly deserve instant and total damnation, that none has any claim upon God's mercy, that salvation is a gracious gift of God through Jesus Christ who died to save sinners, that it is appropriated through faith which itself is a gift of God—all these points were hammered home with a relentless force that scarcely can be appreciated by the reader today. Joseph Tracy observes in all seriousness: "There was a special fitness in those sermons, to produce the effects which followed them." [10] The surprising thing is that Edwards himself was surprised at the results.

They were indeed electric. A frivolous young woman was dramatically converted, and many of the young people followed her in confessing their sins. Religious concern spread throughout the town, until all were convinced that the Spirit of God was at work in an extraordinary way. Conversions multiplied. More than three hundred, aged from four to seventy, professed faith within six months. The news traveled to neighboring towns; visitors came to Northampton to light their own torches and carry home the sacred fire. By next spring the revival was general throughout the Connecticut Valley from Deerfield to Lyme, and from Stratford to Windham. And it was but the precursor of the conflagration which enveloped New England in the forties.

Although the Great Awakening proper broke forth under George Whitefield along the eastern seaboard before it moved overland, and although the promotion and progress of that revival was far different from the frontier awakening which was "very much at a Stop" by 1737, the surprising conversions in the churches of the Connecticut Valley brought several important influences to bear on the later phenomenon. For one thing, they demonstrated as nothing else could the kind of preaching that would arouse sinners; themes like the justice and judgment of God, the awful penalty of rejecting Christ

10. *The Great Awakening* (Boston, 1842), p. 12.

and being rejected by him, the rapturous sweetness of the forgiven soul's repose in God, and the joys of the redeemed throughout eternity in heaven made the intonations of moral homilies from Arminian pulpits seem tasteless and dull. For another, they set the pattern of conversion in a mold which New England, for all the experiential piety of the founders, had never known before. Barely beneath the surface were the emotional pressures of the conversion experience, which would be released in the next decade with devastating results. And lurking in the background of Edwards' break with Stoddardeanism was the whole controversy over the constitution of the church, the way of salvation, and the problem of assurance. It is true enough that this early revival was a relatively innocuous affair when judged by the tumults left in the wake of the Whitefieldian campaign. Seeds were being sown, nevertheless, of tares as well as wheat.

REVIVALISTIC INNOVATIONS

The "time of extraordinary dullness in religion" which Jonathan Edwards bemoaned during his early years at Northampton came to an end with the "great and general awakening" which aroused all New England in 1740–42. Presaged by the earlier and more provincial revivals, and indirectly influenced by the awakenings that had stirred the Middle Colonies since 1726, the revival fires of the fifth decade enveloped all of New England:

> There is . . . abundant evidence that this religious turmoil in New England was in fact "great and general," that it knew no boundaries, social or geographical, that it was both urban and rural, and that it reached both lower and upper classes. . . . [Numerous revivalists] were the occasion of the Awakening's percolating down into every parish, becoming the concern of all the clergy and a reality to all the laity.[11]

During these years ministers were beset on all sides by inquirers after the way of salvation, implored to increase the number of sermons and lectures, and impelled to carry the word of life to distant places. The increase in church membership has been variously estimated at twenty to fifty thousand, and more than a few pastors rejoiced over the noticeable elevation of public morals. Within the next twenty

11. Edwin Scott Gaustad, *The Great Awakening in New England* (New York, 1957), pp. 43, 47. Gaustad notes the various social interpretations of the revival and cites convincing evidence to support his conclusion that it was widespread and of far-reaching influence.

years, more than a hundred and fifty new regular Congregational churches were gathered. In spite of unfortunate excesses which marred the revival and eventually dissipated it in controversy and schism, it amply deserves the name by which it is generally known—the Great Awakening.

It is not necessary here to recount the exciting events of New England's greatest evangelistic experience. The present aim is rather to highlight those aspects of the revival which were quite without precedent in the churches of the region and to show how these innovations led to controversies that provoked numerous and widespread separations from the standing churches.

Itinerant evangelizing. The spark that lit the conflagration was George Whitefield (1714–70), who blazed across the New England landscape for six weeks during the fall of 1740. This evangelistic tour, which took him to all the towns of the seaboard and the Connecticut Valley, set the pattern for revivalism in New England for the remainder of the century.

The tremendous response he received on his first barnstorming tour may be attributed to many causes, not the least of which was the sheer novelty of it. Neither ministers nor people had ever seen anything like it before. A nonplused Hartford pastor confided to his diary, "what to think of the man and his Itinerant preachings I scarcely know: the things which I know not I pray god to discover it to me, wherein I have embraced the truth I pray god that I might hold it fast to the end." [12] Puritan New England believed firmly in a settled ministry, and the Cambridge Platform had refused to sanction the ordination of men to the church at large. Increase Mather, inveighing against the new "liberal" church in Brattle Street, had attacked the pastor's foreign ordination by declaring, "To say that a *Wandering Levite* who has no Flock is a Pastor, is as good sense as to say, that he that has no Children is a Father." [13] Under this kind of thinking, pastors might exchange pulpits occasionally by mutual agreement, or one might assist another in response to an express invitation, but New England knew nothing of an itinerant ministry of the sort exhibited by Whitefield. It was a radical innovation, and set an example destined to be followed by numbers of preachers equally zealous for the salvation of souls if not equally effective in awakening pious concern.

12. *Diary of the Rev. Daniel Wadsworth,* ed. George Leon Walker (Hartford, 1894), p. 56.
13. *The Order of the Gospel* (Boston, 1700), p. 102.

Among the first to imitate "the Grand Itinerant" were evangelistically minded pastors, some of whom attributed their own spiritual awakening to his visit. Whitefield himself prevailed upon Gilbert Tennent, the fiery Presbyterian from New Jersey, to go to New England and fan the flame which had been kindled. Tennent was Scotch-Irish, educated at the "log college" his father founded at Neshaminy, Pennsylvania, and already well on his way to becoming the leader of the revivalistic party among the Presbyterians of the Middle Colonies. After some hesitation, he agreed to leave his churches at New Brunswick and Staten Island and go to Boston. Arriving in December 1740, during one of the most severe winters in New England's history, he stayed until the following March. Returning through southeastern Massachusetts, Rhode Island, and eastern Connecticut, he reported that "divers thousands" had been awakened. By that time some opposition to the revival, or at least to the methods of the revivalists, had appeared; and some had asked what right Tennent had to desert his own charge and invade a territory where there were already enough godly ministers to care for the spiritual needs of the people.

This did not stop others from carrying abroad the torch of truth. There was James Davenport of Southold, Long Island, whose ebullient evangelizing was such a prime factor in the emergence of separatism that he will be discussed in detail later. There was Benjamin Pomeroy of Hebron, Connecticut, a veteran itinerant who enjoyed the full confidence of Jonathan Edwards. Edwards wrote to Eleazar Wheelock on June 9, 1741, requesting "that you and your brother Pomeroy would go to Scantic [East Windsor], my father's parish, and preach there as often as the people will be willing to hear you, and continue so doing as long as the concerns of your own parishes will allow of your being absent." [14] The legislation of 1742 outlawed such activities, and Pomeroy—unwilling to see souls perish because of an arbitrary law—was arrested several times. Eleazar Wheelock, pastor at Lebanon Crank (Columbia) 1735–70, had labored with Pomeroy (his brother-in-law) in Windham and Norwich in 1741. Perhaps Connecticut's most energetic evangelist, Wheelock was frequently berated by the antirevival party, and members of other churches were sometimes suspended for going to hear him. His labors in behalf of the revival

14. David McClure and Elijah Parish, eds., *Memoirs of the Reverend Eleazar Wheelock* (Newburyport, 1811), p. 210. Edwards also invited them to Northampton, though recognizing that other pulpits had been closed to them. Daniel Wadsworth noted that Wheelock and Pomeroy, along with Jedediah Mills of Ripton, were "the principle Itinerant preachers among us" (*Diary of Wadsworth*, p. 72).

were so constant and extensive that in 1741 "he preached a hundred more sermons than there are days in the year." [15] In the fall of that year he made a veritable Whitefieldian tour, preaching across Rhode Island, up to Boston, back through Dedham, Medfield, Bellingham, and Uxbridge, and then home. The Connecticut Valley also had frequent opportunities to hear him.

In eastern Connecticut the numerous pastors who promoted the revival had the willing assistance of Jonathan Parsons, pastor at Lyme 1731–45. As the result of Tennent's visit, Parsons experienced in 1741 a conversion which not only gave him assurance of personal salvation but convinced him of the correctness of Calvinistic principles. He burned his previous sermons as unworthy of preservation and began to preach awakening doctrines with such power that neighboring ministers soon sought his help. His zeal cost him his pastorate, however: the antirevival faction at Lyme secured his dismissal in 1745. Upon the recommendation of Whitefield (ever his close friend) he went to Newburyport, Massachusetts, to become the pastor of a group of separatists who eventually constituted the First Presbyterian Church of that town.

Next to Wheelock and Parsons, eastern Connecticut's most active revivalist was Andrew Croswell, pastor at North Groton 1736–48. The most notable event of his peregrinations was a visit in 1743 to Plymouth, Massachusetts, where he held a protracted meeting (also an innovation of this period)—throwing the town into great excitement and disorder and resulting speedily in a separation. Soon afterward Croswell assumed pastoral charge of a number of separatists at Boston. Samuel Buell, though not a settled pastor until 1746 when he was installed at Easthampton, Long Island,[16] was active in eastern Connecticut, especially at Canterbury, and at Fairfield in the west; and in the fall of 1742 he journeyed up the Connecticut River and spent two or three weeks at Northampton, where his preaching commended him highly to Jonathan Edwards. From there he swung over into eastern Massachusetts, passing through Braintree and Boston, and ended with a riotous revival in Newbury. Philemon Robbins, the largehearted evangelical pastor at Branford, preached as far north

15. F. D. Avery, "Historical Discourse," *The 150th Anniversary of the Congregational Church in Columbia, Connecticut, October 24th, 1866* (Hartford, 1867), p. 10.
16. Jonathan Edwards preached the sermon. Buell had been ordained—irregularly, some thought—as minister at large by the New Haven Association in September 1742.

as Grafton, Massachusetts, and even accepted (at the peril of his legal status) an invitation from the Baptists at Wallingford in 1742. Amos Munson, another of the young ministers "getting into that way" of itinerant preaching, was jailed "for holding forth at Colchester contrary to Law." [17]

Revival fires in the Bay Colony were fanned by the energetic efforts of such itinerating pastors as John White of Gloucester, Joseph Emerson of Malden, and Nathaniel Rogers of Ipswich. Jonathan Edwards engaged in this ministry as far as he was able, though only by invitation, and encouraged others to do likewise. His best-known sermon (though *not* most typical!), "Sinners in the Hands of an Angry God," was preached not at Northampton but on an evangelizing excursion to Enfield on July 8, 1741. Massachusetts' most widely traveled itinerant was perhaps Daniel Rogers (brother to Nathaniel), a Harvard tutor awakened by Whitefield and ordained as an evangelist at large in York, Maine, in July 1742. The Boston *Evening Post* for November 22, 1742, denounced the proceedings as unlawfully designating Rogers "to be a vagrant preacher to the people of God in this land; contrary to the peace of our Lord the King and Head of his Church and to the good order and constitution of the churches in New England as established by the Platform." [18] Notwithstanding this attack, Rogers' fame reached as far as Connecticut, where he was urged to come by Eleazar Wheelock.

It was by such men that Whitefield's novel example of itinerant evangelizing became a primary means of spreading the revival to every parish. As a radical innovation in New England religion that seemed so disruptive to the traditional order of the churches, it soon became a cause of extreme alarm to the conservatives and a prime issue in the controversies that erupted in the wake of the Awakening.

Dramatic conversion. The Puritan founders of New England, with a doctrine of conscious conversion, insisted on a public profession of personal regeneration as prerequisite to church membership. But in the general decline of experimental piety and through the working of the Halfway Covenant, the doctrine of conversion became greatly attenuated. Before the Great Awakening, even those who maintained

17. *Diary of Wadsworth*, pp. 73, 89. Munson (Yale College 1738) was licensed by the New Haven Association but never ordained. He became an original member of the Separate church in New Haven in 1742.

18. Quoted in Thomas Franklin Waters, *Ipswich in the Massachusetts Bay Colony* (Ipswich, 1917), 2, 122. Rogers later became pastor of the Separate church in Exeter, New Hampshire.

some sort of emphasis on conversion held that it was so subtle and inward as not to be cognizable by another person—if indeed by one-self! Anyone who subscribed to the creed of the churches and lived a respectably moral life was presumed to be converted. The Great Awakening marks a recovery of the doctrine of conscious conversion, even setting "experience" over "profession" in a way that the early Puritans had never known. Jonathan Edwards himself articulated this doctrine in such a way as to erect a normative pattern for religious experience among the revivalists.

Edwards applied his idealistic principle of reality not only to the external world but to the human soul, and coupled it with Calvin's insistence on the ministry of the Holy Spirit as inner witness. The result was a statement of the direct action of the Spirit upon the soul as a basis for the doctrine of conversion. Edwards' "Narrative of Surprising Conversions" describes the earlier Northampton revival and portrays three well-defined stages through which the subjects of it passed. The first is characterized by fear, anxiety, and distress at one's sinfulness in the sight of a holy God:

> Persons are first awakened with a sense of their miserable condition by nature, the danger they are in of perishing eternally, and that it is of great importance to them that they speedily escape, and get into a better state. Those that before were secure and senseless, are made sensible how much they were in the way to ruin in their former courses. . . . [Some] set themselves seriously to meditate on those things that have the most awakening tendency, on purpose to obtain convictions; and so their awakenings have increased, till a sense of their misery, by God's Spirit setting in therewith, has had fast hold of them.[19]

This distress is more than "mere legal terrors" arising from threats of punishment over transgressions of God's law. That is part of the picture, but such convictions proceed from "a high exercise of grace, in saving repentance, and evangelical humiliation; for there is in it a sort of complacency of soul, in the attribute of God's justice, as displayed in the threatenings of eternal damnation to sinners." And in this state sinners tend to confess that God's justice would not be compromised if they were to be damned forever. Indeed, "some express themselves, that they see the glory of God would shine bright in

19. *Narrative of Surprising Conversions* (first published 1737), in *The Works of President Edwards* (New York, 1881), 3, 240. This is the standard Worcester edition, with minor revisions; all subsequent citations will be from it.

their own condemnation; and they are ready to think that if they are damned, they could take part with God against themselves, and would glorify his justice therein." [20]

The second stage is absolute dependence on the sovereign mercy of God in Jesus Christ. The conviction of sin, with its accompanying terror of damnation, "has seemed most evidently to be, to make way for, and to bring to, a conviction of their absolute dependence on his sovereign power and grace, and universal necessity of a Mediator, by leading them more and more to a sense of their exceeding wickedness and guiltiness in his sight; the pollution and insufficiency of their own righteousness, that they can in no wise help themselves." [21] The realization of human sinfulness points to the fact that the damnation of all would be just; the realization of divine sovereignty points to the fact that the salvation of any is wholly dependent on grace. Some were convinced, Edwards observes, that God "might justly bestow mercy on every [other] person in the town, and on every [other] person in the world, and damn themselves to all eternity." [22] There can be no quarrel with the way in which a sovereign God bestows or withholds his mercies, which are totally undeserved in any case.

Those upon whom grace is bestowed, however, experience the third stage in conversion, namely a sense of relief from their distress under conviction of sin and a sense of joy at being accepted of God. To those so favored there comes an abiding assurance of eternal salvation, a "calm of spirit" because of the "special and delightful manifestation" of God's grace made to the soul. This is the joy which possessed the new converts; and their numbers, along with the rejoicing of the mature saints, caused Edwards to say that in 1735 "the town seemed to be full of the presence of God; it never was so full of love, nor so full of joy; and yet so full of distress as it was then." [23] The time of extraordinary dullness in religion had come to a very sudden stop.[24]

There were, of course, individual differences in the conversion experience, and Edwards notes them carefully. But in spite of these differences the general pattern is the same. The three-stage process

20. Ibid., pp. 246–47. Samuel Hopkins later made "willingness to be damned for the glory of God" almost a dogma.

21. Ibid., p. 242.

22. Ibid., p. 246.

23. Ibid., p. 235.

24. The remainder of the *Narrative* is composed largely of the testimonies of new converts regarding their new-found joy in salvation. It is worth noting that in spite of "the delightful sense of the safety of their own estate, and that now they are out of the danger of hell," no antinomian tendencies appeared.

of conversion became normative in the Great Awakening and in subsequent revivalism, and those who could not or would not pass through it were in time denounced as unconverted.

This view of conversion as the sole way of salvation is what gave such pointed urgency to the message of the itinerant evangelists. They were out to produce conviction for sin, to portray the justice of God in the damnation of sinners, and to present Christ as the sinner's only hope. On their efforts, they thought, hinged the eternal destiny of multitudes of perishing people. Hence their preaching was directed at one aim: the conversion of sinners in the cognizable pattern enunciated by Edwards. They preached, as has every evangelist since, for decisions. Here also the inimitable Whitefield exerted a powerful—and novel—influence. In the last analysis it is not Edwards the theologian but Whitefield the preacher who founded the revival tradition. His unsurpassed oratorical gifts and theatrical arts combined with a sincere devotion to Christ and concern for souls to give him a most remarkable power over his vast audiences. The persuasive power of his messages made up for their lack of variety and depth. His sermon on "The Kingdom of God" ends with a compelling appeal which is doubtless typical of his procedure everywhere:

> Had I a thousand tongues, they should be employed in inviting sinners to come to Jesus Christ! Come, then, let me prevail with some of you to come along with me. Come, poor, lost, undone sinner, come just as you are to Christ, and say, If I be damned, I will perish at the feet of Jesus Christ, where never one perished yet. He will receive you with open arms; the dear Redeemer is willing to receive you all. Fly, then, for your lives. The devil is in you while unconverted; and will you go with the devil in your heart to bed this night? God Almighty knows if ever you and I shall see one another again. In one or two days more I must go, and, perhaps I may never see you again till I meet you at the judgment day. O my dear friends, think of that solemn meeting; think of that important hour, when the heavens shall pass a way with a great noise, when the elements shall melt with fervent heat, when the sea and the grave shall be giving up their dead, and all shall be summoned to appear before the great God. . . . Come to Christ, and the Lord Jesus Christ will give you a kingdom that no man shall take from you.[25]

25. Quoted in Charles Dargan, *A History of Preaching* (Grand Rapids, 1954 reprint), 2, 314–15. The eschatological element here greatly increases the urgency of the invitation, but it should be noted that Whitefield generally emphasized the love

When appeals like this followed the convincing assertion that all men are sinners and under the curse of God's wrath, that the righteous life and substitutionary death of Christ are the sinner's only hope, and that salvation is the free gift of sovereign grace granted to those who cast themselves in complete trust upon Christ, it is not remarkable that converts were numerous.

Gilbert Tennent, who followed close on Whitefield's trail through New England, sought to feed the flames of revival by stoking the fires of hell. And the difference in his emphasis was matched by a corresponding difference in vocal powers:

> Unlike the mellow-voiced Whitefield, who controlled the emotions of his audiences by subtle inflections, dramatic pauses, and effective modulation of intensity, Tennent, with his strident, unmusical voice, could only flail away at his hearers. His pugnacious Scotch-Irish nature lacked the gentleness necessary for persuasion. His sole technique was to stamp and yell in an endeavor to terrorize individuals into conversion. Whitefield reached the outskirts of the largest crowds by means of perfect enunciation and energetic vocal projection; Tennent frequently so lost himself in his passions that he became incoherent.[26]

This is the verdict of a speech professor, and though so overdrawn as to be almost a caricature of Tennent, it points up an important difference between Whitefield and his most immediate co-worker in keeping New England astir with traumatic religious excitement. Despite their differences, however, Tennent's aim was precisely the same as Whitefield's—he preached for decisions.

> He seem'd to have no regard to please the Eyes of his Hearers with agreeable Gesture, nor their Ears with Delivery, nor their Fancy with Language; but to aim directly at their *Hearts* and *Consciences*, to lay open their ruinous Delusions, shew them their numerous, secret, hypocritical Shifts in Religion, and drive them out of every deceitful Refuge wherein they made themselves easy, with the Form of Godliness without the Power.[27]

and grace of God much more than the preachers whom New Englanders were accustomed to hearing.

26. Eugene E. White, "Decline of the Great Awakening in New England: 1741 to 1746," *New England Quarterly*, 24 (1951), 36.

27. Thomas Prince, *The Christian History* (Boston, 1745), 2, 385.

To the critics of the revival he appeared as "a monster, impudent & noisy," who brayed beastlike that sinners were "damn'd, damn'd, damn'd!" [28] But whether searching or scathing, the sermons had the same effects as Whitefield's pleadings or Edwards' imprecations: they produced conversions.

It is unnecessary to multiply illustrations from the preaching of revivalists who followed in the wake of Whitefield and Tennent. Whether an Edwards was meticulously reading a closely reasoned argument for awakening doctrines or an overwrought Davenport was haranguing his hearers to "Come to Christ!" each in his own way was seeking to elicit a conscious conversion experience. It is said that the ministry of Whitefield alone resulted in the converting of more than twenty Massachusetts ministers. These, and others who were awakened shortly afterward—to say nothing of the horde of lay exhorters who swarmed into the work of evangelism—laid aside their dull homilies on "God's Controversy" and began to preach with new verve on God's judgment and his grace to converted sinners. The personal quality of religious experience which had characterized the first generation of Puritans returned to churches that had long ceased troubling themselves over whether a visible saint was a real saint. There was now a way to tell the sheep from the goats, and a way to bring more sheep into the fold.

Emotional extravagance. If the fundamental principle of the Great Awakening was insistence on personal conversion, its most striking characteristic was religious excitement. The emotional outbursts which eventually discredited the revival have led some to regard it as "a tempest of ungoverned passions that swept over the colonies, leaving wreckage everywhere in the alienations and divisions in families, neighborhoods, and churches, the undermining of cherished institutions, and a relapse into indifference, debauchery, and irreligion." [29] This is because too many historians have seen the Awakening through the eyes of Charles Chauncy, perhaps the most prejudiced observer of the whole movement, and have not corrected his one-sided reporting with the many sober accounts of genuine revival from some of the most eminent and pious ministers in New England. But there

28. Timothy Cutler, letter dated Sept. 24, 1743, quoted in White, p. 37. Cutler's earlier judgment of Tennent was milder; see William Stevens Perry, ed., *Historical Collections Relating to the American Colonial Church* [Episcopal] (Hartford, 1873), 3, 355.

29. Charles Hartshorn Maxson, *The Great Awakening in the Middle Colonies* (Chicago, 1920), p. 139. One should not infer that this is Maxson's verdict, however.

certainly was a strong emotional charge in the kind of preaching that has been described, which should not be surprising in view of the fact that most sermons before the Awakening were directed to the head rather than to the heart. The revivalists' emphasis on experience required, by its very nature, a highly individual approach which addressed itself to the emotions. This was defended by the theologian of the revival. The heart of true religion is holy affection, Edwards insisted: "our people do not so much need to have their heads stored, as to have their hearts touched." [30]

Hearts were mightily touched:

> In many places, people would cry out, in the time of public worship, under a sense of their overbearing guilt and misery, and the all-consuming wrath of God, due to them for their iniquities; others would faint and swoon under the affecting views which they had of GOD and CHRIST; some would weep and sob, and there would sometimes be so much noise among the people, in particular places, that it was with difficulty that the preacher could be heard. In some few instances, it seems, that the minister has not been able to finish his discourse, there had been so much crying out and disturbance. [31]

Whitefield himself was no stranger to these manifestations. But in spite of the excesses of some of his followers, he plainly tried to keep the emotional responses of his own audiences within bounds. Thomas Prince reported, "I don't remember any *crying out*, or *falling down*, or *fainting*, either under Mr. *Whitefield's* or Mr. *Tennent's* Ministry all the while they were here [in Boston]; tho' many, both Women and Men, both those who had been vicious, and those who had been moral, yea, some Religious and Learned, as well as Unlearned, were in great Concern of Soul." [32]

The need for control became apparent early in the revival. Jonathan Edwards noted that the awakening of the forties was accompanied by stronger emotions than that of 1735. Jerking, fainting, crying out, all

30. "Some Thoughts on the Revival of Religion in New England (1742)," *Works,* 3, 336. Edwards expanded this in *A Treatise Concerning Religious Affections* (Boston, 1746). The early Puritans rather distrusted emotion, fearing that it might outrun or completely deceive the mind.

31. Trumbull, *Complete History of Connecticut,* 2, 155–56.

32. *Christian History,* 2, 386. Chauncy's account of the disturbances under Tennent in Boston is most certainly overdrawn; see *A Letter from a Gentleman in Boston, to Mr. George Wishart* (Edinburgh, 1742), pp. 12–13.

appeared.[33] This was most pronounced in eastern Connecticut, where Jonathan Parsons began to notice "plentiful weeping, sighs and sobs" in his congregation at Lyme on March 29, 1741. A few weeks later, preaching in a neighboring parish, he observed more powerful disturbances:

> When Sermon was over, I cou'd better take notice of the Cause; and the Language was to this Purpose, viz. Alas! I'm undone; I'm undone! O, my sins! How they prey upon my Vitals! What will become of me? How shall I escape the Damnation of Hell, who have spent away a golden Opportunity under Gospel Light, in Vanity? —And much more of the like Import. —'Tis true, *Outcries were new and surprising at that Time:* but knowing the Terrors of the Lord, I was satisfy'd that they were but what might be reasonably accounted for; if Sinners were under a true Sense of their Sins, and the Wrath of a Sin-hating God: And therefore I did not use any Endeavours to restrain them at that Time; but the greater Number cried out of themselves and their Vileness, the more I rejoyced in Hope of the good Issue.[34]

The same happened in many other places. When some of the more volatile revivalists fastened on these outbursts as indispensable evidences of God's working, controversy became inevitable.

Even so, perhaps the saner leaders of the revival might have kept it under control had not the fanatical James Davenport injected himself into the situation at this critical juncture. The clerical friends of the Awakening, who were without exception opposed to all the excesses which formed the staple of Davenport's ministry, make it perfectly clear that although there were powerful emotions at work, there had been no hysteria before his ill-starred appearance. Chauncy indeed soon made a blanket indictment of the entire revival on the ground that Davenport's vagaries differed from the novelties of Whitefield only in degree. But there seems to be enough qualitative difference between the two men to warrant the speed with which the revivalistic pastors tried to dissociate themselves from Davenport. It is important, then, to give detailed attention to this man whom many condemned but none could ignore.

33. Edwards' letter to Prince, *Christian History, 1,* 371.

34. Letter to Prince, ibid., *2,* 135; italics mine. Parsons' sermon *Needful Caution in a Critical Day* (New London, 1742) inveighs against lay exhorting, ignorant enthusiasm, spiritual pride, and rash judging, but makes no mention of emotional outbursts. Evidently he still regarded them as indispensable evidence of the Spirit's working.

James Davenport (1716–57) was a grandson of the saintly founder of New Haven and a son of the learned and pious pastor of Stamford, Connecticut. Graduating from Yale (the youngest in his class) in 1732, he remained to study theology under Elisha Williams. During his years at college he was intimate with Eleazar Wheelock, Benjamin Pomeroy, Daniel Bliss, Aaron Burr, Jonathan Barber, and David Ferris. Ferris later became a Quaker minister, and during his college days evidently adhered to inner light doctrines enough to influence the "holy club" which he gathered around him then. He was nine years older than Davenport, and had been one of the leaders in the New Milford revival of 1727; he was fond of insisting on the immediate operation of the Holy Spirit to produce sudden, conscious conversion and to work the assurance of salvation within the believer's heart. He denounced as false a ministry that adhered to the letter rather than the spirit, and a worship that was performed in the will of the creature rather than in the power of the Creator.[35] How far Davenport at this time adopted Ferris' notions is unknown. He appears to have retained the confidence of his tutors sufficiently to be recommended to a pastorate at Southold on Long Island, where he was installed in 1738.[36]

Here he was only twelve miles from Oyster Ponds, where Jonathan Barber was pastor. When news of the evangelical revival in England and of Whitefield's spectacular meetings in America reached them, both reacted strongly. Barber initiated a series of revival meetings in his own parish, and soon claimed a commission to preach abroad the things the Holy Spirit had revealed to him. At about the same time, Davenport confessed to similar impressions. He gathered his parishioners together and addressed them feverishly for almost twenty-four hours straight. The preacher collapsed (nothing is said of the hearers), and when he recovered began to distinguish those in his congregation whom he deemed converted from those still unregenerate. The former he called "brother," the latter "neighbor," and these he excluded from the Lord's Supper. In 1740 he visited Philadelphia to make the ac-

35. *Memoirs of David Ferris*, pp. 20–39. Ferris withdrew from Yale shortly before graduating in order not to receive his ministerial credentials "from the hand of man."

36. Chauncy (*Seasonable Thoughts on the State of Religion in New-England*, Boston, 1743, pp. 202, 207, 212–13) attributed Davenport's later "enthusiasm" to the influence of Ferris. "Enthusiasm" may be defined as belief in immediate inspiration by divine or superhuman power; it leads to acting on impulses thought to come directly from the Holy Spirit. In extreme cases it may lead to a sort of frenzied possession. The Puritan establishment in New England feared nothing more than the vagaries it attributed to the working of "enthusiasm."

quaintance of Whitefield and Tennent, and imbibed the spirit of the New Side Presbyterians who at that time were greatly exercised by "the danger of an unconverted ministry." The next several months he spent in strenuous evangelistic efforts in eastern Long Island. In the fall he accompanied Whitefield on a preaching tour from New York to Philadelphia.

> By mid-1741 Davenport was immersed in the spirit of the Great Awakening. He had had an opportunity to feel the intensity of the revival in the Middle Colonies; he had travelled with the great Whitefield; and in addition to these experiences, he carried the conviction in his heart that he had himself been granted a divine commission. Davenport was like a musket primed to be fired as soon as a target was brought into its line of fire. He found such a target in New England.[37]

Davenport's assault on southern Connecticut was the point at which the note of hysteria was added to the high fever of spiritual excitement. He arrived in New London on July 18, 1741, and preached his first sermon that evening:

> Divers women were terrified and cried out exceedingly. When Mr. Davenport had dismissed the congregation some went out and others stayed; he then went into the broad alley [aisle], which was much crowded, and there he screamed out, "Come to Christ! come to Christ! come away!" Then he went into the third pew on the women's side, and kept there, sometimes singing, sometimes praying; he and his companions all taking their turns, and the women fainting and in hysterics. This confusion continued till ten o'clock at night. And then he went off singing through the streets.[38]

Davenport next went to the North Parish in New London, where he announced his great fear that pastor David Jewett was unconverted. Then on July 23, "Mr. Davenport preached at Groton 4 or 5 days & mighty works followed. near 1000 hearers (near the old meetinghouse) from all quarters held the meeting till 2 Clock at night & Some Stayed

37. Lawrence N. Jones, "James Davenport: Prodigal of the Great Awakening" (Unpublished MS, Yale Divinity School), p. 15; quoted by permission. I confess here my indebtedness to this perceptive paper in interpreting the enigmatic Davenport.
38. *Diary of Joshua Hempstead of New London, Connecticut* (New London, 1901), p. 379. The original is much mutilated at this point; therefore, I have quoted the above passage from the restoration in Frances Manwaring Caulkins, *History of New London, Connecticut* (2d ed. New London, 1860), p. 454.

all night under the oak tree & in the meeting house. about 60 Wounded, many Strong men as well as others." [39] At Stonington on July 24 there were a hundred conversions, and hundreds more "cryed out." The following day was Sunday, and, when pastor Nathaniel Eells, Jr., refused him the meetinghouse, Davenport held forth under the trees; "but he was So Sever in Judging & Condemning Mr Eells that many of the People in the Assembly withdrew into the meetinghouse where Mr Eells preacht to them as he was wont to do." [40] At Westerly, across the Rhode Island line, Davenport stirred up considerable excitement and counted several Indians among his converts.

The results were not so spectacular at Lyme, where Davenport preached in Jonathan Parsons' pulpit, nor at Saybrook, where pastor William Hart refused him the pulpit. Denouncing Hart as a blind guide, a wolf in sheep's clothing, Davenport preached in the field. Everywhere he aroused resentment and suspicion among the ministers by demands to examine them on their experimental knowledge of Christ. Those who submitted rarely received his endorsement, and those who refused were openly denounced as unconverted. He won a hearing at New Haven because of his descent from the famous founder and his reputation for uncommon sanctity in spite of reported idiosyncrasies. After pronouncing pastor Joseph Noyes unconverted, on very frivolous grounds, he was excluded from the First Church. Nevertheless, he remained in town, preaching to a coterie of admirers, some of whom reported trances and visions under his influence; and then he departed to winter in Southold.

The following spring Davenport resumed his westerly course across southern Connecticut, accompanied by Benjamin Pomeroy and some zealous laymen. This brought him to Ripton parish, Stratford, where he ran afoul of the colony's new law against itinerant preaching. Joseph Blackleach and Samuel Adams carried before the Assembly at Hartford a complaint that

> Mr. Davenport had come into their parish between the 21st and 25th of May, 1742, and with "one Pomeroy," and several "Eleterate" men, had acted in a strange and unaccountable manner, and with many expressions unwarranted from the word of God; did affright and terrify the people, and put them into utmost confusion, contention, hate, and anger among themselves.[41]

39. *Diary of Joshua Hempstead*, p. 380.
40. Ibid.
41. E. B. Huntington, *History of Stamford, Connecticut* (Stamford, 1868), p. 385.

The Assembly was in a severe mood, having just passed "An Act for Regulating Abuses and Correcting Disorders in Ecclesiastical Affairs." [42] Jonathan Law, who had just succeeded Joseph Talcott in the governor's chair, was a vigorous opponent of revivalism and in no disposition to indulge its promoters. Hartford itself was substantially antirevivalist. During the two-day trial, which was held in the First Church, the town was in an uproar:

> As the arrested ministers came out on to the meeting-house steps on the conclusion of the first day's hearing, Davenport began a vehement harangue to the crowds about the door. The sheriff took hold of his sleeve to lead him away. He instantly fell a praying, "Lord! thou knowest somebody's got hold of my sleeve. Strike them, Lord, strike them!" Mr. Pomeroy also called out to the sheriff, "Take heed how you do that heaven-daring action; the God of Heaven will surely avenge it on you. Strike them, Lord, strike them!"
>
> The partisans on either side rushed in to aid or to resist the sheriff. For a while it looked as if the prisoners would be snatched away from him. But they were finally taken to a neighboring house; the disappointed portion of the mob crying out, "We will have five to one on our side to-morrow." The night was little less than a riot. An angry multitude gathered round the house where the two ministers were taken, and were with great difficulty dispersed by the magistrates. In the morning forty militia men were ordered on duty to suppress disorder.[43]

The verdict was a foregone conclusion, although the sentence was remarkably lenient. The Assembly decreed that "the said Davenport is under the influences of enthusiastical impressions and impulses, and thereby disturbed in the rational faculties of his mind, and therefore to be pitied and compassionated, and not to be treated as otherwise he might be." [44] They ordered him deported to Southold, which was done immediately.

In Boston three weeks later Davenport was, if anything, at an even higher pitch. The friends of the revival had more to fear from this intrusion than its enemies. Thomas Prince writes of it as the time when

42. See below, pp. 59–62.

43. George Leon Walker, *History of the First Church in Hartford* (Hartford, 1884), pp. 303–04.

44. *Public Records of the Colony of Connecticut*, ed. Charles J. Hoadly (Hartford, 1874), 8 (1735–43), 483.

the showers of blessing that began with the visit of Whitefield "unexpectedly came to an unhappy Period." [45] Davenport arrived at Charlestown on Friday, June 25, reports Prince. Sunday morning he worshiped and communed with the church there, but stayed home in the afternoon because he feared the minister was unconverted. This "greatly alarmed us." On Monday he was summoned to the ministers' meeting at Boston to testify concerning his reputed practices. The ministers were satisfied as to his personal piety and probable usefulness in the ministry, but they felt constrained to publish a "Declaration" against his acting on impulses, judging ministers, singing in the streets, and encouraging private brethren to preach and pray in public. They voted to refuse him their pulpits because his "usefulness in the church is . . . obstructed by his being deeply tinctured with a spirit of enthusiasm." [46] Shortly after this, according to Prince,

> Mr. Davenport thought himself obliged to begin in his public Exercises to *declare* against *Us* also; naming *some* as *unconverted*, representing *the rest* as *Jehoshaphats* in *Ahab*'s Army, and *exhorting* the People to *separate* from us; which so diverted the Minds of many from being concern'd about *their own* Conversion, to think and dispute about the Case of others; as not only seem'd to put an awful Stop to their Awakenings, but also on *all Sides* to roil our Passions and provoke the Holy Spirit in a gradual and dreadful Measure to withdraw his Influence.[47]

Barred from the churches, Davenport took to the fields—as Whitefield had done—and addressed "pretty large Assemblies" daily on the Common. If the report of his conduct in Boston is only partly true, Prince's reference to the "unhappy Period" is understandable. Often after an incredibly boisterous meeting, Davenport would lead a large mob through the streets, all singing at the top of their voices in such disorderly fashion that it shocked the sensibilities of the whole town. He was arrested, tried, and judged "*non compos mentis,* and therefore . . . *not guilty.*" [48] As before, he was deported.

Daunted neither by this verdict nor by the ecclesiastical council at Southold, which on October 7 censured him for neglecting his responsibility to his own people, Davenport went next to New London on

45. *Christian History, 2,* 406.

46. The Declaration was published in Boston July 1, 1742. It is quoted in full in Tracy, *Great Awakening,* p. 242.

47. *Christian History, 2,* 408.

48. Tracy, p. 248.

March 2, 1743, "sent from God" to purify and perfect the organization of a group of his followers who had withdrawn from the church there. "His mind was in a state of fervid exaltation, amounting to frenzy. Bodily ailments and overstrained faculties had so disordered his reason that he could no longer keep within the bounds of order and propriety." [49] He first ordered his devotees to burn all their wigs, fine clothes, and jewelry, in order to cure them of "idolatrous love of worldly things." He then demanded that they bring all their "unsafe" religious books, and on Sunday evening, March 6, he led the company down to the wharf, where they set fire to works by such authors as William Beveridge, John Flavel, Increase Mather, Benjamin Colman, Joseph Sewall, and Jonathan Parsons! They marched around the pyre shouting "Hallelujah!" and "Glory to God!" declaring that "as the smoke of those books ascended up in their presence, so the smoke of the torment of such of their authors as died in the same belief, was now ascending in hell." [50]

For Davenport this was the zenith of his fanaticism and the nadir of his career. He returned home exhausted—physically, mentally, spiritually. For the first time in over three years he began to come to himself, and soon was writing to Solomon Williams and Eleazar Wheelock [51] requesting to be shown the error of his ways. Williams wrote a dissuasive on judging ministers as unconverted, Wheelock on invasions of the ministerial office by laymen. The arguments were no more than those Davenport had faced countless times, but now he was ready to be convinced. Immediately he published his *Confession and Retractations*, in which he professed to be "fully convinced and persuaded that *several Appendages* to *this glorious Work* are no essential Parts thereof, but of a *different* and *contrary* Nature and Tendency, which I promoted under a misguided Zeal and the influence of a false Spirit." [52] He reproduced at the end a letter he had written to

49. Caulkins, *History of New London*, p. 454.

50. Tracy, p. 249. Miss Caulkins remarks that "this ebullition of misguided zeal appears to have operated on the troubled minds of those engaged in it, like a storm upon the moody atmosphere, dispersing the mists, calming the air, and cooling the temperature. From this period the New Light party in New London took reason and discretion for their guides and interpreted more soberly the suggestions of conscience and the commands of Scripture" (*History of New London*, p. 455).

51. Settled pastors in good standing and both strong friends of the revival. Wheelock's wife was Davenport's sister.

52. *Confession and Retractations* (Boston, 1744), p. 3. Benjamin Colman insisted, with good reason, that "Appendages to" be changed to "Things in the Time of" and that "essential" be deleted. Davenport acquiesced and published his revision with the two letters from Wheelock and Williams later the same year.

Jonathan Barber, then superintendent of Whitefield's orphanage in Georgia, confessing deep and lasting humiliation over the debacle at New London in March 1743:

> I was to my Shame be it spoken, the Ringleader in *that horrid Action;* I was, my dear Brother, under the powerful Influence of the *false Spirit* almost one whole Day together, and Part of several Days. The Lord shewed me afterwards [enthusiasm again!] that the Spirit I was then acted by was in it's Operations void of true inward Peace, laying the greatest Stress on Externals, neglecting the Heart, full of Impatience, Pride and Arrogance; altho' I thought in the Time of it, that 'twas the Spirit of God in an high Degree; awful indeed! my Body especially my Leg much disorder'd at the same Time [a footnote here adds, "I had the *long Fever* on me and the cankry Humour raging at once."], which Satan and my evil Heart might make some Handle of.[53]

The remaining four years of Davenport's pastorate at Southold were spent in comparative quietness. He was drawn into closer relations with the New Side Presbyterians and in 1748 was accepted into the Presbytery of New York. He engaged in supply preaching in New York and New Jersey, made a preaching tour to Virginia with Samuel Davies in 1750, and in 1754 was installed as pastor at Hopewell and Maidenhead, New Jersey. Two years after Davenport's death (1757), Samuel Davies, then president of the College of New Jersey, wrote to Eleazar Wheelock, "I have often talked you over, as a familiar subject, especially with my once favorite friend, Mr. Davenport, now *a blessed inhabitant of heaven.*"[54]

One cannot contemplate such a fascinating figure without some attempt at analysis and interpretation. There certainly was some physical frailty that tormented him as a "thorn in the flesh." In college he had suffered a breakdown that forced him to drop out for two or three months; in his itinerations he was assisted constantly by one whom he called his "armor-bearer"; in New London his leg trouble, "long fever," and "cankry humour" were especially bothersome. This febrile state of body, says Tracy,

> predisposed him to unnatural and unhealthy mental excitement; and on the other hand, his splendid dreams, sleeping and waking, of himself as a great reformer and a special favorite of God, his

---

53. Ibid., pp. 6–7. The recantation affected few of his followers, who denounced him as having gone over to the opposers. The brew was now too heady to be capped.
54. McClure and Parish, *Memoirs of Wheelock,* p. 219.

want of sleep while he spent whole nights in prayer, his excessive pulpit labors and the mental efforts they required, the sight of the multitudes that gathered around him, and of the effect which he produced upon them, their outcries, faintings, convulsions, all bearing witness to his power,—all these things acted through his mind upon his nerves, or upon his nerves directly, and kept up the fever.[55]

Something more than this, however, may be required to explain a man who—though twice pronounced judicially insane—promised so much in his youth, led numbers to an apparently genuine saving knowledge of Christ, and died in the good graces of leaders in a church noted for its strictness in approving ministers. It appears that he was subject in an unusual degree to the influence of those who were to him "prestiged others." Not a creative spirit himself, his forte was enlarging—sometimes to an excess that resulted in caricature—upon the characteristics he admired in others. Thus at crucial periods in his life his course was given a decisive turn by associations with such men as David Ferris, Whitefield, Tennent, Jonathan Barber, Williams, and Wheelock. When this personality twist combined with a propensity to revel in popular acclaim, i.e. to become himself a person of prestige to others, all the necessary forces existed to catapult him onto the center of the stage, where unfortunately he lacked the depth and balance to sustain himself.

It is probable that he suffered from deep inferiority feelings which he expressed in terms of superiority as evidenced by his aggressive, non-conciliatory attitudes toward persons who disagreed with him. On the other hand, he longed for acceptance at the hands of the "prestiged others," and when the opposition from this quarter became so strong, and when the accolades of the crowd were only a mental echo in a sickroom, he retreated from his extreme position in order to "belong" again. Perhaps Davenport was not insane, but he was certainly deeply neurotic.[56]

Whatever personal needs Davenport was seeking to fulfill in his blazing course across New England in those hectic years, he infused into the Great Awakening an emotional extravagance that eventually dissolved it in countless controversies among the churches.

55. *Great Awakening*, p. 252.
56. Jones, "James Davenport," p. 44. Even in his retreat to a more moderate position, Davenport had a model in Gilbert Tennent, who expressed regret for his early rashness in a letter to Jonathan Dickinson on Feb. 12, 1742.

Lay participation. Another innovation which the revival brought into the church way of New England was a much larger opportunity for the common man to participate in religious affairs. The social leveling effects of the Great Awakening have been noted by many writers. Its emphasis on individual responsibility ignored class and geographical boundaries; each man stood before God as a sinner in need of salvation, and each man was required to respond in personal terms. This made the whole movement essentially democratic, and gave a tremendous new importance to the common man.[57] Eventually it was to weaken the autocratic parish system and exalt local church autonomy in an unprecedented way. By uniting large numbers of people in all the colonies in common emotional experiences, it was even to awaken a national self-consciousness. Indeed, Whitefield should be reckoned as America's first really national figure. The revival he fostered encouraged men to criticize entrenched conservatism and eventually to revolt against constituted authority, and thus sharpened the sensibilities that led to the Declaration of Independence. Not without reason has the Great Awakening been called "our national conversion." [58]

One of the more important immediate results of the revival was that it opened numerous new avenues for religious expression on the part of laymen. And they were not slow to enter them. Immediate inspiration by the Holy Spirit of all who had experienced the new birth meant that any truly converted man might preach the gospel. Ignoring the ancient Puritan insistence on a qualified and approved ministry, numbers of newly awakened converts hastened to share their experiences with others and exhort them to receive Christ, to such an extent that settled pastors cried in alarm that their office was being invaded. And the same upsurge in individualism which impelled zealous laymen to "go everywhere preaching the word" also guaranteed them a hearing; for, in the general uprising against the old parish despotism, men insisted on their right to seek and find such spiritual food and guides as suited their own personal needs. In a day when organized religion was controlled by the few, it is not too much to say that the itinerant lay preachers fulfilled a social as well as a re-

---

57. This in no way denies what was said (see above, p. 8) concerning the social and geographical non-particularity of the revival. Many of the aristocracy were "awakened" too, but in terms of sheer numbers the response of the masses is obviously a new force to be reckoned with.

58. H. Richard Niebuhr, *The Kingdom of God in America* (Hamden, Conn., 1956), p. 126. Cf. also Alice M. Baldwin, *The New England Clergy and the American Revolution* (Durham, N.C., 1928), pp. 57–58, 80–81.

ligious need. It was through zealous groups of awakened laymen that the Great Awakening became a people's movement.

It is not possible to state now just where and when lay exhorters first appeared. They were certainly in full strength shortly after James Davenport's first assault on Connecticut. Joseph Fish, pastor at North Stonington 1732–81, says that Davenport "was a great encourager, if not the *first* setter up, of public exhorters." Fish regarded these as a great threat to orderly religion because they engaged not merely in private "encouragement of the brethren" but also in authoritative public discourse much like ministers. Though they were "raw and unskilful, in the word of righteousness," they spake very boldly; and soon were preferred by the ignorant people to the "letter-learned rabbis, scribes and pharisees and unconverted ministers" which Davenport had taught them to contemn. "And thus the *exhorters* came into credit, among the multitudes of people; who chose rather to *hear them*, than their old teachers." [59]

On the other hand, Andrew Croswell, the most zealous and headstrong of the Connecticut revivalists, claimed priority in this respect, although he later had second thoughts about the wisdom of it. On May 17, 1743, he wrote to Thomas Prince:

> I may hereafter print something about the times, showing wherein I have seen reason to alter my judgment, particularly with reference to *exhorters*. For though I was the first in New England that set them up, I now see, too late, that the tendency of their ways is to drive learning out of the world, and to sow it thick with the dreadful errors of Anabaptism, Quakerism, and Antinomianism.[60]

Regardless of who may claim credit for opening this Pandora's box, exhorters soon were swarming everywhere. Jonathan Parsons, early in 1742, gave a long section in his *Needful Caution in a Critical Day* to warning his congregation against them. Later that same year a committee of the Connecticut legislature, appointed to investigate "unhappy Circumstances" at Yale College, reported that some of the students had fallen into the errors of the enthusiasts and were going

59. *The Church of Christ a Firm and Durable House* (New London, 1767), p. 119. Jonathan Parsons wrote to Thomas Prince on April 14, 1744, that Davenport doubtless had been the agent of much good; but some of his practices had a hurtful and divisive tendency, "among which was his encouraging persons in a *Lay* Capacity to set up as the Heads of public Assemblies" (*Christian History*, 2, 154).

60. Letter printed in Boston *Evening Post*, May 30, 1743.

about New Haven and the neighboring towns exhorting after the manner of the itinerants.[61] The stern command of the legislature that the rector take immediate steps to get the students in hand may be understood in the light of the disorderly aspect of most of the lay-led meetings. On December 20, 1742, Joshua Hempstead of New London attended such a meeting and reported:

> Mr. Allin of New London was to come & failed them & after Long waiting the young men 2 of them Newlight Exhorters begun their meeting & 2 or 3 Women followed both at once & there was Such medley that no one could understand Either part untill near night Mr Fish came amongst them and Soon began to Pray & one of the Women Speakers kept on praying and Exhorting at the Same time for Several minutes till at Length She grew Silent & Mr fish had all the work to himself who made a short Discourse & So Dismist us.[62]

In cultured eastern Massachusetts things were no better. Charles Brockwell, Anglican rector at Salem, wrote to the Secretary of the Society for the Propagation of the Gospel, February 18, 1742: "It is impossible to relate the convulsions into which the whole Country is thrown by a set of Enthusiasts that strole about harangueing the admiring Vulgar in *extempore* nonsense, nor is it confined to these only, for Men, Women, Children, Servants, & Negros are now become (as they phrase it) Exhorters." [63] Charles Chauncy noted that they were "most commonly *raw, illiterate, weak* and *conceited young Men, or Lads*" who "pray with the People, call upon them to come to Christ, tell them they are dropping into Hell, and take upon them what they imagine is the Business of preaching." [64]

Whereas Chauncy and the Anglicans sought to fasten on Whitefield the responsibility for all the excesses of the revival, most of its friends regarded Davenport as the author of the extravagances which overdid —and thereby undid—the good work. The vagaries he fostered had by this time a full head of steam, and his *Confessions and Retractations*

61. Franklin Bowditch Dexter, ed., *Documentary History of Yale University* (New Haven, 1916), pp. 356–58.
62. *Diary of Joshua Hempstead*, pp. 402–03. Fish, who is quoted above, was pastor at N. Stonington and a genuine friend of the revival. His experience here may demonstrate the problems faced by such men in seeking to keep religious enthusiasm within bounds.
63. In W. S. Perry, *Historical Collections*, p. 353.
64. *Letter to Wishart*, pp. 9–10.

(1744) had no quieting effect whatsoever. Benjamin Colman of Boston prayed fervently that ministers who had been misled might be righted,

> as well as many poor and miserable *Exhorters* who have sprung up under 'em, like *Mushrooms in a Night,* and in the Morning tho't themselves accomplish'd *Teachers* and *called of GOD* to be so; may awake at length out of their *Dream,* or rather *Delirium,* and despise their own *Image* . . . till like Mr. *Davenport* they be seen to *abhor* themselves, *repenting in Dust and Ashes,* for the unknown *Injury* they have done to the *Work of GOD* thro' the Land.[65]

The first rash of wildness soon passed, though not without leaving irreparable damage in its wake, and even the groups who withdrew from the standing churches to enjoy the ministrations of unlettered (and sometimes unordained) preachers soon found it necessary to place a few restrictions on the "improvement" of ministerial gifts. There remained, however, a strong deposit of laicism in the churches which owed their renascence if not their origin to the Great Awakening.

Ministerial factions. A final innovation which New England faced in the Great Awakening was the unprecedented spectacle of an openly divided clergy. There had been some rather deep differences during the first century of American Puritanism, but the ministry had presented to the public a fairly united front. Previous controversies had waxed warm enough, but nothing had ever run a line of cleavage between opposing ministerial factions as did the revival of the 1740s. Beginning with the questions raised by those who doubted the validity of emotional demonstrations and who were disturbed at the threat to ecclesiastical order posed by the itinerant evangelists and lay exhorters, the opposers of the revival soon began to assert openly that the whole movement was spurious. Friends of the revival tried to maintain its genuineness despite certain unfortunate extravagances. Each side drew up its manifestoes, criticisms, and apologies. Party lines hardened, and New England saw for the first time in its history a clerical house divided against itself.

Open warfare among the clergy erupted in 1743. In May of that year the Massachusetts ministers gathered for their annual meeting in Boston. For some reason it was poorly attended, and the anti-

65. *A Letter from the Reverend Dr. Colman of Boston, to the Reverend Mr. [Solomon] Williams of Lebanon* (Boston, 1744), p. 4.

revivalists found themselves a bare majority. Seizing their advantage, they composed against considerable opposition and protest a declaration which was speedily published as *The Testimony of the Pastors of the Churches in the Province of the Massachusetts-Bay in New-England, at Their Annual Convention in Boston, May 25, 1743. Against Several Errors in Doctrine, and Disorders in Practice, Which Have of Late Obtained in Various Parts of the Land; as Drawn up by a Committee Chosen by the Said Pastors, Read and Accepted Paragraph by Paragraph, and Voted to be Sign'd by the Moderator in Their Name, and Printed.*[66] The errors in doctrine testified against were: following secret impulses believed to be from the Holy Spirit (enthusiasm), believing that assurance is the essence of saving faith, and denying that sanctification is any evidence of justification (antinomianism). The disorders in practice objected to were: itinerant preaching, lay exhorting, ordination of persons at large with no specific charges, separations from the standing churches, judging the unconverted (especially ministers), and emotional extravagance in religious meetings. The document was signed only by the moderator of the convention, Nathaniel Eells of Scituate, which implied that the testimony represented the consensus of all the ministers. This was far from the case. Gaustad observes that it "almost certainly represented a minority opinion. That it called attention to and disapproved of many errors and disorders was not the principal point of contention. The objection was rather to its failure to offer any words of praise or thanksgiving for the genuine good done by the revival, thereby tacitly declaring that there had been no real Awakening."[67]

Within a week the prorevivalists served notice of a counterconvention to bear witness to "the remarkable Work of God" and, at the same time, to caution against admitted errors in doctrine and disorders in practice. Some ninety ministers met in July and prepared *The Testimony and Advice of an Assembly of Pastors of Churches in New-England, at a Meeting in Boston July 7, 1743. Occasion'd by the Late Happy Revival of Religion in Many Parts of the Land. To Which Are Added, Attestations Contain'd in Letters from a Number of Their Brethren Who Were Providentially Hinder'd from Giving Their Presence.*[68] After giving their reasons for believing the revival genuine, they admit there have been unfortunate excesses and proceed to warn against enthusiasm, antinomianism, and Arminianism. They caution:

66. Boston, 1743.
67. *Great Awakening in New England*, p. 63.
68. Boston, 1743.

That *Laymen* do not invade the Ministerial Office, and under a Pretence of *Exhorting* set up *Preaching;* which is very contrary to Gospel Order, and tends to introduce Errors and Confusion into the Church. —That Ministers do not invade the Province of others, and in *ordinary Cases* preach in another's Parish without his Knowledge, and against his Consent. . . . That People beware of entertaining Prejudices against their *own Pastors,* and don't run into *unscriptural* Separations. —That they don't indulge a disputatious Spirit, which has been attended with mischievous Effects; nor discover a Spirit of *Censoriousness, Uncharitableness,* and rash *judging* the State of others.[69]

This was signed by sixty-eight ministers, fifteen of whom went on record as desiring a stronger protest against itinerary. In addition there were twenty letters from forty-three other ministers not in attendance, including twelve from eastern Connecticut, making 111 in all. Since this group testifies against essentially the same errors and disorders as the other, it is apparent that the reluctance of the antirevival party to admit that there was any good mixed with the errors was the real point of dispute. "By the end of 1743, it was evident that the New England clergy was divided not on the question of whether there were errors in doctrine and disorders in practice attending the revival, but on the question of whether, notwithstanding these errors and disorders, the revival was a work of God." [70]

Of the four hundred ministers in New England Ezra Stiles estimated that one hundred and thirty were "New Lights—& of these only 30 violent." [71] Probably an equal number were active opposers, the rest uncommitted. But the ministry which had heretofore presented a reasonably solid front was now openly divided. In the emergence of aggressive parties, ministers who had sought to remain neutral were drawn perforce to one side or the other. Those who favored the revival were designated derisively as "New Lights," because of their insistence on the necessity for conscious conversion as the coming of Christ into the soul; this was uncomfortably similar to the "inner light" descriptive of Quakers and other enthusiasts, than whom none were more feared and despised by the established churches. Opponents of the revival by contrast were known as "Old Lights," which soon became

69. Ibid., p. 11.
70. Gaustad, p. 69.
71. *Extracts from the Itineraries and Other Miscellanies of Ezra Stiles, D.D.,* ed. Franklin Bowditch Dexter (New Haven, 1916), p. 414.

synonymous with rationalism in theology and with the substitution of morality for religion. "Such distinguishing names of reproach," wrote Jonathan Edwards in 1742, "do as it were divide us into two armies, separated, and drawn up in battle array, ready to fight one with another; which greatly hinders the work of God," and "tends greatly to widen and perpetuate the breach." [72]

The full development of ecclesiastical fragmentation saw the emergence of three, rather than two, parties. After 1743 the Old Lights under the highly vocal leadership of Charles Chauncy forsook all semblance of reserve and moderation and followed a course of indiscriminate and intransigent opposition. These men constituted the core of the Arminian movement out of which Unitarianism later developed.[73] At the other extreme there were those who went all out for itinerancy and lay preaching, emotional manifestations as evidence of the Spirit's presence, dramatic conversion and extreme censoriousness toward those who were deemed unconverted, and enthusiastic impulses as the rule of judgment and action. These took their initial cue from James Davenport, but their momentum was soon so great that they were unaffected by the retreat of their idol to a more moderate position.

The middle party comprised those who had recognized the hand of God in the revival and had participated wholeheartedly in it, seeking at the same time to restrain the excesses which were the targets of so much Old Light criticism. Besides Edwards, such men as Bellamy and Wheelock served as leaders of this group in Connecticut. Among the pastors of eastern Massachusetts perhaps Thomas Prince, who served as chief intelligencer of revival news, should be named, though others were more active as revival preachers. This was the party which strove to convince the world that this was indeed God's work, however much it may have been marred by human imperfection and folly. Its members rejoiced at the genuine transformations in lives and churches even while they bore testimony against the errors which mingled so disastrously with the revival.[74]

72. "Thoughts on the Revival of Religion in New England," *Works*, 3, 407.

73. Cf. Conrad Wright, *The Beginnings of Unitarianism in America* (Boston, 1955).

74. For a different description of party alignment in terms of theological differentiation after the Great Awakening, see George Park Fisher, *A Discourse, Commemorative of the History of the Church of Christ in Yale College* (New Haven, 1858), pp. 6–7. He delineates the positions as traditional Calvinism ("more a lifeless tradition than a vital, intelligent faith"), departures from Calvinism ("called by their opponents, without proper discrimination, Arminians"), and Edwardsean revivalism (the "New Divinity," or "New England Theology").

The conservative New Lights have been compared to the English Puritans, who sought to reform the Establishment from within, while the radicals who withdrew to form separate churches have been likened to the early English separatists.[75] There is much truth in this. The same factors—extreme individualism and biblical literalism— were operating to produce the centrifugal forces that soon shattered the homogeneous pattern of New England's church way. Inured to both the aspersions of their enemies and the appeals of their friends, the extreme New Lights would not be restrained. As bearers of a new "reformation without tarying for anie," they soon withdrew to form churches where the innovations of the Great Awakening might be normalized—if not stereotyped.

75. M. Louise Green, *The Development of Religious Liberty in Connecticut* (Boston, 1905), p. 238.

2. SEPARATISM EMERGES: THE ISSUES

THE ECCLESIOLOGICAL ISSUE

The first and most basic issue that led the extreme New Lights to withdraw in large numbers from the standing order was concerned with the constitution of the churches. Their protest at this point centered on two things which they thought were inconsistent with spiritual religion: the continued reception and retention of unconverted members by the churches, and an ecclesiastical platform (especially in Connecticut) which vested control of the churches in a clerical class and enforced their support by means of the civil power. These matters are put succinctly in a historical sketch by one of the Separate [1] pastors:

> The three capital articles in our separation from the standing churches, were these, viz. First, Their holding to, and practicing upon, the principle of graceless communion. —Secondly, The ministers, or ministry, ingrossing into their hands, the power of church government, and the power of minister-making, or the sole right of ordination. —Thirdly, The churches submitting under the government of a certain body of ecclesiastical laws, made in this State. [2]

These three complaints are in reality two—the standard of church membership and the ecclesiastical constitution—and will be discussed under those headings.

The standard of church membership. "Graceless communion" is the admission into church membership of those who could not testify to a personal experience of grace. Accessions to the churches during the sporadic revivals which preceded the Great Awakening seem for the most part to have been Halfway members, and even in the Awakening itself this continued to be the case. Nor was the sweeping revival,

1. The separatists will be referred to generally as "Separates," although the more accurate term—used by themselves and made official by an act of the Connecticut legislature in 1777—is "Strict Congregationalists."

2. Eliphalet Wright, *The Difference between Those Called Standing Churches and Those Called Strict Congregationalists Illustrated* (Norwich, 1775 [1778]), p. 20. The author was pastor of the Separate church at Killingly, Connecticut, 1765–84.

for all its emphasis on conversion, deep enough and lasting enough in its effects to lead to a speedy abrogation of the Halfway Covenant. On the contrary, "in churches which seemed to share most deeply in the Awakening, the Half-Way Covenant continued with unabated vigor after the revival ceased." [3] For this reason, separations occurred in revivalistic as well as antirevivalistic churches. Indeed, it was in those very churches where the revival was strongest that separatism most frequently appeared, and the reason given was that the church continued to sanction graceless communion. A convert of the revival wrote later to his former pastor:

> great numbers flocked into the churches; of which I was one, tho' not without great struggles of mind, because I thought the gospel rules about admitting and disciplining of church members, were not so strictly observed as they ought to have been; yet, as I saw no other way to enjoy the precious ordinance of the Lord's supper, I joined with your church; where I continued more than two years, hoping for a reformation; but instead of that, the custom was continued of letting such as did not pretend to be converted, bring their children to baptism; and of receiving members upon written revelations of experiences into the church, which I ever thought to be an unscriptural way; 'till from that, you obtained a vote to admit persons without any relation at all, if they did not see cause to give any.[4]

When the Separates justified their schism on such grounds, the ministerial friends of the revival turned against them in opposition just as truculent as that of the Old Lights.

The admission of unregenerate persons into church membership had given rise to separations from churches in the Puritan tradition even in the absence of revivalism. This was true in seventeenth-century England, where the Established Church was attacked, not only for its "unscriptural" government and corrupt morals, but also because its inclusive constitution had all but obliterated the distinction between the church and the world. In New England the con-

3. S. Leroy Blake, *The Separates, or Strict Congregationalists of New England* (Boston, 1902), p. 55. Evidence of this may be seen in Jonathan Edwards' church, which dismissed him in 1750 for seeking to reinstate the experimental requirement for church membership. An examination of other churches which participated in the revival shows that many manifested a continuing attachment to the Halfway Covenant.

4. Isaac Backus, *A Letter to the Reverend Mr. Benjamin Lord, of Norwich* (Providence, 1764), pp. 32–33.

viction that "visible saints are the only fit matter for a gospel church" had been as dear as life itself. At the very outset, adoption of the Halfway Covenant had occasioned schisms in the churches at Boston, Windsor, Hartford, and Stratford; and the church at Branford had moved completely out of the New Haven jurisdiction (to New Ark, New Jersey) to avoid accepting the odious compromise. Separation on this ground, therefore, was not a new thing, and these precedents supplied many forceful arguments to the converts of the Great Awakening who again became fired with the ideal of the pure church.

The new winnowing had even been predicted. Increase Mather said in 1700, "If the begun apostasy should proceed as fast the next thirty years as it has done these last, surely it will come to that in New England, that the most conscientious people therein will think themselves concerned to gather churches out of churches." [5] This is exactly what happened. The converts of the Great Awakening viewed the Halfway Covenant and Stoddardeanism as having perniciously "turned the world into the church, and the church into the world, in such a manner as to leave very little difference between them." [6] The group which withdrew from the Scotland church (third parish, Windham) stated, in part:

> We dissent from them, because they Admit of Half-membership, or Persons owning the Covenant and coming to the Ordinance of Baptism, and stopping there. . . . [We dissent] Because they (i.e. the Church,) receive Members into the Church, without giving Personal Satisfaction to the Church, that they are true Members of CHRIST, by declaring what GOD hath done for their Souls.[7]

On this ground the Separates undertook a new reformation of the churches, which they thought had been hopelessly diluted in purity and diverted from scriptural standards by three generations of compromising with the world.

The ecclesiastical constitution. The dispute over the rights of the local church was more violent in Connecticut, where the churches had been subject to tighter connection and control since 1708, than in Massachusetts. The Scotland Separates voiced the conviction of all

5. Quoted in Isaac Backus, *Church History of New England, from 1620 to 1804* (Philadelphia, 1839), p. 161. Referred to hereafter as *Abridged History.*
6. Ibid., p. 151.
7. Ebenezer Devotion, *An Answer of the Pastor and Brethren of the Third Church in Windham, to Twelve Articles, Exhibited by Several of Its Separating Members, as Reasons of Their Separation* (New London, 1747), pp. 2–3.

their brethren when they wrote to the parish minister, "That they (i.e., the Church) have not Covenanted together, in any Form of Discipline, according to the Word of GOD; but do Act upon the *Saybrook* Platform, which we think to be disagreeable to the Word of GOD, and therefore reject it." [8] This was still uppermost in the minds of the Connecticut Separates when, at a convention in 1781, they approved a historical narrative and a confession of faith. This document stresses the same two causes for separation: the admission of church members without requiring a credible profession of faith, and a rigid enforcement of the Saybrook Platform:

> We according to our Judgment, looked upon the Ecclesiastical Constitution of this State, and the Traditions thereof, to be a great Departure from the Order of the Apostolick Churches, as well as from the Platform of our Fore Father's in this Land. And although they were called, and importuned to take some Step for Reformation, they refused, and justified themselves in their Constitution, and Practice. Here we judged it necessary, and became our Duty to withdraw from their Fellowship, and Communion; so far as they had departed from the Rule of God's Word. [9]

The Saybrook Platform was an abomination to the Separates because, in most uncongregational fashion, it restricted the ordination and approval of ministers to a clerical association and made the churches too reliant upon the state for their existence and support. To deny the right of "minister-making" to the churches seemed to the Separates a repudiation of strict congregational principles.

The other part of the ecclesiastical constitution, which operated in Massachusetts as well as in Connecticut, was compulsory support of the established clergy through ministerial rates and church taxes, which were imposed on every family in a parish whether they attended the standing church or not. This had long been the traditional church way in New England; voluntary contributions for the support of the ministry rarely found favor outside Rhode Island.[10] But when the New Lights came to regard the established clergy as un-

8. Ibid., p. 1.
9. *An Historical Narrative and Declaration* (Providence, 1781), p. 10.
10. The attempt of early Massachusetts churches to subsist on voluntary contributions was short-lived. John Winthrop (*Winthrop's Journal*, ed. James Kendall Hosmer, New York, 1908, *1*, 299) recorded that on May 2, 1639, John Cotton had preached "that the ministers' maintenance should be by voluntary contribution, not by lands, or revenues, or tithes, etc." But the framers of the Cambridge Platform were not prepared to go this far, and the Separates were the first of the New England Congregationalists to adopt voluntary support as a basic principle.

profitable, in many cases unconverted, and apparently determined to suppress the free exercise of spiritual religion, it is not surprising that they protested loudly against a "hireling clergy" and refused to pay their church rates. The ministers' resort to legal pressures to collect their salaries excited the martyr complex which minority movements frequently manifest, and it also served to heighten resentment against the pastors and their churches. Isaac Backus commented wryly that the hirelings had changed the Scripture to read, "They who preach the gospel shall live of the law." [11] The persecution which arose in the course of the struggle over taxes will be told in another connection, but here the point is that the reliance of the standing churches upon the power of the state was further proof to the Separates that the whole religious establishment had deteriorated so sadly that no conscientious Christian could possibly remain a part of it.

It is important to stress again that these ecclesiological questions raised an issue that cannot be correlated with the attitude of the standing churches and ministers toward the revival. This is not true of the other issues to be discussed. In this sole but crucial instance, the revival merely brought into prominence—by giving birth to large numbers of new converts zealous for the untrammeled expression of experimental piety—a controversy that had long lain barely beneath the surface in New England Congregationalism.

THE THEOLOGICAL ISSUE

It is only natural that questions regarding the standards for church membership should focus attention also on the way of salvation. The revival posed anew a theological issue which soon became a battleground for controversy, namely the age-old question, "What must I do to be saved?" Here the problem is not with the three-stage drama of conversion under revivalistic preaching, but with the agent of salvation. Specifically, what part do sinners play—if any—in saving their souls?

The use of means. Before the Great Awakening, one went to heaven from New England by a diligent employment of the ordinary means of grace offered through the regular ministrations of the churches. No one, neither the most fervent Halfway Covenanter nor Solomon Stoddard himself, denied that the grace was from God and that it was absolutely necessary to salvation. The New Lights were not the

11. *A Fish Caught in His Own Net* (Boston, 1768), p. 75. Backus was not opposed to a salaried ministry; cf. *The Liberal Support of Gospel Ministers, Opened and Inculcated* (Boston, 1790).

only ones to agree with Josiah Dwight of Woodstock that "if un-converted men ever got to heaven, they would feel as uneasy as a shad up the crotch of a white oak." [12] But almost from the beginning many ministers, while still holding verbally to the doctrine of election, had taught the necessity for nurture and had fostered a doctrine of prepara-tion.[13] The result was that regeneration, if it came at all, was so subtle as scarcely to be cognizable; and even before the adoption of the Halfway Covenant it was generally presumed that those who were faithful in the use of means were assured of salvation. The spread of Stoddardeanism accentuated this kind of thinking, so that by the time of the Great Awakening salvation was thought to come chiefly through the performance of religious duties enjoined by the clergy.

Something of this appears in the reply of Ebenezer Devotion, pastor at Scotland, against the Separates who had complained that his church permitted persons to own the covenant for baptism and then stop, which is to say that the church received halfway members. Devotion answered that the church practiced according to the ancient usage of New England: it baptized the infants of those who owned their bap-tismal covenant and expected that when these reached adulthood they would own the covenant for themselves and enter into all the privileges of the church. That they did not was due doubtless to their fear of coming to the Lord's Supper unworthily. But, continued Devotion,

> this Church has admitted none to Baptism in their Adult Years, nor any to Own the Covenant and obtain Baptism for their In-fants, but that they could freely have Admitted to the other Sacrament, and to all the External Privileges of the Church: And we esteem it Wrong, not that they own their Covenant and get their Children Baptized, but wrong that they don't come to the other Sacrament. . . . So that if in this point the Church have Err'd, this must be their Error, *viz.* that they have not Censur'd every Baptized Person for not coming to the Lord's Table.[14]

12. George L. Clark, *A History of Connecticut* (New York, 1914), p. 276.

13. One of the earliest indications was Thomas Hooker, *The Soule's Preparation for Christ* (London, 1632). Cf. Perry Miller, *The New England Mind: From Colony to Province* (Cambridge, 1953), pp. 55 ff.

14. Devotion, p. 2. Devotion unwittingly put his finger on a problem which was soon to plague the Separates just as it had the first generation of "experienced" Puritans—though with a quite different result. He asks: What answer can be made to those "who allow of Infant Baptism, but allow none to be Members in full with their Church, until the Church feels them, or knows they are Converted, by the Relation of their Experiences?" The answer would be either that baptized infants are not in covenant with the church at all and are in no sense members, or that they

Under the impact of the Great Awakening this sort of reliance upon means, and even the value of Christian nurture, came to be viewed with suspicion by those who were overwhelmed at the wave of surprising conversions. The despair of undone sinners and the joy of new-born souls, visibly wrought under the influence of awakening preaching, were so obviously a work of God that no human efforts could possibly prepare for them. They seemed so entirely the doing of the divine Spirit in an operation of sovereign grace that whoever suggested that salvation might be won by any other means was simply a stranger to the wondrous ways of God. Thus it came about that all who denied the genuineness of sudden and sensible conversion were branded, without proper discrimination, as Arminians. In its own way the Great Awakening renewed the controversy between Arminians and Calvinists, particularly as these systems centered on two apparently irreconcilable ways of salvation.

The reassertion of sovereign grace. A classic Reformed doctrine which emerged quite prominently in the revival was that of sovereign —even irresistible—grace. This means that salvation is entirely a free gift of God who bestows it according to his inscrutable purposes upon whomever he will, that no one can possibly merit or deserve it, and that those to whom it comes (the "elect") are completely unable to resist or refuse it. In its starkest form this doctrine would seem to lead not only to antinomianism but to antirevivalism as well; and it required considerable theological acuity on the part of the revival preachers to avoid the Arminianizing tendency inherent in revivalism. After all, the gospel must address the will of the sinner, and salvation must lead to holiness.

Both these problems were treated by Isaac Backus, a Connecticut Separate who later became a Baptist, in *The Doctrine of Sovereign Grace Opened and Vindicated.* . . .[15] The controversy, says Backus, turns on the question of whether the good pleasure of God or the free will of man is the origin of faith, the ground of justification, and the true cause of holiness. Paul's doctrine of holiness is *"He hath chosen us, that we should be holy;* but the modern notions are, that he chooseth us because we *are holy,* making that to be the *cause,* which *Paul* viewed to be the *effect."* [16] It is a weak concept of human depravity

---

are halfway members. Devotion considered the first alternative absurd and naturally chose the second; but many of the Separates chose the first, and consequently became Baptists.

15. Providence, 1771.
16. Ibid., p. 8.

which frustrates the grace of God by making salvation depend on the will of the creature rather than the work of the Creator:

> I have been the more particular here to detect the deceit and blindness of the attempts that are often made, to represent irresistible grace to be inconsistent with the soul's liberty of choice; for there are descriptions of the work of grace that are absolutely irresistible, if any thing can be so; and yet there is not the least violence used with man's will, for the enemy is conquered with the full consent of all his heart: He is slain and made alive by the power of truth.[17]

Backus cites an instance of some besieged rebels: they offer to capitulate (a "work" which merits favor), but are told that they have no choice but to surrender to the king's mercy, i.e. throw themselves without reserve on his grace. Having received mercy, they gratefully submit themselves as good subjects from that time forth.

Divergent views of the way of salvation precipitated considerable controversy within the standing churches themselves. The revival party which arose under the leadership of Jonathan Edwards, though containing the most earnest and able defenders of Puritan faith, recast the traditional Westminster doctrines in bold new forms and maintained them on philosophical grounds. Their system, which came to be known as the New England Theology or New Divinity, ultimately emerged victorious and for a century after the Great Awakening held undisputed sway in the Connecticut Valley. But while the architects of the New Divinity were burying the Halfway Covenant and beating back the Arminians, the more extreme New Lights were deciding that they could not remain under the lifeless preaching of the established clergy. The Scotland Separates informed the pastor that they could not abide the "want of Gospel Preaching in the clear Demonstration of the Spirit and of Power: The Letter killeth, but the Spirit giveth life." [18] Such men left the "cold, dry husks" of the "morality preachers" to seek sounder doctrine from those who proclaimed "free grace." They withdrew in the manner of the Connecticut layman who had his own way of expressing disapprobation of clerical error:

> When doctrine as preached was not in line with his straight-edge [he] went axe in hand to the meetinghouse, chopped out the sheep-pen pew in which he and his family had sat ever since the

17. Ibid., p. 56. How like the modern "rediscoverers" of Luther!
18. Devotion, p. 6.

meetinghouse was built, and transferred it "root and branch and all in all" to his own attic. The uprooted pew became the rallying ground for other aggrieved members, and soon a new church was formed.[19]

THE PRACTICAL ISSUE

It was not enough to settle the theological problem of salvation by grace, or even the ecclesiological question of personal conversion as prerequisite to church membership—the practical problem still remained of discerning accurately who were converted. What were the assurances of one's own salvation, and by what evidences could others be judged? These were dangerous and difficult questions, but they were raised inescapably when the revival disrupted the comfortable complacency of the old order.

The doctrine of assurance. One thing which most sharply differentiated New Lights from Old Lights was the insistence of the former on the possibility and necessity of assurance of salvation. This grew directly out of the revivalists' emphasis on personally experienced conversion, and developed into a pietistic inwardness that even the early Puritans never knew. Whatever assurance came to those in the Puritan tradition usually proceeded from their covenantal theology; they were convinced that God's faithfulness toward his covenanted people would never fail.

The New Lights went far beyond this to claim that genuine faith carries its own assurance. Some even declared that if such assurance were lacking, faith was spurious. They taught that assurance was the essence of saving faith. This meant further that doubting on the part of a believer was sin. The Separate church at Mansfield, Connecticut, declared in its confession of faith that "all doubting in a believer is sinful, being contrary to the command of God, and hurtful to the soul, and an hindrance to the performance of duty." [20] Their proof text was Romans 14:23, "Whatsoever is not of faith is sin."

Ebenezer Frothingham, a leading Separate pastor, defended their position on this point, contending that Christians who doubt their salvation cannot perform properly any duty to God or humanity: they cannot pray in faith, they cannot help the needy in the name of

19. Ola Elizabeth Winslow, *Meetinghouse Hill, 1630–1783* (New York, 1952), p. 236.
20. Article xviii; quoted in *The Result of a Council of the Consociated Churches of the County of Windham* (Boston, 1747), p. 7.

Christ, they cannot confess their faith for the glory of Christ, and so
forth. Such doubters "practically make a middle Way between Heaven
and Hell, and we know not what to call it, unless it is Purgatory; for
these doubting Persons will not own that they are really Saints, and so
belong to the Family of Heaven; neither will they say that they are
altogether in their Sins, and so bound to Hell, and under the Sentence
of Damnation." [21] But the regular clergy regarded the whole doctrine
of assurance as held by the New Lights as dangerous. The Windham
County ministers asserted that it tended to "render all the Warnings
of the Gospel against Hypocrisy vain and ineffectual," and to encourage lasciviousness.[22] As later events were to show, its basis was
altogether too interior and subjective.

Evidences of conversion. If it was necessary to have complete assurance of one's own salvation, it was equally necessary that one be able
to convince others of the fact. Or, put another way, those who had
received the "new light" must be satisfied that a professed convert stood
in the same light before they could admit him into their fellowship.
As this was the basis for constituting churches composed only of the
regenerate, it led to considerable concern over the question of how
the redeemed might be known. This was a problem which plagued all
the revivalists. Jonathan Edwards confessed that many had censured
him for endeavoring to pronounce upon the genuineness of the conversions wrought in the Northampton awakening of 1734–35. About
this time he had noted some "Directions for Judging of Persons' Experiences":

See to it that the operation be much upon the Will or heart, not
on the Imagination, nor on the speculative understanding or motions of the mind, though they draw great affections after 'em as
the consequence. . . . That under their seeming convictions it be
sin indeed; that they are convinced of their guilt, in offending and
affronting so great a God. . . . That it is truly conviction of sin
that convinces them of the Justice of God in their damnation. . . .
That there is to be discerned in their sense of the sufficiency of
Christ, a sense of that Divine, supreme, and spiritual excellency of
Christ, wherein this sufficiency fundamentally consists; and that
the sight of this excellency is really the foundation of their satisfaction as to His sufficiency. . . . Whether their experience have

21. *Articles of Faith and Practice* (Newport, 1750), p. 113.
22. *The Result of a Council of the Consociated Churches of the County of
Windham*, p. 13.

a respect to PRACTICE in these ways. That their behaviour at present seems to be agreeable to such experiences. . . . Makes a disposition to ill practices dreadful. Makes 'em long after perfect
freedom from sin, and after those things wherein *Holiness* consists.[23]

This detailed instruction exhibits Edwards' outline of the stages in
the conversion process and his strong caution against the encouragement of antinomianism. He had emphasized this when he spoke at
New Haven in 1741 on *The Distinguishing Marks of a Work of the
Spirit of God.* The real evidence of genuine religious experience, he
stated there, is an increase of love for Jesus Christ and obedience to
his will as revealed in the Scriptures.[24]

The more extreme New Lights soon grew impatient with insistence
on demonstrated holiness as evidence of conversion. They held that
sanctification is no proof of justification, and even the ministerial
friends of the revival could not control the more exuberant converts
on this point. Joseph Fish, who witnessed at North Stonington "powerful and wonderful operations" of the Spirit, blamed himself for giving too free a hand to the boisterousness of the people in the early
stages of the Awakening. He received 104 new members into his
church in 1742; and although he tried to examine them all very carefully, he had to confess that their subsequent behavior proved their
real ignorance of the great doctrines of the gospel:

> Many gross errors prevail'd . . . the power of godliness [was]
> very much placed in *noise* and *outcry* . . . pure and undefiled
> religion [was] in imminent danger of being lost from among us
> . . . therefore, after mature deliberation, solemn enquiry and
> deep concern, I begun more fully upon the difficult and danger-
> ous work, of correcting the errors and mistakes of the *christians*
> . . . both as to their principles and practices, in *many things.*

What he did was to emphasize the doctrine of sanctification, "preaching
up good works" as the only adequate evidence of saving faith. But

23. Alexander B. Grosart, ed., *Selections from the Unpublished Writings of Jonathan Edwards, of America* (Edinburgh, 1865), pp. 183–85. In spite of his care
and caution, Edwards must have had many spurious conversions—as witness his
church's readiness to dismiss him in 1750 for insisting on regenerate church membership.

24. *Works, 1,* 543. By this time, however, Edwards was more cautious about
trying to pronounce on specific persons, and especially about denying professions
to be genuine (pp. 559–62). His final position was that judging is God's prerogative
and must be left to him.

the people, instead of being convinced, turned on their pastor. "So that what offended them, and finally prov'd an occasion of their separating from us, was, in *general,* the exposing and correcting their *disorders, gross errors and mistakes,* which were a reproach to the religion of Jesus Christ." [25]

In reacting against this "legalism" on the part of their ministers, the New Lights adopted a standard for judging the spiritual state of others which was altogether subjective. Called by some the "key of knowledge," it was the notion that only those with whom they "held communion in the inward actings of their own souls" were true Christians. This key was presumed to be so infallible that those who held it believed that a Christian may be known from an unbeliever "as clearly as a sheep may be known from a dog." [26] Ebenezer Frothingham justified this pretension by claiming that God illuminated the understanding of the believer so that a right judgment could be formed. "A Saint of God having Divine Light shining into the Understanding, and the Love of God (or pure Charity, which is the same), ruling in the Soul, is also to know certainly that such and such Persons are true Converts, or the Saints of God." [27] An illustration of how this key operated may be seen in a record from New London:

> Natt Williams of Stonington Lodged here. he went over in the Evening to Mr. Hills . . . and thare Related his Christian Experiences in order to have their approbation but behold the Quite Contrary, for they upon Examination find him yet in an unconverted Estate & Judged him So & he Confesses the Justice of their Judgment & Says that he hath Judged others Divers times and altho he is unwilling to believe it yet like others is forced to bear it.[28]

Elisha Paine, another leader among the Separates, cited I Corinthians 2:15 as proof that such practice was scriptural: "He that is spiritual judgeth all things." When someone objected that only God can judge men's hearts, Paine replied, "we don't judge by Man's Judgment, but

25. *The Church of Christ a Firm and Durable House,* pp. 132–37. The Separates at Providence accused pastor Josiah Cotton of being a "dull, general preacher—for holding Sanctification the best Evidence of Justification &c" (*The Literary Diary of Ezra Stiles, D.D., L.L.D.,* ed. Franklin Bowditch Dexter, New York, 1901, *1,* 272).

26. Ellen D. Larned, *History of Windham County, Connecticut* (Worcester, Mass., 1874), *1,* 469.

27. *Articles of Faith and Practice,* p. 47.

28. *Diary of Joshua Hempstead,* p. 405.

by GOD in us"; and fell to praying, thanking God for the privilege given him to know the saints and beseeching that his skeptical friend might be enlightened to know the truth.[29]

It is not surprising that the established clergy used every cannon in its arsenal to explode this "enthusiastic" notion. Isaac Stiles of North Haven, preaching the election sermon in 1742, warned the Connecticut magistrates to "Beware of that *Luciferian Pride and Arrogancy*, which prompts some to invade the Divine Prerogative, to anticipate the Work of the Day of Judgment, to take upon them to Judge the Secrets of mens Hearts & determine their State Godward, to Censure & Condemn even those as Unconverted & Hypocrites, *of whom the world is not worthy.*" [30] The ministers of Windham County warned that Christians must not presume to set "soul-satisfying knowledge" in place of God's searching judgment; for this is to make "a Person's Right to be treated outwardly as a Christian . . . depend upon the Fancy or secret Judgment of others who think themselves Christians, which in reality makes a *new Institution* of the Rules and Laws of the *Christian Religion.*" [31] The prorevival ministers, testifying in 1743, were extremely anxious that the new converts should not "discover a Spirit of *Censoriousness, Uncharitableness,* and rash *judging* the State of others."

Despite such cautions, many sincere Christians were labeled as unconverted and attacked as opposers of the work of God simply because they could not (or would not) satisfy the subjective test proposed by the extreme New Lights. The censorious spirit and rash judgment which for a time was a hallmark of New Light practice was most pernicious when directed at the clergy, and this became such a crucial factor in the rise of separatism that it deserves special attention.

Attacks on "unconverted" ministers. There is some justification for attempts to fasten on Whitefield the responsibility for the avalanche of accusations against the standing ministers as blind guides. When in Boston the first time, he was invited to preach the public lecture at the Old South Church; and though he had planned to use another text, it was impressed on him to turn to the third chapter of John's Gospel.

29. *A Letter from the Associated Ministers of the County of Windham, to the People in the Several Societies in Said County* (Boston, 1745), p. 11. After the first flurry of extravagance, the Separates moderated considerably on this point. By 1781, they were at pains to check both antinomianism and enthusiasm; cf. *An Historical Narrative and Declaration,* p. 18. But as an early issue, it was an important factor in schism.

30. *A Prospect of the City of Jerusalem* (New London, 1742), pp. 55–56.

31. *The Result of a Council of the Consociated Churches of the County of Windham,* p. 15.

A large number of ministers were present and Whitefield bore heavily on verse ten, "Art thou a teacher in Israel and knoweth not these things?" Later he wrote in his journal that the Lord had enabled him to open his mouth boldly against unconverted ministers, and to caution churches to inquire carefully into the religious experience of candidates for ordination. When this journal was published in 1741, its aspersions upon the clergy made Whitefield highly unpopular in ministerial circles in New England. Upon leaving Connecticut in November 1740 he had written:

> For I am verily persuaded the Generality of Preachers talk of an unknown, unfelt Christ. And the Reason why Congregations have been so dead is, because dead Men preach to them. O that the Lord may quicken and revive them for his own Name's Sake. For how can dead Men beget living Children? 'Tis true, God may convert People by the Devil, if he pleases, and so he may by unconverted Ministers; but I believe he seldom or never makes Use of either of them for this purpose; No: the Lord will chuse men who are vessels meet by the Operations of his blessed Spirit, for his sacred Use. And as for my own Part, I would not lay Hands knowingly on an unconverted Man for ten thousand Worlds.[32]

Summarizing his New England tour, he wrote: "Many, nay most that preach, I fear do not experimentally know Christ." [33]

Whitefield's barnstorming successor in New England had already distinguished himself as a devastating polemicist against "carnal" clergymen. Gilbert Tennent launched an open attack at Nottingham on March 8, 1740, when he declaimed on "The Danger of an Unconverted Ministry." [34] Attacking the "Orthodox, Letter-learned and regular Pharisees" as "Natural Men [who] have no Call of GOD to the Ministerial Work," Tennent deplored their presence in the church because it left the sheep without a shepherd. Under such "blind Guides" and "dead Dogs, that can't bark," many poor Christians are stunted and starved; "the Ministry of natural Men, is for the most part unprofitable." Tennent compared an unconverted minister to "a Man who

---

32. *A Continuation of the Reverend Mr. Whitefield's Journal . . . the Seventh Journal* (2d ed. London, 1744), p. 40. The entire paragraph is in italics in the original.

33. Ibid., pp. 56–57.

34. For the circumstances of the sermon, which were quite crucial for Presbyterianism in the Middle Colonies, see Leonard J. Trinterud, *The Forming of An American Tradition* (Philadelphia, 1949), pp. 56–58.

would learn others to swim, before he has learn'd it himself, and so is drowned in the Act, and dies like a Fool." [35]

If Tennent's outburst had ended with mere denunciation, he might have been dismissed as an overheated zealot letting off steam at a time when Presbyterian revivalists were about to be squelched by an unspiritual majority. The radical part of his sermon lies in the program of action he offered to whoever might heed his warning about the peril of sitting under a "dead" preacher:

> If the Ministry of Natural Men be as it has been represented; Then it is both lawful and expedient to go from them to hear Godly Persons; yea, it's so far from being sinful to do this, that one who lives under a pious Minister of lesser Gifts, after having honestly endeavour'd to get Benefit by his Ministry, and yet gets little or none, but doth find real Benefit and more Benefit elsewhere; I say, he may *lawfully* go, and that *frequently*, where he gets most Good to his precious Soul, after regular Application to the Pastor where he lives, for his Consent, and proposing the Reasons thereof; when this is done in the Spirit of Love and Meekness, without Contempt of any, as also without rash *Anger* or vain Curiosity. . . . To bind Men to a particular Minister, against their Judgment and Inclinations, when they are more edified elsewhere, is carnal with a Witness; a cruel Oppression of tender Consciences, a compelling of Men to Sin. . . . Besides, it is an unscriptural Infringement of Christian Liberty. . . . [Therefore] let those who live under the Ministry of dead Men, whether they have got the Form of Religion or not, repair to the Living, where they may be edified. . . . Let who will oppose it.[36]

It is true that Tennent never encouraged separation in terms any more drastic than those of the Nottingham sermon. Indeed, he specifically denied that he ever approved the setting up of separate meetings at all, even where the minister's carnal state was painfully obvious.[37] The passages quoted indicate that he had in mind that unfed sheep should seek spiritual food from the hands of some other *approved* shepherd, one known to be regenerate. But his disclaimer was advanced *after* the schism in the Presbyterian synod, when the expelled revivalistic presbyteries were already providing ample opportunity for the expression of New Light sympathies within the

35. *The Danger of an Unconverted Ministry* (3d ed. Boston, 1742), pp. 2–12.
36. Ibid., pp. 12–19.
37. *The Examiner Examined* (Philadelphia, 1743), p. 88.

Presbyterian Church. The ecclesiastical situation in New England was entirely different, and the only way in which dissatisfied parishioners could follow Tennent's advice there was to withdraw from their minister and set up a separate meeting dependent on the ministrations of itinerants. When Tennent carried into New England the sentiments expressed at Nottingham, the only possible result was schism in individual churches. An observer reported that he had "several times heard Mr. Tennent declare that the greatest part by far of the Ministers in this land were carnal, unconverted men and that they held damnable Arminian principles and have heard him pray that the Lord would either convert them or turn them out of his Vineyard." [38] The disaffection promoted by this sort of preaching contributed directly to separatism in New England in a way that it did not in the Middle Colonies.

Whitefield and Tennent stigmatized an unconverted ministry in general. Vastly different, however, was the procedure (and much more pernicious the influence) of James Davenport, who branded individual preachers by name and urged their hearers to forsake them forthwith. He did this on the basis of the "key of knowledge" by which the New Lights supposed that they could discern the true light in others; and thus he gave terrifying particularity to the general charges of his predecessors. "He not only awakened suspicion of ministers, by throwing out in his sermons vague and ambiguous insinuations; but he was wont, in the most peremptory and solemn manner, to declare this or that particular minister an unconverted man, and to call on the people to avoid that minister's preaching as they would avoid poison." [39] On his evangelistic tours he would enter a new town, seek an audience with the parish minister, and inquire into his spiritual experiences. If the man refused to be interrogated, as he usually did, he was immediately denounced as unconverted. Davenport would then announce his verdict to the people, sometimes through the medium of public prayer, and justify the whole procedure on the ground of his concern for souls.

> By this tremendous step of *his*, many people, relying on his judgment to be *right*, were well assured that *they* had unconverted ministers. And others became jealous of *theirs*. And *all* were told, by this wild man, that they had as good eat ratsbane, as to hear an *unconverted minister*. What then could the poor undiscerning

38. Quoted in Waters, *Ipswich in the Massachusetts Bay Colony*, 2, 120.
39. Leonard Bacon, *Thirteen Historical Discourses* (New Haven, 1839), p. 213.

people, who believ'd him, *do,* but think of withdrawing from their respective ministers, and seeking food else-where for their souls? Nay, they were publicly advised and exhorted, by this young counseller, to *leave* the condemned ministers, and their danger-ous improvements, and to join with other churches, that had, in his judgment, converted ministers; sometimes naming the par-ticular men.[40]

All who protested such precipitate behavior were classed as opposers of the work of God.

It was stated previously that although the revival was surcharged with emotion almost from the very first, there was no hysteria until Davenport burst upon the scene. It may be added now, what is even more significant, that *there were no open separations until Davenport began to flail away at individual ministers by name and exhort their hearers to withdraw from their ministry.* The generalized aspersions of Whitefield and Tennent apparently caused as much heart-searching among ministers as uneasiness among the people—some twenty ministers are said to have been converted under Whitefield—but the reckless (one may say, ruthless) charges of Davenport drove a wedge of suspicion and ill will between specific pastors and their hearers. Thomas Prince, who reported so fully on the revival in the Boston area and gathered accounts of it from the rest of New England, had nothing but unqualified praise for the work of Whitefield and Tennent. But after telling of their exploits, he adds:

> And thus successfully did this *Divine Work* as above describ'd go on in *Town,* without any Lisp, as I remember, of a *Separa-tion* either in this *Town* or *Province,* for above a *Year and half* after Mr. *Whitefield* left us, *viz.* the *End* of *June* 1742; when the Rev. Mr. *Davenport* of *Long-Island* came to Boston. And then thro' the awful Providence of the sovereign God, the Wisdom of whose Ways are past finding out, we unexpectedly came to an un-happy Period.[41]

To be sure, Davenport's numerous vagaries made him a handy whipping boy for the friends of the revival who wished to disengage the "Divine Work" from its inglorious "Appendages"; and the enemies of the revival could find plenty in Tennent and Whitefield to substan-

---

40. Fish, *The Church of Christ a Firm and Durable House,* p. 121.
41. *Christian History,* 2, 406.

tiate the charge that they were responsible for the rise of unbridled censoriousness. But even when this argument is weighed carefully, Prince's testimony need not be discounted. There are enough instances where revivalistic excesses were being brought under control by responsible leaders in the manner of Edwards, Wheelock, Parsons, Bellamy, and others, that one may conclude that had Davenport not sowed the seeds of discord so assiduously, separatism would not have assumed such large proportions.

Once the traditional veneration of the clergy was cast aside, however, there was no limit to the kinds of people who might criticize their leaders or the extent to which they might go. Few seemed able to draw the fine line between proper Christian humility and that "hell-peopling charity" whose silence condoned a dead minister and a polluted church. Those who withdrew from the standing churches, in spite of their gross neglect of the demands of Christian love, were undoubtedly sincere in their conviction that they must not help to maintain an order whose leadership seemed to be in unregenerate hands. Those to whom the new birth was of paramount importance saw an unconverted ministry as a ghastly incongruity. Their standard attitude toward an unspiritual clergy was expressed by Frothingham, who excoriated them as "miserable, presumptuous wretches, who have forced themselves into the ministry, for a maintenance, and a purse of honor, or some other selfish motive!" [42] Davenport's influence, moreover, lasted a long time. Robert Ross, pastor at Stratfield (now Bridgeport), wrote in 1762:

> Some Time ago a Fellow, who was an utter Stranger to me, called at my House, and immediately addressed me thus. "As I understand you are the Minister of this Parish I want to ask you one or two questions." I told him he might ask me as many reasonable Questions as he pleased. Then he proceeded without further Ceremony. "Do you look upon yourself to be in a State of Grace? What are your religious Experiences?" I answered him; his Questions appeared to me very improper, both as he was an intire Stranger whom I had never seen nor heard of before, and as he was not invested with any proper Authority, that I knew of, to

42. A Key to Unlock the Door, That Leads in, to Take a Fair View of the Religious Constitution, Established by Law, in the Colony of Connecticut (n.p., 1767), p. 233. Maxson notes that such charges were often near enough to the truth to give power to the accusers and arouse much resentment in the accused (Great Awakening in the Middle Colonies, p. 144).

make such Enquiries, and therefore I should not answer them. Upon this he went off saying he believed I had no Grace.[43]

Who could keep such inquisitors in his church? Indeed, who would want to? In the social and ecclesiastical climate which followed the outbreak of the Great Awakening, the practical issue of who was converted—and could prove it—could hardly help but lead to schism.

THE EVANGELISTIC ISSUE

The quarrel over itinerant preaching by properly ordained ministers and exhorting by laymen who assumed ministerial prerogatives constitutes the evangelistic issue. Itinerant preaching was one of the chief novelties of the Great Awakening; but however much it offended the proprieties of staid New England, it quickly commended itself to ardent revivalists as a most effective means of evangelism. They regarded any attempt to interfere with their work as hindering the salvation of souls. The same may be said of lay preaching, and efforts to suppress all such activities quickly sparked a spirited controversy. Since the phenomenon itself has already been described, attention here will be focused on the opposition to it which became another cause for schism.

Opposition to itinerant preachers. When the General Association of Connecticut met in June 1741, all the ministers present expressed gratitude for the extraordinary revival of religion in the colony and passed a resolution recommending that preachers maintain frequent lectures for the people and assist each other in the great work of evangelism. A year later, while still grateful for great numbers concerned for eternal verities, the ministers observed that the devil had been busy sowing tares among the wheat. In particular, they bore testimony against

> the Errors & Irregularities as doe already prevail among some persons, As Particularly the Depending upon & following Impulses & impressions made on the mind as tho' they were immediate

43. *A Plain Address to the Quakers, Moravians, Separatists, Separate-Baptists, Rogerenes, and Other Enthusiasts; on Immediate Impulses and Revelations, &c.* (New Haven, 1762), p. 74. I see little justification for Isaac Backus' distinction between two phases of separatism. He says that the earliest separations were from particular ministers who were thought to be unconverted; "whereas, our separations began several years afterwards, and upon quite different principles . . . [i.e.] the general constitution of the churches" (*A Fish Caught in His Own Net,* p. 33). This indeed points up the crucialness of the ecclesiological issue, but it seems to me impossible to divorce one issue from the complex of causes which provoked separations early and late.

Revelations of Some truth, or Duty that is not Reveald in the Word of God—Laying too much Weight upon bodily agitations, Raptures, Extacies, Visions &c—*Ministers disorderly intruding into other Minister's parishes*—Laymen taking it upon them in an unwarrantable manner publicly to teach and Exhort—Rash Censuring & Judging of others. . . . [We advise] that they [the elders] Endeavour to heal the unhappy Divisions that are already made in Some churches: and that the like may in the future be prevented. That a just defference be paid to the laws of the Christian Magistrate: lately made for the Suppression of Disorder.[44]

At first glance this quotation may seem to be longer than necessary to illustrate the point at hand, but it reveals several things. It shows how the revival itself was beginning to be dissipated in emotional and enthusiastic froth, and also what official steps were being advocated to curb its intensity. More important, it suggests how the practice of itineracy was spreading disorder by carrying into every parish the excesses which disgusted and alarmed the settled pastors. Swarms of itinerants were not only disrupting the traditional church way in New England by disregarding parish lines to preach in other ministers' domains, but they also were subverting long-accepted religious customs in many other ways. This is the first disorder in practice scored by the antirevival ministers in their convention of 1743; and even the prorevivalist counterconvention six weeks later felt constrained to recommend that "*Ministers* do not invade the Province of others, and in *ordinary Cases* preach in another's Parish without his Knowledge, and against his Consent." [45]

Settled ministers were not alone in their opposition to the revival and especially to the itinerants. Some churches were substantially Old Light, and if the pastor happened to be a New Light, friction developed over the issues created by the revival, and often it increased until either the pastor was dismissed or the antirevival party with-

44. *Records of the General Association of the Colony of Connecticut* (Hartford, 1888), p. 12. Italics mine.
45. *The Testimony and Advice*, p. 11. It should be recalled that fifteen of the fifty-three signers of this document went on record as preferring a stronger protest against itinerancy. Cf. also *The Declaration of the Ministers of Barnstable County* [*Massachusetts*], *Relating to the Late Practice of Itinerant Preaching* (Boston. 1745); and *The Declaration of the Association of the County of New-Haven in Connecticut, Conven'd at New-Haven, Feb. 19.1744,5. Concerning the Rev. Mr. George Whitefield, His Conduct and the State of Religion at This Day* (Boston, 1745).

drew. Thaddeus Maccarty was settled at Kingston, Massachusetts, in 1742. His active support of the "Whitefieldians" soon aroused the church to vote that no itinerant preachers should be allowed to use the meetinghouse. On January 29, 1745, a committee was appointed

> to see that there be hooks and staples put to the casements in the meeting-house, that nobody may get in at unseasonable times to do damage in the meeting-house. Also that this committee shall have a prudential power relating to the meeting-house and other parish affairs, and particularly to itinerant ministers, who having of late been troublesome in many places, and as Mr. Maccarty may be in danger of being overborne by their insolence, the said committee are desired to use their good office to prevent the same and to guard the meeting-house from them, viz.: itinerant ministers.[46]

Whitefield returned to New England later that year, and when it was rumored that the pastor had invited him to preach in defiance of the church's wishes, Maccarty was dismissed. The same thing happened at Grafton, where pastor Solomon Prentice with boundless zeal gave unqualified approval to all the more extravagant aspects of the revival. He opened his pulpit not only to regularly ordained ministers such as Philemon Robbins of Branford but to others like Solomon Paine, Separate preacher from Canterbury, Connecticut, and Ezekiel Cole, an Indian exhorter. A mutual council, probably containing as many pastors friendly to the revival as unfriendly, recommended Prentice's dismissal in 1747. He went to Easton, where we shall hear of him again.

On the other hand, an Old Light pastor of a church containing a vocal (if not numerous) New Light party also faced a situation in which controversy was inevitable. His unwillingness to invite "dear Mr. Whitefield" and other evangelists into his pulpit was sure to expose him to the charge that he was hindering the work of God. Many separations were occasioned by such a minister's attempts to prevent his parishioners from hearing the itinerants. It is well known that the Second Presbyterian Church in Philadelphia, to which Gilbert Tennent later went as pastor, was built in 1740 for the express purpose of providing Whitefield a pulpit when he visited the town. The same thing happened in Boston. When Whitefield returned there in 1745 his reception was as cool as the previous one had been warm. Harvard College had denounced him as an "enthusiast, a censorious, uncharitable person, and a deluder of the people"; and President Holyoke told him in an

46. Quoted in D. Hamilton Hurd, ed., *History of Plymouth County, Massachusetts* (Philadelphia, 1884), p. 260.

open letter, "the furious zeal with which you had so fired the passions of the people hath, in many places, burnt up the very vitals of religion; and a censorious, unpeaceable, uncharitable disposition hath, in multitudes, usurped the place of a godly jealousy."[47] In such an atmosphere there were few pastors who would manifest cordiality even if they had felt it.

But Whitefield was not without supporters, nor did Boston lack for New Lights. Aggrieved members from every Congregational church in the city withdrew to augment the little band of Separates that had been forming since 1742, and they covenanted together as the Eleventh Congregational Church. Having called Andrew Croswell of Groton, Connecticut, as pastor in 1748, the new church petitioned for a council to install him. When the council convened, the church stated that "our leaving the other Ministers and coming together into a Church-State, was not for such Disaffection as you seem to imagine, but for our better Edification, and also, that we, being professed Friends of the present Reformation, might have a Pulpit open to receive Mr. *Whitefield*, and others whom we look upon to be the zealous and faithful Ministers of Jesus Christ, who are so commonly shut out of other Pulpits."[48] After his installation Croswell wrote to the ministers of the Old South Church, who had opposed the whole proceeding, "You cannot reasonably expect *much of the Presence* of Christ in your Assemblies, while Mr. *Whitefield* and other godly Ministers, who occasionally come to *Boston*, are industriously *kept out*."[49]

This was so much the feeling elsewhere that a minister's refusal to receive an itinerant evangelist into his pulpit almost certainly created intense disaffection—if not open separation.

Opposition to lay exhorters. The animosity of pastors toward itinerant ministers was nothing compared to their antagonism toward the spate of lay preachers who rushed into evangelistic work in the wake of Whitefield. Even among the most zealous friends of the revival, no one approved of them in any way except a few erratic hotheads like James Davenport, Andrew Croswell (both of whom later repented), Solomon Prentice, Daniel Rogers (whose own ordination was

47. Josiah Quincy, *The History of Harvard University* (Boston, 1860), 2, 48, 51–52. Prince indeed labors to show that on this second visit Whitefield's meek and pacific spirit convinced "People of their Mistakes about him"; but though numbers attended his ministry, there was no revival as in 1740 (*Christian History*, 2, 336).

48. Croswell, *A Narrative of the New-Gathered Congregational Church in Boston* (Boston, 1749), p. 13.

49. Ibid., p. 16.

considered invalid by many), and Nicholas Gilman (of Durham, New Hampshire). The lay exhorters constituted still another rebuke to the unevangelistic clergy of the establishment. New Lights openly preferred an uneducated lay preacher to an unconverted minister, and claimed that "at such Meetings of Lay-preaching and Exhorting they have more of the Presence of GOD, and in His Ordinances, than under the Ministration of the present Ministry, and Administration of the Ordinances in these Churches." [50] This was so galling that even the prorevival ministers' convention in 1743 protested vigorously "That Laymen do not invade the Ministerial Office, and under a Pretence of *Exhorting* set up *Preaching;* which is very contrary to Gospel Order, and tends to introduce Errors and Confusion into the Church." [51]

In every way possible the most vigorous promoters of the revival— to say nothing of the antirevivalists—sought to restrain what they considered an unwarranted and dangerous usurpation of their rights and duties.[52] Backus said that this attempt to stop the work of lay evangelism was such a source of consternation that "sundry ministers who had been greatly engaged in the work of God, turned and joined with others that had called it a delusion of the Devil, and united all their force to crush these *exhorters:* and the public were cautioned against admitting any into the ministry, but such as *man had taught* for that purpose *from their youth.*" [53] But repression accomplished little. Men who had seen the new light simply would not, or could not, keep it under a bushel.

THE LEGAL ISSUE

In addition to all the other grievances, determined attempts were made to coerce the New Lights to conform by the exercise of civil and ecclesiastical authority. There were a few—very few—instances where pastor and church brought the disaffected ones back into the fold through love.[54] In the main, however, Old Light strategy was to tighten

---

50. *A Letter from the Associated Ministers of the County of Windham*, pp. 5–6.
51. *The Testimony and Advice*, p. 11.
52. See, e.g., Parsons, *Needful Caution in a Critical Day*, pp. 47–52; S. E. Dwight, *Life of President Edwards* (New York, 1830), p. 153; Edwards, *Works, 3,* 399; Solomon Williams and Eleazar Wheelock, *Two Letters* (Boston, 1744), pp. 28–29.
53. *A Letter to the Rev. Mr. Benjamin Lord*, p. 33.
54. A noteworthy instance was at New London, where pastor Eliphalet Adams did a remarkable job of steadying his church and pacifying the Separates at the scene of Davenport's wildest disorders. See Blake, *The Later History of the First Church of Christ*, pp. 55, 66, 78.

controls and apply pressures even to the point of persecution. The guardians of orthodoxy and preservers of order were not discerning enough to see that such tactics would only aggravate the animosity of the Separates, stiffen their resistance, and (for a time at least) inspire them to greater cohesion and determination.

Coercion in Connecticut. It was possible to apply much greater pressure to nonconformists in Connecticut than elsewhere in New England. The Saybrook Platform had made possible a tighter control of the churches and a much closer relation between church and state than that which obtained in Massachusetts. As a result, there developed in Connecticut an immense concern for the stability of the establishment. The shock of a large-scale defection to Anglicanism in 1722 had caused the colony to triple its concern for uniformity and to believe that such uniformity must be maintained through militant ecclesiastical supervision. When the revival began to manifest unruly centrifugal forces, the first thought of the men who controlled political and ecclesiastical affairs was to tighten the screws and prevent any further weakening of the religious establishment. That is why "the Old Guard Congregationalists of that day speak of the Awakening in terms reminiscent of an Archbishop Laud harrying an upstart and loud-mouthed meeting of Dissenters"; [55] and why the oppressive legislation of 1742–43 "enabled Connecticut to usurp the leadership in religious intolerance among English-speaking peoples previously enjoyed by Massachusetts." [56]

An "Act for Regulating Abuses and Correcting Disorders in Ecclesiastical Affairs" was passed by the Connecticut Assembly in May 1742.[57] The Assembly moved decisively to halt violations of ecclesiastical order by decreeing (1) that if any ordained or licensed minister should enter any other parish not immediately under his charge and there preach or exhort without the express invitation of the settled minister and a majority of his church, such an intruder would forfeit his legal right to support under the laws of the colony; (2) that if any association of ministers should meddle in any of the affairs properly under the jurisdiction of another association, including the licensing of ministers, every member of the offending association would forfeit his legal maintenance; [58] (3) that before any minister could receive a war-

---

55. Clarence M. Webster, *Town Meeting Country* (New York, 1945), pp. 63–64.
56. John M. Mecklin, *The Story of American Dissent* (New York, 1934), p. 218.
57. For the circumstances behind the Act, see Philemon Robbins, *A Plain Narrative* (Boston, 1747).
58. This was against the Fairfield East Association, whose New Light majority

rant from a justice of the peace for the collection of his stated salary, he had to present a certificate from the clerk of his parish stating that no other minister or members of other churches had lodged a complaint against him for disorderly conduct in violation of these laws; (4) that if "any persons whatsoever" (i.e. laymen) should preach or exhort without the permission of the settled minister and a majority of the church, they must deposit a peace bond of one hundred pounds until the county court should meet to determine their cases; and (5) that if a stranger from outside the colony should come and preach in any parish without the consent of the minister and a majority of the church, whether he had an "ecclesiastical character" or not, he should "be sent (as a vagrant person) by warrant from any one assistant or justice of the peace, from constable to constable, out of the bounds of this Colony." [59]

Benjamin Trumbull calls this law an outrage to every principle of justice and an abridgment of the rights of all residents. It was "partial, inconsistent, and highly persecuting. . . . Instead of preserving the peace and order of the churches, it was a means of separation and division." [60] This is the law under which James Davenport was arraigned at Hartford on a complaint by two laymen of Ripton parish in Stratford. Benjamin Pomeroy, who was with him but acquitted for lack of evidence, was later deprived of his salary for seven years because he preached to a group at Colchester without the express approval of pastor Ephraim Little. John Owen of Groton was cited before the Assembly in 1743 to answer accusations that he "from the pulpit did utter, speak, publish and declare, divers false words and sentences, unjustly reproaching and scandalizing the laws and ruling part of this government, and did broach sundry seditious principles, tending to bring the authority and laws of this government into contempt and reproach." [61] Eleazar Wheelock also was "Deprived of my Living, at Least of the Benefit of a Law to secure it to me . . . Whereby [I] have Suffered much already & am Like to Suffer more." [62]

---

had licensed several zealous young revivalists who hardly limited themselves to Fairfield County. In defiance of this law, Fairfield East proceeded to license David Brainerd after his expulsion from Yale College (July 1742).

59. *Public Records of Connecticut, 8*, 456.

60. *Complete History of Connecticut, 2*, 166.

61. *Public Records of Connecticut, 8*, 519. At Owen's trial the charge was reduced from contempt of the laws to following "a misguided conscience and overheated zeal" (*ibid., 9*, 20).

62. Letter to Thomas Clap, dated Sept. 1743, in Dartmouth College Library; quoted in Gaustad, *Great Awakening in New England*, p. 75.

The ministerial associations, especially that of New Haven, did all they could to implement the Assembly's act. Timothy Allen of West Haven, a zealous revivalist, was reported to have said that the reading of the Scriptures apart from the operation of the Spirit of God "will no more convert a sinner than the reading of an old almanack." When it was rumored that he had compared the Bible to an old almanac, the Old Lights convoked the consociation and secured his dismissal. Then they chortled that they had blown out one New Light and would blow them all out.[63] The boast was made good: Philemon Robbins and Daniel Humphreys of Derby were both suspended from the association for preaching to the Baptists; and when a church was formed at Salisbury in 1744 on the Cambridge Platform, all who participated in the installation of its pastor (Jonathan Lee) were expelled. These were Humphreys, Mark Leavenworth of Waterbury, and Samuel Todd of Northbury. The churches of the disfranchised ministers, however, rallied to them and supported them with voluntary contributions until they were reinstated.

An instance of the force of the law against "vagrant persons" occurred at Milford. Samuel Whittelsey, Jr., son of the veteran Old Light pastor of Wallingford, had been settled here in 1738 over the protests of a sizable group. During the Awakening, these persons determined to sit no longer under his ministry. They withdrew, declared themselves Presbyterian, and applied to the revivalistic New York Synod for preaching. The Synod sent Samuel Finley, afterward president of the College of New Jersey (Princeton), who was promptly arrested and transported out of Connecticut as a vagrant. Nothing daunted, Finley returned a few months later to preach to those who had recently withdrawn from the First Church in New Haven.

> The tradition is, that Finley having been arrested on Saturday, in anticipation of his preaching, was kept in custody by the officer of justice on the Sabbath, and by him was taken to Rev. Mr. Noyes's church, and made to sit in the aisle—probably to expose him as an offender against the laws, and to give him the privilege of hearing preaching and praying especially designed for his benefit.[64]

After this blessing, Mr. Finley was deported once again. His audacity in flouting the authority of the colony, however, moved the Assembly

63. Trumbull, *Complete History of Connecticut*, 2, 196. Allen went to New London and placed himself at the head of the emerging Separate party there.

64. S. W. S. Dutton, "The Safety and Wisdom of Complete Religious Liberty, as Illustrated in Connecticut during the Last One Hundred and Fifty Years," *Contributions to the Ecclesiastical History of Connecticut*, p. 120.

to put teeth in its law against foreign preachers. The "Act in Addition to one Law of this Colony entituled An Act for regulating Abuses and correcting Disorders in Ecclesiastical Affairs," passed in October 1743, provided that second offenders should be fined one hundred pounds and pay the cost of their transportation out of the colony.[65]

There is nothing that reveals the mood of the reactionary Old Lights who controlled Connecticut at this period better than the sermon preached by Isaac Stiles of North Haven at the opening of the Assembly in May 1742. Using a text regarding the building of Jerusalem, Stiles likened his magisterial hearers to Nehemiah. There are many, he said, "that conspire to discourage, obstruct, retard and hinder the Work: Insomuch that you may find occasion while you are building on the Wall, and have one Hand Employed in the Work, with the other to hold a Weapon. And God grant you may *not bear the Sword in vain*." [66] This was an ominous note. Deploring the divisions of the day, which are sins "not of *Ignorance* but of *great Light*," he advised the rulers to waste no love on those that hate the Lord:

> We hope You will take due care that such be preferr'd to places of Publick Trust, as dare put the Laws of Men in Execution against them that trample on the Laws of God. Whosoever breaketh any of the wholsome Laws of the Government himself, and (at least by his Example) teaches others so to do, must needs be unfit to be a Judge of the Law, or a Justice of the Peace.[67]

This was to say that not only must action be taken against ministers who did not attend strictly to their own charges and would-be ministers who invaded clerical prerogatives, but the colony must also have civil officers who would keep close watch on disturbers of the ecclesiastical peace. In accordance with Stiles' recommendations, all who were suspected of New Light sympathies were removed from public office, and representatives from towns having New Light majorities were denied seats in the General Assembly.[68]

Another way in which the Old Guard moved to suppress the New Lights and Separates was to short-circuit the latter's plans to establish a school for the training of their ministers. It was very plain that

65. *Public Records of Connecticut, 8,* 569–70.
66. *A Prospect of the City of Jerusalem,* p. 42.
67. Ibid., pp. 48–49.
.68. The latter class included Capt. Obadiah Johnson of Canterbury, Capt. Thomas Stevens of Plainfield, and Capt. Nathan Jewett of Lyme. These men were all of decidedly separatist tendencies.

Yale College was unfriendly to the revival. It had responded quickly to the instructions of the Assembly in 1742 to squelch the prorevival activities of its students; and during the next two years it documented its position by expelling David Brainerd for doubting the religious experience of his tutor, by expelling also the sons of a Canterbury New Light for attending an "unauthorized" religious meeting with their parents during vacation, and by declaring its violent disapproval of George Whitefield. The Separates therefore needed their own seminary. In 1742 they opened the "Shepherd's Tent" at New London in the home of Samuel Harris, which had become the gathering place of those who had withdrawn from the First Church there. Timothy Allen, recently dismissed from West Haven, was both pastor of the Separate church (not yet organized) and teacher of the school. The obvious purpose of the Shepherd's Tent was to train pastors for the people who were unhappy with the dull preaching of unconverted ministers. Yale's officials noted in 1745 that some of their students had withdrawn earlier to "that Thing call'd the Shepherd's Tent"; [69] and while in Boston James Davenport raised money for its support.[70] In February 1743, one month before Davenport's execrable bonfire brought the New London New Lights into disrepute, it had fourteen students.[71] The school was a thorn in the flesh to the ecclesiocrats, who had outlawed such enterprises in October 1742.

There was still one more piece of repressive legislation by which Connecticut sought to preserve its ecclesiastical establishment. Recalling that when the Saybrook Platform was enacted into law in 1708 there had been a provision "for the ease of such as soberly dissent from the way of worship and ministry established" by that law, the Assembly voted in May 1743 that "those commonly called Presbyterians or Congregationalists should not take benefit by said law." By those who un-

69. "Declaration of the Rector and Tutors against Whitefield" (Feb. 25, 1745), *Documentary History of Yale University*, p. 370.

70. This was in obvious imitation of Whitefield's efforts in behalf of his Georgia orphanage. Charles Chauncy observed caustically that Davenport's concern for his academy contradicted his preaching that the end of the world was imminent: "To be sure, if your *impression* about the *nearness* of the *judgment* was from GOD, your *proposal* soon after it, to *raise monies* for the building [of] a *school* or *college*, under the name of a *Shepherd's Tent*, that the churches might be supplied with *converted ministers*, must be own'd to have had its rise from *meer fancy*" (*Enthusiasm Described and Caution'd Against*, Boston, 1742, p. vi).

71. Timothy Allen, letter dated Feb. 27, 1743, to Eleazar Wheelock, in Dartmouth College Library; cited in Gaustad, p. 108. Joshua Hempstead noted in 1749 that six years earlier there had been "12 Refined Scholars at the Shepards Tent so Called" (*Diary of Joshua Hempstead*, p. 528).

warrantably claim the benefit of the toleration act, it continued, the legal parishes of the colony "have been greatly damnified, and by indirect means divided and parted, without any sufficient reason for the same." To prevent this mischief, "the said law, entituled An Act for the ease of such as soberly dissent, &c., shall be repealed and made void, and the same is hereby repealed and made void." Hereafter, dissenters had to apply to the Assembly for exemption from the ecclesiastical laws; and it was made plain that only "such persons as have any distinguishing character, by which they may be known from the presbyterians or congregationalists, and from the consociated churches established by the laws of this Colony, may expect the indulgence of this Assembly, having first before this Assembly taken the oaths and subscribed the declaration provided in the Act of Parliament in cases of the like nature." [72]

This incredible act audaciously assumed that the original toleration clause had *never* applied to any but those who dissented totally from the Congregational (or semipresbyterian) way, i.e. Anglicans, Quakers, Baptists, etc. It forms the finishing stroke in a series of arbitrary fiats "which for bigotry, intolerance, and disregard of the rights of conscience is without parallel in the legislation of Connecticut." [73] After the implementation of "this remarkable expedient for promoting peace, love, and Christian unity," says Miss Larned, "the inevitable results followed. The revival element was at once arraigned against the Government. Social religious meetings . . . had now become lawless and disorderly conventicles, liable to be interrupted by the warrant of the constable. The attempted suppression of free speech in a time of high religious excitement greatly increased the existing evil." [74] The oppressive laws were so overreaching in their severity that they not only aggravated the separatistic tendencies of the New Lights but also gave rise to a party of political New Lights which eventually outnumbered and overthrew the reactionary Old Guard.

The use of church censures. One other aspect of the legal issue which deserves mention is the effort on the part of the standing churches to pass censures on those who were conducting themselves in "disorderly" fashion. In some instances this behavior might be no more than attending private meetings for the exchange of religious ex-

72. *Public Records of Connecticut, 8,* 521–22.

73. James Hammond Trumbull, "Sons of Liberty in 1755," *New Englander, 25* (1876), 302.

74. Ellen D. Larned, *Historic Gleanings in Windham County, Connecticut* (Providence, 1899), p. 21.

periences, going to hear an itinerant evangelist in a nearby service, or remonstrating with the minister for not preaching enough on awakening themes. The invoking of church discipline in cases of this sort had the same effect as the passage of civil legislation—it increased the disaffection. When the disaffected began to absent themselves from the stated services of the church, they were censured, usually on the ground of covenant-breaking. As is well known, the Puritans did not take their church covenants lightly. When this charge was made against the separatists, their answer was that the church itself had broken covenant by departing from true gospel order. John Cleaveland, who became pastor of the Separate church at Chebacco (second parish, Ipswich; later Essex), wrote that a church covenant was a contract between the church itself and its individual covenanting members. The church's performance of its ministry in preaching the word, administering the ordinances, exercising proper discipline, etc., is presupposed. "But if this be neglected by the Church, then that Covenant is by them vertually dissolved, and the Party injured [i.e. the aggrieved member] . . . at Liberty from his obligation to that Church." The correction of disorders and delinquencies is normally the function of the minister, but if he himself is involved in the dereliction, recourse must be had to extrajudicial means, i.e. separation, "since the main Thing in Religion, viz. The Edification of the Person can't be obtained otherwise." Whatever injury is done to the order of the churches by this procedure must be blamed on those who were guilty of the first error.[75]

This argument, which in Cleaveland seems too much ad hoc, was stated more precisely by Isaac Backus. In 1768 he undertook to answer all the calumnies that had circulated against the Separates for two decades. To the charge of covenant-breaking he replied: "The engagement to God is perpetual, and that to one another is conditional, *by the will of God:* which makes it to be an incumbent duty to withdraw from persons or churches, who are evidently corrupt, and will not be reclaimed, as to walk with those who are not so." [76] He quoted at length from John Owen, who justified separation under certain conditions: "*Churches* are not such *sacred machines* as some suppose, erected and acted for the outward interest and advantage of any sort of men; but only means of the edification of believers, which they are bound to make use of, in obedience unto the *commands of Christ,* and no

75. *A Plain Narrative of the Proceedings Which Caused the Separation of a Number of Aggrieved Brethren from the Second Church in Ipswich* (Boston, 1747), pp. 3–4.
76. *A Fish Caught in His Own Net,* p. 82.

otherwise." [77] Backus concluded that the standing ministers and churches have broken covenant with God, leaving no alternative to true believers but to break with them. Separation in such cases is no sin; rather, it is a virtue.

The outcry against repressive legislation and church discipline brought the controversy back to the ecclesiological issue, which was unquestionably the basic cause of rupture. Other factors became contributing causes only when the Old Guard invoked the powers of the constitution as a means of sanctioning pre-Awakening conditions and suppressing the awakened reformers. Solomon Paine, Separate pastor at Canterbury, put this quite clearly:

> The cause of a just Separation of the Saints from their fellow Men, in their Worship, is not their being worse by Nature than themselves, nor their being unconverted. . . . Nor is it because there are Hypocrites in the visible Church, nor that some fall into scandalous Sins in the Church; or because the Minister is flat formal, or saith, that he is a Minister of Christ, and is not, and doth lye. . . . But affirmatively, it is their being yoaked together, or incorporated into a corrupt Constitution, under the Government of another supream Head, than Christ, and governed by the Precepts of Men, put into the Hands of Unbelievers, which will not purge out any of the abovesaid corrupt Fruit, but naturally bears it, and nourishes it, and denies the Power of Godliness, both in the governing and gracious Effects of it. So that the sound Doctrine in the Demonstration of the Power of the Holy Ghost, and the Discipline of Christ, and the true Worship of God in Spirit and in Truth, must of Necessity make a Division and Disturbance in the Body; and the Saints must either be ashamed of Christ and his Word, or else they must be treated as Disturbers of the Peace (of that Community) who turn the World upside down; doing contrary to the Decrees of Men, saying, there is another King, one Jesus, who alone hath Right to govern in his Worship, *Acts 17*. And a Man must separate from that to join to the Church of Christ, and separate from the Church of Christ to join with that.[78]

To men of that conviction there was no middle ground.

But such arguments were lost on ecclesiastics who assumed that their long tenure in the establishment gave them a privileged position almost

77. Quoted ibid., pp. 85–86.

78. *A Short View of the Difference between the Church of Christ, and the Established Churches in the Colony of Connecticut* (Newport, 1752), pp. 52–53.

amounting to divine right. In their opinion, therefore, the dissidents were to be censured, the churches were to acquiesce in the protective laws passed by their nursing fathers,[79] and no quarter was to be given those who prated in impossibly idealistic terms of "the rights of conscience."

> The evangelicals were compelled to insist on the right of the individual to a wider liberty than the conservatives were disposed to grant him. The battle cry of the conservatives was therefore "order and discipline." Of the evangelicals it was "the right of conscience." [80]

The future lay with the evangelicals, but they were to experience many hardships before reaching their goal.

79. Cf. the protest of the Scotland Separates: "[We withdrew] because of the Persecuting Spirit among them against those that hold to the present Work, and especialy against those that improve the Gifts that GOD has given them, by Imprisoning them, or Vilifying them, or executing Laws upon them, to bind the Consciences in matters of Religion; which we never find to be in the Church of Christ." The answer of the church to this charge sidesteps the issue by disclaiming any power to pass or enforce civil laws; the church has imprisoned nobody, nor has it ever entertained a complaint against any of its members for being "of a Persecuting Spirit" (Devotion, pp. 10–11). But some went beyond mere acquiescence to the laws. Pastor Benjamin Lord of Norwich called the separations a *rebellion against the state,* which was to level the age-old charge of sedition against religious dissenters (Backus, *A Fish Caught in His Own Net,* p. 23).

80. Maxson, p. 144.

3. SEPARATISM EMERGES: THE CHURCHES

"My God commanded me to go from you, and I know it, and that is all my reason." [1] Thus did one New Light take his leave of the pastor whose sermons were no longer edifying and of the church with which his soul no longer had communion. The Great Awakening had thrust a two-edged sword into New England; and in the "separatical times" that followed, this man was legion. He and others like him formed nearly a hundred churches constituted of saints saved by grace, assured of salvation, zealous to preach the pure Word of God, and contemptuous of the state-supported establishment. Perhaps most of them only dimly understood the issues that impelled them to separate. But there is no doubt that they *felt*—and this was the decisive force—an inescapable compulsion to become the bearers of a new reformation. Few parishes escaped the separatist ferment, although in some cases the disaffection was ephemeral and no separate church was formed. It is not necessary (nor is it possible), to describe the controversy in each parish; therefore, I have selected several cases which illustrate the general situation. All the separations discovered in this study are summarized in the Appendix and are charted on Map 1.[2]

IN CONNECTICUT

New London. This town has been mentioned as the scene of James Davenport's most unrestrained fanaticism, but the spirit of separatism was manifest here some time before his appearance. It may be that the boiling New Light activity in this region was what led him to believe that he would find here the most promising beachhead from which to direct the Lord's controversy with New England. At all events, New London witnessed one of the earliest instances of open separation. Gilbert Tennent had preached three sermons there on March 30 and 31, 1741. By June pastor Eliphalet Adams was urging Jonathan Parsons to come from nearby Lyme and help him reconcile differences that had arisen between "a number of new converts with a flaming zeal" and

1. Quoted in Fish, *The Church of Christ a Firm and Durable House*, p. 152.
2. See below, p. 115. For interpretive discussion of the geographical distribution of the Separates, see below, pp. 186–88.

those who had "opposed themselves to the work going on among them." Parsons came on June 16 and preached twice. Later he wrote:

> The Success was not according to my Wishes. I found *mutual* rising Jealousies, and, as I tho't, *groundless* Surmisings in some Instances, prevailing among them. These Difficulties increas'd afterwards; and for want of Charity and mutual Condescension and Forbearance, they have produc'd an open Separation.[3]

Such was the situation when Davenport arrived on July 18 and led the hysterical meetings described earlier.[4] From this time forward, New London "was regarded abroad as the focus of enthusiasm, discord and confusion." [5]

By the beginning of 1742, though no one had as yet withdrawn from the church, private meetings were numerous and boisterous. The justice of the peace noted that on February 22, "Mr. Curtiss & his Companion were preaching or praying together att Peter Harris's Sautterday with Great Crying out of many & yesterday up in the Town att his house." [6] Such activity is probably what attracted Timothy Allen to New London after he was dismissed from his West Haven pastorate.[7] On July 10, 1742, Hempstead went "with the Rest of the Authority to Speak with Mr Allin a Suspended minister who is Come here from N: Haven West Side & Sets up to preach at private houses." [8] Being permitted to stay, Allen soon became the recognized leader of the disaffected party. The fateful step of withdrawal was taken on November 29, when five prominent members of the First Church absented themselves from communion. The informal meetings they had been holding quickly crystallized into a semiformal church organization; services were conducted regularly at the home of Samuel Harris, which also housed the Allen family and the infant seminary called the Shepherd's Tent. The number of separatists here has been estimated at one hundred.[9]

The authorities decided to deal leniently in this case, and the Sepa-

3. Letter to Thomas Prince, dated April 14, 1744, in *Christian History, 2,* 143.
4. See above, p. 25.
5. Caulkins, *History of New London,* p. 452.
6. *Diary of Joshua Hempstead,* p. 389. John Curtis (Yale College 1719) had studied for the ministry but abandoned it before being ordained. During the Great Awakening he became a disciple of James Davenport, and in 1748 left his business at New London to preach to the Separate church at New Haven.
7. See above, p. 61.
8. *Diary of Joshua Hempstead,* p. 395.
9. Caulkins, p. 453.

rate society was permitted by the County Court to conduct its meetings without molestation. Justice Hempstead betrays no rancor in his early diary references to them. Such was not the case, however, after Davenport instigated his infamous purge of March 6, 1743.[10] The published reports of his sacrilegious bonfire alarmed the ministers—the prorevival ones most of all—and they hurriedly called a council to meet at New London on March 30 and bear testimony against these wild disorders.[11] The next day Hempstead convened the court, which arraigned the incendiaries and assessed moderate fines. Jonathan Edwards preached in the courthouse "a Lecture Sermon . . . very Suitable for the times to bear Wittness against the prevailing disorders & destractions that are Subsisting in the Country by means of Enthusiasm." [12] The entire episode seemed to have a calming effect; no more is heard of Timothy Allen,[13] Davenport retracted his errors, and the Separates dispersed in a short while. Most of the members returned to the First Church, where they were received with kindness; the others joined themselves to a group of separatists in the west part of town (Waterford, now Niantic). The latter were under the leadership of Nathan Howard and most of them subsequently became Baptists.

Canterbury. The first instance in which an entire church became "new-lighted" and withdrew from the communion of the established churches was at Canterbury. A number of circumstances conspired to produce an unusual situation there. Located in Windham County, which was still practically frontier territory, the town had always included a strong radical element and the church was accustomed to large liberties in administering its affairs. It entered the Great Awakening in the throes of a long meetinghouse controversy and in a dejected state because of the moral defection of its pastor. Notwithstanding these distractions, it experienced a stirring revival. Having dismissed

10. See above, p. 25.
11. The council included Jonathan Edwards, Solomon Williams of Lebanon, Benjamin Lord of Norwich, Joseph Meacham of Coventry, Benjamin Pomeroy of Hebron, Joseph Bellamy of Bethlehem, Ebenezer Rosseter of Stonington, and Samuel Buell (no charge). Of the eastern Connecticut men in this list, all but Rosseter had concurred with the prorevival *Testimony and Advice*, sending a letter to that effect to Thomas Prince on Jan. 23, 1743 (*Christian History, 1*, 196).
12. *Diary of Joshua Hempstead*, p. 407.
13. Allen does not reappear in a ministerial capacity until 1748, when he assumed charge of the Presbyterian church at Maidenhead, New Jersey. His later pastorates were at Providence, New Jersey (1752–56), Ashford, Connecticut (1757–64), Granville, Massachusetts (1782), and Chesterfield, Massachusetts (1785–96). He died in 1806, aged 90.

John Wadsworth in 1741, it offered a fertile field for the labors of the itinerant evangelists—notably Eleazar Wheelock, Jonathan Parsons, Benjamin Pomeroy, and Samuel Buell—and also provided an unparalleled opportunity for the activities of its own aroused laymen. Foremost among these were Elisha Paine and his brother Solomon, both converted in the Windham revival of 1721 and now active and influential in both church and town. But these activities which sustained the new religious excitement were all outlawed by the legislation of 1742, which had the effect of increasing their tempo among the resentful Canterburians. A "gentleman of veracity" wrote to the Boston *Gazette* (Dec. 16, 1742):

> Canterbury is in worse confusion than ever. Their minister has left them, and they grow more noisy and boisterous so that they can get no minister to preach to them yet. Col. Dyer exerted his authority among them on the Lord's Day, endeavoring to still them when many were exhorting and making a great hubbub, and ordered the constable to do his office, but they replied, "Get thee behind me, Satan!" and the noise and tumult increased to such a degree, for above an hour, that the exhorter could not begin his exercise. Lawyer [Elisha] Paine has set up for a preacher . . . and makes it his business to go from house to house and town to town to gain proselytes to this new religion. Consequences are much feared.[14]

The revival party was thus in open collision with the government and its ecclesiastical constitution.

At a church meeting on January 27, 1743, it was voted that "the Platform of church disapline, agreed upon by the Synod at Cambridge 1648 Consisting of Learned persons from the four Colonys of New England, is most agreable to the former and designed practice of this church, Excepting ther having Ruling Elders as distink offecers; and most agreable to the Scriptures—".[15] This was a unanimous vote, and not even Colonel Dyer, leader of the antirevival party, pretended that the church had ever been subject to the Saybrook Platform. There was a difference of opinion, however, over whether the church might receive members in the absence of a pastor. The prorevival majority insisted that it could; and in April accepted ten new members over Dyer's protest, greatly alarming the conservatives. Two

14. Quoted in Larned, *Historic Gleanings in Windham County*, p. 22.
15. *Records of the Congregational Church in Canterbury, Connecticut, 1711–1844*, ed. Albert C. Bates (Hartford, 1932), p. 7.

antagonistic parties developed: a majority of the church, which was New Light and congregational; and a minority of the church, backed by practically the entire town, which was Old Light and inclined toward Saybrook regulation.[16]

In this situation it was impossible to agree on a new pastor, and several candidates were rejected seriatim. The town appealed to the consociation, but the church refused to recognize its authority and would not appear before it, calling instead a council of New Light ministers. Both bodies met at Canterbury on December 12, and recommended that the town and church apply either to Jonathan Lee or James Cogswell as prospective pastor. This resulted in a temporary truce, and the church consented to listen to Cogswell (Yale College 1742), the candidate selected by the town. But when the church perceived that Cogswell supported the Saybrook Platform, allowed the Halfway Covenant, and dispensed with public professions of faith, the armistice was over. The New Lights withdrew and resumed their private meetings at the home of Samuel Wadsworth, whereupon the town and a minority of the church proceeded with plans to settle Cogswell. The church protested that by the unanimous adoption of the Cambridge Platform the town had no legal right to ask the consociation to proceed with Cogswell's installation, but to no avail. Tension rose during 1744 and was increased by Yale's expulsion of John and Ebenezer Cleaveland for attending the New Light meeting at Canterbury during vacation with their parents,[17] and by the resolution of the Windham County Ministerial Association against lay preachers. Open division came at a church meeting on November 27, 1744. Colonel Dyer "Declared that he was for Saybrok Platform &c. and desired as many as were for the Platform Established by the Law of

16. Miss Larned comments that the town had always harbored a number of "vagabond fellows" who could be counted on to oppose the church in everything. "An unusually large proportion of its population was without the church, and indifferent or hostile to religion. The bold denunciations of the Revival preachers and exhorters had aroused the hostility of this irreligious class, and they gladly cooperated with Colonel Dyer in enforcing the laws and resisting the encroachments of the church" (*History of Windham County*, 1, 407).

17. Cf. *Judgment of the Rector and Tutors of Yale-College, Concerning Two of the Students Who Were Expelled* (New London, 1745). The students' mother was a sister of the Paines, their father one of the leading men in the town. The fact that the College had to publish an apologia for its action indicates something of the widespread resentment over its course. Robert C. Learned says: "This highhanded transaction roused a strong feeling throughout the colony," and did as much as anything to make the Canterbury schism irreconcilable ("The Separatists of Eastern Connecticut," *New Englander, 11,* 1853, 199).

this Colony to move or with draw to the other side of the meeting house . . . and after a little spell Coll Dyer Declared they were the Church." [18] Fifteen persons aligned themselves with Dyer, declared themselves under the Saybrook constitution, and called for the ordination of Cogswell.

When the ordaining council met on December 26, the church protested that in view of the previous action of the church repudiating the Saybrook Platform, "those sixteen brethren who actually voted with the church in accepting Cambridge Platform and now acted separately from them, were necessarily *separators* and guilty of schism." [19] The council replied that the church and its ministers, by previously cooperating in the association and consociation of the county, had tacitly affirmed their consent to the Saybrook constitution and that those who voted later to be governed by the Cambridge Platform

> are to be esteemed by that explicit act *to have denominated themselves another church, and separated themselves from those who adhered to Saybrook Regulation;* that this vote could bind none but themselves and those who adhered to it, and that, therefore, those who on November 27, 1744, called Mr. James Cogswell for their pastor as the church remaining and abiding by Saybrook Regulation, were declared to be and should thenceforward be esteemed—*The Church of Canterbury.*[20]

One concession was made to the New Lights: Cogswell was ordained only over the people who had concurred in his call and those who

18. Canterbury Separate Papers, No. 22. This large collection of original documents is at the Connecticut Historical Society.

19. Quoted in Larned, *History of Windham County,* 1, 424.

20. Ibid., p. 425. Miss Larned comments: "The absolute supremacy of the form of church discipline established by the Government of Connecticut, was affirmed in this remarkable decision. Every church in the Commonwealth was assumed to be subject to Saybrook Platform except by formal dissent at the time of its organization, and no subsequent vote or protest by any number of its members, could change its status. The Canterbury Church, by declaring itself 'Congregational according to Cambridge Platform,' had forfeited its ecclesiastical standing and legal privileges. As the vote was unanimous and not a member for a time adhered to Saybrook Regulation, the original church, according to this decision, was virtually abrogated, but after a lapse of twenty-two months was restored by a touch of this magic Platform. Sixteen brethren, who had once voted for Cambridge Platform, now manifested their determination to adhere to Saybrook, and were pronounced by the Council the Church of Canterbury and vested with all its rights and privileges."

should willingly place themselves under his pastoral care. Dissenters were to be released from obligation for his support as soon as they might gain parish privileges for themselves, and the leaders of the Saybrook party even offered to assist them in presenting their application to the Assembly. But the New Lights spurned the proposal, denounced the establishment as contrary to their principles, and declared that no consideration of personal benefit could induce them to submit to its onerous requirements. This decision, noble as it was, left them without legal rights, the underdogs in a prolonged struggle with civil and ecclesiastical authority which eventually was to deprive them of adequate leadership, stable constituency, and ultimate existence.

For a long while, however, the disfranchised church manifested considerable vigor. They met on January 6, 1745, to renew their covenant and voted that "all that shall hereafter be admited to Communion and fellowship with them to sine said Covenant." [21] Again they repudiated the Saybrook Platform, and very carefully spelled out the points wherein they differed from the Cambridge (denying the magistrate's power over the church). This was signed by thirty-two men and twenty-five women, "representing some of the oldest and most respectable families in Canterbury." [22] They had considerable difficulty in settling on a pastor. Their first choice was Elisha Paine, but he felt impelled toward an itinerant ministry among the Separate churches. They appealed to John Cleaveland, but he preferred to continue his private studies at Branford. Finally they turned to Solomon Paine, already approved as an exhorter, recognized as sound in the faith, and though of lesser abilities than his brother, acceptable as a preacher of the Word. After a long period of indecision, brought about by doubts as to the propriety of infant baptism (he could find no direct command for it in the Bible), he gained satisfaction by means of a vision and accepted the call.[23] He was ordained on September 10, 1746, the services being performed with the assistance of officers from the newly organized Separate church at Mansfield.

The Canterbury Separate church, when thus at length formally organized and furnished with requisite officers was a strong and united body, comprising about one hundred and twenty members, "known to be regenerate," professing a high degree of spirit-

21. *Records of the Congregational Church in Canterbury,* p. 10.
22. Larned, *History of Windham County, 1,* 438.
23. His letter of acceptance, describing his wrestling with these doubts, is in Canterbury Separate Papers, No. 28.

uality and consecration. With some errors in doctrine and practice, and a tendency to fanaticism and extravagance, it was still a church of strong faith, ardent prayers and great spiritual vitality, and for a time increased in numbers and influence. Its pastor, if lacking in judgment, was honest and earnest. Many of its members lived devoted Christian lives, and died in the triumphs of faith. Special seasons of quickening and revival were enjoyed, when many were added to the church.[24]

Solomon Paine died in 1754. Joseph Marshall served the church from 1759 to 1768, after which it had irregular preaching and eked out an increasingly tenuous existence until becoming extinct in 1831.

Mansfield. The Separate church at Mansfield was organized on October 9, 1745.

> The Manner, in which they formed themselves into a visible Church, was this; they gave a verbal Relation to each other, of their Experience, of a Work of Grace upon their Souls, to the Satisfaction of each other; a special Respect being had to the Fruits of Grace, that discover themselves in the Lives and Conversation of such as are truly godly, or gracious Persons: And also subscribed to Articles of Faith, and Practice, and a Church Covenant, that had been previously drawn up, and in their Opinion, agreeable to the Word of God.[25]

Unlike the Canterbury church, which bore with it the history of the original church, the group at Mansfield was composed of dissidents in schism from the original church. As such, it was the first really "Separate" church in Windham County, and it horrified the established ministry all the more on that account. Whereas the Canterbury New Lights retained the covenant and confession of faith of the original church, the Mansfield Separates drew up entirely new documents which constitute the first deliberate manifesto of the Separate party. These will be considered in detail later.[26]

The Mansfielders also carried through the first, formal, congregational ordination of a pastor among the Separates. Thomas Marsh, a deacon in the Second Church Windham, had been chosen as teaching elder. January 6, 1746, was the date appointed for his ordination. But on January 5 he was jailed for unlawful preaching. Ignorant

24. Larned, *History of Windham County, 1,* 438.
25. *An Historical Narrative and Declaration,* p. 11.
26. See below, pp. 150–51.

of this turn of events, a large crowd gathered the next day for the ceremonies. Elisha Paine preached a "suitable" (and doubtless inflammatory) sermon. Thirteen ministers of the Windham County Association appeared to read a testimony against the unlawful proceedings. The Separates, highly incensed, drowned their remonstrance with "Tumult and unchristian opprobrious Language and Revilings," and forced them to retreat in undignified haste.[27] Nothing daunted, the Separates (on advice from Marsh) chose John Hovey and carried through his ordination the next month.

> This was the *first Ordination* among the Strict Congregational Churches,—and was performed in the following Manner, viz. The Church chose Three Brethren, out of their own Number: Men of approved Gifts, and Abilities, to personate the Church, as their Presbytery, in ordaining Mr. Hovey to the pastoral Office over them.[28]

When Marsh was released from jail in June, he was quickly ordained as colleague pastor with Hovey. The church met with severe persecution, however. A group removed to Wantage, New Jersey, in 1751, and by 1765 only four members remained at Mansfield. These went to the Separate church at South Killingly, and the Mansfield Separate Church passed out of existence.

Plainfield. At Plainfield the situation was exactly the reverse of that in Canterbury. The church, led by its aged and ultraconservative pastor Joseph Coit, was substantially Old Light. The converts of the Great Awakening had been unwilling to unite with such a church, and while remaining aloof had attracted a large number of sympathizers. Therefore the town, in opposition to the church, was strongly

27. *The Result of a Council of the Consociated Churches of the County of Windham*, p. 5. Some of the ministers who had been active in the revival were hissed at for now being among the "opposers."

28. *An Historical Narrative and Declaration*, p. 12. A footnote adds that one of the three men was Thomas Denison, who had been ordained as pastor of the Separate Baptist church at Ashford by Dr. Thomas Green of Leicester and Ebenezer Moulton of South Brimfield. But Moulton had been ordained by John Callender of Newport, who had been ordained by his uncle Elisha Callender of First Baptist Church, Boston, who in turn had his "ministerial powers" directly from the hands of the famous Mathers (see below, p. 237). Jeremiah Condy, the next pastor at Boston, also participated in Moulton's ordination; he likewise had been ordained by Boston Congregationalists. Now Denison assisted in most of the Separate ordinations (eight in 1746 alone). Even the high churchmen of Connecticut should have granted the "regularity" of these who stood in such a noble succession of "true" ministers!

New Light. A Separate church was formed, and Thomas Stevens, Jr., one of their number, was ordained as pastor on September 11, 1746, with the assistance of Thomas Denison, Thomas Marsh, and Solomon Paine. Stevens was zealous and popular, and attracted so many to his ministry that the standing church asked the town to retire Coit and call a younger preacher. David Rowland [29] was called on July 13, 1747, with the understanding that he would preach the doctrines of grace; but when the town discovered his attachment to the Saybrook Platform, it refused to confirm his call. The Separates felt secure in their political control, but they soon grew careless about attending town meetings. On December 3 Rowland's friends found themselves unexpectedly in the majority and voted promptly to settle him. The church quickly confirmed and Rowland accepted. On March 15, 1748, against the opposition of the town, he was ordained by the same ministers who had ordained Cogswell at Canterbury against the opposition of the church.

The Separatists were dismayed by this *coup d'église* but were powerless to revoke it. They still had the power of the purse, however, and resolutely withheld Rowland's salary, forcing him to sue yearly for his maintenance. This shifted the focus of the controversy from the ideal of the pure church to a litigious squabble over taxes, which led inevitably to spiritual decline.

All was not lost, however. A Separate church sprang up at nearby Voluntown which, on April 17, 1751, ordained Alexander Miller as pastor. When Thomas Stevens left Plainfield in 1755, his church proposed union with the Separates of Voluntown. This was consummated by consent of a Separate council in 1758. Miller served as pastor of the united church until his death about 1761, at which time David Rowland resigned to go to Windsor. Both of the Plainfield churches were by that time in a feeble state, and after much discussion they agreed to unite. John Fuller, who had preached to the Separates at Lyme and Bean Hill (Norwich), was called as pastor. Upon renouncing the principles peculiar to the Separates, he was ordained on February 2, 1769, in regular fashion by the ministers of Windham County.[30]

29. Yale College 1743. The Hartford North Association refused to ordain him in 1746 because he would not subscribe to the Saybrook Platform, and he had secured ordination from the (New Light) Fairfield East Association. After his installation at Plainfield, he had a change of heart with regard to the ecclesiastical constitution. One often sees things differently from a position of authority.

30. Fuller's deposition at his reordination is printed in *The Itineraries of Ezra Stiles,* p. 295. At the end he avowed a desire "to unite with the regular Ministers

Lyme. Separates formed churches in all three parishes of Lyme. In the First Church, Jonathan Parsons' conversion to revivalistic Calvinism and his zeal in itinerant evangelizing evoked dissatisfaction among his conservative members.[31] They contrived his dismissal in October 1745, and the next year the prorevival party withdrew to form a Separate congregation. On December 25, 1746, they ordained John Fuller, one of their number, as pastor. He remained through various vicissitudes until 1759, when he assumed the leadership of the Separate church at Bean Hill (Norwich). The church at Lyme probably became extinct soon afterward.

In the second parish (East Lyme) a Separate church was formed in 1749 under Ebenezer Mack. Three years later this church became Baptist in a body. In the third parish (North Lyme) some Separates organized a church at Grassy Hill in 1755 and Daniel Miner served as pastor from 1757 until his death in 1799. At Hadlyme, which in 1742 had been set off from North Lyme and Haddam as a regular parish, there was a Separate meeting which included some thirty families by 1768. Religious conditions in the town of Lyme that year were described in typical gossipy style by Ezra Stiles:

> In Lyme are seven Congs—4 of the regular standing Chhs. —3 of the Separates of which two are Baptists. But the paedseparates in the Vicinity of the Bapt. attend the Baptist Teachers, & I think the Bapt. allow some Paedob. to partake in Lds. Supper. . . . The E. or 2d Par. had no Min. since Mr. Griswold's Death 1760. The Majority being partly Bap. & partly Sep. —both fond of exemption from Rates. . . . [In 1746 the first parish] consisted of about 120 Fam. of which 16 or 18 Separates, the most of them Baptists, & formed a Bap. Chh.
>
> The Sep. in Mr. Beckwith's [North] Society are between a Quarter & Third of the Parish. Most or Majority of East Parish are Bapt. & Separates. Hence perhaps One Third of the whole Town may be Sep. & Baptists.[32]

North Stonington. Separatist activity was equally fervid in North Stonington. A Separate church of thirty-one members gathered on September 11, 1746. It chose Matthew Smith as its pastor on Novem-

---

& Churches of Christ in every Thing wherein we are agreed; & to forbear one another in Love in circumstantial Matters, wherein we cannot be perfectly united."

31. See above, p. 11.

32. Ibid., pp. 266–67. The rise of Baptist sentiments among the Separates, which unavoidably appears in much of this discussion, will be treated in detail in Chap. 7.

ber 27 and ordained him, with the assistance of other Separate pastors, on December 10. Joseph Fish, the parish minister, wrote in 1767, "Not less than two thirds of the congregation, formerly under my care, having, for many years, withdrawn from my ministry, and form'd themselves into baptist and separate churches or assemblies." [33] By 1765 there were three such churches in the town: this first one, which remained properly Separate, and two Separate Baptist churches. One of these was formed in 1743 under Wait Palmer, and the other (formerly a part of the Separate church at Westerly, Rhode Island) in 1765 under Simeon Brown. The strength of these churches is indicated not only by the fact that all of them achieved permanent status but also by Fish's plaint in 1767 that most of his remaining church members were "favouring the separate teachers, *so far* as to frequent their meetings, and, thereby, promoting a-fresh the cause of separation: while others renounc'd their *infant baptism,* and, too hastily, run *into the water.*" [34]

South Killingly. The church in this parish began as a Separate congregation in 1746. On June 3, 1747, it ordained as its pastor Samuel Wadsworth, whose home in Canterbury had housed the earliest meetings of Separates there. The church adopted the confession of the Mansfield Separates and pursued a peaceful and prosperous course. It was the only Separate church in Windham County to meet with no open opposition, the reason being that it was in a remote corner of a fairly large and sparsely settled parish. "These distant residents had long been practically a distinct branch, and were allowed to withdraw and develop as they chose without remonstrance or excommunication, but as members of the society they were still obliged to pay rates for the support of the [parish] church on Break-neck." [35] This onerous burden was removed in 1755 when the Separates petitioned the Assembly for relief, and South Killingly became the first Separate church to be relieved of taxation for the support of the establishment.[36]

Wadsworth served until his death in 1762. Thomas Denison spent two troublous years here, after which Eliphalet Wright discharged a fruitful ministry from 1765 to 1784. Under his leadership the church

33. *The Church of Christ a Firm and Durable House,* p. iii.
34. Ibid.
35. Larned, *History of Windham County, 1,* 451.
36. This particular action, however, applied only to the signers of the petition, and future members of the church (including the children of the signers) were taxed until the parish church itself quit trying to collect the rates in 1770 (ibid., 2, 95–96).

revised its covenant and articles of faith to agree with those in use at Plainfield, which in turn had been adapted from the Mansfield Confession. Wright himself, in spite of his vigorous attack on the establishment, recognized that there were real Christians in the standing churches and proposed that the Separates resume communion with the more evangelical churches with whom they agreed in essence.[37] Under his successor, Israel Day 1785–1826, the church re-entered the communion of the standing churches and its pastor was received as a member of the Windham County Association in 1799.

Windham. The Separate element in Windham township was quite disorderly. This only reflected the general state of the area, however, for when Thomas Clap was pastor of the First Church 1725–39 his chief problem was the disciplining of unruly church members. When the flaming sword of the Great Awakening was thrust into this rambling parish, many of its eight hundred souls were seared. The church received more than one hundred new members during the revival, and many of these withdrew to the Separate church organized in 1747. Elihu Morse, ordained as pastor on October 7, 1747, soon left, and the church fell into confusion.

> It does not appear that this church was ever very thriving or vigorous. Mild Mr. White [Stephen White, pastor First Church 1740–93] persuaded the more rigid disciplinarians "not to drive things," and apparently allowed seceding brethren to fall away without resistance. The Separate church, thus left to itself, soon fell to pieces. Its pastor became a Baptist, its more moderate members returned to their allegiance, while others were absorbed into the more vigorous [Separate] churches of Mansfield and Scotland Parish. . . . The separation in Windham evidently embraced a very lawless and disreputable element, and falling into gross error and extravagance, gained no permanent footing in the community.[38]

37. Eliphalet Wright, *The Difference between the Standing Churches and the Strict Congregationalists,* p. 23.

38. Larned, *History of Windham County,* 1, 458–59. I have used Backus' name for the pastor. Miss Larned calls him Elisha Marsh. Neither says what became of him other than that he later became a Baptist. The historian of New Milford, Connecticut, says that a lay preacher named Elihu Marsh was at the head of the Separates in that town (1753), and that he owned sufficient property to enable him to serve the church without salary (Samuel Orcutt, *History of the Towns of New Milford and Bridgewater, Connecticut,* Hartford, 1882, pp. 192–98).

It is entirely possible that what is called lawless here was no more than individualism and independency asserting itself in an area which was still practically frontier. For example, Joshua Abbe, a man of substance in North Windham, seems to have joined the Separate movement more as a protest against the abridgment of free speech than out of religious conviction. When Elisha Paine was imprisoned at Windham, Abbe helped build bleachers (out of county lumber!) in the jailyard so that the crowds could hear Paine preach from prison. Upon Paine's release, he offered his home to the Separate meeting, demanding, "Why in God's name shouldn't Lish Paine preach if he wants to? By God, I'll have a church of my own, and it'll be free to everybody!" [39] But while such a spirit might swell the size of a separation, it was hardly adequate to sustain the ongoing life of a Christian church.

A more stable Separate church was formed in the third parish (Scotland), where dissatisfaction with pastor Ebenezer Devotion dated back to 1741. Seeing that he was very attached to the Saybrook Platform and little disposed to grant them any concessions, the disaffected withdrew from his ministry in 1745. Cited to appear before the church on January 22, 1746, they gave eight reasons for separating (later expanded to twelve), all of which were voted insufficient by the church.[40] On March 17 the church excommunicated some twenty of the more refractory Separates, who promptly organized themselves into a new church. John Palmer, one of the original number, served as chief exhorter—which earned him a stay of four months in Hartford jail—and eventually was chosen pastor. Ordained on May 17, 1749, he served faithfully until his death in 1807.

The Scotland separation included many of the better members formerly of the standing church, and Palmer himself was representative of the better class of Separate ministers. "Though deficient in education and somewhat rough in speech and manner, Mr. Palmer was a man of estimable character and sound piety, and under his guidance the Brunswick church, as it was called, maintained for many years a good standing in the community, comparatively free from those excesses and fanaticism which marred so many of its contemporaries." [41]

39. Webster, *Town Meeting Country*, p. 75.
40. See Devotion, *An Answer of the Pastor and Brethren*, for the twelve articles and the church's answer. Most of these were quoted at various points in the preceding chapter.
41. Larned, *History of Windham County*, 1, 464.

Ebenezer Devotion, however, was never reconciled to this intrusion into his bailiwick:

> Every Sunday he was accustomed to send his negro servant with a paper forbidding Mr. Palmer, or any person, to preach in the Brunswick meeting-house that day. This prohibition served only to increase the number of attendants upon the preaching of Mr. Palmer, and fan the spirit of separation and opposition into a brighter flame.[42]

After the death of Palmer, the church dwindled. It voted in 1813 to dissolve, and most of the remaining members went to the Canterbury Separate Church, itself in the last stages of life.

Preston. Another of the more stable Separate churches which endured beyond the end of the century was formed in the north parish of Preston. The first page of its record book, in the handwriting of Paul Parke, who served as pastor from 1747 to 1802, reads:

> This Church is called the Seperate Church because the firsts Planted; in this; Came out from the old Church in the Town. which Caled its Self Partly Congregational and Partly Presbeterial: who Submitted to the Laws of the Govemments to settle articals of faith; to govern the gathering of the Church the settlement and support of its Ministors building of meeting houses Preaching Exhorting &C: as also the Church Refuses the members should Improve there Gifts of Preaching & Exhorting Publickly &C: as also were offended at the Powerfull opperations of the Spirits of God: and Did Not Make Saving Conversion the necesary termes of Communion: but admitted unbelievers to Communion: also made half Members: Baptized there Children &C:—
> We bore our testimony to them and Came out from them: to Carry on the worship of God according to our Knowledg of the will of God: and gathered into Church ordor: and the Lord has graciously owned us ever sence.[43]

The church was organized on March 17, 1747, and Parke ordained on July 15. Although only six people covenanted together at the beginning, the movement represented a rather large degree of disaffection in both parishes of Preston. The historian of the First Church says that the number who separated from it nearly depleted the

42. Blake, *The Separates*, p. 174.
43. The record book is at the New London County Historical Society.

church, reducing the membership from 106 in 1744 to 17 in 1781.[44] With their meetinghouse located in North Preston (now Griswold), the Preston Separates became one of the leading churches of their order. A tax relief petition presented to the Assembly in 1751 indicated that its members came not only from the Preston parishes but also from North Groton (now Ledyard), North Stonington, and the fourth parish of Norwich ("Preston Long Society"), and that all these members lived within eight miles of the Separate meetinghouse. They secured tax exemption in 1784, after which they entered into increasingly fraternal relations with the standing churches about them. The last entry in the records is dated July 27, 1817, by which time the standing church had revised its covenant to agree with the practice of the Separates so that reunion became desirable.

Norwich. In Norwich township there were five parishes, all of which were powerfully affected by the revival and subsequently witnessed the formation of Separate churches. When twelve prorevival ministers met at Norwich on June 23, 1743, to add their witness to the Boston *Testimony and Advice,* there were already signs of internal commotion in the churches over errors in doctrine and disorders in practice. As elsewhere, the churchmen finally decided that the best preventive was closer adherence to the ecclesiastical constitution, and the Norwich First Church was led by pastor Benjamin Lord to declare its adherence to the Saybrook Platform in 1744. If this course proved effective anywhere, which is doubtful, it was least so in the church which had dismissed its former pastor for his part in the Saybrook Synod and settled his successor (Lord) on the express condition that he would adhere to the ancient congregational way.[45]

Schism swiftly followed this vote. The group which had been meeting privately in the home of Hugh Caulkins organized a church early in 1745 and built a meetinghouse at the foot of Bean Hill. On August 28, the day before Whitefield arrived in Norwich on his second visit to New England, the standing church arraigned thirteen Separates to hear their reasons for "disorderly" withdrawal.[46] These reasons being judged insufficient, the church suspended the offenders on November

44. R. H. Gidman, "The First Church in Preston: An Historical Survey," *The Bi-Centennial Celebration of the First Congregational Church of Preston, Connecticut* (n.p., 1900), p. 27. The effects of the Revolution and postwar emigration should be taken into account in interpreting these statistics.

45. See above, p. 3.

46. Their depositions, copied from Dr. Lord's records, are in Frederick Denison, *Notes on the Baptists, and Their Principles, in Norwich, Conn.* (Norwich, 1857), pp. 21–27.

10. One of this number, Jedediah Hyde, was ordained as pastor two years later (October 30, 1747). His ministry was troubled by frequent discord, as is shown by the records of other Separate churches which were besieged for appeals to help resolve the difficulties, and he was finally dismissed on September 22, 1757. John Fuller, who was called from the Lyme Separate Church, fared little better and remained only two years. His successor, Gamaliel Reynolds, is reported to have become a Baptist in 1766.[47] The remainder of the church fell under the influence of the Universalist John Murray, who preached there in 1772. By 1788 Dr. Lord noted that the Separate church was meeting "in the character of Universalists."

The other four separations in Norwich deserve brief mention. The second parish, called West Farms (now Franklin), was in the throes of a bitter dispute regarding its meetinghouse when the disorders of the revival refocused the controversy on the issues of ecclesiastical authority. Thomas Denison appeared on the scene in 1746 and gathered the dissidents into a Separate church, of which he became pastor on October 29. The church sold its meetinghouse and went out of existence in 1784.[48] The third parish, called Newent (later Lisbon), initiated disciplinary proceedings with some Separates in 1746, noting that "one Jeremiah Tracy, Jr., has taken upon him to be a preacher, a calling which we don't apprehend God has called him to." [49] Tracy seems not to have been ordained, and the next year Thomas Denison came as pastor of the church. There being some hesitation regarding his previous ordination as a Baptist, he was reordained by several Separate ministers, many of whom he himself had helped ordain. He remained only a few years, being succeeded in 1753 by Bliss Willoughby. In 1761 practically the entire church migrated to Bennington, Vermont, taking with them the church covenant and records.[50] The sixteen remaining members either returned to the standing church or sought communion with the Separate churches at Preston, Canterbury,

47. Ibid., p. 27. A Baptist by the name of Reynolds is noted by Ezra Stiles as being at Mansfield in 1769. Probably it was the same man.

48. *Records of the Congregational Church, Franklin, Connecticut* (Hartford, 1938); and *The Celebration of the One Hundred and Fiftieth Anniversary of the Primitive Organization of the Congregational Church and Society, in Franklin, Connecticut* (New Haven, 1869).

49. Quoted from church records in Henry F. Bishop, *Historical Sketch of Lisbon, Connecticut* (New York, 1903), p. 16.

50. These are printed in Isaac Jennings, *Memorials of a Century. Embracing a Record of Individuals and Events Chiefly in the Early History of Bennington, Vt. and Its First Church* (Boston, 1869), pp. 400–3.

or Scotland. The fourth parish, East Norwich, or "Preston Long Society," had a separation over which Jonathan Storey was ordained as pastor on May 20, 1752. It eked out a tenuous existence for thirteen years, after which it dissolved and commended its remaining members "to any Church they were minded to join with of the same Constitution." [51] The fifth parish, called Norwich Plains (later New Concord, then Bozrah), seems to have fallen almost entirely into the sentiments of the Separates, at least for a time; but no certain knowledge of details has come to light. Most of these Separates went over to the Baptists, and were constituted into a church in 1788 by messengers from the Waterford Baptist Church west of New London.[52]

Enfield. While Separate activity was especially prominent in eastern Connecticut, the central portion of the colony was also affected. The Connecticut River Valley was the scene not only of the frontier revival of 1734–35, but of Whitefield's circuit in 1740. Among the communities where a strong Separate church appeared was Enfield. The exact organization date is unknown, but it was sometime in the forties because extant correspondence between this church and the Canterbury Separates, dated 1751–53, indicates a fully organized church with a covenanted pastor.[53] The documents reveal further that the church was unhappy with its pastor (not named) for neglecting certain duties and for expressing doubts regarding infant baptism. The first formal record from the church itself is dated April 13, 1762, when it was preparing to call Nathaniel Collins, Jr., as pastor. On August 20 Collins "made a gospel Dedication of him selfe to us as on his Part Ready to comply with that Call Which Seamed so Evidently from God and man." [54] When he came, the church took a new lease on life, renewing its covenant and beginning a vigorous campaign for legal status. Its members had managed to retain voting rights in the town; and when Peter Reynolds, pastor of the First Church, died in 1768, they were numerous enough to prevent the settlement of a successor. They bargained with the standing church to drop their opposition to a new minister on condition that the regulars would not oppose the Separates' petition for legal recognition by the Assembly.

51. Quoted from Preston Separate Church records in Blake, *The Separates,* p. 195. Blake has pieced together the whole history of the Separate church in the Long Society from extant records of other churches in the vicinity.

52. Denison, *Notes on the Baptists,* p. 70.

53. Canterbury Separate Papers.

54. Quoted in Oliver William Means, *A Sketch of the Strict Congregational Church of Enfield, Connecticut* (Hartford, 1899), p. 30. This Collins was the son of the first pastor of the Enfield Congregational Church 1699–1724.

This was agreed, and in 1770 the Separates were designated the Second Ecclesiastical Society in Enfield.[55]

Apparently Collins served until his death in 1787. The Separate church lost some of its members to the Shakers about that time, some returned to the First Church, and several more went to the Baptists, who had organized a church in the town sometime previous to 1785. It was difficult for the Separates to obtain regular preaching, and equally so for the Baptists. For several years they shared in supporting men who preached to both groups, and they seem to have merged about 1806. In 1842 the church succumbed to the Millerite excitement and the property passed into the hands of the Adventists.

Wethersfield and Middletown. A Separate church was organized in Wethersfield on January 7, 1747, and Ebenezer Frothingham was ordained as its pastor on October 28 of the same year. Its members seem to have come from several towns up and down the Connecticut River. Because of severe persecution, many of the members moved to New York in 1754, and Frothingham led the rest to Middletown, where they established themselves permanently as a Strict Congregational Church. Separate sentiment reappeared in Wethersfield about 1782 when another dissenting group began to meet. In two years it announced itself Baptist and petitioned for release from ecclesiastical taxes to the standing church. The Middletown church meanwhile grew to such an extent that it divided into two parts in 1788, a branch being formed in Westfield under Stephen Parsons. The latter group became Baptist in 1795. Frothingham was dismissed about the time of the division, probably on account of failing health. He remained in Middletown until his death in 1798 at the age of 81. The church attracted members from a number of smaller towns in the area, and is still in existence as the South Congregational Church of Middletown.[56]

New Haven. When the Great Awakening came to New Haven, pastor Joseph Noyes was in the twenty-fifth year of his ministry and the forty-ninth of his age. According to Leonard Bacon, "no doubt of his piety or orthodoxy, and no complaint against his ministry, appears to have found public utterance."[57] Nevertheless, Davenport's attacks on Noyes in 1741 seem to have touched some hidden strand of discon-

55. Francis Olcott Allen, *The History of Enfield, Connecticut* (Lancaster, Pa., 1900), 2, 1526. All the extant records of the Enfield Separate Church, beginning with 1762, are printed here, 2, 1551 ff.

56. The work which gathers up most of the information to be found in various sources concerning this church is David Dudley Field, *Centennial Address* (Middletown, 1853).

57. *Thirteen Historical Discourses*, p. 211.

tent, because soon after his visit a considerable number of "aggreaved brethren" presented fourteen articles of complaint to the pastor. Instead of consenting to their request for a council, Noyes demanded that the consociation be called. When the dissidents pointed out that the church had never adopted the Saybrook Platform (though the previous pastor, James Pierpont, had been one of its chief architects), the church met hastily on January 25, 1742, and formally subscribed to the platform at a meeting from which the dissidents were "secluded." It was claimed that this vote merely declared what had always been a fact, but the action shifted the main point of controversy from the pastor's preaching to his stand on the ecclesiastical constitution— where it usually came to center in all the contention of the New Lights with the standing order. The dissenting party, some sixty persons of considerable political influence led by James Pierpont, Jr., received from the County Court permission to set up separate worship; and on May 7, 1742, they embodied themselves into a church.[58] Known first as the "Tolerated Church" because it successfully claimed the benefits of the Act of Toleration, it later chose the name "White Haven." After worshiping for a time in the home of Timothy Jones, it began in 1744 to erect a meetinghouse. This audacious move was so obnoxious to the people of the First Church that some of the more violent objectors cut the long timbers one night, and the building was completed only under constant surveillance.

Preaching was difficult to secure after passage of the repressive acts of 1742, though sympathetic ministers from neighboring churches had helped freely before this legislation. John Graham of Southbury, Joseph Bellamy of Bethlehem, Jedediah Mills of Ripton, Philemon Robbins of Branford, and Benajah Case of Simsbury all preached here. Then itineracy was outlawed. Samuel Finley of New Jersey was arrested in New Haven more than once. The first preacher to remain any time was the Separate exhorter from New London, John Curtis, who served from October 1748 to October 1750, though without formal ordination or settlement.

The first ordained and settled pastor was Samuel Bird, who had

58. The moderator of the constituting council was Samuel Cooke, the zealous New Light pastor at Stratfield. He had been a candidate for the pastorate at New Haven when Noyes was chosen, and may have felt a peculiar satisfaction in that minister's present difficulties. The New Haven Association censured him for aiding the Separates, and Yale College contrived his removal from its board of trustees in 1745. The Fairfield East Association, of which Cooke was scribe, retaliated by voting that none of its members were responsible to the Yale Corporation for his doctrines or conduct. Cf. Samuel Orcutt, *A History of the City of Bridgeport, Connecticut* (New Haven, 1887), pp. 21–23.

been expelled from Harvard shortly before graduation in 1744 for New Light sentiments, and who had been preaching at Dunstable, Massachusetts. Two notable events characterized Bird's ministry. First, the White Haven Church obtained from the legislature legal standing in 1759, at which time it outnumbered the First Church 179 to 147. The division obviously could not be made along geographical lines; by necessity each citizen was permitted to choose the church to which he would belong, and a committee assigned persons who had no choice. This voluntaristic plan marked the beginning of the end for the traditional parish pattern in Connecticut.

The second event, which is surprising only if one ignores the largely personal issues which brought this church into being, is the adoption of the Halfway Covenant in 1760. This set the stage for a new controversy when Jonathan Edwards, Jr., called to be pastor in 1769, demanded its abrogation as a condition of his acceptance.[59] The anti-Edwards faction withdrew after sitting restively for eight months under his preaching, and in June 1771 it decided to form the Fair Haven Church. The group persuaded Samuel Bird to serve as pastor, among other reasons because he had an estate in town and could subsist on little salary. "Thereupon they applied to Mr. Mills & Pumroy, Veterans in Separation-makings, and they came, & under their Guidance, a new Church of about a dozen Male Members was gathered." [60] After Edwards' departure there was little reason for the division to continue; the two groups reunited in 1796 as the North Church.

In a sense, the Church of Christ in Yale University is a Separate church, though for somewhat different reasons. The growing New Light sentiment throughout the colony tended to bring the school into disfavor with the public; and the increasing strength of New Lights in politics led President Clap, who had vigorously opposed the revival and the Separates, to establish worship in the College Hall in order to keep clear of the controversies in the First Church. For Clap this was probably a change of strategy more than of personal conviction: where he had previously sided with the Old Lights in defense of the establishment, he now sided with the New Lights in defense

59. The most recent study of this controversy is J. Robert Livingston Ferm, "Jonathan Edwards, Jr., and the American Reformed Tradition" (dissertation, Yale University, 1958), pp. 14–87. Ferm says: "There is no certain evidence that this [the abandonment of the Halfway Covenant] was done at Edwards' request, but it is a probable supposition" (p. 147). The most immediate issue was Edwards' insistence on a public testimony of religious experience, as Ferm indicates later (p. 170).

60. *Literary Diary of Ezra Stiles, 1,* 118.

of orthodoxy (for he *was* a strict Calvinist)—and did both in the interests of the college. The Anglicans were also exerting pressure to secure permission for students of their persuasion to attend their own worship. Thus caught between two fires, Clap determined to procure a professor of divinity for the college and establish private worship under his lead. In 1753 the General Assembly, with political New Lights in the majority, ordered a contribution throughout the churches in behalf of the project. The Rev. Naphtali Daggett was chosen in 1755, and the church was formed on June 30, 1757.[61]

New Milford. Of the three or four Separate churches in western Connecticut, the one selected for description here is that at New Milford. This town will be remembered as the home of David Ferris, who shared in the revival of inner light doctrines there in 1727 and later became a minister in the Society of Friends. The historian of the town says that in 1731–2 nineteen persons "fell away to Quakerism" —a sizable schism considering that the total church membership at that time was less than one hundred.[62] The Great Awakening made no immediate impact on the town, although the people soon became acquainted with the controversies that arose in its wake. Party spirit appeared in the calling of a new minister after Daniel Boardman's death in 1744. One faction wanted to submit to the recommendation of the New Haven Association, because of its known opposition to New Lights and its support of the Saybrook Platform; the other wanted a revivalistic minister who would help to set aside the Halfway Covenant. The first party had its way, over the written protest of thirty-five men. In 1747 the church extended to Nathaniel Taylor of Danbury a unanimous call—unanimous because all who opposed the Saybrook scheme had withdrawn. This secession marks the beginning of the Separate church, although no formal organization was projected for several years.

Taylor was ordained over the divided church with the understanding that if he deviated in his faith and practice from the Saybrook Platform, he should return to the church the one thousand pounds given him at his settlement. With the pastor's immobility thus assured, the dissatisfaction of the New Lights increased. All disciplinary efforts

61. Fisher, *A Discourse, Commemorative of the History of the Church of Christ in Yale College;* and Ralph Henry Gabriel, *Religion and Learning at Yale* (New Haven, 1958), chaps. 1, 2. Roland Bainton, in one of his illuminating metaphors, says that in the gradations of light, "Clap was of medium intensity" (*Yale and the Ministry,* New York, 1957, p. 35).

62. Orcutt, *History of New Milford and Bridgewater,* p. 109.

of the church failing, as well as all protests from the dissenters, a Separate church was organized on May 1, 1753. The constituting council included John Palmer of Scotland and Jonathan Storey of Preston Long Society. The Separates were treated leniently by the town, which exempted them from taxes to the standing church in 1754 and granted them permission to erect a meetinghouse in 1759. They enjoyed preaching at first by Elihu Marsh; later pastors were Robert Campbell 1772–84, Barnabas Lathrop 1791–93, and Daniel Hine 1797–1812. After the last man left, the church disbanded, some members going to neighboring congregations and quite a few to the Baptist church at Northville which had been organized a few years previously.

IN RHODE ISLAND

Except for those questions directly related to attempts at civil and ecclesiastical coercion, Congregational churches outside Connecticut faced all the issues leading to schism that arose in connection with the revival, and these were sufficient to occasion a number of separations. In Rhode Island the two main centers of separatist activity were at Westerly, in the southwest corner of the colony, and at Providence.

Westerly. In 1733 the New England Society for the Propagation of the Gospel (Congregational) had sent to Westerly a missionary to the Pequot Indians. This was Joseph Park, a graduate of Harvard, who became "more evangelical" during the Great Awakening and formed a New Light church on May 5, 1742. Joseph Fish of North Stonington and Nathaniel Eells, Jr., of Stonington participated in Park's installation. This church had fourteen original members and received many others after its formation, among them some sixty Indians, many of whom were converts of James Davenport's ministry. The revival proved an uncontrollable ferment among the members of this church, and, despite an attempted reorganization on the Cambridge Platform in 1745, by 1750 there had been two separations.

One of these groups was led by an Indian exhorter, Samuel Niles, who had been disciplined for exhorting in a disorderly fashion in Park's congregation. He and about one hundred Indians withdrew and established a Separate church at Charlestown. Since none of the Separates would ordain Niles, the new church appointed three of its own members to do so. Baptist sentiments appeared early, and the church adopted the policy of mixed communion. Ezra Stiles noted after Niles' ordination:

> Ever since he has ministered there in holy Things, *preaching, baptizing* and *breaking bread*. He himself was baptized a second

Time, and this was by plunging, and I think by an Indian not an Elder. Yet he professes to hold it indifferent: and it was agreed that baptist or paedobaptist principles and practices should be no Term of Communion. Accordingly Samuel baptizes both Infants and Adults, and the latter by Sprinkling or plunging, as any are persuaded in their own Minds.[63]

Niles' church was also beset with apocalyptic vagaries and was highly unstable in other ways. In 1752 a number of the congregation fell out with the pastor and began to prefer the preaching of another Indian exhorter, James Simon. A division was narrowly averted. During the controversy the church wrote for help to the Canterbury Separate Church:

> Dear Brethren We are Wading through many Tribulations Toward the Blissfull Shores of Eternal Day where we Shant Stand in Need of Councils to Inlighten and Direct us into the True worship and Discipline of the House of God. Neither shall we stand in Need of your Witness to Direct us in the Choice of a Pastor. But O Dear Brethren we are in the Militant State and Stand in Need of your help in all These. Therefore our Cry to our God and to you his Witnesses; Help, help, help . . . the Battle goes hard on the side of the Faithfull; therefore again we Cry Gird on your Sword, Mount the White Horses, and Come forth to the help of the Lord against the Mighty; and as you hear the Trumpet sound on this part of Zion's walls, the Certain Sound is, *viz.* We have been in Search of a Pastor till many of us is Lost in the Wilderness; for our Evidences Cross each other, some for James Simon and some for Samll Niles. The grace of our Lord Jesus Christ be with you. Amen.[64]

Simon seems to have carried the majority, for an entry in the records of the Preston Separate Church (June 5, 1752) states that messengers had returned from the ordination service for Simon. Backus says that this church dissolved when depleted by death and the removal of its chief members to New York.

The other separation from Joseph Park's church in Westerly was also a mixed group of Separates and Baptists. It was led by Stephen Babcock, a deacon in the church and justice of the town. They

63. *The Literary Diary of Ezra Stiles, 1,* 232–33.
64. Quoted in George Leon Walker, *Some Aspects of the Religious Life of New England with Special Reference to Congregationalists* (New York, 1897), pp. 118–19.

formed "The Church of Christ in Westerly and Stonington in Union"
on April 5, 1750, and Babcock was ordained pastor the same day by
David Sprague, pastor of a Separate Baptist church in Exeter, Rhode
Island, and Solomon Paine of Canterbury. Babcock himself accepted
believer's baptism, and this church is usually reckoned as a Baptist
body, although it continued to admit members sprinkled in infancy.
Members living on the Connecticut side secured certificates showing
that they regularly attended and contributed.[65] One of the deacons of
this church, Simeon Brown, became a strict-communion Baptist and
in 1765 established a church of that order at his Connecticut home,
which became the Second Baptist Church of North Stonington.

Providence. Congregational work in Providence dates from 1722.
A meetinghouse was built in 1723, and the first minister, Josiah Cotton
(a descendant of John), was ordained in 1728. For many years the
church was little more than a mission of Massachusetts Congregationalists, and progress was slow. Cotton gave only token approval to the
Great Awakening and took rather high ground in opposing its disorders. Many of his members, however, were powerfully affected by
the visits of Tennent, Wheelock, and Buell in 1741. Criticisms of Cotton's preaching began to increase rapidly. The New Lights gave formal
notice of their uneasiness in a letter on April 2, 1743, and at a church
meeting in September of the same year. On March 22, 1744, the church
abandoned all hope for reconciliation and suspended the malcontents
—ten men and fifteen women—who remained under censure for a
year:

> Five of the Separates wrote a Letter to Mr. Cotton May 25, 1745,
> desiring him to call a Council, by Advice of Rev. Geo. Whitefield.
> Mr. Whitefield had advised them—to take back their Admonition
> —return to the Lord's Table—Mr. Snow to leave off preaching—
> and call a Council to conciliate them.[66]

Neither church nor Separates regarded this advice. The latter maintained worship continually from 1743 on, meeting in private houses or
under the trees. They were supplied by preachers from eastern Connecticut, who came along the road between Providence and Windham
County which was opened in 1722. Elisha Paine, who preached here
frequently, was called as pastor in 1744 but declined. The man finally
chosen was one of their number, Joseph Snow, Jr., who had been

65. A number of these interesting documents are printed in Frederick Denison,
Westerly and Its Witnesses (Providence, 1878), pp. 104–05.
66. *The Literary Diary of Ezra Stiles*, 1, 274. Stiles here draws on a collection
of papers regarding the Providence separation which he had seen recently.

exhorting ever since his conversion under Gilbert Tennent. He was ordained in February 1747 by Solomon Paine, Thomas Stevens, and Samuel Drowne (a lay member of the congregation, later a Baptist preacher); and during the half-century in which he served the church it became one of the strongest congregations in Providence. Indeed, the First Church had only four families left in 1763, while the Separates numbered 140 families in 1771. Snow's meetinghouse was the largest in town, and the commencement exercises for Rhode Island College (later Brown University) were held there until the First Baptist Church built its commodious house of worship in 1775. Relations with the Baptists were always good, and some Baptists were included in its membership; although when controversy between Separates and Baptists arose in New England generally, Snow sided with the pedobaptists. Ezra Stiles predicted in 1772 that "the Majority of the Church being Baptists, will chuse a Baptist for their next Minister after Mr. Snows Death, and so that church will terminate Baptists, some few perhaps in that Case returning to the original Church." [67] He was wrong. The church achieved stability, was received eventually into the fellowship of regular Congregational churches, and still exists as the Beneficent Church in Providence.[68]

IN MASSACHUSETTS

Old Plymouth Colony. Separatism in Massachusetts was strongest in the southeastern part of the commonwealth, the territory of the Old Colony. Typical of separations in that region was the one at Attleborough, where Habijah Weld was pastor from 1727 until his death in 1782. The church shared so largely in the Great Awakening (as did all this area) that 192 new members were received in the years 1740–43. This led to the peaceable and perfectly legal formation of the Second Church in 1743, to which Peter Thacher, Jr., was called. He did not accept until five years later, giving as his reasons for the delay "the death of my Rev. and Hon'd. Father, April 1744, at Middleboro', and a sad, unchristian separation from the church at Attleboro' together with some discouragements of my own." [69] The separation to which he referred was primarily from the First Church, though it

67. Ibid., p. 278.

68. See James Gardiner Vose, *Sketches of Congregationalism in Rhode Island* (Boston, 1894); and Arthur Edward Wilson, *Weybosset Bridge in Providence Plantations* (Boston, 1947).

69. Quoted from Thacher's account of his ordination in John Daggett, *A Sketch of the History of Attleborough from Its Settlement to the Division* (Boston, 1894), p. 246.

included some from his own also. Seventy-four persons formed them-selves into a Separate church on January 20, 1747, stating their dis-satisfaction with "the Constitution of the standing order of Churches in the land," i.e. the continued reception of halfway members.[70] The same day the Separates, assisted by Solomon Paine, Thomas Stevens, and Matthew Smith, all from eastern Connecticut, ordained as their pastor Nathaniel Shepard, a Boston tailor converted by James Daven-port, who served them until his death in 1752.

Other notable separations in the territory of the Old Plymouth Colony were at Rehoboth, Freetown, and Middleborough. At Rehoboth the Separate church was gathered in May 1748. It wrote to the Canter-bury Separates to send messengers for the ordination of John Paine to the pastorate on the first Wednesday in August. Paine was a brother to Solomon and Elisha, and had already been seasoned by spending eleven months in Hartford jail for illegal preaching. He seems to have remained about three years, for in 1751 Samuel Peck became pastor of the Rehoboth church, being ordained by Solomon Paine, Thomas Stevens, Nathaniel Shepard, and a deacon from Joseph Snow's church. Peck was pastor until 1788.

A Separate church was organized at Freetown under Silas Brett in 1747. There was no regular Congregational church here previously, and where these New Lights came from is uncertain; most of the evidence points to the Middleborough-Bridgewater area. After Brett's departure in 1775, the church passed into the Baptist fold. Six years later it moved to Fall River, where it became the First Baptist Church of that town. Separate activity at Middleborough, perhaps the most important center in this whole region, will be discussed in connection with the story of Isaac Backus in chapter 6.

Cape Cod. The Cape, also, was the scene of considerable Separate activity. All but two of the thirteen ministers of Barnstable County were strongly opposed to the revival and published a blast against Whitefield and the itinerants in 1745. But Elisha Paine, the far-rang-ing Separate evangelist, hailed from Eastham and was hardly disposed to let the land of his birth lie in "heathen" darkness. In the summer of 1744 he preached through all the towns of the Cape and en-couraged separatist tendencies that were already appearing. Writ-ing to his wife from Chatham on July 3, he said:

> I am purposing every day to come home, but dare not leave the
> Lord's harvest lest the wild beasts should devour and the wild

70. Quoted from church records, ibid., p. 271.

boars should root up what the Lord seems to be doing here, with the greatest power that ever I saw here, or, I think, anywhere. The Lord is doing wonders in this sandy land; but as Christ triumphs, Satan rages. The Lord hath hitherto sustained me and delivered me from the rage of the adversary. O pray for me and the cause of dear Jesus. The pine woods in Harwich ring hallelujahs and hosannas, even from babes; I never heard the like before; from little ones from six years old and upwards, saying, "Holy, &c.," "Hallelujah, &c.," God is bringing of them in from the hedges.[71]

On February 23, 1749, a Separate church was constituted in the south parish of Harwich, and Joshua Nickerson was ordained pastor with the help of Isaac Backus, John Paine, and Nathaniel Shepard. "This church admitted to communion all Christians whether they had been sprinkled in infancy, or been baptized by immersion." [72] Nickerson remained until 1772. A second Separate church was formed in 1751 under Richard Chase and became Baptist in 1757. Chase remained until 1777. The Separates at Chatham worshiped at Harwich. At Barnstable, where the First Congregational Church is a direct descendant of Henry Jacob's Independent Puritan congregation in London, a Separate church was formed of which Nathaniel Ewer was pastor from 1750 to 1760. This church included members from Yarmouth and Hyannis. At the latter place a Baptist church was formed by the Separates in 1771.

Easton. Solomon Prentice, whose dismissal from Grafton for extreme New Light sentiments has been noted,[73] assumed the pastorate of the Congregational church at Easton in 1747. Here he soon induced the church to adopt a new covenant, receive only experienced Christians as members, and establish stricter discipline. Perhaps all would have gone well had not the town become embroiled a few years later in a controversy over where to erect a new meetinghouse. Bitter disputes led to a division in which a majority of the church adhered to Prentice on the old site, while a majority of the town built a new meetinghouse on their preferred site. The latter accused Prentice's company of being separatists, which Prentice hotly denied:

71. Quoted in Backus, *History of New England,* 2 (2d ed. Newton, Mass., 1871), 67 n.

72. Josiah Paine, *A History of Harwich, Barnstable County, Massachusetts* (Rutland, Vt., 1937), p. 364.

73. See above, p. 56.

> I Humbly Beg the faviour of this Hon'ble Court [he said in one
> of their petitions], that the church & Pastor may be acquitted
> from that Infamous term of Seperatists fixed upon us by the
> Town's Com'tee in their Petition. Because it is an epithett we
> renounce with abhorrence and Detestation.[74]

In the long and acrimonious controversy the church party decided it
might be better to establish themselves completely independent of
the town by building their own meetinghouse on land belonging to
the pastor. When the townsmen threatened to tear it down, Prentice
bellowed:

> Let them Come into my field, I will breake theare Heads; when
> it was answered to Him that the Genaral Cort's Committey might
> Command Assistance, and he would not be abel to do it, and
> His reply was this: I do not fear it, I can have anofe to assist
> me in that afare; Let them Come in to my field if they Dare, I will
> split theaire braines out.[75]

Accusation and recrimination, petition and counterpetition, all failed
to solve the problem; but nobody's head was broken. A council
called in 1751 even succeeded in bringing the two parties together
for a few months' worship in the town's new meetinghouse.

The final break came on November 5, 1752, when Prentice's group
served notice to the town that restoration of amicable relations was
impossible and that after much heart-searching and prayer they had
voted "to Come off from the broken Congregational Ecclesiastical
Constitution, and declare for and Come in with the Disapline and
order of the Ancient & Renownd Chh of *Scottland*." [76] This rather
surprising turn to Presbyterianism can be explained only by the
fact that it offered at the time the only respectable direction in which
to flee from the standing order. The church revised its rules and usages,
and was accepted by the Presbytery of Londonderry, New Hampshire.
"Mr. Prentice so enjoyed his new associations under the Presbyterian
order of things, that he went to other towns and preached to the
quickening of their congregations, and awakened new religious interest among his own people." [77]

His peace, however, was short-lived. His wife had already imbibed

74. Quoted from *State Papers, 13*, 219–20, in William L. Chaffin, *History of the Town of Easton, Massachusetts* (Cambridge, 1886), p. 115.
75. Quoted from *State Papers, 13*, 760, ibid., pp. 116–17.
76. Quoted from church records, ibid., p. 130.
77. Ibid., p. 133.

Baptist opinions. Her dissent had been noted at the baptism of their ninth child in 1748, and in 1750 she herself had been immersed by an unordained preacher. Prentice recorded the event with disgust: "Ipsa Anna baptista; Immersa Indignissimo Laico, Viz., ——— ———, Decembr 5, 1750, absente marito." [78] Soon she had groups of her Baptist friends holding prayer meetings in the parsonage, which so offended her husband's parishioners that they forbade him to celebrate the sacrament for nearly a year. Although he disagreed with Baptist sentiments, he would neither deny that these folk were Christians nor cast them out of his house. For this his church complained to the Presbytery and he was suspended from the ministry in 1754. "And because by sd Vote I was Deprived of ye small Subsistance I had among my People at Easton, I thought it Necessary, for the Honr of God and good of my famaly, to Remove with my famaly to Grafton; which accordingly was Done, April 9th, 1755." [79] The Presbyterian church in Easton never succeeded in gaining separate parish privileges and gave up the struggle in 1762. The Baptists, however, continued to gain strength and organized an independent church in the year the Presbyterians disbanded.

The Boston area. Separatism in Boston has already been mentioned.[80] Those who withdrew from the Congregational churches in the town were estimated by Timothy Cutler in 1743 to number about five hundred. These sat under the preaching of John Cleaveland between 1745 and 1747, but he declined to be settled formally over them and they called Andrew Croswell from Groton, Connecticut, in 1748. Known as the Eleventh Congregational Church, it dissolved shortly after Croswell's death in 1785. There are suggestions of Separate congregations in the outlying towns also. At Newton, Nathan Ward was pastor of such a church from 1753 to 1758, when he left for Maine. This church then coalesced with the Separate church at Brookline, which had been under the care of Jonathan Hyde since its formation in 1751; he remained as pastor of the combined congregation until his death in 1787. Those of this group who became Baptists formed a church at Newton in 1780 under Caleb Blood. A Separate church at Cambridge under Nathaniel Draper 1751–53 also

78. Quoted from baptismal records, ibid., p. 136. Translated: "She is an Anabaptist, immersed by an unworthy layman, namely [Peter Sullard?], Dec. 5, 1750, her husband being absent."

79. Quoted from church records, ibid., p. 138. Chaffin observes that Prentice had rebelled against the "broken Congregational order" only to fall victim to the stricter order he had chosen as a substitute.

80. See above, p. 57.

included some Baptists. It never flourished and seems to have broken up sometime between 1784, when it complained of oppression by the standing church, and 1817, when the First Baptist Church was organized. At Charlestown a group of Separates signed a petition for tax exemption in 1749, but it is not clear whether they completed a church organization.[81]

Ipswich. The second parish in Ipswich (Chebacco, now Essex) witnessed one of the most notable separations in the Bay Colony. Theophilus Pickering, pastor of the regular church 1727–47, professed to favor revivals conducted by settled ministers in their own churches, but he distrusted the new methods fostered by Whitefield and the itinerants. Most of the wandering evangelists came through his parish, and his neighboring pastor in the First Church, Nathaniel Rogers, was an ardent advocate of the new measures. Caught in a storm center of revivalistic turbulence, Pickering was, according to the New Lights' complaint, "very reserv'd and cautious." [82] At the insistence of those who had discarded reserve in religion, he allowed "occasional Preaching from others under certain Restrictions," and promised to hold his own lectures more frequently—which he did for two weeks. But beyond this, "we don't remember any Thing that he did to encourage or assist us; or that he adapted his Preaching any otherwise to the Times (as we apprehend) than by taking Advantage of the Failings that attended, to blacken and disparage the whole." He never counseled with the concerned, attended a prayer meeting, or offered any guidance whatsoever to his awakened people. "This Carriage, together with his *old Way of Preaching* (which now was become very unsavoury to us) caus'd great Uneasiness." Twenty-three of Pickering's sixty-three parishioners presented to him their grievances in writing, which he spurned. In 1744 several more exchanges took place, which only made the aggrieved brethren feel that their pastor had treated them with cruelty and their church with neglect. "Whereby our consciences were so offended as that, we could not in Charity

81. G. L. Walker, *Some Aspects of the Religious Life of New England,* p. 115, lists Charlestown as one of the better known Separate churches. I am unable to verify this. It is possible that he confused it with the Indian church at Charlestown, Rhode Island.

82. All quotations in this and the next paragraph are from John Cleaveland, *A Plain Narrative,* pp. 4–15. This was in answer to Pickering's *A Bad Omen to the Churches of New-England* (Boston, 1747), which centered entirely on the irregularity and offensiveness of Cleaveland's ordination over the Separates, and ignored the grounds of separation which were present before Cleaveland ever came to town.

and Love commune with them; and then this must be construed as cutting our selves off from all Right to a Church-meeting for our Help! What could Men do in such a Case?"

Thus at an impasse, the dissidents proposed that the church hear their case (which it had steadfastly refused to do), call a mutual council, dismiss them to another church, or permit them to embody into a church themselves. Rejecting all these propositions, Pickering told them curtly, "It is of no avail for you to keep tugging and striving with your Pastor." Neighboring pastors interceded with Pickering in behalf of the dissenters, but to no avail; and the Third Church (Hamilton) chided the Second for its neglect of their grievances. Pickering once agreed to resign, then reneged; he agreed to call a council, but before it could meet he died. In the divided state of the church, the New Lights felt they had no choice but to withdraw, for which they were excommunicated—the only formal action ever taken by the church in the whole affair. The Separates summed up the matter:

> We can truly say, that we dislike Seperations on trivial and flighty Reasons, as much as any Christians, and would with Humility caution against such, or of taking Example by us, to separate without weighty Reasons: But where Christians are treated by the Churches and Pastors, as we have been treated by ours, we have Freedom to say, that we have no great Concern about preserving the outward Peace of such Churches; and we think it highly offensive to God if they do not separate, since we can't see what Gospel End can be served, for Persons to be held down under spiritual Tyranny, in order to support & maintain such a Peace.

There is no hint here of wild enthusiasm, disorder, or harsh censoriousness. Cleaveland's *Narrative* implies only the determined seriousness of men faced with the disagreeable choice of violating their consciences to maintain a dishonorable peace by acquiescing in a dead religion, or of inviting the misunderstanding and censure of others by following their firm convictions.

The dissidents, on advice of the Separate churches of Boston and Plainfield, covenanted together as a church on May 20, 1746. John Cleaveland, who had been expelled from Yale in 1744 for the Separatist activities of his parents at Canterbury, and who had been preaching for two years to the Separates at Boston, was ordained as pastor in an outdoor service on February 25, 1747. The church grew rapidly, became strong and stable, and in 1774 received the remaining members of the original church into its fellowship, thus ending the schism. Cleaveland, whose degree Yale granted belatedly in 1764, remained as pastor until his death in 1799, serving with distinction as a chaplain in both the French and Indian and the Revolutionary Wars.

Newbury. An equally notable separation in the territory north of Boston occurred at Newbury. The revival had been quite strong here also. Matthias Plant, Anglican rector, wrote in 1742:

> I do not know but before these six months to come most of my hearers will leave me for all the country near me is taken with this new scheme (as they call it.) Within one month 53 have been taken into communion in one dissenting [Congregational] meeting house. Some of them belonged to another meeting house, and the dissenting teacher not approving of said scheme they forsook him to [attend] at the other meeting house.[83]

The withdrawal here mentioned was from the First Church, where pastor Christopher Toppan was totally opposed to the revival. But the New Lights were scarcely more satisfied at John Lowell's Third Church (Newburyport). An anonymous article in the Boston *Evening Post* for May 3, 1742, charges Nathaniel Rogers of Ipswich, Daniel Rogers (his brother, a New Light evangelist at large), and Samuel Buell "with having come into Newbury and formed a party and taken possession of Mr. Lowell's meeting house without his knowledge, or asking leave of the proprietors of the house, or the consent of the church or congregation and so forth and that an attempt of the like factious nature was made upon the reverend Mr. Toppan's meeting house, but Mr. Toppan being present the party was repulsed." [84] The Separate church, when formed in 1746, included about one-third of the membership of each of these churches.

For two years this group enjoyed the informal ministrations of Joseph Adams, "a young zealous new-light preacher." All efforts at reconciliation failing, the Separates on July 24, 1744, convened a council of New Light ministers who advised them that their charges against Toppan were justified, that they had exhausted every reasonable means of reconciliation, and that "however we utterly disapprove of unnecessary separations as partaking of great guilt and accompanied

83. Quoted in Joshua Coffin, *A Sketch of the History of Newbury, Newburyport, and West Newbury* (Boston, 1845), p. 212. The letter is dated March 2, 1742.

84. Quoted ibid., p. 212.

with great scandal, yet looking upon your circumstances as extraordinary and deplorable we cannot think you blameworthy, if with good advice you seek more wholesome food for your souls and put yourselves under the watch of a shepherd in whom you can confide." [85] This so strained relations in the First Church (in spite of the fact that Toppan hastily convened a council of Old Light ministers to acquit him of all the allegations of the disaffected brethren and to admonish them for their disorderly withdrawal) that it was thought best to secure a colleague pastor. John Tucker was called in 1745 over a sizable opposition—the vote carried with a majority of twelve in the parish and two in the church—and was ordained on December 20. Twenty-three dissidents served notice to the church that the peace of their consciences and their desire for spiritual edification demanded that they withdraw from Toppan and Tucker and seek a pastor in whom they might have more confidence.

Whitefield, visiting the town for the second time in 1745, had already advised them that their man was Jonathan Parsons, recently dismissed from Lyme, Connecticut, by the Old Light party in his church. Parsons arrived in November; and on January 3, 1746, nineteen members of the First Church organized themselves into a Separate church. Two months later they received a considerable number of persons who had withdrawn from John Lowell's church in Newburyport, and a meetinghouse was built on the line between the two parishes. Parsons was settled over them in March 1746. The church grew rapidly and soon reached a membership of several hundred. Tax exemption was difficult to secure; consequently, in September 1748 the church voted to unite with the Boston Presbytery. Parsons wrote in his diary: "they deemed it expedient to take the Presbyterian form." [86] This was the first Presbyterian church in Massachusetts to achieve permanent standing.

Sturbridge. Eastern Massachusetts was not alone in witnessing separations. Separate churches were formed at several places in the Connecticut River Valley, in the less developed territory between there and the seaboard, and even farther west. One of the more interesting of these was at Sturbridge, where Caleb Rice was pastor 1736–59. In May 1747 a large number of New Lights withdrew from his ministry and on November 10 organized a Separate church. Several letters in which they furnished their reasons to the standing

85. Quoted ibid., p. 214.
86. Quoted in Jonathan Greenleaf, *Memoir of Jonathan Parsons* (Boston, 1841), p. 8.

church are preserved in the Congregational Library in Boston and have been printed in a recent work by Ola Elizabeth Winslow.[87] They are all dated 1749. Hannah Cory wrote:

> One time as I was coming to the Lecture the words come to me in Cor. come out from amongst them, and then these words in Amos, can two walk together Except they be agreed, so I went to the meeting house, and when I came in there was no body & as I set there these words came to me my house is a house of prayer but ye have made it a den of thieves, then sudden fear came over me so I Got up and went out and walked over the burying place and I thought I had rather lie down among the Graves than go into the meeting house, but when I se Mr Rice comeing I went in but it seemd to be a dark place Ministers deacon and people lookt Strangely as if they were all going Blindfold to destruction, and tho my body was there, my soul was with the Seperates, praising God as soon as I was dismysd at the meeting house I went to Brother Nevils where my Soul was sweetly refresht, the Lord alone be praised for it was he alone who Brought me out and not any Creature . . . . yet altho I was not free of some degree of rising against some outward actions or noises of the Seperates yet this avanisht upon the sweet oneness of soul I felt toward them.

David Morse wrote that after his conversion he had joined the standing church, ignorant of the fact that it was "Right the Reverse" of the true church described in Scripture. Jerusha Morse was distressed by the apparent "wants of Gods Presents" in the church meetings; after "laboring long in the darkness," she went to Pastor Rice, who told her he could not advise her and that maybe the Separates were right. This compounded her confusion, whereupon she determined to trust her own impressions more than the advice of men. Having sought out the Separates, she became convinced that their way was "of the Lord," and admonished her former associates in the church to remember that "whatsoever is not of faith is sin." Several others avowed that the Lord had impressed upon them, through certain crucial texts or directly by the Spirit, that they must join the Separates. Sarah Morton at first was "a fraid of the Seperate teachers because they had no larning," but when she recalled that the apostles had been "unlearned and ignorant men" she had no more qualms. Sarah Blanchard confessed to attending the Separate meetings at first "more to find what I could git against them than to finde the truth,"

---

87. *Meetinghouse Hill,* pp. 232–36.

and even when convinced against her will, "could not bear to be cald a Sepperate and bare the flouts & scoffs of those my Companions." But she finally had to confess that the truth was with them, and she cast her lot there.

John Blunt, one of the members of this Separate church, was ordained its pastor on September 28, 1748. Although at first a pedobaptist, he led the congregation in a study of the New Testament on the subject of baptism, with the result that the church accepted Baptist sentiments en masse. In May of 1749 over sixty persons, including the pastor, were baptized by Ebenezer Moulton of Brimfield, for which audacious act he was seized as a vagabond and imprisoned. The church practiced mixed communion until about 1780. Blunt himself reverted to pedobaptism in 1752 and was excommunicated by the church, causing the Separates of Connecticut to remonstrate with the Separate Baptists of Sturbridge. In 1753 Blunt was a member of the Preston Separate Church, whose records show that some of its members could not forgive him for his inconstancy in submitting to "rebaptism." At Sturbridge some of the Separates returned to their original affiliation after ten or fifteen years. One penitent came back thankful that at least she had not consented to "reBaptism by being dipped." But the Baptist church that came from these events proved to be permanent.

IN NEW HAMPSHIRE

There are indications of at least nine Separate churches formed in New Hampshire. The majority of these fall more into the category of frontier phenomena—that is, they were organized and/or led by Separates and New Lights who had moved out to the fringes of civilization from some more settled area. Frontier separatism is discussed in the next section; here attention is given to three notable separations from older and better established churches in the southeastern corner of the district.

Whitefield made three visits to this area, and was greeted each time by the determined hostility of most of the regular ministers. Indeed, the New Hampshire Convention of Ministers, formed on July 28, 1747, seems to have had its origin in opposition to itineracy. Here as elsewhere the clergy's attitude led to the withdrawal of those who were convinced that they had never heard the gospel until they listened to Whitefield and his kin.

Exeter. The separation which caused the most commotion was at Exeter, a town important enough to become the capital of the "state" in 1775. The Old Light pastors here were John Odlin 1706–54 and his son Woodbridge, who was installed as colleague in 1743 and remained until 1776. Disaffection in this church first appeared when the Odlins refused to allow Whitefield and other itinerants to preach here. Soon the revival party was charging that neither Odlin nor his son preached the gospel. The town tended to side with the pastors; it was anxious to hold the Separates in line so as to lose no more names from the tax roll. (It had lost Epping in 1741 and Brentwood in 1742, and calculated that a New Light defection now would cost them a third of the remaining taxable citizens.) But party lines were sharply drawn by the beginning of 1743. Both sides held an ex parte council condemning the opposing faction, which only served to widen the breach.[88] The Separate church was formed on July 7, 1744, by fifty-four persons whose names indicate that the schism cut across the most prominent families of the town.[89] In spite of the indefatigable opposition of the Odlins, Daniel Rogers was installed as pastor on August 30, 1748, the church having been supplied in the meantime by itinerants.[90] When the New Light councilors arrived in town for the installation—a term which the Old Lights resented because it implied the legality of Rogers' previous ordination at York—the Odlins sent two remonstrances, both of which were ignored. The last note concluded:

> But if you are determined to proceed, we look upon ourselves obliged to testify against it, and to let you know we look upon such a Procedure to be contrary to the Order of the Gospel, and has a Tendency to break up the Communion of Churches, and opens a Door for Disorder and Confusion, and will be very hurtful to the

88. Cf. *The Result of a Council of Ten Churches; Conven'd at Exeter, Jan. 31, 1743* (Boston, 1744). This was the Old Light council; the New Lights apparently left no record.

89. John Taylor Perry, *The First Church in Exeter, New Hampshire* (Exeter, 1898), p. 74.

90. Rogers, who was to serve this church for thirty-seven years, was the grandson of President John Rogers of Harvard, the son of John Rogers of Ipswich, and the brother of Nathaniel (who succeeded his father at Ipswich) and John Rogers, Jr. (pastor of the Second Church in Kittery). He graduated from Harvard in 1725, third in his class; then tutored and supplied various pulpits. At the time of Whitefield's first visit, he and all his family became devoted followers of the evangelist and ardent promoters of the revival. Daniel had been ordained as an evangelist— a vagrant preacher, his opponents said—at York, Maine, on July 13, 1742 (see above, p. 12).

Churches, and the real Interest of Religion, as well as to this Church in Particular.[91]

In 1755 the Separates obtained legal recognition as an independent parish. A mutual council met this year and voted that the Separates had acted disorderly, but if they would accept this judgment and agree to walk in harmony with their sister churches they might be recognized. The council then advised the First Church to forgive the seceders. Though neither party was overly conciliatory for some time, relations gradually improved between the two churches and later they were receiving members by transferral from one another. Rogers, though extremely careful to give no offense and to show himself agreeable toward his fellow ministers, did not receive fraternal recognition for a long time. He did exchange pulpits with Joseph Adams, the Separate pastor at Stratham, and with some of the Massachusetts New Lights; and he enjoyed further visits from Whitefield (who preached here the day before he died in Newburyport in 1770), but otherwise his relations with surrounding churches were not very pleasant. Rogers died in 1785, after which the two churches contemplated reunion. This was not consummated, however, and the later history of the two churches became involved in controversies over Hopkinsianism and Unitarianism.[92]

Portsmouth. In the middle of the eighteenth century, Portsmouth boasted a more elegant social life than any other town in New England. Whitefield said after his first visit here that his small audience had been polite but so spiritually unconcerned that he scarcely knew whether he spoke to rational or brute creatures. The response was somewhat better on his second visit in 1745, so much so that the Second Church sent its pastor to the installation of Daniel Rogers at Exeter. Soon after 1750, however, the churches seem to have settled back into their lethargic ways once again, much to the distress of those who had been awakened. In 1757 a number of people withdrew from both Congregational churches and began to hold private worship led by one Walton, a lay exhorter. Samuel Drowne, formerly a deacon in the Separate church at Providence and later pastor of the Baptist church at Coventry, Rhode Island, came in 1761; and these people

91. John and Woodbridge Odlin, *An Account of the Remonstrances of the Church in Exeter and of a Number of Neighbouring Ministers, against the Installment (So Term'd) of Mr. Daniel Rogers, over a Number of Separatists Belonging to Said Church* (Boston, 1748), pp. 8–9.
92. J. T. Perry, *First Church in Exeter,* pp. 100 ff.

organized the Independent Congregational Church and ordained him as pastor. Although Drowne was willing to sprinkle infants, his presence undoubtedly sowed Baptist ideas early among these Separates, and when a Baptist church was formed in Portsmouth in 1780 they tended more and more to pass into its communion.[93]

Newcastle. Even if they did participate briefly in the revival movements of the day, the pastors at Newcastle (Portsmouth's neighbor at the mouth of the Piscataqua River) were also far from sympathizing with the more fervent New Lights. Although the separation in this place came much later than elsewhere, it is notable for its subsequent results. The story revolves around the experience of Benjamin Randall, who came under the influence of powerful religious concerns in the summer of 1773 and began to speak to individuals regarding their relation to Christ. The response encouraged him to begin private meetings at his home "every Sabbath and every Thursday evening, for the purpose of singing, praying, and reading a sermon or some other good book." [94] He invited the minister of the town, Stephen Chase, who attended only one of the meetings: "the probable reason why he did not attend more, might be that he heard the *old Whitefield sound* among them." [95] On a visit to Portsmouth, Randall heard a Separate preacher and was so impressed that he invited the man to Newcastle, but his guest met only with abuse and insults. Because of growing dissatisfaction with his pastor and church, Randall "came out and separated himself from the congregational church, and met with them no more. He was not cast out, but so oppressed [i.e. depressed] that he came out." This was in May 1775. Soon he was followed by others who were convinced by his example. These, though few in number, held "a constant meeting by themselves," which exposed them to public ridicule. The next year they began to question infant baptism, and Randall's biographer would have it that each man in private study of his Bible reached independently the conclusion that the ordinance was for believers only. Attending the ordination of William Hooper at the Baptist church in Berwick, Maine, Randall and three others were immersed; they returned home and persuaded others to follow their example. Up to this point, there was no question of doctrinal deviation from the Calvinism of the orthodox Congregationalists, the Separates, or the Separate Baptists. Ran-

93. Robert Sandeman also had a church in Portsmouth 1764–71.
94. John Buzzell, *The Life of Elder Benjamin Randall* (Limerick, Me., 1827), p. 30.
95. Ibid., p. 31.

dall, as is known, soon began to deny the doctrine of election and the other distinctive points of Calvinism, and subsequently became the father of the Freewill Baptist movement.[96]

ON THE FRONTIER

Migration of the New Lights. Most of the emigrants from the older parts of New England into the frontier areas of Maine, New Hampshire, Vermont, and New York were to some extent New Lights, whose religious radicalism formed a part of the discontent which led them to seek larger opportunities in newer regions. After the fall of Montreal in 1760 these restless folk pushed up the Merrimac River to the "Great Lake" (Winnipesaukee), and up the Connecticut River toward its head. Often their points of origin are indicated in the place names they brought with them, and Connecticut names are most prominent. "Movers from eastern Massachusetts and Rhode Island, to be sure, joined the trek, but the Connecticut people by sheer weight of numbers so dominated the development of both sections [Vermont and western Massachusetts] that they became, in substance, new Connecticuts."[97] Nearly all of these people were from areas where the Great Awakening had been strong, and their migration meant the transplanting of the revival spirit to new areas. For a number of years trained preachers were few—a situation that began to change only after the founding of Dartmouth College at Hanover, New Hampshire, by Eleazar Wheelock in 1770—but this was no handicap to settlers who were largely prejudiced against an educated and salaried ministry anyway. The same training which qualified a minister in the eyes of the traditional churches made him less able to reach these pioneers who preferred to listen to itinerant exhorters. The uneducated preachers who often accompanied the immigrants were on the same social and intellectual level as their hearers, and found favor not by preaching doctrinal discourses but by aiming at an experience of heartfelt religion. The independent settlers were glad enough to leave behind the aristocratic established ministers and hear the New Light exhorters who swarmed into the new regions.

An illustration of this may be seen in the case of Richard Elvins. On February 18, 1742, the Anglican rector at Salem, Massachusetts, wrote that Nathaniel Rogers of Ipswich, "one of this Pseudo Apostle

96. See Norman Allen Baxter, *History of the Freewill Baptists* (Rochester, N.Y., 1957).

97. Rising Lake Morrow, *Connecticut Influences in Western Massachusetts and Vermont* (New Haven, 1936), p. 1.

displayed his talent in the Town on Sunday the 24th January & continued here so doing until the Thursday following, when he left his auditory in charge to one Elvins a Baker, who holds forth every Thursday, and tho' a fellow of consummate ignorance is nevertheless followed by great multitudes and much cried up." [98] Two years later this Elvins appeared at Dunston, Maine (near Portland), gathered a church among the new settlers, and served with such acceptability that he remained until his death in 1776. Not all the Separate preachers lived up to the accusation of their traducers that they were "like Reuben, unstable as water."

The first church in Vermont. The most outstanding instance of how the Separates established themselves on the frontier is at Bennington, Vermont. The town was settled in 1761 by families from Amherst, Hardwick, and Sunderland, Massachusetts; and Newent, Connecticut. All except those from Amherst had been Separates in their former places. One of the original settlers was Joseph Safford, who had been a deacon of the Newent Separate Church and had brought with him the records of that church. The group from Sunderland had withdrawn from the standing church there in 1749 and had met as a Separate congregation until an opportunity to make a new start in Vermont came at the close of the French and Indian War. The Hardwick emigration was distinctly a religious pilgrimage, the people seeking larger freedom in ecclesiastical affairs.[99] The Bennington church was formed in 1762 and the next year was greatly augmented by the arrival of a Separate congregation from Westfield, Massachusetts, formed there in 1748. Its pastor, Jedediah Dewey, though a carpenter with only a common-school education, was respected for sincerity and sobriety; and when his church moved to Bennington, he became pastor of the entire settlement. The Westfielders originally had planned to merge with the Separate church at Amenia, New York, but instead accepted the invitation to join with the Bennington people. Their move was approved by a council of Separate preachers at Westfield on August 14, 1763.

The united Separates at Bennington thus became the first church of any denomination in the state, where they were free to carry their cherished principles into practice without molestation. Their first minutes read:

98. W. S. Perry, ed., *Historical Collections, 3,* 354.
99. Cf. Lois Kimball Mathews, *The Expansion of New England* (New York, 1909), p. 117.

It is agreed . . . [to] make an exception in the fourth paragraph, in the eleventh chapter in Cambridge Platform, in respect of using the civil law to support the gospel; and also the ninth paragraph in the seventeenth chapter, in respect of the civil magistrate's coercive power.[100]

This church, established in its own way and with no competitors, in time became almost as conservative as those from which its members had separated. For example, some wanted a strictly voluntary method of supporting the pastor; there was controversy on this point for a number of years, and at length it was found expedient to assess some sort of ecclesiastical rates.[101] Differences on this point and others resulted in a schism, and the stricter party removed to Poultney in 1780 and formed a church under Ithamar Hibbard. Interestingly enough, differences among the Connecticut Separates were reflected here: in the debate over whether to call a council to adjust their differences, the strict party was anxious to have Ebenezer Frothingham, while the others wanted the more catholic-spirited and liberal-minded Alexander Miller and Paul Parke.[102] But in spite of the "jars and jangles" due to this controversy, an unpopular pastor (David Avery 1780–83), and various other things, the church prospered. There were numerous additions, and the church was stirred anew from time to time with seasons of revival.

New York. The eastern edge of New York, especially between the Hudson River and the Connecticut-Massachusetts border, was quite attractive to Separates seeking more room in which to implement their religious and political ideals. A speaker at a ministerial convention in 1773 enumerated various sects in New York, and added:

There is beside a considerable number of *separates* or lay preachers in the province who have congregations to which they statedly preach, and some of them large. Some of these people call themselves Presbyterians or Congregationalists, and some Anabaptists. [No Baptist ever called himself an Anabaptist!] They are pretty numerous in the new counties in the north and north easterly parts

100. Quoted in Jennings, *Memorials of a Century*, p. 32.
101. From 1783 to 1801 every resident was taxed for the majority worship unless he had a certificate stating he was of another persuasion. After 1801 certificates required no signature save that of the dissenter himself, and by 1807 they were abandoned altogether.
102. Jennings, p. 342.

of the province, and parts adjacent, and on the east end of Long Island, where they have two ministers.[103]

An illustration of this Separate immigration into eastern New York is the church at Amenia, which invited the Westfield Separates to join them in 1762. This church was located in the tract of land called "The Great Nine Partners," which included part of the "Ob-long," a strip of land down the Connecticut boundary which was ceded to New York in return for a clear title to 61,440 acres in the southwest corner of Connecticut. Abraham Paine, the eldest brother of Elisha, Solomon, and John, was ordained pastor of the Separate church here in 1750; and it became a haven of refuge for radicals from eastern Connecticut and elsewhere who were looking for a free place to make a new start. It apparently had some of the same difficulties that plagued the other Separate churches, for in the records of the Preston church, under date of June 3, 1756, there is a request for a peace council from "some agreived Br of a *Church* in the Nine Partners."

Another church was at Canaan, New York, under Jacob Drake, a Separate who came from Windsor, Connecticut, in 1769. Finding a number of Separates already in the vicinity, he organized them into a church in 1770; a decade later this body numbered five or six hundred members and had embraced Baptist principles. They were spread over a large territory, and by 1791 the parent church had set off seven branches as independent churches. The next year Drake moved to Wyoming, Pennsylvania, and repeated the same process along the Susquehanna River.

Another group of Separates migrated from Mansfield, Connecticut, to Newtown (later Wantage), New Jersey, and formed a church in 1756. Two years later they adopted Baptist principles. In the summer of 1750 Paul Parke, Solomon Paine, and Thomas Stevens went with a group of Separates to ordain a pastor over a new church at "Rocksberry, in the Jerseys." This body soon became Baptist also. Both the Roxbury and Wantage churches were accepted into the fellowship of regular Baptists in the Middle Colonies, being admitted to the Philadelphia Association in 1753 and 1758 respectively. Thus

103. John Rodgers, "A Brief View of the State of Religious Liberty in the Colony of New York, Read before the Reverend General Convention of Delegates from the Consociated Churches of Connecticut, and the Synod of New York and Philadelphia, Met at Stamford Sept. the 1st. 1773," *Collections of the Massachusetts Historical Society, 1,* Series 2 (1814), 152. A footnote adds, "There are seven Baptist separate preachers in the colony, and some of them have pretty large congregations."

the Separate movement fanned out on the frontier, not only geographically but doctrinally.

OLD LIGHT SEPARATIONS

The story of separatism would not be complete without pointing out that it was not always the revivalists who withdrew in disgust from churches with whose practices they no longer agreed. There were several instances in which the New Light activities of the pastor and a sizable proportion of the church caused the conservatives to separate. In most such cases the schism was temporary. Where it was permanent there was often a change of affiliation, the Old Lights usually finding a resting place among the Anglicans. "The Great Awakening in large part flowed around the Church of England; yet the latter, sometimes fearful for its safety, more often concerned with maintaining and strengthening its position, did by its orderliness and calm prove attractive to many in the rough waters outside." [104] The letters of the Anglican rectors of the period show that they hoped the turbulence of the times would drive many into their haven of refuge. The rector at Braintree, Massachusetts, wrote to the Secretary of the S.P.G. that he had visited Taunton, where people "are in great confusion on account of the New Light as they call it, and I am informed that some of the most considerable Dissenters [Congregationalists] are inclined to come into the Church of England if they may be favoured with a Minister." [105] A few instances of Old Light separatism, some of which led into Anglicanism, follow.

Stratfield. The accessions that the Church of England gained from those who were unable to find peace in their own churches were limited chiefly to isolated individuals. Only in a very few cases was there a defection of such proportions as to form an Episcopalian church. One of these was at Stratfield (now Bridgeport), Connecticut. The pastor, Samuel Cooke, was a close friend of Whitefield, and as moderator and scribe of the revivalistic Fairfield East Association wrote to the great evangelist urging him to come and preach in the churches of Fairfield County. Cooke also itinerated widely, and was active in encouraging the separation from the First Church in New Haven.[106] Those in his church who were opposed to the revival withdrew from his ministry; and although he died in 1747, they proceeded with their plans to organize an Episcopalian church (St. John's) the

104. Gaustad, *The Great Awakening in New England,* p. 119.
105. Letter of Ebenezer Miller, dated Jan. 17, 1742, in W. S. Perry, p. 360.
106. See above, p. 87, n. 58.

next year. The Congregational church, alarmed at the loss of some
of its most substantial members, called an Old Light minister, Lyman
Hall, who served only four years.[107] This reversal of leadership
antagonized the New Lights in the church, and they withdrew to
form a Separate Baptist church in 1751. The temper of the times was
such that it was most difficult to find middle ground in the disputes
that arose out of the Great Awakening.

Northbury. Old Light reaction was even more severe in Northbury
(Watertown), Connecticut, where pastor Samuel Todd was installed
as pastor in May 1740. At first he was indifferent to the revival; but
when he experienced its power firsthand, his zeal knew no bounds.
He introduced "conference meetings" in an effort to rouse the feelings
of his church, and adopted other novel measures to such an extent
that many of his parishioners, and finally a majority, turned against
him. At length they obtained control of the meetinghouse and established it in Episcopalian worship, leaving the Congregationalists to
shift for themselves the best way they could. This group met in private
homes until a new building could be started, but it was a slow process because of their depleted numbers. The town's historian concludes
that "the meeting house was probably begun in 1746; that it was
occupied in mild weather, in 1750; that it was glazed and the lower
part put in order for use throughout the year in 1753; that the galleries
were not fitted up till 1762; and that the house was not finally finished
till 1768." [108] This indicates something of the severe trials even in
practical matters brought on a church by schism. Concerns of the
spirit were sometimes even harder to rebuild.

Concord. A recent study of the records of nearly every Congregational church formed in colonial Massachusetts indicates that the
very first of the open schisms over the revival was an Old Light separation from the church at Concord. Here pastor Daniel Bliss became
an exceedingly vigorous revivalist. Accused of neglecting his charge
by itineracy, of encouraging lay exhorters, and even of antinomian
doctrines, he justified himself before a council and was acquitted. A
second council, called at the insistence of the church members who
were still offended, allowed that Bliss' conduct had been injudicious
and his statements of doctrine somewhat dubious, but it declined to

107. Hall left the ministry to become successively a school teacher, a physician,
and a political leader in Georgia—becoming the first governor of that state in
1783.

108. Henry Bronson, *The History of Waterbury, Connecticut* (Waterbury,
1858), p. 274.

censure him. The dissidents remained aloof from the church from 1741 to 1765, then grudgingly returned. No Separate church, however, was formed.[109]

Plymouth. Old Light Congregationalists organized a separatist church in Plymouth as a result of the protracted meeting held there in 1743 by Andrew Croswell.[110] At communion Croswell had caused consternation by declaring that three-fourths of the church members were unconverted. A number of the offended communicants withdrew and held a consultative meeting to debate whether,

> 1st a sudden and short distress, followed by a sudden joy, amounted to true repentance; 2d, whether the judgment and censure of good men as unconverted was not contrary to the rule of charity contained in the Scriptures; 3d, whether disorder and confusion in religious meetings was not opposed to the Scripture rule; and 4th, whether, as three-fourths of the church had been declared unconverted, they were really so or not.[111]

When the pastor continued to approve the proceedings of Croswell and other revivalists, this group withdrew and formed the Third Congregational Church in Plymouth. In 1744 they built a meetinghouse and called Thomas Frink as pastor. Charles Chauncy preached the ordination sermon on November 7, five days after Whitefield landed at York for a second visit to New England. One may safely assume that the Old Brick controversialist took full advantage of the occasion to point out the follies of revivalistic religion. Frink stayed until 1748, when he removed to Barre; and the church called Jacob Bacon, who remained until 1776.

Noteworthy in this separation was the conciliatory attitude of the New Lights in the First Church toward their separating brethren. Pastor Nathaniel Leonard, whose name appears often in the lists of prorevival pastors, wrote to Thomas Prince describing the separation with no trace of rancor or derogation. After recounting the revival under Croswell, he said:

> A violent Opposition presently arose, and prevailed so far, that a number of this Congregation went out from us into a *distinct Society,* and *nine* of the Brethren *asked a Dismission* from us to

109. Emil Oberholzer, Jr., *Delinquent Saints* (New York, 1956), pp. 107–08.
110. See above, p. 11.
111. Quoted in William T. Davis, *History of the Town of Plymouth* (Philadelphia, 1885), pp. 122–23.

embody into a Church by themselves. *We readily granted* their Request, and they have lately had a Minister set over them. My Prayer for Him and Them is, "That God would pour out his Spirit abundantly upon them, greatly enrich them with heavenly Blessings, and fill them with all the Fulness of God." [112]

In 1783 the schism was healed. The Third Church disbanded, and its members returned to the First Church.

Ipswich. The only Old Light separation that resulted in a permanent Congregational church was at Ipswich. The prorevival activities of pastor Nathaniel Rogers in the First Church met with a peculiar challenge when some of his parishioners proposed the settlement of John Walley as his colleague. Rogers would not consent to this because Walley refused to recognize John Cleaveland, now securely installed as pastor of the Separates in the second parish. In 1747 the dissidents, most of whom lived in the south part of the first parish, withdrew and petitioned for independent status. This was approved by the General Court, and they promptly formed a church with Walley as pastor.

112. *Christian History, 2,* 315–16.

MAP I. The EXTENT of SEPARATISM

- Separate Church Organized
- ▲ Temporary Separation, No Church Organized
- ■ Old Light Separation or Separate Church

4. SEPARATE LEADERS AND DOCTRINES

Separatism is not fully illuminated without more detailed attention to some of its guiding lights. Even though it was almost entirely a people's movement in which few men were really outstanding, it produced some who are typical enough to be called representative and about whom there is enough information to enliven the previous account of new churches aborning. Five different types of leaders have been selected for biographical exposition, to be followed by a brief examination of Separate doctrines.

REPRESENTATIVE LEADERS AMONG THE SEPARATES

An evangelist: Elisha Paine. Beyond question the ablest leader of the Separates during their early formative years was Elisha Paine (1693–1775). There was scarcely a Separate congregation to which he did not preach, and few of them did not try at one time or another to induce him to become pastor. Isaac Backus called him the "Moses" of the Separates. The ministers of Windham County, in their published blast against the Separates, centered their attack on Paine, "who is by most in this County known to be of much superiour Abilities to the others," thinking that if they could unhorse him they would have routed the whole Separate phalanx.[1] A résumé of his life, therefore, even though information is meager, will do much to elucidate the character of the whole Separate movement.

Paine was born in 1693 at Eastham on Cape Cod, the second of four sons. His father was a prominent man in that town, and also in Canterbury, where he moved his family about 1706. He was one of the seven men who formed the Canterbury church in 1711. Elisha's mother was from the family of Deacon John Doane, one of the early magistrates of Plymouth Colony. Young Paine showed an aptness for learning, and chose law as his vocation. Although he seems not to have had the privilege of formal education, he became a renowned lawyer. Backus, who does not often use superlatives, says he was "one of the greatest lawyers in Connecticut, and was in very pros-

---

1. *A Letter from the Associated Ministers of the County of Windham*, p. 6.

perous circumstances in the world." [2] Of his early religious interests, Paine wrote:

> God hath so ordered it in his providence, that ever since I was a child I have had an inquiring mind after knowledge, of almost all sorts; but religion bore the sway. I seemed to have a regard for good men, and therefore took great care to watch persons, especially to see how they kept the Sabbath. Before my conversion I had the curiosity to hear all the different worships in New England, and inquired into their principles, and observed their behavior, both in and out of their worship. And I saw so little, or rather nothing, of the power of godliness in any of them, that I was then, even in my carnal estate, afraid that the true religion was not in this land. Yet worldly pleasure, and the form which was most acknowledged, would soon make me easy again. But when conviction came to lay hold of me, let who would be of the true religion, I saw mine was of no value.[3]

The conversion of which he speaks here probably refers to the Windham revival of 1721, during which both Elisha and his brother Solomon professed religion.

That experience, however, was nothing compared to the one which came when the revival of the forties irrupted into their remote community. Under the convictions which then seized him, Elisha became convinced that he was "called of God" to preach the gospel. "He then quitted their courts, and went forth preaching the gospel through the land." [4] Doubtless this decision was influenced by the example, if not the explicit encouragement, of revivalistic ministers such as Eleazar Wheelock and Benjamin Pomeroy. Because of his friendly relations with the clergy at that time, Paine applied in July of 1742 to the Windham County Ministerial Association for license to preach. They agreed that he was qualified, and were willing to license him on condition that he would subscribe to the Saybrook Platform. Neither he nor his family, however, had ever liked the close union of church and state which prevailed in Connecticut, and he hesitated. Upon further reflection he considered that his call from the Head of the Church was a more valid license than any which could be granted by a human—if not downright unscriptural—association, and he began to preach from house to house and

2. *History of New England, 2,* 64.
3. Private paper, printed ibid., pp. 64–65.
4. Backus, *Abridged History,* p. 162.

from town to town. The remainder of 1742 was spent in this fashion, and he does not seem to have been molested even though such activity on the part of unauthorized laymen was now illegal.

On February 19 of the next year, however, he was arrested at Woodstock (then in Massachusetts) while conducting a service at the home of John Morse. Haled before a justice, he refused on ground of conscience to give bond, and was taken to Worcester to "the dirtiest prison I ever saw." He had to "beg" a broom to sweep a place to walk in. Nevertheless, he "had a sweet contentment in and resignation to the will of God, and have had ever since first taken." [5] He steadfastly refused the many efforts to extort from him the required bond.

> The imprisonment of a man of such high character and standing upon so trifling a charge . . . excited much talk and indignation, especially when it was found that such confinement was not warranted by the laws of Massachusetts. Many visited him in prison, and many petitions were sent for his release, and after holding him three months the authorities were fain to bid him depart, somewhat after the fashion of Paul's release from Philippi. Continuing his tour he was everywhere received with enthusiasm, his bonds falling out rather for the furtherance of the Revival movement. [6]

One of the measures contrived to effect Paine's release was a letter formally attesting his piety and character signed by four well-known Connecticut ministers, Benjamin Pomeroy, Eleazar Wheelock, Joseph Meacham, and Samuel Mosely. All but Pomeroy were in Windham County, and the last-named man sent a personal note to Paine encouraging him to constancy:

> Dear Sir, stand fast in the faith; be strong. They that be with you are more than they that be with our adversaries. Never think it hard to suffer for Christ. It is enough for the servant that he be as his Lord. [7]

Later, when party lines were hardened and the standing ministers could find nothing good in those who had aligned themselves against the establishment, these gentlemen were much chagrined over their hasty approval of one who was to become their inveterate enemy.

Released from Worcester jail on May 13, Paine preached another

5. Paine's *Journal*, quoted in Backus, *History of New England, 2,* 65.
6. Larned, *Historic Gleanings in Windham County*, p. 23.
7. Quoted in Backus, *History of New England, 2,* 66.

fortnight under the haughty noses of the Massachusetts authorities at
Shrewsbury, Grafton, and Upton, returning home at the end of the
month. On July 8 he set off again, traveling to Providence, Bristol,
Boston, Cambridge, Chelmsford, Dunstable, and Lancaster. On his
arrival back home on December 3, he had preached, according to
his journal, 244 sermons. The following summer (1744) he itinerated
the length of Cape Cod, renewing fellowship with many of his friends
and kinsmen, preaching New Light doctrines, and encouraging his
converts to withdraw from their "unspiritual shepherds" and form
churches of the regenerate. In the revival at Chatham [8] he wrote of
what probably was a typical experience of the Separate evangelists:

> I preached from Ez. 14.3. and from Rev. 2.21. After service we sang
> a hymn. I felt the Spirit of the Lord come upon me. I rose up and
> exhorted and persuaded them to come to Christ; and immediately
> there was a screeching and groaning all over the multitude, and
> hath ever since been very powerful. Some whole families, I hope,
> have received Christ, and others continually crying out against
> their own hearts. I hope the Lord will carry on his work in his way,
> and by his own means.[9]

He rejoiced that although the devil's crew was assiduous in their
opposition, "the Lord reigns and the saints shout aloud for joy."

Paine returned home just in time to lead the New Light party in
the crisis at Canterbury, which was rapidly coming to a climax.[10]
The Saybrook party had just called a committee of neighboring ministers to advise on the proposed settlement of James Cogswell. They
asked Paine to state the objections of his party, but he refused on the
ground that the committee was called without the consent of a
majority of the church. The ministers recommended that the parish
proceed with Cogswell's ordination, upon which Paine wrote them a
sharp letter of reproof for "wronging the truth." For this impudence
he was seized on September 22 and imprisoned at Windham jail on
the charge of having preached illegally in the town the preceding
spring.[11] As before, he suffered with utmost cheerfulness. To his wife
he wrote:

8. See above, pp. 94–95.
9. Letter to his wife, dated July 3, 1744, printed ibid., p. 67.
10. See above, pp. 71–73.
11. He had preached at the home of Benjamin Cleaveland in the third parish
(Scotland) on April 10. Tried before Justice Nathaniel Huntington on September
22, he pled that "this Court hath not Jurisdiction of this Case; for that the Facts

I know not when I shall be delivered from this pleasant house;
I seem to be willing to tarry here just as long as my Father and
your Father shall see cause to use me here; though I seem to have
a strong persuasion that I shall not tarry here long; but how the
Lord will bring it about I know not. . . . if I go from prison to
Paradise, it will be as sweet as if I went from a throne.[12]

In the meantime Paine felt that no opportunity should be wasted.
By giving security to the jailer, he obtained liberty to preach in the
jailyard. His congregations were soon so large that the authorities
finally thought it best to release him, which they did on October 19.

From this time forward Paine carried on a running battle with the
ministers of Windham County, and the documents of that controversy
do much to reveal his personal beliefs and public teaching. A major
instance may be seen in the published letter of the Association dated
from Mansfield December 11, 1744. The letter began by enumerating
the errors of the Separates under five headings, then proceeded to
blame them all on Paine's heresies. To expose his deviations, the
orthodox divines cited first a letter from James Cogswell of Canterbury, who had been taken to task by Paine for a sermon on faith.
Paine had declared that he had rather be burned at the stake than
hear such a sermon, accusing Cogswell of relying on the letter of
Scripture apart from the Holy Spirit for the conversion of sinners
(this is reminiscent of Timothy Allen's "old almanack"), and of holding
to "universal provision," i.e. Arminianism. Cogswell asked:

> Mr. *Paine,* do you not think there is sufficient Merit in the Blood of
> Christ to procure Pardon for the Sins of the whole World? He
> [Paine] answer'd, GOD has made Provision sufficient for the Salva-
> tion of them that are saved, and no more; and to suppose other-
> wise would be to render GOD unjust. . . . I will tell you how GOD
> convinced me of this; In the first Place he convinced me I was a
> Sinner; then he shewed me there was enough in Christ for Sinners;
> and then he discovered [revealed] that Christ died for me. . . .
> I [Cogswell] asked him, whether he thought that was saving Faith.

complained of, are warranted by the Law of God and the King, and therefore not
tryable by any Court of Law inferior thereto." The court refused this plea and assigned the standard peace bond of £ 100. Refusing to give bond, Paine was committed to prison immediately after the trial. The whole record is printed in
Solomon Paine, *A Short View of the Difference between the Church of Christ and
the Established Churches in Connecticut,* pp. 20–22.

12. Quoted in Backus, *History of New England,* 2, 69.

He answered in the Affirmative. I told him, I thought it was not.
. . . He replied, that I talked like the Papists, or that this was
Popish Doctrine; and that this was the very Dispute between the
Papists and the Protestants; that this Doctrine which he held was
the old Puritan Doctrine, and that it was much safer to hold so
than that a Person might be Converted, and not know it.[13]

Elizabeth Darbe and Jabez Fitch wrote from Canterbury that they
had heard Elisha Paine declare that "it was made manifest to him,
that Christ was about to have a pure Church; and that he had not
done his Duty in Time past in promoting Separations and Divisions
among the People, and that for Time to come he should endeavour to
promote and encourage Separations." Churches and ministers who
failed to divide the converted from the unconverted in their membership, Paine insisted, deserved to have their churches taken from them.

A much more serious charge was brought in a letter from Stephen
White and Eliphalet Dyer, who accused him of denying the doctrine
of the Trinity. Paine is said to have taught that "he never understood
that they were three Persons [in the Godhead] any otherwise than
that they were three Offices." He had illustrated this by the fact that
a man may stand before the law in several offices without being several persons. He rejected philosophical niceties as tending to run into
absurdities, "for he could not conceive of three Persons . . . unless
making them three Gods." [14] If his accusers were quoting him cor-
rectly, Paine was a modalist; he nevertheless refused to be trapped
into an open admission of antitrinitarianism. He wrote quickly to his
accusers:

> I was taught from my Youth, that there were three Persons in the
> Godhead, viz. the Father, Son and Holy Ghost; and that these
> three were one GOD, the same in Substance, equal in Power and
> Glory; and that I had never been taught to distinguish or knew
> them apart by any Thing but their Offices and Names. . . . But
> how the Personality of these three Persons exist in the divine
> Mind, was always a Mystery to me, although I verily believe it,
> yet I cannot comprehend it, and I dare not be wise beyond the
> Word, in so great a Mystery as the Trinity.[15]

He thought it safer not to probe this mystery, "lest it end in Error, as
at the Council at *Nice*, Anno 325, some did by being too critical to

13. *A Letter from the Associated Ministers of the County of Windham*, p. 8.
14. Ibid., p. 13.
15. Ibid., pp. 13–14.

find out how that Christ the Son, and GOD the Father, were of the same Substance or coequal, were left to deny it." The Windham ministers' commented that this is what happens when a man, "who in other Things is known to be a Man of the most Sense of any in these Parts," sets himself above the Word of God. In other words, they avoided an explicit refutation of his "heresy" by implying that he stood self-condemned.

The Windham County Association met again on January 13, 1747, to inquire into the state of ecclesiastical affairs. They summoned Elisha Paine and other Separate preachers to appear before the "lawful ministers" and give answer for their errors. He disdained to appear, replying instead that they exalted themselves above God and his Word, that they were "sitting to receive the Devil's Trumpery against GOD's Children," that their methods were the same as the papists used to take, and that they would receive the most dreadful damnation for leading their flocks down to hell.[16] The council responded by retracting the letter written by some of their members when Paine was imprisoned at Worcester in 1743, explaining that their purpose had been not to "encourage him in his profess'd Inclination to preach the Gospel," but only to keep him from being falsely accused as a rabble-rouser. Since that time they had had abundant cause to alter their judgment that he might be "useful in the Church" and to regret their weakness in writing at all. They were especially offended by Paine's use of their letter to claim that they had approved his whole course.

The Canterbury Separate Church had been quite insistent at the first that their own Elisha Paine become their pastor. He had felt then that his calling was to an itinerant ministry and that in this way he could make his maximum contribution to the Separates' cause. In 1752, however, he accepted the pastorate of a church at Bridgehampton on Long Island. Although he served here until his death, he seems to have remained about as troublesome as ever to the Connecticut authorities. Having been installed at Bridgehampton in May, he was in jail again at Windham in November—this time for an unpaid church tax to James Cogswell. Debarred from preaching, he took up the pen. After chiding his captors for forgetting that persecution drove their fathers to seek freedom in this land, Paine pointed out that he had as much right to tax Cogswell for his preaching as Cogswell had to tax him. The only difference was that Cogswell was upheld by the power of the state.

16. *The Result of a Council of the Consociated Churches of the County of Windham*, p. 19.

I believe the same people, who put this authority into the hands of Mr. Cogswell, their minister, to put me into prison for not paying him for preaching, would think it very hard for the church I belong to, and am pastor of, if they should get the upper hand, and tax and imprison him, for what he should be so unjustly taxed at; and yet I can see no other difference, only because the power is in his hands; for I suppose he has heard me as often as I ever have him, and yet he hath taken from me by force two cows and one steer, and now my body held in prison, only because the power is in his hands.[17]

A few weeks later he wrote comparing the ecclesiastical power in Connecticut with the "beast of Rome," declaring that both had conspired with the civil power to suppress true religion. He cited Psalm 94:20, "Shall the throne of iniquity have fellowship with thee, which frameth mischief by a law?" and accused his assessors of resting on that throne more than on the "rock of Jesus Christ." He challenged them to prove otherwise "by Scripture and reason"; if they could, he would confess his fault and "soon clear myself of the prison."

But if this constitution hath its rise from that throne, then come forth to the help of the Lord against the mighty; for it is better to die for Christ, than to live against him. From an old friend to this civil constitution, and long your prisoner.[18]

This was apparently the only protest by any individual Separate that ever dented the thick skin of the Connecticut ecclesiocrats during the turbulent years before the New Lights were able to bring about a change in the political climate of the colony. Paine's question was never answered; but five days after his letter was delivered, he was released. He had been kept through the extremities of a severe winter, and his family in Bridgehampton had "suffered much in an unfinished house for want of his help." [19]

Unlike some of the Separates, Paine held fast to his ideas to the end. The last notice of him in Connecticut is from the diary of James Cogswell under date of March 26, 1769:

Lawyer Paine sent for me in the evening, said that he wanted to see me but did not desire I should tarry [for his] lecture . . .

17. Quoted in Backus, *Abridged History*, pp. 174–75.
18. Printed in Larned, *History of Windham County*, 1, 480.
19. Backus, *Abridged History*, p. 175.

however, when I came there the old gentleman said he had nothing special to say, and that he only sent word that he was going to preach, and began lecture soon. But I thought I would not go away immediately—was not sorry I tarried as I have not heard a Separate teacher in a great while. He is much more moderate than formerly and indeed is a dull preacher; some part of his discourse was good but he preached many things erroneous as I thought, as that all religion which was established by civil authority was false . . . that all Christians have assurance, and those who think they have not are to be suspected of knowing nothing of Christ's beauty experimentally. That though men should live peaceably together yet it was a vain and wicked attempt to reconcile converted and unconverted men for they would always have implacable enmity; and tho' they should agree ever so well on an outward plan of church government which he called a *hiarchee*, meaning as I suppose an Hierarchy, it would be of no service unless men were converted—and several other exceptional [exceptionable] things.[20]

The next day Paine visited his old antagonist, and they "discoursed in a friendly manner." Cogswell took him to task for errors in the previous evening's sermon, and they argued at length—as old men will about bygone issues—but without the acrimony that characterized their earlier controversies. Cogswell wrote that Paine spoke "with a pleasant countenance and to appearance with a temper much less bitter and severe than when he lived in town—but I believe he holds much the same doctrines." Paine spent the rest of his life in peaceful seclusion, ministering to his flock at Bridgehampton, and preaching until two weeks before his death. His final separation from all earthly ties came on August 26, 1775, in his eighty-fifth year.

A pastor: Paul Parke. The pastor of the Preston Separate Church appears in the record as abruptly as Melchizedek. Little is known of his life before the Preston Separates announced on June 18, 1747, that their spiritual "evidences" pointed to the choice of Paul Parke (1721–1802) as its pastor. He was then twenty-six years old. It is said that he had been preaching for one or two years at North Stonington, but beyond this his early life is shrouded in obscurity. In spite of this almost total lack of information—and the situation is little better for his later life—Parke deserves high priority in a list of Separate leaders because he proved to be one of the most stable pastors among them. For fifty-five years he shepherded one flock, which, although it died

20. Quoted in Larned, *History of Windham County,* 2, 40.

with him, stood during his lifetime as one of the more prominent
Separate churches.

The chief source of data regarding Parke's half-century of ministering to the Separates at Preston is the record book of that church, kept
by the pastor in a very legible hand.[21] The first entry is dated June 18,
1747:

> At this meeting the minds of the Bretheren was (if the Lord wood
> give lite) to Chuse one to take the Pastoral Care of this Church;
> as an under Sheperd; The Lord as a faithfull Sheperd Sent Down
> the Holy Ghost which gave Cleare witness in Gospill Lite: who
> the Holy Ghost had appointed for that worke. Whereupon the
> Church manifested there Evidence that—Paul Parke—was Chosen:
> And upon there Call: and the witness of the holy Ghost in his
> own Soule: (through the glass of God's word) that he was ap-
> pointed by the Sheperd; to that worke; he submitted himself; to
> be there Servent, for Christ's Sake; in that worke.

On July 15 a council composed of "gifts," i.e. ministers similarly chosen,
from the Separate churches at North Stonington, Norwich, Canterbury,
and Plainfield were convinced that God had manifested his will in the
call, and proceeded to "the laying on of hands upon this there Brother
to witness that he was ordained of God to Preach the Gospill and to
Administor all Gospill ordinances to the whole Church universal so
far as he is Called But to this flock in Perticular: which ordination
was attended with much of God's Presents." Trumbull claims to have
been informed that the brethren at Parke's ordination enjoined him
"by no means to study or premeditate what he should say in public;
but to speak as the spirit should give him utterance." [22] Although the
new pastor is listed as one of the six charter members of the church,
his wife Sarah was not received until January 29, 1749, when she
"told her experience with God" and came into full communion. This
could mean that he was unmarried at the time of his ordination, and
took a wife shortly before the time she united with the church.

The new pastor and various members of his church were kept busy
in the larger fellowship of Separate churches, assisting in organizing
churches, ordaining pastors, and settling disputes. On such missions,

21. At New London County Historical Society. The record book is not paged;
references are given by date of entry.

22. *Complete History of Connecticut*, 2, 195. If this was actually said, it has
been taken to mean more than perhaps it actually did. For the Separates' manner
of preaching, see below, pp. 174–80.

Parke went as far as Bennington, Vermont; Amenia, New York; and Roxbury, New Jersey. But there is no evidence that he ever neglected his ministry to his own flock. One of the striking things about the Preston Separate Church is the frequent calls it received from sister churches for help in resolving difficulties between private members or between a pastor and some opposing faction, yet no appeal of this sort was ever made by Preston to the other churches. This was very unusual among the Separates, and was not because the Preston church always had smooth sailing—there were plenty of unruly members to rock the boat at frequent intervals—but was due to the wise and patient guidance of the pastor in dealing with troublemakers early and effectively. Two things may be suggested to account for the stability of Parke's church: its prayerful, evangelistic spirit; and its moderate but firm disciplining of those who violated the rules of Christian charity. As an illustration of the first, one finds the church praying often for the salvation of the unconverted, recognizing (as good Calvinists) God's initiative in redeeming the lost. A minute of November 15, 1751, reads:

> Daniel Whipple, being called of God and made willing (after a Sweet travel [travail] in the Church for him) he did Give up him Self to God and to the watch and Care of this Church which was done in a Sweet felloship: and he was Received to full Communion.

This kind of thing happened often. The church made "Sweet travel," and soon saw the object of its prayers "made willing" to answer the call of God to faith and fellowship among those who had interceded for his salvation.

An illustration of how Parke and his church labored to maintain Christian love within their fellowship may be seen in the fact that while other Separate churches were resorting to discipline in cases of petty personal disputes over picayune problems, the Prestonites cited members only for real breaches of proper conduct.[23] For example, on August 28, 1751, the church met to consider the case of Sarah Rennals (Reynolds?), who had absented herself from Communion:

> Upon Examination it was found: that she was full of Prejudice and an Accusing Spirit: and made light of the Necessity of a Gospill

23. Conversion to Baptist beliefs was in this category, and the Preston Separate Church was exercised almost as much as any other over this problem. This is discussed in detail below, Chap. 6.

temper of Mind in order to the Right Pertaking of the Sacry-
ment, and appeared Ignorant of Gospill felloship which the
Church Indeavoured to Convince her of.

This apparently succeeded, for no further labor with Sister Rennals
is recorded, nor was she excommunicated as would have probably
been done had she proved to be intractable. Others were convinced
in the same sweet spirit, and the Preston church seems never to have
been torn with the strife and dissension that plagued so many of her
sisters. In all of this, one can only conclude that the beneficent influence of the pastor pervaded the whole church.

In 1797 Pastor Parke preached a half-century sermon, which is said
to have taken several Sundays for its delivery and to have been heard
by large audiences. It unfortunately is not preserved (if indeed it
was ever written down), but undoubtedly it would have revealed, like
the church records, how inseparably the life of the church was intertwined with that of its pastor. It is almost literally true that the story
of this church is his biography. "For [more than] fifty years he held his
flock about him, ministering to them as pastor, kept with his own
hand the records of the church, maintained regular Sunday services,
participated prominently in every council in which his church was
represented, while at the same time supporting himself and family
upon his farm, without ever receiving one dollar as salary or state
remuneration." [24] The only material assistance he ever received, apparently, was the aid his parishioners gave him with his farm work
from time to time. When he died in 1802, it was neither possible nor
necessary to secure a successor. The church had imbibed his largehearted spirit so that by then fraternal relations with the regular
churches had been restored, and the remaining members were able
to return to their original communion in peace.

An apologist: Ebenezer Frothingham. A man of quite different
temper, but just as important to the life of the Separate movement,
was the pastor of the Wethersfield-Middletown Separate Church,
Ebenezer Frothingham (1719–98). His main contribution was not
in the field of preaching or pastoral ministry but in the writing of
two pungent apologies for the Strict Congregationalists. What Ezra
Stiles said of other Separate writers could be said with equal propriety
of Frothingham:

He [Samuel Hyde of Brookline] has written some things very
sensibly. This with the Writings of *Backus* & [Israel] *Holly,* might

24. Amos A. Browning, "The Preston Separate Church," *The Bicentennial Celebration of the First Congregational Church of Preston, Connecticut,* pp. 56–57.

be shewn as a specimen of the Abilities of the Illiterate Men of New England even in Writing as well as the Things of Religion. These productions would be considerable even for University Men.[25]

Frothingham's two works are *The Articles of Faith and Practice,* a volume of 432 pages, and *A Key to Unlock the Door,* with 252 pages.

What is known of Frothingham's life may be summarized briefly. He was born in Cambridge, Massachusetts, in 1719, and spent most of his early life in the Boston area. It is not known when he came to Wethersfield, but he was one of the original Separates there and became their pastor on October 28, 1747. The next year he was jailed for preaching without the permission of the parish minister. In a paragraph on persecution he says:

I myself have been confined in Hartford Prison near five Months, for nothing but exhorting and warning the People, after the public Worship was done, and the Assembly dismissed. And while I was there confined, three more Persons was sent to Prison; one for exhorting, and two for worshipping God, in a private house, in a separate Meeting. And quick after I was released, by the Laws being answered by natural Relations unbeknown to me, then two Brethren more was committed for exhorting and preaching, and several others afterwards, for attending the same Duties; and I myself twice more was sent to Prison for the Minister's rates.[26]

Because of these severities, many of his church members moved to New York, and Frothingham led the remaining ones to Middletown in 1754. Stiles noted that the Middletown church included some forty or fifty families who maintained their pastor by voluntary contributions. "They have built a house, the Chambers of which are all in one & serve as a Meetingh. —the lower part a Parsonage House where Mr. Froth. lives." [27] When the church divided in 1788, Frothingham was dismissed, probably by his own request because he was then approaching seventy years of age. He remained in Middletown and died on November 30, 1798.

In the early days of his separatism Frothingham seriously considered becoming a Baptist, and "says he went so far, that if he had met with

25. *Literary Diary of Ezra Stiles, 1,* 68.
26. *A Key to Unlock the Door,* pp. 51–52.
27. *Itineraries of Ezra Stiles,* p. 237.

a baptist elder, he should have been re-baptized." [28] He eventually decided against it on the ground that the Bible contained no express prohibition of infant baptism, and became one of the most strenuous opponents of the Baptists. His greatest contribution, however, was his constant effort in behalf of religious liberty; and the records of other Separate churches show that they relied on him more than on any other single man to draft their petitions and carry them to the authorities. He was chosen in 1754 to carry a memorial to the king in England, but for some unexplained reason he had to relinquish that responsibility to another. His activity in this regard was important enough to earn for him special treatment in Louise Greene, *The Development of Religious Liberty in Connecticut.*[29] For this reason, he is treated here under the rubric of the Separates' apologist. That he himself envisioned this as his major task is indicated in the following statement: "The main thing which I have in view . . . is free Liberty of Conscience . . . the Right of thinking, and choosing and acting for oneself in the matters of Religion, which respect God and Conscience, and to contend for this important Privilege, I nor any other person should not be ashamed to do." [30]

In the preface to the "Discourse" which accompanies *The Articles of Faith and Practice* (and is the main part of the book), Frothingham confesses lack of formal education which normally would be required for a work such as he undertakes. He had hoped that some more qualified apologete would come forth in behalf of the Separates; but since none has, he determines to take the task upon himself. "I am chosen by infinite Wisdom to be a publick Witness for God and his despised Cause and Interest, and to contend earnestly for the Faith once delivered to the Saints." [31] He plunges immediately into an argument for carrying forward the Reformation, quoting a passage from Stoddard that it is no sin to question the old ways of the fathers, because failure to do so would prevent any reform; and one from "old Mr. Mather" to the effect that all the Reformation churches carried with them "something of Rome," which implies that new reformations are always required. Frothingham adds that "the Bane of Reformations, or what has hindered their Progress from time to time, has been the first Reformers stopping in the Light that they was

28. Isaac Backus, *A Short Description of the Difference between the Bond-Woman and the Free* (Boston, 1770), p. 48.
29. Pages 284–97.
30. *A Key to Unlock the Door*, preface.
31. Page 23.

first brought into, and so not duly pressing forwards for further Attainments."[32] He believes that the last five or six years have brought the Church to a pinnacle of spiritual power transcending anything since the apostles; "yet notwithstanding, if the Saints of God rest in the Light that they now have, then all comfortable Hopes of a further Reformation for the present, will be cut off." So the saints must press on to perfection.[33]

The Discourse proper is an attempt to prove from Scripture certain of the crucial articles of faith printed at the front of the book. Among these are: the belief that only real believers are to be members of the true church of Christ, how such believers may and should be discerned, the necessity of assurance and the sinfulness of doubting, how a visible church is formed, and the nature of the officers in a true church. This leads him to state the fundamental conviction of the Separates, that a true church has the right to determine its membership and select its officers without any outside interference whatsoever. Since it is the body of Christ, it receives all its power from its holy Head; and no other authority has the right to usurp the place of Christ in presuming to rule over his churches. Christ alone has given to his church the rules for the exercise of discipline in order that its purity may be kept undefiled. He has given also all the graces and gifts necessary "for the Comfort, Edification, and Well-being" of his Church.[34] Those who seek to take this control and authority out of the hands of Christ and the church to which he has committed it—such as associations of ministers, consociations of churches, authoritative councils, ecclesiastical constitutions based on civil power—are all of Antichrist and hence enemies to Christ's true church. In fact, the state-supported religious establishment is precisely what is signified by the second beast of Revelation! To substantiate this, Frothingham accuses the established ministry of perennial concern for self and worldly advantage, rather than a hearty interest in the kingdom of Christ and the souls committed to their care. He caricatures ministerial behavior at councils and conventions to show how the established clergymen like to "lord it" over God's churches.[35]

The apologist next turns his attention to answering the objections

32. Ibid., p. 28.
33. Ibid., p. 29. This is reminiscent of John Robinson's advice to the departing Pilgrims that "God always has more light to break forth from his Holy Word."
34. Ibid., p. 204.
35. Ibid., pp. 265 ff. This is followed by a long section on supporting the gospel ministry by voluntary contributions from convinced believers.

brought against those who are seeking to return to "the Order of the Gospel, and the Way of walking with God in practical Godliness." The first is that the pretended work of God splits the churches. Frothingham answers that they are not true churches to begin with, because they hold "that external Morality is the Door into the Church, and that the Lords Supper is a converting Ordinance; or that all have a Right to join with the Church, that will make an outward public Profession of Christianity, altho' they may be unconverted." This is why they have dwindled away into a "dead, dry, lifeless Form of Godliness" which denies the power thereof.[36] A second objection is that good and learned ministers disown the work. Frothingham replies that their judgment must not be set over the authority of Scripture, especially when it is recalled that the leaders of institutionalized religion invariably oppose new movements of the Spirit toward reform. Even those that are not thoroughgoing hypocrites are induced by motives of pride and profit to stand with the world like Peter among the priestly servants, denying that they know Christ in his true work.[37] A third objection is that the Separates encourage disorder and confusion: disorder by withdrawing from standing churches without regular dismission, confusion by permitting lay and women preachers. The accusation of disorder is answered by pleading conscientious conviction in fidelity to God's Word; that of confusion by reference to the doctrine of spiritual gifts. As for women, they do not preach but sweetly declare in all humility what Christ has done for their souls—of which there are numerous examples in the Bible. A fourth objection is that the Separates manifest an uncharitable, censorious spirit and thereby break the peace of the churches. In answer, Frothingham asks whether this did not happen when the apostles preached the true gospel: is not the world always in opposition to those who expose its sinful ways? Admitting that there had been at times too much of a harsh spirit among the Separates, he yet insists that their criticisms were necessary in order to call attention to the dangerous deadness of the churches and their ministers. He deplores hasty and rash judging, though not judging itself. "But to say, A Person is such a One, from the Fruits made manifest, is not rash judging; but is a Judging a Tree by the Fruits, according as Christ would have us judge." [38]

36. Ibid., pp. 340–42.
37. This is Davenport's old charge that many converted ministers were like "Jehoshaphat in Ahab's army." In his second work, Frothingham returns to a scathing attack upon both unconverted ministers and professing Christians who will not "come out from among them" and be separate (*A Key to Unlock the Door*, pp. 223 ff.).
38. *Articles of Faith and Practice*, p. 369.

It is plain from the four objections which Frothingham has already considered that he is not merely setting up straw men, and the fifth one is further proof of his honesty as an apologist. It is: the divisions and contentions among the Separates argue against the truth of their cause; if God is with them, if they know each other infallibly, why all the discord that proceeds from their midst? In answer Frothingham admits the shameful truth of the charge but denies that it invalidates their claim to be trying to follow sincerely the true light of God. "To take the Sins and Infirmities of the Saints for a Rule, to know whether God is amongst them with his gracious Presence, is a very wrong Way of Tryal; and this Objection stands as much against the Work of God in all Ages of the Church, as it doth against us in God's present Work." [39] Many illustrations are cited to show that the most eminent saints have been divided among themselves, and the reason in every case is neglect of the first step in "the Gospel Rule of Discipline," Matthew 18:15, "Go tell him [an adversary] his fault between thee and him *alone*." [40] Further divisions have arisen over the erratic conduct of a few who claim to have premonitions of future events and declare that God will do certain things for them merely because they desire it so fervently. Others have been led to do things which they supposed to be the will of God because human nature opposed it. Here Frothingham preaches to his coreligionists:

> When a Person has had something presented before him, as a Duty to be done: and upon it, an Opposition has arisen in his Mind against the performance of the Thing which has brought the Person into great distress, not knowing what the Mind and Will of God is in that Particular; and by and by the Lord conquers his Will, and takes away that Opposition that was in his Mind, so that he finds a Peace and Serenity in his Mind, and a Willingness in his Mind to be at God's Disposal in all Things; and from hence takes a Belief, that the Thing should and will be done, when at the same Time the Person has never seen the Thing to be directly of God, and for his Honour and Glory to be done, but takes his Faith from the Opposition which he had, and his being conquer'd, and so makes a dreadful Mistake.[41]

39. Ibid., p. 374.
40. Ibid., p. 379.
41. Ibid., p. 380. At the same time this was being written, another Separate was wrestling with his conscience over the question of baptism. When Isaac Backus finally agreed to submit to believer's baptism, one of his reasons was that "the Baptist principles are certainly right, because nature fights so against them." See below, p. 218.

At this point Frothingham confesses to many heart-searchings among the more sober Separates as to whether their leaving the standing churches was really and solely for the glory of God. "And in these Straits and Tryals, the Lord has been pleas'd to give us to see in Divine Light[!], that it was his Honour, and the Good of poor Souls, that first mov'd us to give our Testimony in such a Manner." [42] The remaining objections are variations of the ones already treated, and are answered with nothing new. The book closes by summarizing the Separates' reasons for a "just" separation.

Frothingham's first foray into the field of apologetics attracted immediate attention and drew upon him "the concentrated odium" of several defenders of the establishment. For the most part their chief weapons were scurrility and slander, and few attempts were made to meet his charges as honestly as he had met theirs. A scorching sermon was published by Moses Bartlet, pastor of the Third Church in Middletown (Portland), revealing his dismay that the notorious Separate had become his near neighbor.[43] Out of all the 432-page book of the "false and seducing teacher," Bartlet cited only one objectionable sentence, filling his sermon instead with raillery against the Separates at large. A more formidable attack, though in the same uncharitable spirit, was launched five years later by Robert Ross of Stratfield.[44] He prefixed to his book of 213 pages accounts of the Dutartes (an incestuous group of semireligious fanatics in North Carolina) and of John Lewis (who murdered his wife at the bidding of an inner voice); throughout the book he made invidious comparisons with the Münsterites, French Prophets, and similar wild groups. He classed Frothingham, Solomon Paine, and other Separates with Robert Barclay and George Fox in regard to their attitude toward the Bible. Ross brought out the strongest polemic of the time against the doctrine of enthusiasm, but his extremely unfair representation of his opponents weakened, rather than strengthened, its impact.

Frothingham's reply to both attacks was ready in 1767. Bartlet, he said, had "begged the whole Matter in Debate, for he has settled the Point, that he and his Confederates in the Ministry are right and their Churches; and never bro't a Scrap of Scripture or Reason to prove that they are so." [45] His sermon, continued Frothingham, reveals none of his knowledge (if he has any) about the new birth or a work of God's Spirit in his own heart. He has ranked me with the worst of

42. Ibid., p. 385.
43. *False and Seducing Teachers* (New London, 1757).
44. *A Plain Address.*
45. *A Key to Unlock the Door*, p. 13.

heretics without a shred of proof, and the one sentence which he quoted to show my errors was so out of context that its intended meaning was completely obscured. Bartlet reveals nothing but his own poverty of spirit by railing against me instead of instructing his congregation; "for a Cart-Load of Sermons upon the Negative, will never produce the Positive, and Negative, Negative, is the Sum total of the Author's Sermon." [46] Ross likewise "has charged the Separates almost with every-Thing, but what is good, in his Book; insinuating to the Public, as though we was some of the wildest Sort of Enthusiasts, setting as a Scarecrow in the Front of his Book, an Account of the Dutartes, and the Life of John Lewis; which Accounts are very shocking Instances of dreadful Delusions." [47] He has, moreover, "ranked me among a Number of Persons and Professions that I stand no more in Connection with, than he himself"; he has quoted passages from unknown authors and attributed them indiscriminately in the footnotes to me and Paine. To set the record straight on my attitude toward the Bible: "I hold that the written Word of God is the alone, and only Rule of Faith and Practice, and contains all that is needfull for us to know in Time, to fit us for a happy Eternity." [48]

But the main body of the book is its "Remarks upon the Religious Constitution of the Colony of Connecticut, established by Law." This is a bold explication of the thesis that liberty of conscience is the inalienable, unalterable right of every person. In the preface Frothingham said, "I am bound in Charity to believe, that those that deny ecclesiastical Councils having Right to give Rules and Laws for Conscience, or usurp over the Church and People of God, must also deny civil Ruler's exercising the same Power; and that the ecclesiastical Laws of this Colony, denies Liberty of Conscience, and robs the Church of Christ of her sacred Rights and Privileges, I think cannot be deny'd." He observed tartly that those who justify the Puritan and Pilgrim fathers in their contending for the rights of conscience cannot condemn the Separates for doing essentially the same thing now. His assertion of religious tyranny is documented by reference to the many petitions which the Separates have presented to the General Assembly from year to year, "asking nothing but their just Rights, full and free liberty of Conscience, and have been, and still are, denied their Request." [49] Again he advances the argument that it belongs to Jesus Christ alone to constitute and rule his churches;

46. Ibid., p. 17. This is close to an accurate judgment.
47. Ibid., p. 28.
48. Ibid., p. 30.
49. Cf. M. L. Greene, *Religious Liberty in Connecticut,* p. 296.

but if the Lord himself came personally to Connecticut, he could not gather a church "unless he would crouch, and come down to this Constitution Plan." [50] Declaring that Connecticut leaves "no Gap for one Breath of gospel Liberty," he proceeds to cite instances of persecution for conscience' sake. He reviews the experience of the church at Canterbury, where, for the sole crime of seeking to follow their religious convictions and walking all the while in peace with their neighbors, the people of this church have suffered unspeakable loss:

> I ask in Meekness, who shall answer at the Bar of God, for all the abominable Oppression and Persecution done to this Church, for fifteen Years together, notwithstanding all their voting; not only pushing them out of the Meeting-House that was built for them, in that Principle and Profession to worship God in, and robbing them of their Property in it; but, additional thereto, straining away their Substance, Horses and Oxen, stripping them out of their Teams, in the midst of Business; seizing Cows, Sheep, and poor People's Meat out of their Tubs, and other Utensils, exceedingly wanted in their Families? And what is still beyond, seizing and imprisoning the Bodies of the Flock of Christ, whilst their poor Families are left to shift as they can! [51]

And how does the establishment pervert the laws of Christ! Under the ecclesiastical constitution the inhabitants of the town share in the vote to call a minister for the church—a travesty on the sacred office of the ministry because it allows every nondescript person, whether immoral or profane, drunkard or atheist, to have a voice in the selection of spiritual leaders. Further, to force such people to attend the worship of God under penalty of law is "to commit a Rape upon Christ's chaste Spouse which he has bought with his precious Blood." [52] Frothingham criticizes another aspect of the platform, that which required a major part of the ministers of a consociation to concur in order to determine a matter. His illustration here is the Wallingford case, where in 1758 the Old Lights forced the settlement of James Dana over the protests of the church, the town, and even the (New Haven) consociation. What impressed him in this case was that the arguments advanced by the Old Guard revolved entirely around the construction to be placed on the platform rather than

50. *A Key to Unlock the Door,* p. 50.
51. Ibid., pp. 68–69.
52. Ibid., p. 61.

on the requirements of the Word of God. "Indeed, this affair at Wallingford, has been a preaching Providence to me, and has been instrumental with other Things to introduce me into the Labor of Writing this Book." [53] He protests the requirement that a ministerial association must approve candidates for the ministry and advise bereaved churches whom to call; it also has the final word in cases of discipline, and the part played by lay messengers in all these proceedings is insignificant.

To the objection that chaos would result if the churches were disestablished, Frothingham replies that both church *and* state will be ruined if the churches are not freed from state control immediately. There must be a careful distinction between civil and ecclesiastical power. The state is, under God, to preserve the life, property, and liberty of its subjects:

> Life when it is exposed by the designs of wicked men, or otherwise, the rulers aid is wanted; property, by the execution of wholesome and righteous laws to preserve every one in their just, legal rights and properties. Liberty by defending every one of different sects, in their sacred rights of conscience, not allowing one sect to disturb another, while they are peaceably & publickly worshipping God, as they think is best pleasing in his gracious sight. [54]

This is the limit of the ruler's work, and he should have nothing more to say about the constitution, worship, ministry, boundaries, or anything else concerning the church. Thus Frothingham pleads not merely for toleration but for absolute religious liberty. What civil disability would come to anyone, the dogged Separate demands, if the whole ecclesiastical constitution were scrapped and every man left to worship as he pleases?

> Since I have liv'd in Middletown, there has been 5 different worships in the town, within the compass of a mile on the Lord's Day, besides the consocation, and church of England, and separates, there was a number of Dutch, in one private house, and the neutral French, in another, and no damage accrued to any man's property, or civil interest, any more than if they had all worshipped under one roof; and had there been added, Baptists, Quakers, and Moravians [the worst he could think of], it makes no odds, as to mens civil property. [55]

53. Ibid., p. 75.
54. Ibid., p. 153.
55. Ibid., p. 155.

Even if it did, such pragmatic considerations are secondary. What if disorder did result? The real question is, is it right or wrong? If it is wrong according to the Word of God, it ought to be rejected, "let the consequence be what it will." [56]

Frothingham treats a final objection, the casuistical claim that the Connecticut ecclesiocrats feel themselves bound in conscience to maintain the establishment, and he who respects the rights of conscience must allow them to do so. He almost gives away his previous argument by retorting that if he has crossed his neighbor's conscience, it must be a wrong conscience—this answer works too easily both ways. But he gets quickly to the point by adding that nobody has the right, even by pretending conscience, to *force* others to violate their consciences. It is the use of force that makes for tyranny.

If it had been published twenty years sooner, Frothingham's second work probably would have earned him another term in Hartford jail. In 1767, however, the political climate was much changed. The "Sons of Liberty" had successfully resisted the imposition of the Stamp Act on Connecticut, the New Lights were a political force to be reckoned with, and some of the Separates had won limited rights to exist without molestation. Miss Greene remarks that Frothingham's *Key to Unlock the Door* "was probably the strongest work put forth from the dissenter's standpoint, and within three years it was followed by a legislative act granting a measure of toleration." [57] Although the aged apologist did not live to see the day when complete separation of church and state was won in New England, he died (November 30, 1798) knowing that his efforts had brought about much progress in that direction.

A layman: Nathan Cole. It has been observed that the Great Awakening was largely a popular movement stirring the common man as nothing else since the planting of the colonies. It is entirely fitting that some attention should be given to one who was in no sense a preacher or pastor, but whose leadership in a strictly lay capacity illustrates the response of the common people to the religious issues of the day. Such a man was Nathan Cole, the semiliterate farmer of Kensington, Connecticut. His manuscript biography, "The Spiritual Travels of Nathan Cole," is in an excellent state of preservation at the Connecticut Historical Society. [58] The first sentence reads: "I was

56. Ibid., p. 167.

57. *Religious Liberty in Connecticut*, p. 297.

58. The work is in the handwriting of a copyist, but has been interlined and corrected presumably by Cole himself. It is accompanied by several fragments dealing with other matters, most of which seem to be in Cole's hand.

born Feb 15th 1711 and born again Octo 1741—". Typical of his over-powering religious concern is the fact that his whole life before conversion is covered in one sentence: "When I was young I had very early convictions; but after I grew up I was an Arminian untill I was near 30 years of age; I intended to be saved by my own works such as prayers & good deeds."

He then launches into a detailed description of how his spiritual pilgrimage began with the hearing of Whitefield at Middletown in 1740.[59] The evangelist's sermon, he says, "gave me a heart wound"; but he was not converted on the spot. He was convinced of the doctrine of election, but "went right to quarreling with God about it" because it seemed to make God unjust. "I began to think I was not Elected, and that God made some for heaven and me for hell. . . . [And] if as I thought; I was made to be damned; my heart then rose against God exceedingly." This distress lasted for a full year, during which Cole could think of little beside his sinful and undone condition:

> Poor me it took away most all my Comfort of eating, drinking, Sleeping, or working. Hell fire was most always in my mind; and I have hundreds of times put my fingers into my pipe when I have been smoking to feel how fire felt: and to see how my Body could bear to lye in Hell fire for ever & ever.

Others noticed his morbidity; family and friends tried to comfort him, but all to no avail. Finally one night he had a vision of God and was made to see that he could trust God completely for his eternal soul's salvation:

> My heart was broken; my burden was fallen of my mind; I was set free, my distress was gone, and I was filled with a pineing desire to see Christs own words in the bible; & I got up off my bed being alone; And by the help of Chairs I got along to the window where my bible was and I opened it & the first place I saw was the 15th Chap: John—on Christs own words & they spake to my very heart & every doubt & scruple that rose in my heart about the truth of Gods word was took right off; and I saw the whole train of Scrip-

59. Cole's story of how he left his tool in the field, called his wife, and rode the twelve miles to Middletown "dubbel in littel more then an hour" is one of the classics of the Whitefieldian impact on New England. In spite of the fact that it has been printed several times, the temptation to repeat it here is great. However, the reader is referred to Stuart C. Henry, *George Whitefield: Wayfaring Witness* (New York, 1957), pp. 68–70; G. L. Walker, *Aspects of the Religious Life of New England*, pp. 89–91; Gaustad, p. 54; or *William and Mary Quarterly*, 3rd ser. 7 (1950), 590–91.

tures all in a Connection, and I believe I felt just as the Apostles felt the truth of the word when they writ it, every leaf line & letter smiled in my face; I got the bible up under my Chin & hugged it; it was sweet and lovely; the word was nigh me in my hand, then I began to pray & to praise God. . . . I was swallowed up in God.[60]

Here once again is the familiar pattern of conversion which became typical during the Great Awakening: deep distress over sin, utter despair of salvation, surging joy of forgiven sin. Cole passed through this traumatic experience, however, only to face another one—the problem of assurance. When he related his experience to other Christians, they told him he had been converted. This was something he had not thought about and scarcely dared believe for fear it might not be genuine. But after listening to revivalistic preachers and other experienced Christians, he had "the sealing evidence." Praying in the field one day, he saw another vision:

It seemed as if I really saw the gate of heaven by an Eye of faith, & the way for Sinners to Get to heaven by Jesus Christ; as plain as ever I saw anything with my bodily eyes in my life . . . I saw what free Grace was; I saw how stubborn & willfull man was; I saw it was nothing but accepting of Christs Righteousness & the match was made; I saw I was saved by Christ, I thought here I had the sealings of the Holy Ghost; & here I had evidences clear. What I saw here is unspeakable, I could do no work here but lay down for want of bodily Strength untill this view was a little abated.[61]

There followed several weeks during which Cole was sorely tempted to test his assurance by committing suicide. The devil seemed to say, "If you're really saved, you can prove it in a minute; if you're not, you never will be anyhow." Cole asked advice of several esteemed Christians, none of whom could help, and was again on the verge of despair. Then he recalled that even Christ had been tempted to destroy himself and had routed the devil by relying on the Word of God. Cole did the same, and peace returned. He recounts many such trials: doubts arise, struggle ensues, assurance returns. The episodes always climax with a couplet, presumably of Cole's own composure:

60. "The Spiritual Travels of Nathan Cole," pp. 7–11.
61. Ibid., p. 14. Several pages later (p. 49) he quotes from the Larger Westminster Catechism, Questions 80 and 81, concerning assurance, and assents to them "because I find them true."

Jesus and me ye ne'er shall part,
For God is greater than my heart.

Next he began to see that the standing churches were not in a true gospel order. "I was called a member of this old Church for 14 or 15 years; but now I saw Ichabod was written upon it, the Glory of the Lord was departed, for they held several things contrary to the Gospel . . . that unconverted men had a divine right to come to the ordinance of the Lords supper." [62] To Cole this was a double lie: the unregenerate communicant and the church were both lying in permitting such persons to own the covenant and receive privileges that rightfully belonged only to true saints. "I tryed to have these things mended but all in vain: Then I came out & seperated or dissented from them, for I could not see them to be a Gospel Church." [63] For a time he found fellowship with the Separates at Wethersfield, and went regularly to their "Conference meetings," where he learned more from "them Dear Children of God" than he had "learnt in all my Life before." He seems not to have joined this church at that time (1748), however, but to have bent his major efforts toward establishing a Separate church in Kensington. A fragment dated 1771, which accompanies the "Spiritual Travels," reads as follows:

I Nathan Cole Separated from the Saybrook Churches in the year 1747 & kept metings in my own house on the Sabbath with a few others that came to me & some times we had preachers came to us: & Isaac Hurlbut after some time began to preach & continued about 2 years & our number increased & in the year 1750 we sent for mr John Fuller & he came from Lime to us & preached to us six months & now in our meetings on the sabbeth there was about 20 or 30 persons but when mr Fuller left us then the people began to fall away thinking we never could set up a church hear & some went back to the old meeting house again & some moved away to new towns & some of the best were taken away by death all gone but sister pack wife to samuel pack & she came hear on the sabbeth so long as she lived & she & i kept meetings together some years & she died & i was left alone some years

During these years Cole had more than his share of both joy and sorrow. He was troubled frequently by "wounds" on his legs, for which he could get little relief. The year 1763 was a particularly

62. Ibid., p. 21.
63. Ibid.

difficult time: in June his wife fell "into a melancholly way; & she was in great darkness so as at last to border hard upon despair, & then lost the use of her reason & understanding." She apparently remained in this condition the rest of her life, which continued at least five years, and Cole had to care for her as he would a helpless child. In December, "the dropsy & Scurvy humours fell down again into my leggs; and the Doctors used many means; but all seemed to be in vain, so that about the mid of winter the Doctor yeilded to let it have its course; only to try things that were thought likely to kill or cure; which things did help me some." His friends added their comfort by saying that he had not long to live, or at the very most could never work again; while his enemies said it was his just desert for withdrawing from the church, and expressed satisfaction that soon the town should be rid of its last Separate. Poor Cole must have felt something like Job:

> Now all this time my wife was by me Crying out in her distress Oh dreadfull Oh dreadfull Oh dreadfull dreadfull, dreadfull, dreadfull, and I was sitting three months or thereabouts in the furnace of purification & the sound of dreadfull from my wife continually in my ears night & day almost: Now all this time God gave me a sweet Submission to his will, & a sweet measure of patience.[64]

Joys came too, in the form of fellowship with the saints. After he had joined with them in praising God, Cole testified, his heart and soul were "in a sweet frame" for many days. "When I was with them I seemed to feel perfectly their feeling, they felt all as one as if they had been made up all into one man, all drinked into one Spirit & oneness, & whatever trouble or affliction they went through in this world they had borne it patiently as Coming from the hand of God it turned into sound joy in their heart." [65] Even in the midst of his affliction, he found no room for sorrow and grief.

The crisis of 1763, however, proved something of a turning point in Cole's life. He felt that his trials had been God's way of showing him that he had not been zealous enough in Christian service, and that he should remain no longer isolated as a lone Separate in Kensington:

> Now the Lord bid me arise & go forward after the flock; & make speed to go forth by the footsteps of the flock; now my heart says

64. Ibid., p. 50.
65. Ibid., pp. 37–38.

> Dear Lord blessed be thy name I will obey; now my mind looked away into Gods word to find the footsteps of the flock, & as my mind was following the footsteps of the flock in the bible; I came right upon Mr. Frothinghams Congregational Church in Middletown.

A remarkable revelation indeed! At the time of his conversion, Cole had seen in a vision "the form of a Gospel Church, and the place where it was settled, and Angels hovering over it, saying, the Glory of the town, & strangers that came pressing by had the same to say." [66] He saw exactly the form of the house, the place where it stood, the minister who dwelt there, the people who worshiped there—all the details are described. When Cole later saw the meetinghouse of the Separates in Middletown, exactly according to the details of his vision (even with the angels hovering over it), he knew he had found the pure and true gospel church. Now they stood right before him, as it were, on the pages of his Bible.

> I purposed fully if the Lord should give me a measure of healing I would endeavour to Joyn my self with them the first opportunity: Their watchman being a faithfull Servant of Jesus Christ, kept a faithfull watch round about his Church & happened to see me a coming in hast to joyn in their Church, it seemed as if I heard him say, pointing at me
>
> > Oh he was once a lump of Sin
> > But now he's Just a entering in
> > And here he comes a lovely Soul
> > I say to you make room for Cole
>
> I joyned to them on friday the 29th day of June 1764 a fast day, & sat at the Lords table with them the next Sabbath. [67]

Cole was troubled from time to time by the tax collectors for rates to support the "hireling minister." Though threatened with imprisonment occasionally and at least once deprived of ten pounds worth of his estate for an unpaid tax, he seems to have been treated fairly leniently by the standing church in Kensington. The town usually voted year by year to abate his rates, always testifying (if his own record is true) to the beneficent influence of his godly life. One dis-

---

66. Ibid., p. 11. This "vision" was recorded twenty years later, after Cole was already active in the Middletown congregation.

67. Ibid., p. 56. The verse is also part of an "epic poem" on Cole's experience, found in another fragment from his hand.

gruntled deacon, as the annual vote was taken, had said: "As to Brother Cole his morals are lovely, & I love them but as to his rates we have a law, & by our law I do not know why he ought not pay as well as we." [68] But there was not the deep animosity between Cole and his former church as in so many other cases. However, in 1764, the year he joined Frothingham's church, there was quite a debate over the question. At a town meeting the pastor stated flatly that all ought to obey the law which the civil authorities had made for supporting a godly minister and that even Christ paid tribute to the civil power. Cole, having learned rapidly from his new pastor at Middletown, arose and replied with spirit that this was "mans law; not Gods Law; & God says men frame mischief by their laws; &c." [69] This was a reference to Psalm 94:20, the same text that had won freedom for Elisha Paine in 1752. Cole went on to distinguish between obeying civil laws in civil matters and disobeying them when they contravened God's laws. He declared, "Gods law to support the Gospel is free will offerings all over the Bible." Nor was this merely a ruse for him to avoid paying at all:

> I have done ten times more to support the Gospel by free will offering this last year than any man in Kensington according to his list; yet you must fall to Robbing your neighbour Churches by force of law, to get money to pay your ministers; which the Church of Christ never did, in all the whole bible, no nor no saints in all the whole book of God, & yet you call your selves a church of Christ.[70]

Cole recorded that after this spirited speech before the whole town, the citizens released him, the church members marveled, and the minister turned pale.

Although he continued as a member of the Middletown Separate Church for fourteen years, Cole also revived the Separate meeting in his Kensington home. In a vision of 1764 he had seen himself as "a poor old coal buryed up in the ashes as if there was no fire to be seen but the Lord seemed to shew that in time a little spark of fire would come out of these ashes from that coal & catch fire to a brand that was neer & that brand catch fire to some brands that lay hear & there & the fire began to burn more & more & keept increasing until it arose to a much greater height then ever it was before in Kensington." In a fragment of 1771 he testified:

68. Ibid., p. 35.
69. Ibid., p. 60.
70. Ibid., p. 61.

i have stood in the separation now stedfast 24 years this year 1771 but in the year 1770 they began to come out too me one hear & another there & the Lord seemed to convert them into the separation sweetly & now others keep comeing to us & our meeting keeps incresing so that some times we have a considerable number.

In 1778 Cole "got more light" and discovered, as many other Separates were doing, that "there is no other church to be found in the bible or new testament but a real baptist church." The last we hear from him, he is contending for his Baptist faith against the pedobaptist Separates as warmly as he formerly contended for the Separates against the standing order.[71]

A frontiersman: Joseph Marshall. Typical of the restless spirit which led many Separates to scatter themselves profusely along the New England frontier was Joseph Marshall (1731–1813), who began as a youthful exhorter, preached all across Connecticut, evangelized in New York, and wound up as a wandering preacher in Vermont, "respected for his piety and wondered at for his eccentricity." [72] He was born in Windsor, Connecticut, on February 17, 1731, the sixth son of Samuel and Abigail Marshall.[73] His father was converted during Whitefield's first visit; and Joseph himself, though only nine years old at the time, was deeply affected and professed faith soon afterward. A few years later he joined the Separate church under Thomas Marsh at Mansfield and began to travel in company with the Separate preachers. It was said that he made a practice of stopping every individual he met to inquire into his personal religious experience and ask whether he had been born again. Arrested at a Separate meeting in Tolland, Marshall exhorted bystanders continually during his trip to jail, trial for disorderly conduct, and time in the stocks. Refusing to pay his fine, he was bound over to a farmer to work out his penalty. He preferred to attend Separate meetings rather than work, however, and to prevent his church-going the farmer hid his clothes. But his behavior was still unsatisfactory, and he was sent to Hartford jail where he was confined with Ebenezer Frothingham until a kindly neighbor paid his fine. Upon being released, he made his way to Amenia, New York, where a group of Separates had set-

71. Nathan Cole, *Dialogue Between a Separate Minister, and One of His People, and Cole* (Hartford, 1779?), pp. 11, 12.

72. *Historical Notices of the First Congregational Church in Canterbury, Connecticut* (Northampton, 1853), p. 7.

73. Samuel Marshall was the son of Deacon Thomas Marshall and the brother of Daniel Marshall, who became a pioneer Separate Baptist preacher in the South and founded the first Baptist church in Georgia.

tled under Abraham Paine. After preaching in this vicinity for a while, he came to New Milford, Connecticut, and remained until 1751. Then he assumed the pastorate of a Separate church at Somers, Connecticut. Here he became agitated over the baptismal question— a struggle which few Separates escaped—and eventually he was immersed. In three or four months he retracted his Baptist sentiments and remained a stedfast pedobaptist.

Marshall's next and perhaps most distinctive pastorate was at Canterbury, where he served some ten years. Solomon Paine had died in 1754, and the Separate church had been pastorless three years. Its records for September 8, 1757, read:

> A Record How the Congregatinul Church of Christ in canterbary was Leade according to the Ruels of the Gospel in Chuseing & ordaning Bro Joseph Marshal to the Pastoral Charge of the Church of Christ in Canterbury at a Regaler Meting of the Congregatinul Church of Christ of Said twone thay made Cheise of Bro Joseph Marshel to be their Pastor under Christ according to the Rules of the Gospel [74]

On September 18, at a regular church meeting called to receive Marshall's answer, "he Sollomly Declared that he accepted there Call & freely gave himself to God & by the will of God to the Church to be there Pastor the Church voted that they accepted his anser[.]" It was not until April 18, 1759, however, that Marshall was ordained.

> Deacon Obadiah Johnson of Said Church mead the first Prayer: Our Beloved Brother Paul Parks Pastor of the Church of Christ in Presson Gave the Solloum Charge our Beloved Bro Bliss Willoughby of the Church of Christ in Norwich Gave the Righthand of Fellowship our Belved Bro Alexander Meller Pastor of the Church of Christ in Plainfield made the Last Prayer all don according to the Ruls of the Gospel and under the ades & assetance of the Holy Spirit of God all Glory to God the father & God Son & God the holy Gost Amen [75]

The question of why two years elapsed between the church's choice of Marshall and his ordination is answered in part from the records of the Preston Separate Church, which indicate some hesitancy on their part to proceed with the ceremony. On September 10, 1758, the Canterbury church had requested (apparently not for the first time)

74. *Records of the Congregational Church in Canterbury*, p. 12.
75. Ibid., pp. 12–13.

that brethren be sent to join them in ordaining Marshall, and the Preston church had appointed its pastor and two deacons "to assist as far as they Should have felloship." They evidently decided not to extend fellowship until the next year; but then, as appears from the Canterbury record quoted above, they were satisfied and went ahead with the ceremony. One can only surmise the reason for this hesitancy, but more than likely it was due to Marshall's reputation for erratic conduct.

This is confirmed by the fact that his pastorate at Canterbury was a stormy one. After various strivings, the church found itself in such a trial respecting Brother Marshall that it could not join together in the Lord's Supper, and voted on June 30, 1767, to "Call a Councell of the Elders & Bretherin from Such of the Sister Churches as Waire present att the ordination of Brother marshal" in order that they might have help in resolving their difficulties.[76] The council met and recommended that the church "Seek to Obtaine an able minnister that might Serve and Sattissfy the Whole Church," which the church immediately voted to do.[77] But matters dragged along for another year, and it was not until August 29, 1768, that the church voted "that Brr Joseph marshal be Dismissed from the pastoral Charge of this Church on account of the Contentions in this Church Respecting his giftes & ordination Which Rendors his Improvement unprofitabel as a pastor over Said Church." [78] To soften the blow, the church on December 9 "Voted to give and Did give to mr Joseph marshal a Letter in these Words (Viz) the Congregational Church of Christ in Cantrbury unto the Churches and peopel of god to Whome these may Conserne these may Certify that mr Jos marshal is in good Regaler Standing in this Church and allso we Do recommend Said marshal to [be] good in his morral Conduct and Sound in the faith an art [?] that we Beleve that god hath given gifts unto and hath Called him to prech the gospel of Jesus Christ." [79]

A rather amusing sequel to this series of actions came when Marshall received a call to become pastor of a newly gathered church in Brentwood, New Hampshire. The Canterbury Separates revoked their act of dismissal and refused to release him because the Brentwood church had offered him a fixed salary. On April 5, 1769, it was voted that

76. Ibid., p. 27.
77. Ibid., p. 28.
78. Ibid., pp. 29–30.
79. Ibid., p. 31.

this Church Did Not Dismiss Said marshal Because thay had No fellowshipp with Said Brintwood Church in their Call given Said mr marshal, in that thay in Writing promis to Support him the Said marshal and his famely While he Remaines With them in the minstry Which is an Obligation Not Warranted in Scriptuer (to wit) to maintain the gospell is Right But to Enter into Bonds to maintain any a perticuler man & his famely While Said man is With any perticuler peopel in the ministery is unwarrantabel [80]

Unable to go and unable to stay, the unhappy pastor finally freed himself from the strife-torn church in November, 1769. As a parting gesture, the church voted that "Brother Joseph marshall have Liberty to Joine With any other Church of Christ in fellowship with this Church of the Same prinsaples & when he hath So Joined & given this Church Notis there off then he Shall be Desmissed from this Church." [81] With his wife, whom he had married in 1760, and three small children Marshall moved to Canaan. Here, in the northwestern corner of Connecticut, he preached as an itinerant evangelist for sixteen years. Then he moved to Green River, New York, and lived with his eldest daughter for about ten years, after which he came to Starksborough, Vermont. Although past sixty years old, he ranged far and wide in that frontier territory, preaching with the same blunt speech and inflamed passion that characterized him everywhere.

Of the anecdotes which are preserved from this period of his life, one of the more interesting tells of his visit in the home of Ethan Allen, of "Green Mountain" fame. After furnishing him shelter for the night, Allen invited the preacher to lead family devotions the next morning. Colonel Allen handed him a copy of *Reason the Only Oracle*, saying, "This is *my* bible; I suppose you have no objection to reading out of it in my home." Mr. Marshall replied, "Let us sing a few verses first. Have you any objections to the psalm-book?" His host did not, so Marshall turned to the selection which began:

> Let all the heathen writers join
>   To form one perfect book.—
> Great God, if once compared with thine,
>   How mean their writings look!

Allen, who in spite of his infidelity was unusually cordial and candid, interrupted him to exclaim, "Floored, Father Marshall; take your own Bible." [82]

80. Ibid.
81. Ibid., p. 32.
82. Told in Jennings, *Memorials of a Century*, pp. 118–19. Allen recently had

Not only infidels but Baptists found it hard to get ahead of this salty old Separate. From time to time he consented to preach for them, and occasionally would be asked to administer communion, although he would be expected not to commune. "On one such occasion, a piece of bread fell from the table to the floor; he picked it up, and ate it, saying, 'The dogs eat of the crumbs that fall from the master's table.'"[83]

Two years after Marshall died at Starksborough, one of his Vermont contemporaries ventured a "memoir," which essayed not the customary eulogy—though it was by no means unappreciative—but something of a critical evaluation of this eccentric preacher.[84] This writer offers the interesting information that Marshall often manifested a constitutional tendency to dejection. When he was in his teens he was haunted at times by fear that he had committed the unpardonable sin. These periods of extreme distress returned rather often throughout his life. Yet when he preached, he would manifest some of the extreme emotional flights of which the more enthusiastic Separates were capable. And Marshall certainly was as tinctured with enthusiasm as the headiest of the Separates. His memoirist attributes this unbalance to lack of proper education and culture:

> Many of the irregularities into which he ran, were caused by the warmth and vehemence of his feelings not being tempered and restrained by ample and correct views of the spirit and dictates of religion, and of the nature of that propriety and decorum of conduct, which christianity is very far from authorizing her votaries to trample under foot. Much of the distress also, which so often and so keenly tortured his mind was occasioned by the narrowness of his information and the inaccuracy of his opinions. He experienced a powerful excitement of the passions, and his conscience was tremblingly alive to every impression. But, his understanding was not sufficiently enlightened and his notions were not sufficiently just and scriptural to guide and control the emotions of his mind and the operations of his conscience.[85]

This is doubtless true, and is what Puritans from Sibbes to Edwards feared might happen if the wrong kind of emotions got the upper

lost an entire edition of the *Oracles* in a print-shop fire which some accused Marshall of setting. This was never proved, however.

83. Ibid., p. 119.

84. "Memoir of the Rev. Joseph Marshall," *Adviser; or Vermont Evangelical Magazine,* 7 (1815), 207. I have not been able to identify the author of this informative piece.

85. Ibid., p. 203.

hand in religion. If Marshall's analyst had been able to bring to bear modern psychological concepts, he perhaps would have concluded that the subject of his memoir was at least a mild manic-depressive. To Marshall's credit it can be said that his judgment matured with the years, his prejudices were subdued, and at length he entered into fraternal relations with the regular churches and ministers. In all of this he serves as a good illustration of the typical Separate: by the time of his death in 1813, he had made the full round of emotional conversion, enthusiastic excess, precipitate separation, zealous evangelism, contentious strife, and gradual reconciliation. His was the kind of spirit that had to seek the frontier, and having found it, could then afford to share in the transition of his new home to a more conservative and refined culture.

DOCTRINES OF THE SEPARATES

Many of the doctrinal beliefs of the Separates have been exhibited in connection with the leaders discussed above, as well as in the course of describing the issues between them and the standing order.[86] The picture is not complete, however, without a survey of some of the more important confessions of faith that they put forth from time to time, and in which may be found not only individual tenets and controversial issues but the doctrinal consensus of all who shared in the shaping of the Separate movement. The first thing to be said is that, apart from the enthusiastic vagaries which did so much to discredit the movement in its early years, the discipline and doctrine which eventually emerged from the Strict Congregationalists stood squarely in the tradition of the Westminster Confession of Faith and the Cambridge Platform of polity. The Killingly Convention of 1781 made this plain:

> As Churches, we have ever acknowledged Westminster Confession of Faith; and Cambridge Platform of Church Discipline, as to the Substance of them (some few things excepted) to be orthodox Systems of Faith, and Practice.[87]

The qualifier, "some few things excepted," is important. This is best illustrated in the case of the Canterbury Separate Church, which, to support its claim to represent the original church, carried with it

86. See above, Chap. 2.

87. *An Historical Narrative and Declaration*, p. 17. The Separates here make it plain, however, that they are bound by no creeds "any further than they agree with the Word of God, contained in the Scriptures of the Old and New Testaments."

the covenant and confession adopted in 1711. Both of these were significantly revised in 1746.[88] In the excerpts below, the original form is used as a base; the additions of 1746 are printed in small capitals, the omissions in italics.

The first difference to be noticed is the Separates' emphasis on a particular and cordial faith. Article x of the Canterbury Confession reads:

> That in the new Covenant God hath promised Life unto all THOSE that HEARTILY AND WITH THE FULL CONSENT OF THEIR SOULS believe in him through Jesus Christ. . . .

The first article of the Canterbury Covenant reads:

> That we do EACH ONE OF US IN PERTICULAR unfeignedly resign up ourselves and our seed to the Lord Jehovah, Fat[her] Son and, holy Ghost; receiving Jesus Christ AS *ye* very God, and very man, and the only Mediator between God and Man as our Lord and Saviour; FREELY GIVEN OF GOD TO EACH OF US IN PERTICULAR AND SEALED TO EACH OF US BY THE HOLY SPIRIT OF PROMISE, relying upon the [free] grace of God for that salvation and Blessedness, which Christ hath purchased, [and] we *do* hope to have by faith in and dependance upon his merits.

These additions indicate the Separates' concern for heartfelt religion as against the intellectual acceptance of certain doctrines, and they reinforce the insistence on personal, i.e. particular, faith in the redemptive work of Christ for the individual.[89] A second point to notice is the Separates' denial of the Halfway Covenant, a subject on which the original (1711) documents are completely silent. Article xiii of the Confession reads:

> We beleive that there are two seals of the Covenant of grace *Viz* B[aptism] and the Lords Supper; that Baptism BELONGS TO NON BUT TRUE BELIEVERS WHO ARE RECIEVD BY FAITH AND LOVE AND THEIR SEED IN THEIR INFANCY AND is a sign of our entrance in [to Christ] and the Lords Supper is a Sign of our groth in grace:—

The most extensive changes in the Separates' revision come when they spell out the requirements of church discipline and emphasize

88. All the documents are in *Records of the Congregational Church in Canterbury*, pp. 1–4, 16–20.
89. For a New Light defense of this doctrine see Andrew Croswell, *What Is Christ to Me, If He Is Not Mine?* (Boston, 1745).

strict congregational principles of polity. The first of these matters
will be left for future consideration,[90] and of the other it is necessary
only to repeat that they rejected entirely the semipresbyterian system of the Saybrook Platform and the sections of the Cambridge
Platform which granted to the magistrate power to enforce ecclesiastical discipline and church support. In an entirely new addition to the
original covenant, the Canterbury Separates say (capitals omitted):

> The Power granted by Christ unto the body of the Church and
> brotherhood, is a prerogative or priveledge which the Church doth
> exercise (1) in admiting of their own members (2) in Chusing
> and ordaining their own officers (3) in Removing them from their
> office and allso from their fellowship in cace of Scandal or any thing
> that by the Rules of the Gospel Renders them unfit therefor (4) in
> supporting and maintaining the Gospel Ministry ordinances and
> the poor of the Church without useing the Civel Sword or any
> Coercive means to force men thereto; which Disipline we desire
> may ever take place; and that the worship of God in all the parts
> thereof may evermore be kept up in the power and spirituality
> thereof among us—:

While the Canterbury Confession and Covenant were adopted by
the Separate churches at Scotland and Newent, the doctrinal standards of the Mansfield Separates (used also at Plainfield and South
Killingly) were entirely new and original.[91] They represent the first
such attempt among the Separates and because of their early date
(1745) reveal more of an enthusiastic bent than that which became
general even among the more "high-flying" Separates. This so distressed the ministers of Windham County that they declared (in a
characteristic overstatement):

> there is not one single Instance wherein they have varied from the
> Confession of Faith professed from the Beginning by the Churches
> of Christ in this Land, but that they have therein marred the Sense,
> or perverted the Scripture Doctrine of *Faith,* or at least rendered
> them ambiguous and uncertain; and in most of them have cor-
> rupted the Faith which was once deliver'd to the Saints. . . . So
> that under Pretence of greater Purity and Reformation they have
> opened a Door and paved the Way to let in *Moravian, Antinomian,*

90. See below, pp. 164–67.
91. These are printed (to be "refuted") in *The Result of a Council of the Consociated Churches of the County of Windham,* pp. 5–10.

Anabaptistical and *Quakerish* Errors into the Church: And also under a Pretence of Congregational Discipline, have set up as absolute an Independency as ever was heard of in the Church.[92]

The Mansfield Confession of twenty-two articles is perhaps not quite this heretical, but it does contain some indiscreet statements, to say the least. It may be described as trinitarian (with emphasis on three offices rather than tri-personality), infralapsarian (God is not the author of sin), antinomian (external morality is "no Part of the Essence of the Religion of Christ"), and fideistic (faith is necessary for any deed to receive God's approval). An especially obnoxious statement was in Article xv:

> We believe that we are of that Number who were Elected of GOD to eternal Life, and that Christ did live on Earth, die and rise again for us in particular; and that He doth now, in the Virtue of his own Merits & Satisfaction, make Intercession to GOD for us; and that we are now Justified in the Sight of GOD, for the sake of Christ, and shall be owned by Him at the great and general Judgment, which GOD hath made us to believe, by sending according to his Promise the Holy Ghost into our Souls, who hath made a particular Application of the above Articles; first convincing us of our lost Condition by Nature; as being under a full Sentence of Condemnation for our Original Sin, and also for our actual Transgressions; of the heinous Nature of Unbelief, which keeps us off from GOD and all Duty, till GOD by his Spirit brought into our Souls the Grace of the Gospel; so humbling us by Gospel Grace has made us Partakers of the Divine Nature, which being added to Christ's taking the Humane Nature makes up the Union between Christ and our Souls.

Here is an extreme form of insistence on a particular faith and an assurance that "*we* are of the elect." This conviction is obviously necessary to maintain the spirit of separatism in any age, and, because it unchurches all but the dissenters, always draws the fire of established conservatism. It did here. But what the ministers objected to most in this article was the way it asserted the believer's mystical union with Christ even to a partaking of the divine nature. "This, if any thing, is little short of the Blasphemy of *Jacob Bekman* [Boehme], our being *godded* with GOD, and *christed* with Christ." [93] Also singled out for special attack was the grounding of assurance in religious

92. Ibid., p. 17.
93. Ibid., p. 12.

feeling rather than in a moral life. That antinomianism was a problem among the Separates cannot be denied, and often it shaded over into perfectionism. The ministers quote one Caleb Hide as saying that "the New Nature, which was implanted in every converted Soul, was as holy as GOD, and as perfect as GOD was." Elisha Paine defended him by demanding:

> What if he did say so? What harm was there in it? Does not the Apostle *Peter* say, We are made Partakers of the Divine Nature? And all the Works of GOD are perfect; and it is said the Saints shall be perfect as their heavenly Father is perfect: Indeed (said he) if he had said *he* was so perfect and holy, it would have been another Thing; but there is a Distinction between the Person and the Principle.[94]

This distinction, unfortunately, was not always kept in mind.

The most comprehensive statement of faith to issue from the Separates jointly before 1781 is the one printed in the first seventeen pages of Ebenezer Frothingham's *Articles of Faith and Practice*.[95] Published in 1750, it is modeled on the Mansfield Confession but shows an awareness of the criticisms that had been leveled at that document's incautious affirmations, and on the whole indicates that a measure of self-discipline was beginning to take hold of the Separates. It therefore deserves a more complete exposition than has been given to the more local confessions. Its Westminster flavor is apparent in the first article, which confesses "one only living and true God, who is a Spirit of himself, from eternity unchangeably the same, Infinite in Wisdom, Power, Holiness, Justice, Goodness, and Truth; merciful, gracious, and omniscient God, and incomprehensibly glorious, and eternally happy in the possession and enjoyment of himself." The next article defines the Trinity as three persons in one essence, co-equal and co-eternal; "a mystery too deep for men or angels to unfold." A striking change appears in the third article, by the insertion of a phrase given here in small capitals:

> [We believe] That God, being infinite in knowledge, doth from all eternity perfectly see and know all things past, present, and to come; even to eternity did fore-ordain THAT whatsoever came to pass either by his order or permission, SHOULD BRING ABOUT HIS HONOR AND GLORY; and though God did not fore-ordain men to sin,

94. Ibid., p. 18.
95. Printed also in Denison, *Westerly and Its Witnesses*, pp. 95–98.

yet he did for the glory and honor of his great name fore-ordain the punishment for sin.

The Mansfielders had said simply that God foreordains whatever comes to pass.[96] The revision, it will be observed, greatly weakens the predestinarian character of the confession.

One of the criticisms of the Windham ministers against the Mansfield Confession was that while it mentioned the sin of Adam it neglected to say anything of the imputation of sin to his posterity. This was probably an unintentional oversight, rather than any weakening of the doctrine of original sin, and is corrected in the Frothingham version: the first man acted as the "public head or representative for all his posterity," and his fall "brought upon himself, and all his race, death temporal, spiritual, and eternal." The doctrine of the atonement in the first confession was quite Anselmian (this doubtless from Jonathan Edwards, who developed the theory of sin as "infinite" because against an infinite God and therefore requiring an infinite, i.e. eternal, punishment) and remains so here. But the typical Reformed insistence on a limited atonement is not quite so strong: Christ died "the accursed death for sinners," not for the elect. Later, however, it is said that he "made full satisfaction to the Infinite Justice of God for all elect."

In place of the much-protested Article xv of the Mansfield Confession, the Frothingham version has an entirely new declaration of the nature of salvation and assurance:

[We believe] That the Holy Spirit of God (proceeding from the Father and Son), he only can and doth make a particular application of the redemption (purchased by Christ) to every believer, as it is revealed in the word of God, namely, by convincing us of sin, of righteousness, and of judgment, and being utterly slain by the holy law of God, and completely conquered into the hands of a sovereign and absolute God, where we see Justice clear and God's throne guiltless if we were eternally damned. Thus being conquered, God the Holy Ghost revealed Jesus Christ in our souls, in his glory, power, love, and all-sufficiency; and for what we beheld in Jesus Christ, or the attributes of God, our souls accepted him freely upon gospel terms; and so the Lord wrought in our souls

96. Compare the Westminster Confession of Faith, chap. 3: "God from all eternity did, by the most wise and holy counsel of his own will, freely and unchangeably ordain whatsoever comes to pass; yet so as thereby neither is God the author of sin, nor is violence offered to the will of the creature."

faith and love, which was accompanied with a living union to Jesus Christ, and a new obedience which flows from an immortal principle of holiness and likeness to God; and hereby we are brought to trust our eternal all into the hands of this unchangeable and faithful God; and thus we come to the knowledge that we are elected òf God to eternal life, and that Jesus Christ has wrought out a pure, spotless righteousness for us, and is now, by virtue of his merits, interceding before the Father for us.

Several things are interesting here. The "particular application of redemption" is prominent at the beginning of the article. The revivalistic pattern of conversion, including an acknowledgment of the justice of God in the damnation of sinners, is set forth. The initiative of God in granting freely of his grace as the sinner's only hope is clearly asserted. The believer's union with Christ is made to depend upon the working of faith and love in the soul rather than on a mystical "partaking of the divine nature," and is explicitly said to issue in obedience to God. Thus at one stroke the antinomian and pantheistic tendencies of the Mansfield Confession are set aside. And to deny the possibility of perfection in this life, it is stated that the hope of sinners is never their own righteousness but Christ who continually intercedes in their behalf. As a further response to the prodding of their critics, the Separates omit entirely the article stating that all doubt in a believer is sinful and that faith is required before any act can be pleasing to God. An interesting sidelight on this last point is the fact that the Mansfielders (like so many pure church idealists before them) had demanded that the administrators of the ordinance must have faith to validate their ministry. The later version requires faith only in the participant, and makes no mention of the attitude of the administrator.

Many of the Articles of Practice in Frothingham's work were subsumed under Article xxii of the Mansfield Confession, and in both cases comprise statements about the church and its relation to the civil state. The emphasis of the Separates upon regenerate church membership is, if anything, stronger in the later document. And as a corollary to this belief, they will not relinquish the necessity of "good scriptural evidences and soul-satisfying knowledge of one another's union to Jesus Christ." Articles v and vi read:

> That, in order to the church's having a gospel evidence and knowledge of each person's qualifications for communion, we believe it is expedient and according to God's word, that every member admitted into the church do, before the church, publicly

make manifest of what they have experienced (more or less) of God's grace upon their hearts; and, upon the church's fellowship and satisfaction, be received into the privileges and watch of the church.

That at all times the door of the church shall stand open to every meet member, and at the same time be carefully kept against such as cannot give a satisfying evidence of a work of God upon their hearts, whereby they are united to Jesus Christ.

The rights of strict congregational churches with regard to determining their membership and disposing the officers are asserted in familiar terms. The privilege of laymen to respond to the promptings of the Spirit in the exercise of their gifts is jealously guarded. Local church members are qualified to act in the administering of church discipline or the determining of any matters of difficulty, although it may be advisable at times to seek the assistance and advice of sister churches; "yet their advice and counsels are not binding any further than they are instrumental of giving light."

Several additional articles in Frothingham's work are completely new, having appeared in no previous Separate confession of faith. They mostly express convictions which have been touched upon already. The gospel is to be supported by voluntary contributions, and those who neglect to give according to their ability may be subject to divine, but never civil, punishment. The seventh day commemorates God's finishing the work of creation, the first day commemorates Christ's finishing the work of redemption; therefore the seventh part of man's time is "to be spent in religious worship and improvement," and this is specifically to be the first day of the week. Marriage is appointed of God that male and female might become mutual helpmates (this is the only reason given, in contradistinction to traditional moral theology which usually adds the purposes of procreation and prevention of sin); it is for all persons that are "qualified to answer the end that God has proposed in that relation," but curiously the Separates do not add that it is the duty of Christians to marry only in the Lord.[97] Christians ought not to go to law with one another, "but all their differences and difficulties ought to be decided by the brethren." The article on the function of the magistrate is important enough to be given in full:

We believe God has ordained and appointed the ordinances of civil justice, to rule under God in the Kingdom of Providence,

97. Cf. Westminster Confession, chap. 24.

for the protecting and defending the poor as well as the rich in their civil rights and privileges, without either the major or minor having power to oppress or lord it over the one or the other. The work of the civil magistrates is to execute, and to punish the breaches of, moral precepts; they have no right to touch that which does infringe upon the conscience, nor order, nor dictate, in the worship of the living and dreadful God, for that belongs entirely to Jesus Christ, the great law-giver and head of the church.

Thus they do not reject magistracy, or say that no Christian should take part in government, but they deny the power of the state over individual conscience and corporate worship. Finally, there is a closing statement on eschatology—the first to appear in any Separate confession. Its presence here indicates, at the very least, the desire of the framers of this document to round out a complete doctrinal statement and not merely to deal with points in immediate controversy:

We believe there will be a general and final judgment, when all the sons and daughters of Adam (that have been, are, or shall be till Christ comes in like manner as he ascended) shall be summoned up into the awful, sweet, and glorious presence of the dreadful God, to be rewarded according as they have obeyed or disobeyed God, in the gospel of Jesus Christ; the righteous will be received into full, complete, and everlasting enjoyment of God; and the wicked will stand like ghastly damned ghosts, to receive a dreadful, heart-rending sentence from the Great Judge of quick and dead,—"Depart ye cursed into everlasting fire prepared for the devil and his angels"; and all heaven will own the sentence just, saying, "Amen, hallelujah, for the Lord God omnipotent reigneth. Amen, and Amen."

The Killingly Convention of 1781 gave some attention to doctrinal beliefs in its *Historical Narrative and Declaration*. This was not so much a confession of faith as it was an irenicon exploring the possibility of union with the regular Congregationalists. Like Melanchthon and Contarini, the framers of this document stress the similarity, rather than the differences of the two groups in schism. This was possible because by that time the regular churches had already restored many of the principles for which the Separates contended. The consociational system was much less authoritarian,[98] the Halfway Covenant

98. The Saybrook Platform was dropped from the statute books in 1784.

was falling into disuse, and toleration of dissent was substantially larger. The Strict Congregationalists at Killingly, therefore, reiterated their doctrinal concord with the best tradition of New England Puritanism in the hope of smoothing the way for further rapprochement with the "reformed" establishment.

> We agree to the Confession of Faith, agreed upon by the Synod at Boston, May 12, 1680 [the Reforming Synod approved the Savoy Declaration], and to the longer and shorter Catechisms, agreed upon by the Assembly of Divines at Westminster, as orthodox Systems of the Doctrines of the Christian Religion, as to the Substance of them. Ever holding the Word of God, contained in the Scriptures of the Old and New Testaments, to be the only perfect Rule of Faith and Practice.[99]

They enunciated their principles of polity in the familiar pattern of strict congregationalism, stressing the fact that "there is no Jurisdiction, to which particular Churches are or ought to be subject, by Way of authoritative Censure; nor any other Church Power, extrinsical to such Churches, which they ought to depend on any other sort of Men for the Exercise of." [100]

Nothing better illustrates the Separates' attitude toward the standing order in 1781 than "A Serious Address," a sort of circular letter to the churches appended to the Killingly *Declaration.* After observing that some forty years have passed since the "Great Reformation," it records encouragement over the slackening of persecution—though freedom is far from complete. But "the Lord hath inclined many of the established Ministers, and Churches, to adopt the same Principles, and Practice in Reformation, that first influenced us." [101] The best way of showing gratitude to God for this, the letter continues, is by walking purely, peaceably, and humbly according to the truth of God. The writers are especially sensitive about the censoriousness which has hampered their churches in the past, and advise now a more charitable spirit:

> We recommend to you to put away all rash, and party Zeal, in Matters of Religion; and to be cloathed with an humble, meek, and quiet Spirit. . . . to speak Evil of no Man, and especially

99. *An Historical Narrative and Declaration,* p. 25.

100. Ibid., p. 26. Here again an appeal is made (in a footnote) to the opinions and practices of the early Puritans of New England.

101. Ibid., p. 36.

not to traduce any Sect of Protestant Professors, by the hard harsh Names of Babylon, and Antichrist; knowing that others have as good a Right, to think and act for themselves as we have. But let us endeavour in Meekness, to instruct those that we think are out of the Way. We would put you in mind of the Sin of speaking Evil of Civil Rulers, a Sin that is too much prevailing at this Day we live in: It is a special Command of God, not to revile the Gods, nor speak Evil of the Ruler of thy People. We ought to consider their Administration, in this Day of Trouble, and Perplexity, and to pray for them according to the Direction given in the Gospel.[102]

This is followed by a warning to avoid "those damnable Errours, and Heresies, that are spreading in our Land"—not Arminianism but Universalism—and a caution to pay particular attention to the religious instruction of "our baptized Children," some of whom are following the ways of the world. The letter closes with the reminder that "practical Godliness is the final, and last Evidence you can give of your being the chaste Spouse, or true Church of Christ." [103] Thus, while by no means sacrificing any of the basic convictions which inspired their separation at the first, the Killingly Convention documents the moderating process which calmed the Separates in the passing of time.

102. Ibid.
103. Ibid., p. 38.

5. CHARACTERISTICS OF THE SEPARATES

John Leland once told a congregation, "My father was a Presbyterian and my mother a high-flying separate new-light." [1] This expresses succinctly the difference between the established churches and the Separates: the latter flew a little higher. In their striving for a pure church, in their strictness of congregational polity, and in their free forms of spiritual worship, they were quite conscious of moving on a level far above earthlings who groveled among traditions of human origin. Often accused of assuming a holier-than-thou attitude toward the established churches, [2] the Separates insisted that they were only returning to the more scriptural way of the early Puritans. Indeed, they considered that they were the real descendants of the Puritans and were now seeking to repurify churches which had apostatized from their original ideals. In this may be seen the classical pattern of religious reform: exaltation of an earlier era as the golden age of the church, belief in a decline or fall from that period of pristine purity and vital piety, and a striving to reproduce—usually without taking account of a changed social situation or the historical development of the church itself—the pattern of the golden age. Because of the limited historical understanding and social consciousness of many self-styled reformers, such movements sometimes become tragicomic caricatures of the ideal toward which they strive. In some ways this happened to the Separates; in other ways they contributed to a real reformation. The difference between caricature and contribution can be made clear by describing the characteristics of the Separate congregations, which will show how far they were able to implement their lofty claims in actual practice.

THE IDEAL OF THE PURE CHURCH

Erecting a pure church. The golden age for the Separates lay no farther back in history than the early Puritan era, when a testimony

1. "The History of Jack Nips," *The Writings of the Late Elder John Leland,* ed. Louise F. Greene (New York, 1845), p. 73.
2. This charge, of course, was easily turned back on the accusers. When a state-supported clergyman stigmatized a Separate as having gone "in the way of Cain and the rebellion of Korah," he implied that he alone was in the way of truth.

of personal religious experience was expected from everyone who applied for membership in a visible church. Though some doubts regarding the propriety of this were already arising in 1648, the Cambridge Synod nevertheless affirmed:

> The like tryall is to be required from such members of the church, as were born in the same, or received their membership, & were baptized in their infancy, or minority, by vertue of the covenant of their parents, when being grown up unto years of discretion, they shall desire to be made partakers of the Lords supper: unto which, because holy things must not be given unto the unworthy, therfore it is requisit, that these as well as others, should come to their tryall & examination, & manifest their faith & repentance by an open profession thereof, before they are received to the Lords supper, & otherwise not to be admitted there unto.[3]

In the decline of Puritan piety, and through the compromises represented by the Halfway Covenant and Stoddardeanism, the churches by the time of the Great Awakening were confessing that it was impossible to tell a true believer from a hypocrite and therefore useless to insist on a confession of faith. Under these conditions a church composed only of real saints was not to be expected or even an approximation attempted. This is why the ministers of Windham County could peremptorily condemn the Separates for saying "that it is the Will of GOD to have a pure Church on Earth, in this Sense, that all the Converted should be separated from the Unconverted."[4] But the revival reopened this issue with compelling force, convincing the New Lights that the churches not only could but must be purified.

The classic defense of the pure church ideal was put forth in 1749 by Jonathan Edwards, whose *Humble Inquiry into the Rules of the Word of God, Concerning the Qualifications Requisite to a Complete Standing and Full Communion in the Visible Christian Church* cost him his pastorate at Northampton the next year.[5] A few years earlier he had been unwilling "to meddle with that controversy" in public, although some unpublished notes indicate that he had already reached the conviction that a church should be a society of visible saints

3. Cambridge Platform, XII, 7. Admission to the Lord's Supper represented full church membership.
4. *A Letter from the Associated Ministers of the County of Windham*, p. 5.
5. Printed in *Works*, *1*, 83–192.

who are visibly *real* saints.[6] Edwards stood unalterably opposed to separatism, and hesitated to announce his view for fear of being branded as a Separate. But he was just as opposed to an artificial division of church members into professing saints and real saints, and the central thrust of his *Humble Inquiry* was an attempt to restore sincerity and meaning to the profession of sainthood.

> The question is not, whether Christ has made converting grace or piety itself the condition or rule of his people's admitting any to the privileges of members in full communion with them. . . . It is the credible profession and visibility of these things, that is the church's rule in this case.[7]

That is to say, to be a visible saint is to appear to be a real saint, not only to the eye of God (who cannot be fooled in any event) but also to human eyes. Such a standard deals with probability rather than certainty, offering no ironclad guarantee to keep out all hypocrites and thus establish a perfectly pure church. Edwards endorsed the use of both extreme care and Christian charity in judging the sincerity of professions of faith, and made it very plain that he would not countenance any sort of inner witness like the Separates' key of knowledge. Referring to them as "that wild enthusiastical sort of people, who have of late gone into unjustifiable separations, even renouncing the ministers and churches of the land in general, under pretence of setting up a pure church," he vehemently disowned their "notion of a pure church by means of a spirit of discerning." [8]

The Separates accepted his arguments for a church of real saints, but disagreed that it could be only approximated. One wrote to Edwards inquiring pointedly how, since he had described such an excellent new house, one could enter it without going out of the old one which was in such a ruined condition? Edwards answered that although the old house did seem to be in a sorry shape, he thought there was no call as yet to leave it.[9] It was Ebenezer Frothingham who joined the issue, publishing his *Articles of Faith and Practice* the year after Edwards' work appeared. His Discourse launches immediately into a proof of the proposition that "real believers in Jesus Christ, and

6. "Thoughts on the Revival of Religion in New England, 1740," *Works, 3,* 395. The unpublished miscellanies are cited in Thomas A. Schafer, "Jonathan Edwards' Conception of the Church," *Church History, 24* (1955), 58–59.

7. *Works, 1,* 90.

8. Ibid., pp. 86–87.

9. Backus, *History of New England, 2,* 92.

none but such, are members of the true church of Jesus Christ, and
have a right to all the gifts and privileges which Christ has left for
his church in this world." [10] After deploring Edwards' prejudice
against the Separates, which has caused him to judge them on the
basis of the errors of a few rather than the principles of the many
(thus violating the rules of his own "distinguishing marks" and opening him to the charge of censorious judging on his own part!), Frothingham gets to the main point of difference: Edwards would accept
a mere *profession* of godliness, which any hypocrite could make,
whereas the appellation "saint" is "peculiar to real Converts, or them
that have a living Union to Jesus Christ." [11] By requiring only a verbal
profession, Edwards has opened a door "wide enough for all moral
Hypocrites to come into the Church that can parrot or say over a Form
of Christian Experience." [12] To prevent this, Frothingham would substitute for Edwards' Christian charity the illumination of the understanding by divine light so that a right judgment could be formed:

> A Saint of God having Divine Light shining into the Understand-
> ing, and the Love of God (or pure Charity, which is the same),
> ruling in the Soul, is also to know certainly that such and such
> Persons are true Converts, or the Saints of God: And this Dis-
> cerning Knowledge, is not an immediate Discerning, like that of
> *Peter's* discerning *Annanias* and *Saphira;* no, but mediate in an
> ordinary Way, judging and knowing from the Fruits of the
> special sanctifying Grace, made visible and manifest to the
> spiritual Understanding, by the Improvement and Practice of the
> Saints. [13]

This is the basis on which the Separates claimed certain knowledge
of the saints, "so far forth as we stand in Divine Light," and on which
they formed their churches.

Such saints become a visible church, according to Frothingham,
"by being made visible by their visible Fruits of Holiness, and their
publickly declaring to each other their experimental Acquaintance
with Jesus Christ; by which Means they make Manifest to each other,
visible Fruits of their Saintship and Union to Christ, and so publickly
and solemnly renew their Covenant with God, and enter into Covenant
with each other, promising, that by the Grace of God assisting them,

10. *Articles of Faith and Practice*, pp. 8–9.
11. Ibid., p. 45.
12. Ibid.
13. Ibid., p. 47.

they will maintain the publick Worship of God, and carefully attend all the Institutions of the Gospel, walking as becomes the Followers of the Lamb of God." [14] Such a church once formed received new members upon the relation of their Christian experience only if the present members discovered "fellowship" with the applicant. A minute of the Preston Separate Church reads:

> Keziah Randal Desired to be Received Into ye felloship of this Church; at first felloship seemd to be wanting but after Strict Examination and Prayers mad for Direction the witness was obtained so far that she was Received Into full Communion: to be one with us to Injoy all Gospill Previledges.

If fellowship was wanting, the applicant was not admitted.

Even evangelicals in the standing order objected to the substitution of "soul-satisfying knowledge" for more objective evidences of conversion because it made "a Person's Right to be treated outwardly as a Christian . . . depend upon the Fancy or secret Judgment of others who think themselves Christians." [15] Robert Ross carried this critique further by pointing out that there might be a community of feeling between hypocrites just as easily as between real saints. In fact, he averred, the scheme of the Separates practically encouraged hypocrisy for the sake of being accepted:

> There is a probability that Hypocrites will have Fellowship with Hypocrites from the sameness of their Experiences. As they are not much restrained by Modesty and Humility, but ambitious to be accounted eminent Christians, their open Freedom and Forwardness will give them great Influence.

By the same token, the modesty of true Christians will open them to suspicion and thus tend to exclude them from the "pure" churches. Continual recitation of intimate religious experiences not only fosters ostentation but furnishes a ready device to censure and condemn all with whom the Separates disagree for any reason.[16]

14. Ibid., p. 152.
15. *The Result of a Council of the Consociated Churches of the County of Windham,* p. 15.
16. *A Plain Address,* p. 72. This point is developed at length by Tracy in a paragraph of real insight: "A man may very naturally 'feel his heart going out in love' towards another, when both are deeply tinctured with the same faults, and especially if both are sinfully bitter against the same enemies. . . . Among those who are thus bound together, party spirit naturally usurps the name and place of brotherly love; hatred of opponents passes for zeal for God; and defamation and bitter railings are counted Christian boldness" (*Great Awakening,* p. 321).

The granting of Christian fellowship only on the basis of an inner witness, however, was but a temporary phase of the Separate movement. The claim that a true Christian might be known from a hypocrite "as easily as a sheep might be known from a dog" was later abandoned. But the ideal of the pure church remained at the heart of their convictions. The Killingly Convention of 1781 explicitly disclaimed the possibility of absolute knowledge of any person's spiritual state. What their churches generally demanded, they said, was credible profession of genuine repentance, vital faith, and personal relation to Jesus Christ.

> In order for a Church to receive a Person into Membership, it is Necessary, that they be well satisfied of the Truth and Reality of what he professes to have; and the most proper Means to be attended to, in Order to obtain a satisfaction, is to examine the Person, into his Knowledge of his lost and undone Estate by Nature; and of the Way of Salvation through a Redeemer; and of the Exercises of his Heart towards God: And also to consider and view the Life, and Conversation of the Person in the World. In which Things, if the Church be satisfied, they have good Right to extend their Charity to such an One, as a real Disciple of Jesus Christ, without pretending to an absolute Knowledge, of the Estate of his Soul.[17]

To answer the charge that the Separates alone considered themselves to be true Christians, the brethren at Killingly made it plain that all who offer themselves "in a professed Heart Subjection to Jesus Christ, as their rightful Lord and Sovereign, to be ruled and governed by his Law prescribed in his Word" are to be accepted as the friends of Christ. But those who do not make this profession, and disclaim or doubt that they are truly regenerated, cannot be considered as true Christians nor their so-called churches true churches. Thus at the close of the first generation of Separates, they returned to essentially the same position for which Jonathan Edwards argued in 1749.

Maintaining a pure church. The pure church ideal demands not only care in admitting members but the exercise of strict disciplinary watch over those already admitted. Most of the church covenants used by the Separates included an explicit agreement to be subject to the discipline of the church. The Canterbury Separates carefully spelled out all that this involved:

17. *An Historical Narrative and Declaration*, p. 18.

We do allso promise by the grace of God to oppose all sin and Error in our selves as far as in us Lyes and in others allso when Ever they appear viz: all foolish talking and Jesting, Chambring and Wontoness all Vaine disputings about words and things that gender strife and doth not Edifie to more Godliness, allso vaine Company keeping and spending Time Idlelly at Taverns; typling Houses or Els where; Evil whisperings or Backbiting of any Persons, allso Carnal and unnecessary forsaking the Assembling our selves in private Conveniant Conferences, and allso on the Sabath days, and all other Sins whatsoever both of Omition and Commition— [18]

They took this obligation quite seriously, and whenever any breach of conduct came to the attention of the church the offender was cited to appear and give account of himself. For example, the Canterbury church voted on January 28, 1746/7 that "with Refferrance to those persons who . . . have not held Comu'n with this Church in Renewing Cov'nt &c: will Call upon them by our pastor to appear or meet with this Church at their meeting house on the first thirdsday of march next at ten oClock in the moring to give the Reasons of their neglect &c." [19] Such cases were frequent.

When a church did not take steps to discipline an unruly member, or when the steps taken were not considered stringent enough, an aggrieved party might carry his appeal to other Separate churches. Extant records are filled with pleas for help from churches which could not solve their problems of spiritual delinquency or personal differences. On November 28, 1751, Joseph Markham of Enfield wrote to Canterbury in great distress:

Beloved in the Lord for help I wright to you by an agreement with the church of Enfield: for we have had two metens & a:jurned meten with the helps from Som other Churches as witness in the Case of Dificolty wich you may Com to the understanding of my Coming to the help of the Lord for the honer of god lyes at Stake & Siners are going bleeding to hell—Non as a body Stands as a witness in that Case to them for there is the mystrey of enecyty Got into this Church where as if it is not Searched out it will Destroy this body of Saints as a Church here wich will be grately to the wounding of the Cause of Christ

18. *Records of the Congregational Church in Canterbury*, pp. 19–20.
19. Ibid., p. 15.

> & to Strengthen of the hands of siners, there fore help help help for the Cause of god: amen, we have a greede that on the 18 day of December Next to met on the Case a gain with the helps of other Churches they agree for Elder molten with Som other helps to be here on said day where as I Desire that gods witness as maney as god Shall Call may apear here on Sd day—& O that the living Child may Not be denied—& So I wright as a witness for god desiren your help [20]

This extremely weighty case, which, judging from the urgent plea, seems to have been about to tear the church apart, arose over the perfidy of Markham's servant, Benjamin Simons. Not only had Simons married against the advice of his master but he had proved a poor steward of his master's goods while the latter was in prison "for the testimony of Jesus." That the church had refused to discipline Simons (who was also a member) for this "Damig to my outward Estate and wounding of the Cause of Christ" grieved Markham sorely. The council, which included Solomon Paine of Canterbury and Thomas Stevens of Plainfield, upheld Markham, admonished Simons to make "gospel satisfaction," and advised the church to keep a closer watch on discipline.

Dragging into the arena of church action this personal quarrel, which eventually required several councils before it could be settled to the complainant's satisfaction, points up a serious problem in the inner life of the Separate societies. Their extreme concern that nothing be allowed to mar the purity of the fellowship in Christ led to a morbid preoccupation with the private life of each member. And since every member possessed the key of knowledge by which he might know the state of every other member's soul, it was all too easy to turn the key against anyone who might appear the least bit disagreeable. Thus a person admitted to the church in absolute certainty that he was truly a saint was never immune from later suspicion about his spiritual state:

> If a brother or sister did not feel a positive interflowing of sympathy and affection with some particular person, some hidden sin was the cause which must be sought out, detected, confessed and brought to judgment before they could commune together at the Lord's table. Every church member considered himself his brother's keeper. The most trivial derelictions from duty were noted and

20. Quoted in Means, *The Strict Congregational Church in Enfield*, pp. 40–41.

reported, and espionage and tale-bearing encouraged as if they were cardinal virtues. . . . Every man was at the mercy of the "inward actings" of his neighbor's soul.[21]

Illustrations of this are legion. More than one-third of the perfectly known, fully assured saints of the Canterbury church were suspended or expelled during the first three years of its existence. John and Ebenezer Cleaveland, who were expelled from Yale College for loyalty to this church, were both excommunicated from it in 1749 for presuming to question its infallibility. At Norton, Massachusetts, one brother claimed that a sister church member had broken fellowship with him and joined with the world simply because she preferred to walk to the meeting with her husband who was not a Christian rather than with the complainant who was.[22] At Westerly, Rhode Island, a raging dispute over church discipline eventually split the church; pastor Stephen Babcock thought all matters should be settled by the "divine testimony," i.e. certain impulses and impressions, while the faction under deacon Simeon Brown maintained that such questions were to be decided by moral and scriptural evidence. Pastors were frequently in trouble because they did not conform to every contentious member's idea of what they ought to be and do. This sort of uninhibited fault-finding and invoking of disciplinary procedures to settle real or fancied personal grievances was undoubtedly a major factor in the disintegration of many Separate churches. The crossing of evidence in charges and countercharges left many to wonder where the truth really lay. One woman cried in dismay, "I would not write a line counter to the work of God if I knew where it was, but I have got so bewildered and sunk that I can't tell where the work of God is." [23] The ideal church, which the Separates hoped to erect and maintain by withdrawing from those churches that had already traversed the long road of declining piety and diluted purity, proved for them also to be an ever-eluding *ignis fatuus*.

Mutual Relations of the Churches

Because of the strenuous opposition of the Separates to the authoritarian consociational system, it is pertinent to inquire how they conducted their own interchurch affairs. Already there have been numerous references to councils called by the Separate churches to

21. Larned, *History of Windham County, 1,* 470.
22. Chaffin, *History of Easton,* p. 175.
23. Larned, *History of Windham County, 1,* 475.

discuss specific problems. It has been pointed out repeatedly that the churches were jealous of their independence and regarded a conciliar decision as purely a piece of advice with no ultimately binding authority. A summary of the functioning of councils will show, however, that in spite of strong centrifugal forces among the Separates these gatherings helped to foster a corporate consciousness that at one time promised to produce a self-sufficient denomination. Interchurch meetings were generally of two sorts: occasional councils called by some individual church or group to deal with a specific need of the moment, and the larger general conferences which dealt with matters that affected all the Separate churches.

Occasional local councils. These meetings were called usually for one of two purposes, either to organize a church and/or ordain a pastor, or to adjudicate a church quarrel. The number of councils called for the first purpose was highest during the decade of 1745–55, when most of the Separate churches were being formed; after 1755 most of the occasional councils were attempts to restore peace in churches plagued by friction and dispute.

It is clear that whenever neighboring ministers were invited to assist in ordaining a pastor, they appeared as representatives of their own churches and acted on the authority of the ordaining church. That is to say, the power of ordination was vested in the local church, not in the ministers; and the presence of other ministers at a service of ordination was not a necessity but a courtesy to sister churches. Yet their presence was an admission that even independent churches were to some extent interdependent.

The form of service usually followed that of historic Congregationalism, and differed little from the practice of the standing churches except in where the locus of authority was thought to lie. The candidate would be examined as to his doctrinal soundness and "denominational loyalty"; the evidence was inward fellowship, of course, and sometimes it pointed to the rejection of the candidate.[24] One who met the test would be charged with his awful responsibility as a spiritual leader, and given the hand of fellowship in his new undertaking. One of the more mature ministers present would preach a suitable sermon.

Ordinations were doubtless pleasant occasions, "attended with much

24. A group of Separates near New London asked for the ordination of a pastor on Sept. 9, 1752. Parke wrote in his church records: "Upon Examination the Council Concluded the Man Purposed for to be ordained was not Qualifyed: Where upon he was Not ordained."

of Gods Presents." It was quite otherwise when it became necessary
to draw "the Sword of Disapline" in answer to a church's request
"to advise in sartaine Diffecolties sabsisting amongst them." [25] Pleas
of this nature came with increasing frequency from such places as
Lyme, East Lyme, North Groton, Norwich (Bean Hill), Franklin,
Newent, Canterbury, and Enfield. In 1756 there was an urgent call
for a peace council from "some agreived Br of a *Church* in the Nine
Partners," i.e. Amenia, New York, where Abraham Paine had been
pastor since 1750. Paul Parke recorded on May 21, 1758, that he had
"Received a lettor from the Remaining Part of the *Church* of Christ in
the [Preston] long Society desiring us to Send Brn to give them advise Respecting there Broken scatred Conditton." More often than
not, the difficulties revolved around professed dissatisfaction with
the pastor. This brother found himself in the same position as many
of the members—an infallible approbation of his gifts at the time
of his call did not save him from criticism later. Because the person of the minister was in no case sacrosanct, he was subject to conciliar
admonition and censure, just as any other member.

Two illustrations of this situation will suffice. The Enfield Separate
Church was far from calm after Joseph Markham had won his point
before a series of councils. Some of the members (probably the Markham faction) commenced a labor with the pastor for alleged inat-
tention to duty. A council—convened on June 24, 1752, and moderated by Solomon Paine—censured the pastor for infidelity to his
ordination vows, saying:

> altho the pastor hath walked Clear of Scandal as a member except
> this wrangling and Confessed the Substance of what the brethren
> had Charged him with (viz) that he had neglected to feed and
> lead the church and to disapline them that were out of the way,
> yet it is Evident that he hath broken his Solemn ordination pastoral
> Covenant and all his Renewidly promising to do better hath been
> only saying I go sir—and went not and the flock Rent with divitions
> and he Still neglected to take them by the hand as a pastor ought
> to do to heal and lead them there fore Stands guilty of Breach of
> Covnant.[26]

Another case was at New London, where Joshua Morse, pastor of
the Separate church in the north parish, was already under admoni-

25. Request from Colchester Separate Church, in Records of the Preston Separate Church, Sept. 28, 1755.
26. Quoted in Means, p. 43. The pastor's name at this date is not known.

tion for broaching views that eventually led him into the ranks of the Baptists. The pedobaptist party in his church called for another council, which found him openly in contempt of the previous admonition. He was unrepentant and "slited the admonition, Where upon he was Excommunicated." [27]

Actions of this sort obviously invested the occasional council with a measure of ecclesiastical authority, indicating that, in spite of themselves, the very men who had complained so loudly of conciliar power in the establishment could not resist the temptation to meddle in the internal affairs of their own churches. Backus says that when peace councils were called, "they were received into fellowship with the church that wanted advice; and when they had heard the case, and given their advice, in many instances the council acted with the church in censuring delinquents; though sometimes there were more of the council than of the acting members of the church." [28] Two passages from his diary indicate this peculiar practice:

> Wednesday, May 8 [1751]. We met together, and there came brother S. Paine, T. Stevens, S. Wadsworth, Drown, Shepherd, Carpenter and some others; and, after prayer, brother John Paine said that our work he viewed to be this: that because they were so broken that they were not capable of acting as a church in dealing with some that had sinned, therefore we should embody together there as a church to hear and try those cases.

> Wednesday, January 15 [1752]. I went, being sent for, to Bridgewater Town, to a church meeting, and brother Carpenter was there; and we were taken into their fellowship to act with them upon the case of some that have transgressed in this church.[29]

Thus the authority of the local church was transferred to the council, from whose decisions there was no appeal—except perhaps to another council with different composition. This seemed to preserve the autonomy of the individual churches, which would never have granted to a general body (consociation, synod, convention, etc.) the powers they gave readily to the occasional councils. While no visible coercion appeared, the acceptance of conciliar authority even under the guise of church power marks the decline of extreme independency among the Separate churches. Through the use of these councils in-

27. Records of the Preston Separate Church.
28. *History of New England, 2,* 90.
29. Ibid., p. 90 n.

telligence passed freely, advice was readily asked and offered, and a feeling of oneness began to emerge.

General conference meetings. Three matters of common concern drew together all the Separate churches into gatherings of a more denominational character: the need to make a concerted attack on the oppression of dissenters by the standing order, the desire to formulate a generally acceptable platform of faith and practice, and the effort to work out a viable relationship with the increasing numbers of Baptists within their ranks.[30]

The disability of the Separates before the law was the primary catalyst in their earliest cooperative endeavors. For example, Solomon Paine and Matthew Smith carried to the General Assembly in 1748 a petition bearing the names of 330 persons in eastern Connecticut who desired exemption from ecclesiastical taxes to the established ministry. The next year Isaac Backus traveled the length of Cape Cod and visited nearly every Separate church in southeastern Massachusetts gathering signatures for a similar petition to be presented to the General Court. Efforts like these created a sense of unity among the scattered Separate churches. The first general meeting of Separates in Connecticut was called by the Preston Separate Church to consider methods to free themselves from the onerous tax. Their records for January 17, 1753, read:

> This Church meet to Consult whether we ought not to Send to our Cyvil Rulers: to Request them to Put an End to the Oppression; for it is very greate and many Suffer &c. And we agreed to Send to the Churches in General to meet on the Second Tuesday of March Next to Consult what Israel ought to do.

This meeting was held at Norwich on March 21, and Paul Parke noted with satisfaction that the churches "were very wonderfully all of one Mind." Other general conferences for the same purpose followed this one, and it is not difficult to see how such meetings operated to create a unity of common purpose.

Drawing together for mutual defense, of course, produces a purely negative union which may hide temporarily some rather deep differences. The Separates sensed this, and were soon exploring areas of positive agreement. Their first public manifesto which had more than local significance consisted of the confession and the covenant published by Ebenezer Frothingham in 1750. These were drawn and subscribed by a large convention of churches, and were intended to

30. On the last point, see below, pp. 260–64.

represent the doctrinal consensus among the Separates at that time. Like the decision of a council, they were binding no further than they were believed to agree with God's Word; and like previous Congregational confessions of faith, they were subject to revision as need dictated. In printing the articles, Frothingham observed that though they had summarized the truth then grasped, the saints must not rest in the light they now have but press on to deeper apprehension and understanding.[31] Following this reasoning, both individual churches and general conferences met from time to time to revise their articles of faith. The first call for a general meeting to consider a new confession came apparently from the Preston Separate Church on March 21, 1759. The results of this meeting, if it was ever held, have not come to light; but doubtless the subject came up from time to time and was discussed energetically even if no decisive action was taken.[32]

The year when the Separates may be said to have emerged as a denomination is 1781. On September 9, the Preston church chose four messengers "to attend a General meeting of all the Churches of our constitution, to agree upon a general confession of faith; and Rules of Disapline for said Churches to meet at Killingly September 19th 1781." This was the Killingly Convention, whose published *Historical Narrative and Declaration* has already been discussed. This convention represents the fruition of the tentative expressions of interdependency implied in the earlier occasional councils and general conferences. The assembled messengers declared: "We agree that particular Churches ought not to walk so distinct, and separate from each other, as not to have Care and Tenderness one towards the other; but ought by mutual advice and brotherly Intercourse, to strengthen and encourage each others Hearts and Hands in the ways of the Lord."[33] That this points toward some sort of permanent organizational structure is made clear in a later paragraph:

> In order to maintain Fellowship and Union among the Churches, and for the Assistance of each other, in some difficult Cases, it is

31. *Articles of Faith and Practice*, p. 29. The doctrinal content of the confession was summarized above, pp. 152–56.

32. On June 13, 1766, the Canterbury Separate Church voted to "answer the Request of the Eldors of our sister Churches By Sending our paster (Br marshal) and Brr Josiah Cleaveland to Carray our Confession of faith and Covenant to Norwich att their meeting att Norwich on the Next thirsday after the Last Wensday in this month" (*Records of the Congregational Church in Canterbury*, p. 26).

33. *An Historical Narrative and Declaration*, p. 30.

expedient that Churches meet together by their Delegates, or otherways, to consult, and advise with each other about such Things, as shall be for their general Good and Benefit. . . . [We agree] that we will have a General Meeting of our several Churches, by Delegation, annually on the Third Wednesday of September, for the Purpose abovesaid; the First to be at Plainfield, September next.[34]

The convention closed with the adoption of "A Serious Address," a circular letter of advice and encouragement to the churches of their constituency—a practice for which there was ample precedent among the Baptist associations that had been functioning for many years prior to 1781.[35]

This meeting marks the beginning of the Strict Congregational Convention of Connecticut. The intention to meet annually was fulfilled, and each year the delegates gathered at some place designated by vote the previous year. The records of the Separate churches show that shortly before the time for the annual meeting, delegates were duly elected to represent them. Separate churches on Long Island were a part of this body until 1791, when they were dismissed to form the Long Island Convention of Strict Congregational Churches. The parent body probably did not survive the end of the century, since by that time most of its constituent churches had dispersed, emigrated, rejoined the regular Congregationalists, or passed into the Baptist fold; but the Long Island Convention in 1839 counted nine churches with over one thousand members.[36] The next year these were absorbed into the association of regular Congregational churches, which were in close relations with the Presbyterians of the Middle Colonies. It is interesting to notice that the Connecticut Convention began to function more and more as an ecclesiastical body rather than as a voluntary association for inspiration and mutual counsel. Ministers apparently were ordained by it for the churches, rather than as before when the churches themselves handled ordinations. It is significant that this development took place only in Connecticut, always the home of closer ecclesiastical connectionalism. The Separates of Massa-

34. Ibid., pp. 31–32.
35. The Philadelphia Baptist Association, formed in 1707, began the practice of sending out an annual circular letter in 1729. Other associations formed later followed suit and likewise exchanged letters of correspondence among themselves, which had no small influence in developing a self-conscious unity among American Baptists in the eighteenth century.
36. Blake, *The Separates,* pp. 138–39.

chusetts and elsewhere made little attempt to develop an organic denominational life.

Manner of Preaching and Worship

There is perhaps no area in which the "high flying" of the Separate New Lights is more apparent than in their manner of preaching and worship. In their early and enthusiastic stages, their unrestrained response to the promptings of the Spirit in worship resulted in a type of pentecostal fervor. Candid observers had difficulty at times in separating the expressions of the Spirit from the excesses of the flesh.

The improvement of spiritual gifts. A fundamental tenet of the Separates was that every converted man not only stood in divine light but had some sort of gift by which he could reflect that light to others. This usually took the form of exhorting, which passed quickly into lay preaching; and those who by trial of their gifts convinced their fellow church members that God had indeed called them to preach could be set apart for the ministry of the Word. If a lay brother evidenced a gift for preaching, the church expected that he would exercise it as a faithful steward. A minute of the Canterbury Separate Church illuminates this point:

> Voted that this Church give Br Cleaveland fellowship in his gifts and Calling and Desier that he Improve as god Shall give him grase and opertunity and allso that Every member of this Church Cum forward to Improve the giftes god hath given for the Edifycation of the Body.[37]

This was, in fact, the way most of the Separate churches obtained their pastors. After the trial of several members' gifts, the church could examine the "evidences" and discern the one to whom the Spirit was directing them.

In spite of the freedom they allowed in the improvement of spiritual gifts, the Separates strove to maintain a measure of order and propriety. Persons who did not subject the exercise of their talents to church control were censured. By the time of the Killingly Convention, the limits of lay preaching were firmly established. Disowning the notion that every brother in the church has an unrestrained right to preach, pray, or exhort publicly, the assembled messengers said:

> Now to set this Affair in a true Light, we say, that we believe it to be the Duty of all professing Christians, to let their Light shine

37. *Records of the Congregational Church in Canterbury*, p. 25. Josiah Cleaveland was the father of John and Ebenezer.

in the World, so that their Life, and Conversation, might be one continued Preachment to others: But that every Brother hath a Right to set up to be a Publick Teachers, or Exhorter in the Church, we deny: It is our Opinion, that all those Brethren in a Church, that have Gifts given them, that are for the Edification of the Church, ought to be improved in the Church, in their proper Place; and to be subject to the Government and Direction of the Church. And in order that a Church may know the gifts they have among them, it is necessary that there be an open Door for the Proof, and Trial of those Gifts that they have; and when the Church has made Proof and Trial of the Gifts, and Abilities of any one Brother, and find them to be for the Edification of the Church; then the Church ought to approve of them, by giving them their Fellowship, or Approbation to improve their Gifts among them, and to recommend them to the Acceptance of others. And this we apprehend is a sufficient Licence, for any Man to preach, as a Candidate for the Gospel Ministry.[38]

Just as in the effort to approximate the ideal of the pure church, the Separates here returned to a position quite similar to that outlined by Jonathan Edwards in 1742.[39]

Mouthpiece of the Spirit. Preaching was serious business. The Separate preacher had an immediate sense of speaking under direct inspiration. This implied several things. First, it meant that previous preparation was unnecessary. The often-repeated charge that the Separates repudiated all human learning is not exactly true; it was mainly the *substitution* of literary polish for the leading of the Spirit to which they objected. Many of the Separates conceded the desirability of ministerial training, and endorsed the establishment of the Shepherd's Tent at New London. Only after such schools were outlawed did some of the more radical ones fall back on the all-sufficiency of immediate inspiration.

If the Separates are accused of making ignorance a theological virtue, it could be retorted that the standing order left them no alternative. They were neither permitted to attend the established schools nor conduct their own, which in itself was enough to provoke vigorous antieducation sentiments. In any case, the doctrine of immediate inspiration was of considerable comfort to men who could not obtain formal instruction even had they desired it. One Separate

38. *An Historical Narrative and Declaration,* p. 19.
39. See above, p. 58, n. 52.

was anxious not to be known as an enemy to learning, "for true Learning is what I highly prize"; but he insisted "it is horrid Presumption to pretend to limit the Most High to any Schools, or Bodies of People whatsoever, and to say that he shall have none for his *Ambassadors* but such as Men have trained for that Purpose in their way." [40] An internal call to preach was after all the only *essential* qualification for a minister.

Secondly, the use of notes in preaching was leaning on the flesh rather than listening to the Spirit. In fact, one reason for separating had been that the minister brought a manuscript into the pulpit, then prayed for divine assistance in delivering his sermon—rank hypocrisy! [41] This is what was behind Trumbull's assertion that Paul Parke was advised at his ordination not to premeditate what he should preach but to rely completely on the Spirit for both content and delivery of his sermon. Backus feared that the use of notes in preaching permitted unscrupulous men to impose on their congregations by reading high-sounding works of other divines. Besides, "I am sensible that many will own that when a minister has faith in exercise, he can preach better without *notes* than with them." [42]

A third implication of the preacher as a mouthpiece for the Holy Spirit was that spiritual rapport with the congregation was absolutely necessary if Separate sermonizing was to be successful. Rapport is a mutual affair, obviously, and it was as necessary for the congregation to empathize with the preacher as vice versa. The Separates' extreme emphasis on inward religious experience meant that they judged the preacher according to whether he furthered or hindered those experiences. This was the test of whether he really was a spokesman for God or not.

A most notorious problem with rapport occurred at North Stonington, where Matthew Smith served as the first pastor of the Separate church.[43] He had been a deacon in the Separate church at Mansfield

40. Backus, *All True Ministers* (Boston, 1754), preface, p. xii.

41. Cf. Fish, *The Church of Christ a Firm and Durable House,* p. 149. The Separates regarded the reading of sermons as another departure from early Puritanism. Backus pointed to Stoddard's reference to it as "a *late* practice of *some* ministers" (*A Fish Caught in His Own Net,* p. 72).

42. *A Fish Caught in His Own Net,* p. 74.

43. There are four primary accounts of this controversy, all differing in several details. I have attempted to reconstruct what actually took place from the following sources: Fish (pastor of the standing church in North Stonington), *The Church of Christ a Firm and Durable House,* p. 145; idem, *The Examiner Examined* (New London, 1771), p. 106; Backus (who was present at Smith's elec-

before he began to preach on trial to the Separates at North Stonington. According to Joseph Fish, he was chosen pastor by revelation:

> The brethren, at a meeting, appointed for the purpose, having an
> *impression,* that if it was the Lord's will that they should have a
> minister, he would shew it to them, and *reveal* the *man's* name, or
> shew them *the very man.* Upon *this,* one of their number, in a
> vision or swoon, had a revelation that he *himself* was to be their
> minister: but the brethren not having fellowship with him in that
> discovery, rejected *his* revelation; though he declared to me he
> knew it to be from heaven.

Isaac Backus said that on this occasion (Nov. 27, 1746) several Separate preachers were present and advised that if any man felt called to
assume the pastorate he should make it known. The man of whom
Fish speaks "fell into a strange frame, and then made the declaration
which Mr. *F.* speaks of: which struck a visible damp upon the assembly, as being an *unexpected* thing, and none concurred therewith." The rest of the day was spent in worship. A case of discipline
was attended to; and when the guilty brother confessed his fault, it
"gave as visible a quickening to their minds, as the other declaration
had a damp: and a leading brother in the church being much over-
come, took hold of Mr. *Smith* (who was expected before to be their
minister) and told him he was the man to go before them; and all
concurred therewith."

Smith was ordained on December 10, and it would seem that after
this marvelous concurrence of spiritual evidences he should have had
a happy and fruitful pastorate. His testimony, however, indicates quite
the contrary:

> Soon after I was ordained at Stonington I preached to the people
> from Ephes. ii, 22, in a clear Line of Gospel Truth: all on a sudden
> I perceived that the Church did not give me Fellowship . . . we
> parted in great Confusion. . . . We must see Eye to Eye or my
> lips will be forever sealed. The labouring point [whatever it was is
> never described] could not be gained. I took a tour into the
> Country—returned before sacrament day. The Church desired me
> to proceed as usual. I objected and refused. Then the Church called
> a Council and charged me with Neglect of Duty [but said] we
> have nothing against Brother Smith, and so every man went to his

---

tion), *A Fish Caught in His Own Net,* p. 92; and Smith's own version, told to
Ezra Stiles and printed in *The Literary Diary of Ezra Stiles, 1,* 203.

Tent. —After a few Sabbaths my Mouth was quite stopped that I could not speak for Want of Fellowship. All this happened in about the space of one year after my ordination.

Smith must have thought that the situation was hopeless, for soon after this he moved his family back to Mansfield. Another year passed. The church called a second council to deal with the delinquent pastor; it met at North Stonington on July 20, 1750, and summoned him to answer the charge that he had left without proper dismission. Paul Parke, who was present at this council, wrote in his records:

We met on the Day aforesaid with many Bretheren frome several Churches: the Cause was Diligently looked into: and it appeared he had Causlessly Rent away: and was gilty of Breach of Covenant; and stood now in opposition to the work of God; the holy Ghost witnessing: unreclaimed and Blinded with Error: Wherefore the Command of God upon us was to Excommunicate him from our felloship: and Pronounce him uncleane Which was done in the Power of our Lord Jesus Christ.

Smith said, after there had been a full hearing of the charges against him,

The Moderator turning to me says—there is some accursed Thing with you, that you, by your softness, hide from us: and for which I now, in the Name of the Lord Jesus, declare you unworthy to have a standing in his House, and hereby cut you off from all Priviledges in the same, and deliver you over to the Buffettings of the Devil. Another of the Council says, I as a Friend to the Bridegroom, and in the Name of the Bride the Lamb's Wife, declare you unfit to walk the streets of the New Jerusalem, and hereby do cast you out of the same, and set you down in the cold Shades of Antichrist and the dark Lanes of Babylon, to be buffetted by the Devil, and eat no more of the Children's Bread. Another says, as you are now excommunicated by the holy Ghost you will soon *feel* and *curse* like a Devil. And so the matter ended.

Backus, who rather deplored the entire incident, adds that three or four years later Smith revisited the church, confessed his fault, and was forgiven. This is admittedly an extreme case throughout, and is hardly typical of general Separate practice, but it illustrates the extent to which belief in immediate spiritual inspiration was sometimes pushed.

A final aspect of speaking in and for the Spirit was the notion that an inspired preacher must even *sound* different. The "holy whine" became so characteristic of Separate preaching that it deserves examination. The father of persuasive intonation in revivalistic sermonizing is unquestionably George Whitefield, whose dramatic delivery was made doubly impressive by "that godly tone." In this, as in other respects, Whitefield had imitators who were hardly more than caricatures of the great master. None was more determined a copyist, or more perverse an influence, than James Davenport. It was from him that the holy whine was taken up, to become a hallmark of Separate preachers. At North Stonington, Joseph Fish said that Davenport extended his voice to the highest pitch.

> And all this, with a strange, unnatural *singing* tone, which mightily tended to *raise* or *keep up* the affections of weak and undiscerning people, and consequently, to heighten the confusion among the *passionate* of his hearers. Which odd and ungrateful *tuning* of the *voice*, in exercises of devotion, has, from thence, been propagated down to the present day [1765], and is become *one* of the characteristicks of a *false spirit*, and especially of a *separate*; that sect being almost universally distinguished by such a *tone*.[44]

The adjective "universally" is well chosen. This tone was carried wherever the Separates went, to the northern and western frontiers, and to the South by the Separate Baptists. Thus the memoirist of Caleb Nichols, who went from Rhode Island to Vermont, could say that "his preaching is spiritual and animating, pretty full of the musical 'New Light' tone"; and one who had firsthand acquaintance with the Separates in the South could write:

> The *Separates* in N. England had acquired a very warm and pathetic address, accompanied by strong gestures and a singular tone of voice. Being often deeply affected themselves while preaching, correspondent affections were felt by their pious hearers, which were frequently expressed by tears, trembling, screams, shouts and acclamations.[45]

John Leland reported that sometimes he was laughed at in school for reading with the New Light tone; "once, in particular, as I was

44. *The Church of Christ a Firm and Durable House,* pp. 116–17.
45. Henry Crocker, *History of the Baptists in Vermont* (Bellows Falls, Vt., 1913), p. 24; Robert B. Semple, *A History of the Rise and Progress of Baptists in Virginia* (Richmond, 1810), p. 4.

reciting a lesson, to a Latin master, he told me 'not to preach like a new-light, but to speak like a scholar.' " [46]

There is perhaps a partly natural explanation for the holy whine. Most of these preachers spoke frequently in the open air to large crowds under great excitement for a long time. Under such conditions, an overstrained voice finds relief by rising and falling much as a person standing still does by shifting his weight periodically. Witness, for example, the singsong tones of auctioneers and newsboys. This natural necessity, combined with a desire to imitate the master revivalists of the past, surrounded the holy whine with an aura of sanctity. A professor of homiletics noted that such preaching was still in vogue in certain circles more than a century after the Great Awakening. "The whine of the preacher, associated for many ignorant hearers with seasons of impassioned appeal from the pulpit, and of deep feeling on their own part, has become a musical accompaniment which gratifies and impresses them, and like a tune we remember from childhood, revives 'the memory of joys that are past, pleasant and mournful.' " [47] To the first generation of Separates, it was an unmistakable mark of a man who spoke as a mouthpiece of the Holy Spirit.

The Spirit and the flesh. Persons under the influence of powerful religious feeling often found it difficult to control the physical effects of their overwrought emotions. At any rate, "crying out,—falling down, —Twitchings and convulsive Motions,—Foamings and Frothings,— Trances and Visions and Revelations" [48] which early began to mar the revival were taken by the Separates as evidences of the power of God in their midst. The opponents of the revival undoubtedly exaggerated these manifestations, just as the more sober friends of the Awakening tried to minimize them; but Davenport and the Separates after him were ready to pronounce the subjects of seizure as genuinely converted. Unconvinced, Ezra Stiles described the heydey of the New Lights as a time when "multitudes were seriously, Soberly and solemnly out of their wits." [49] The story of the Separates must include some description of this queer behavior.

46. "The History of Jack Nips," *Writings of John Leland,* p. 73.

47. John A. Broadus, "The American Baptist Ministry of One Hundred Years Ago," *Baptist Quarterly,* 9 (1875), 18–19.

48. Charles Chauncy, *The Late Religious Commotions in New-England Considered* (Boston, 1743), p. 35.

49. *A Discourse on the Christian Union* (Boston, 1761), p. 50.

The Anglican rector at Salem described the meetings conducted there by the "set of Enthusiasts that strole about harangueing the admiring Vulgar in *extempore* nonsense" in a letter to his superior:

> Their behaviour is indeed as shocking, as uncomon, their groans, cries, screams, & agonies must affect the Spectators were they never so obdurate & draw tears even from the most resolute, whilst the ridiculous & frantic gestures of others cannot but excite both laughter & contempt, some leaping, some laughing, some singing, some clapping one another upon the back, &c. The tragic scene is performed by such as are entering into the pangs of ye New Birth; the comic by those who are got thro' and those are so truly enthusiastic, that they tell you they saw the Joys of Heaven, can describe its situation, inhabitants, employments, & have seen their names entered into the Book of Life & can point out the writer, character & pen.[50]

This was from an unfriendly observer. However, the same behavior was sometimes recorded by revivalists. Samuel Chandler of Gloucester, Massachusetts, and Jeremiah Wise of Berwick, Maine, two active friends of the revival, visited Durham, New Hampshire, on a preaching mission in August 1746. Nicholas Gilman, Jr., pastor of the regular Congregational church there, had become one of the most fanatical followers of Whitefield, and in his congregation were some of the wildest enthusiasts in New England. Chandler's diary describes the almost incredible events of their visit:

> Mr. Wise preached from John 15, 5, and concluded with prayer. In the exercise were a number, 4 or 5, that were extraordinarily agitated. They made all manner of mouths, turning out their lips, drawing their mouths awry, as if convulsed, straining the eyeballs, and twisting their bodies in all manner of unseemly postures. Some were falling down, clapping their hands, groaning, talking. Some were approving what was spoken, and saying aye, that is true, 'tis just so and some were exclaiming and crying out aloud, glory, glory. It drowned Mr. Wise's voice. He spoke to them, entreated them, condemned the practice, but all to no purpose.
>
> Mr. Gilman came in, and after him a number of these highflyers, raving like mad men, reproaching, reflecting. One, Hannah

50. Letter of Charles Brockwell to the Secretary of the S.P.G., dated Feb. 18, 1741/2, in W. S. Perry, *Historical Collections, 3,* 354.

> Huckins, in a boasting air, said she had gone through adoption, justification and sanctification and perfection and perseverance. She fell to dancing round the room, singing some dancing-tunes, jiggs, minuets, and kept the time exactly with her feet.

The next day Chandler preached, and Gilman's party made the same offensive gestures as an indication of their displeasure.

> I desired and entreated, if they loved the souls of sinners, that they would suffer them to hear what I had to offer to them, but all to no purpose. Mr. Gilman says he has a witness within him that I neither preached nor prayed with the Spirit. I told him I had a witness within myself that I did both. He said, "how can that be when you have your thumb papers and you can hardly read them?" [51]

Visions and trances, reported soon after the first visit of Whitefield, continued among the Separates for a short time. In most cases, the subjects of them told of such experiences as are described in the rector's letter above. But there is little evidence that these things continued long among the Separates. The visions that were claimed after the first few years were usually much less sensational.

It remained for the members of the Killingly Convention to clarify the entire issue of enthusiasm by a candid admission of intemperate zeal and a clear statement of their mature understanding of what it meant to worship in spirit and truth:

> Our first withdrawal from the established Churches, was much like Israel's coming out of Egypt, a mixed Multitude came out also; and served to answer the same Purpose, i.e., to be a Trouble and Vexation to us, and to bring a Reproach and Scandal upon the Work of God. . . . Many that appeared forward in the Separation fell into notorious, scandalous Sins: —Others there were who ran into Errors and Extremes, in Matters of Religion; holding to an absolute Knowledge of the Brethren, upon an invisible Evidence, as they called it. —Others there were that made *Faith, Conscience,* and *Good Feeling* in Religion, their Rule of Duty, and did not pay that Honor to the revealed Will of God, in his Word, as they ought to have done.—Some there were that held that Church Discipline might be proceeded in without visible Evi-

51. Quoted in D. Hamilton Hurd, ed., *History of Essex County, Massachusetts* (Philadelphia, 1888), 2, 1167. Notice that Chandler betrays a tincture of enthusiasm himself.

dence to prove Facts alledged. —Some held that Ministers ought to have no previous Study before Preaching; but that they ought to have their Sermons immediately from God. —Others there were that seemed to strike at the Foundation of Civil Government, to overthrow it entirely; and were for destroying human Learning, and even human reason itself, as useless in Religion; and were for introducing unqualified Persons into the Ministry, upon the Belief, that their Qualifications were in Heaven, and would be sent down when they needed them. . . . Yet through the distinguishing Goodness and Mercy of God to us, there is a Number, who have so far escaped the Snares and Devices of the Gates of Hell, in those searching and perilous Times, that we are agreed to declare our Understanding of the Times: —Our Agreement as to Articles of Faith: —and our Judgment respecting Church Discipline.[52]

The allusion to the "mixed multitude" (Exod. 12:38) is quite apt. The presence of wild enthusiasts and undisciplined libertines almost prevented the Separates from reaching a Promised Land where they could conserve the best fruits of the new reformation. It took them a full forty years, from the Great Awakening to the Killingly Convention, to emerge from their wilderness wanderings into a sober state of self-conscious integrity. Their "Moses," as Backus called Elisha Paine, was removed prematurely; and there was no Joshua to take his place.

Fresh outpourings of the Spirit. Lest one think that the Separate churches were hotbeds of confusion and contention, it is well to point out that at times their meetings seemed to be graced with a genuine divine presence. One such occasion was at Canterbury on October 5, 1746, "the first sac[rame]nt after Sol[omo]n Paine was Ordained Pastor." The record reads:

It being the first day of the week the Church Came togather to break Bread were Entertained in the forenoon with a discorse from mat 26. 26, 27, 28, 29 in the demonstration of the spirit & with power many were addid to the number declaring their faith &c which Continued till in the night & then the Lords supper was Administred and Recieved By faith in and Love to the Glorious Broken Bleeding Saviour in a wonderfull flame of Love one to another, flowing from the Glorious Sweet & awfull Love of God to our souls senesably flowing to us thro & in his Dear son who

52. *An Historical Narrative and Declaration*, pp. 12–14.

was Broken for our Sins, Oh Lett us Remember this Love more then wine Amen.[53]

There are many similar occasions when it is said that the worshipers had "much of the gracious presence of God."

It is worth while to inquire also, since the Separate churches were born in the fires of revivalism, whether seasons of revival returned at various intervals. The question is phrased this way in deliberate recognition that it is both physically and spiritually impossible to maintain a consistently high level of revivalistic fervor under any conditions. But it is pertinent to ask whether there were any new harvests from time to time after the first bumper crop. The answer is that individual churches did experience seasons when religious concern increased and when numerous conversions were counted. Since the techniques of revivalism were imperfectly understood, revivals were still said to "break out," and both time and place were unpredictable. Without a protracted meeting, and perhaps even apart from the visit of an itinerant evangelist, a Separate (or Separate Baptist) church might receive upwards of a hundred new members in the space of a few months. But these were mostly isolated instances.

Between the Great Awakening of the forties and the Second Awakening at the end of the century, the only approach to general revival occurred in the sixties. Large areas were relatively untouched, but numbers of churches in widely separated places were visited. Easthampton, Long Island, which experienced its first revival under James Davenport in 1741 and its second soon after Samuel Buell's installation in 1746, was stirred again in 1764.[54] Buell was a strict Calvinist, and his account of some hundred pages describes the conversion of numbers of people in the same pattern as seen in the Great Awakening: legal terrors, unconditional submission to the sovereign purposes of God, rejoicing in the freeness of divine grace. Although there were intense emotions, there do not appear to have been the wild excesses which marked the earlier revivals. The same year, John Cleaveland was refreshed by the breaking out of a revival at Chebacco which reminded him of the good old days at Canterbury. The separation of which he was pastor was almost twenty years old, a vigorous church; and it now received ninety new members.[55] At Bennington,

53. *Records of the Congregational Church in Canterbury*, p. 36.
54. Buell, *A Faithful Narrative of the Remarkable Revival of Religion* (2d ed. Sag Harbor, 1808).
55. *A Short and Plain Narrative of the Late Work of God's Spirit at Chebacco in Ipswich* (Boston, 1767).

Vermont, a revival broke out in 1765. This was the fourth year of the town's settlement and the third of the church's formation, by which time numerous settlers—many professing no religion at all— had arrived. Exactly half of the seventy-two members received by the first pastor, Jedediah Dewey, in his fifteen-year ministry came into the church during this revival.

Within the triangle bounded by Easthampton, Chebacco, and Bennington, there were numerous revivals during the sixties. The Preston Separate Church records for June 15, 1764, say: "It has Pleased the Lord of Late to Pour out of his Spirit in a very Extraordinary Manner to the awakning of Greate numbers that the Cry of the Convicted & Destressed Souls was very Greate; and number appeare to be Converted." At Woodstock, Connecticut, where Elisha Paine had first faced persecution, a single sermon by a traveling evangelist in December 1763 resulted in the outbreak of a revival among the young people which led to a separation from the standing church and the formation of a Separate Baptist church in 1766.[56] Middleborough, Massachusetts, experienced such a shower of blessing in 1762 that many people "neglected their worldly business" for religious pursuits. Backus' church received more than sixty converts in six months, and other churches were proportionately increased. The sight of a revival in his home town of Norwich quite overcame his sorrow at the death of a brother there in 1764, and he reported on similar works of grace in Providence and Newbury, as well as in parts of New York and New Hampshire. It is clear that the in-gathering of the sixties was strong enough and widespread enough to remind many of the Separates and Separate Baptists of the halcyon days of the Great Awakening. Individual churches continued to report sporadic revivals and large harvest of converts until the end of the century, when there occurred another general awakening. But whether languishing in spiritual drought or caught up in a new spurt of spiritual concern, all the churches with separatist origins continued to cherish the revivalistic tradition.

NONTHEOLOGICAL FACTORS IN THE SEPARATE MOVEMENT

This entire study has proceeded on the premise that the phenomena described issued mainly from genuine religious conviction, in much the same way that the American Revolution issued from genuine political conviction. In neither case, however, does such an assumption deny that a number of other factors helped to determine the

56. See below, pp. 228–29.

place, manner, and degree in which the convictions were advocated and accepted. Max Weber's dictum that certain religious ideas have an elective affinity with the social circumstances of particular groups applies in a limited way to the present case. Intertwined with the influence of social factors is the important way in which psychological forces were at work.

Geographical distribution. The location of the Separate churches indicates something of their character. Map 1 [57] gives the impression at first glance that separatism was fairly widespread, as indeed it was—much more so than previous writers have suspected. This geographical nonparticularity may be more apparent than real, however, especially when one considers the pervasiveness and strength of Separate sentiments in eastern Connecticut. In spite of the undeniable virility of many Separate churches elsewhere, this was the real stronghold of separatism.[58] Several factors account for this. First, eastern Connecticut was not safe for settlement until after 1675, when King Philip's War cleared out the Indians; and the comparatively late influx of settlers meant that during the first half of the eighteenth century the region was still practically frontier territory. The character of the people here was noticeably different from that of those who stayed in coastal towns like Boston and New Haven. To make matters worse, because of technical irregularities in the expropriation of land from the Indians, there were no clear land titles to be had in this sector; this in itself is enough to explain the restlessness of people in these parts during the time under discussion.[59] Many of the early settlers, moreover, were from the Old Plymouth Colony, where the spirit of independence and separatism were traditionally strong (notice the great number of Separate churches in that area). Isaac Backus, who came from such a family himself, said that "many who now came out in a separation from these churches, descended from those Plymouth fathers, and meant conscientiously to follow their

57. See above, p. 114.

58. Separate churches are fairly plentiful in eastern Massachusetts, especially in the territory of the Old Plymouth Colony, but apparently they were not sufficiently massed to warrant an attempt to interpret any unusual pattern. Separate activity was rife from Boston northward into southern New Hampshire, but most of this is explained by the repeated visits of Whitefield and other itinerants to an area where the established religion had already moved far in a direction opposite to that taken by revivalism generally. The presence of Separates on the frontier has been discussed above, pp. 107–11.

59. Edith Anna Bailey, "Influences toward Radicalism in Connecticut, 1754–1775," *Smith College Studies in History*, 5 (1920), 188–89.

good principles." [60] There were also many settlers from northeastern Massachusetts (Ipswich, Haverhill, etc.), where proposals for a stronger ecclesiastical platform had been strenuously opposed by a traditional love of congregational independence.

Radical influences probably came from another near neighbor as well: Windham County was closer culturally to Rhode Island, the center of individualism and independency, than to the Hartford-New Haven axis; and after a road from Canterbury and Plainfield to Providence was opened in 1722, the intercourse between Rhode Island and northeastern Connecticut increased considerably. This all adds up to the fact that in the eighteenth century eastern Connecticut was the home of radical sentiment. There had been little opportunity for conservatism to develop here, and this part of Connecticut did not become a "land of steady habits" until its radicals emigrated to new homes in Vermont, New York, and parts west, leaving it to the moderating influences of other social forces.[61]

The radicalism was reflected in religious affairs. Ezra Stiles commented that, "whatever be the reason, the eastern part of Connecticut . . . [is] of a very mixt & uncertain character as to religion." [62] Documenting this observation is the experience of the church at North Stonington, formed in 1720 but unable to secure a permanent pastor until 1727:

> There had been lacking a spirit of cooperation almost from the first, a disposition to contend for individual preferences, and a tendency to harbor grudges against each other. . . . [A ministerial candidate] in 1722, spoke of "the party spirit and self-willedness which hath showed itself from time to time, even in trifles . . . to the making of schisms and breaches, so as to render your minister the most uncomfortable of any man in the world.[63]

60. *Abridged History*, p. 172. Of his own ancestry, Backus said, "My mother sprang from the family of Mr. Winslow, who came over to Plymouth in 1620" (quoted in Hovey, *Memoir of Isaac Backus*, p. 31).

61. The fact that eastern Connecticut furnished most of the settlers to Vermont and western Massachusetts explains the early radicalism of these regions (above, p. 107). "It is not surprising, under the circumstances, that the first organizer of the movement which culminated in Shay's Rebellion was a deposed [Separate] clergyman who had come to Hampshire county from Somers, Connecticut [Samuel Ely]" (Morrow, *Connecticut Influences*, p. 13).

62. *Itineraries of Ezra Stiles*, p. 299.

63. Edna Hewitt Tryon, "From Congregational Records," *Papers and Addresses Delivered at the Dedication of a Granite Memorial on the Site of the First [Baptist] Church Edifice September 23, 1934* (Westerly, 1936), p. 43.

In this territory uncomfortable ministers met with strong resistance in their efforts to impose the Saybrook Platform at the time of its formulation, and the resulting controversies served to make people sensitive to issues of church polity and resentful of authoritarian encroachment. Finally, there is personal influence to be taken into account: here is where James Davenport was most active and where his most uninhibited enthusiasm broke forth. In contrast to an area like Boston, which had developed effective ways of dealing with disturbers of the ecclesiastical peace, eastern Connecticut was easily swept off its feet by the overwhelming force of such a demagogue. Here, too, nearly all the strongest leaders among the Separates arose —though that may have been a result as well as a cause. These factors combined to make eastern Connecticut the place where separatism was most widely influential, most deeply rooted, and least effectively stamped out. It was also the place where the Separates came nearest to developing a denominational cohesiveness and self-conscious integrity. The forming of a convention of Strict Congregational churches was almost entirely the achievement of the Separates of eastern Connecticut.[64]

Social status. The social distribution of the Separates is much more difficult to assess. Separatism is such a complex phenomenon, with so many mutually interacting variables, that class analysis can be quite misleading.[65] Religious groups indeed may give evidence of a certain correlation with existing social strata, but it is more than probable that religion sometimes operates to *reduce* social differences. There has been very little investigation of this rather crucial point. The

64. It is interesting to observe that in the growing political power of the New Lights after 1750, the concentration of Separates in eastern Connecticut shifted control of public affairs to Windham and New London counties. Against this "eastern faction" the conservatives, aided by the salty pen of Dr. Benjamin Gale, bent all their force. They were able to regain control in 1754, when Thomas Fitch displaced Roger Wolcott in the governor's chair. But when Fitch complied with the Stamp Act in 1765, popular opposition blazed forth from the east stronger than ever. The "Sons of Liberty" arose and ousted Fitch with all his followers the next year. See Trumbull, "Sons of Liberty in 1755," *New Englander,* 35 (1876), 299–313; Edmund S. and Helen M. Morgan, *The Stamp Act Crisis* (Chapel Hill, N.C., 1953), chap. 13; and Oscar Zeichner, *Connecticut's Years of Controversy* (Chapel Hill, N.C., 1949), pp. 25–27, 99–102.

65. Some writers, overpowered by the temptation to equate religious radicalism with social inferiority, have concluded erroneously that the Separates were entirely from the lower classes. See Maurice Whitman Armstrong, "Religious Enthusiasm and Separatism in Colonial New England," *Harvard Theological Review,* 38 (1945), 133; and John Chester Miller, "Religion, Finance, and Democracy in Massachusetts," *New England Quarterly,* 6 (1933), 41, 49.

Separates certainly represent a sect, as sociologists presently define that term, but this is far from implying that theirs was a "religion of the disinherited." J. Milton Yinger defined a sect:

> We shall broaden the meaning of the term sect somewhat to refer to any religious protest against a system in which attention to the various individual functions of religion has been obscured and made ineffective by the extreme emphasis on social and ecclesiastical order. . . . [It includes] religious groups that represent protests against the failure of the established churches to deal successfully with feelings of inadequacy, confusion, ennui, pain, and guilt. If these are included in the same concept, *we may define a sect as a movement in which the primary emphasis is the attempt to satisfy, by religious means, various basic individual needs.* It is usually seen as a revolt against a religious system in which these needs have been inadequately dealt with.[66]

When applied to the separatist patterns under study, this definition, resting as it does more on psychological than sociological distinctions, explains why the Separates were not merely a group on the cultural periphery seeking to solve their problems by substituting religious status for social status.

How the class structure of the Separates compared with that of society as a whole, however, is an unavoidable question. It must be stressed that a complete answer would require minute examination of the membership of every Separate church. The examiner would find enormous differences between churches. One would also find that almost every Separate church included members who were upper class in relation to their immediate cultural milieu. The writers of local histories, who are always sensitive to the names of outstanding families, indicate that many of the Separates were among the most prominent people in their community. Miss Larned, whose *History of Windham County* is unsurpassed in the field of local history, affirms this with respect to Canterbury, the first church formally to avow New

66. J. Milton Yinger, *Religion, Society and the Individual; an Introduction to the Sociology of Religion* (New York, 1957), p. 146. Italics mine. Ernst Troeltsch gave the classic definition of the "church" and "sect" types of religious groups in *The Social Teachings of the Christian Churches,* trans. Olive Wyon (New York, 1931), pp. 331–41. Yinger's "Refinements of the Typology" into a broader spectrum are much more useful; see *Religion, Society and the Individual,* pp. 147–55. For discussion of "churches of the disinherited," see H. Richard Niebuhr, *Social Sources of Denominationalism* (New York, 1957), chaps. 2, 3.

Light principles as a body. After studying the list of persons signing their covenant, she states:

> Fifty-seven subscribed their names on this occasion, and many others a few months later, representing some of the oldest and most respectable families in Canterbury, viz.: Paine, Backus, Cleveland, Adams, Johnson, Fitch, Bacon, Hyde, Bradford, Brown, Parish, and Carver. Whatever the character of the Separate element in other places, in Canterbury it was respectable and influential, and under favoring circumstances might have become a permanent power in the community.[67]

The historian of Norwich says of the Separates there: "They had among them several of the most wealthy and respectable men in the Society." [68] At one time the Separates had a majority in this parish, and counted nearly all the more influential families.

The Separates at Enfield likewise were of incontestably high status. That town had an able historian, who wrote:

> It has been supposed by some that the "Separates" of Enfield were poor, ignorant, shallow persons who separated from the Established Church in order to enjoy more freely religious hysterics and disorderly physical demonstrations in their worship. To correct this impression it is only necessary . . . to study the lists hereafter given of the Enfield "Separates." . . . [They are persons] of high character [and] were certainly among the best citizens of Enfield.[69]

The petition of the Enfield Separates in 1769, asking permission to embody into a distinct ecclesiastical parish, was signed by seventy-eight men whose names represent the old and honored families of the town. They not only won the rights for which they petitioned but continued to serve locally in positions of trust and influence. "It is reasonable to infer that in its earlier years this Separatist congregation must have been a considerable body, including a number of persons of undoubted social standing, and entitled, both by numbers and worth, to the respect of their fellow citizens." [70] The same certainly could be said of the separation at New Haven. Along with other people of prestige, Roger Sherman, the town's leading citizen, signer of the Declara-

67. *History of Windham County, 1,* 438.
68. Frances Manwaring Caulkins, *History of Norwich, Connecticut* (Norwich, 1845), p. 194.
69. F. O. Allen, *The History of Enfield, 2,* 1526.
70. Means, p. 50.

tion of Independence, participant in the Constitutional Convention, treasurer of Yale College, and a prominent man in other ways, was a pillar in the White Haven Church during the ministry of Jonathan Edwards, Jr. The chronicler of New Milford concludes his account of the schism there by observing that "a fair proportion of the men and women who went from the First to the Separate Church, were among the very best, most faithful, true Christians, in the town." [71] The historian of Exeter, New Hampshire, demonstrates conclusively that the separation there cut across some of the town's most prominent families.[72] Studies of other towns suggest much the same thing.

The fact that most of the Separate churches included socially prominent members does not mean that they did not count numerous adherents from the lower strata of society. This was especially true in eastern Connecticut, where all of life was less cultured than it was, for example, in New Haven, Enfield, or Exeter. In that entire area, where separatism was strongest, there were few genuinely upper class families in the first place. Miss Larned confesses that when she describes some of the Separates as being among the most notable families in a town, she does not imply that these were drawn from a silk-stocking set. Most of the residents of Windham County were in fact farmers in a homespun economy. In view of this, it might be argued that here and in areas where similar social conditions obtained, the Separates were predominantly poor, ignorant, and uncultured. The point, however, is that everywhere they reflected a fair cross section of the society in which they existed. It is the conclusion of this study that the class structure in most of the Separate churches was about the same as that of the surrounding society. Nearly all of them, notwithstanding emotional extravagance and enthusiastic excess, included members of a fair degree of social elevation *for their particular area,* as well as many others of lower status. A recent study of the Great Awakening in New England has concluded that the revival itself was not confined to any one particular social stratum: "Whether the population was dense or sparse, the mode of living primitive or moderately luxurious, the class high or low, the economy agricultural or mercantile, the revival was there." [73] Perhaps such an unequivocal statement regarding separatism would be less appropriate, but to affirm the opposite would be even more false. The Separate movement clearly was not just an uprising of the rabble.

Psychological factors. As has been suggested, the chief differentiat-

71. Orcutt, *History of New Milford and Bridgewater,* p. 198.
72. J. T. Perry, *First Church in Exeter,* p. 74.
73. Gaustad, *Great Awakening in New England,* p. 52.

ing factor underlying the religious issues in separatism was probably more psychological than sociological. It is a commonplace of modern psychology that in any given situation individuals will react in different ways determined largely by their basic personality traits, ancestral background, early experiences, and a complex of nonrational factors as yet dimly understood. The suspicion grows, moreover, that there emerges at times a collective mentality which finds in the *crowd* an outlet for repressed emotions. At times of great group excitement,

> it is as if all at once an unspoken agreement were entered into whereby each member might let himself go, on condition that he approved the same thing in all the rest. . . . [A crowd] is a device for indulging ourselves in a kind of temporary insanity by all going crazy together.[74]

There are many who will accept this as a satisfactory explanation of some of the more aberrant mass behavior which has been described. Caution, however, cannot be urged too forcefully against unsubstantiated speculation at this point. Many attempts to psychologize religious behavior have been dismal failures.[75] Even competent psychologists differ widely over the significance of apparently irrational aspects of religious behavior, and their disagreement over a well-documented life such as that of Martin Luther points up some of the problems arising when psychological analysis is attempted on a movement which is at once vastly more complex and much less illuminated.

These difficulties notwithstanding, it is impossible to deny that certain types of people found their psychological as well as religious needs answered in part by the Separate movement. This again focuses attention on the relevance of the definition of a sect as "a movement in which the primary emphasis is the attempt to satisfy, by religious means, various basic individual needs." In their awakened state, the Separates desperately needed larger opportunities for emotional self-expression, avenues of group participation, a sense of sharing and belonging, and an assurance of ultimate vindication—which things were

74. Everett D. Martin, *The Behavior of Crowds* (New York, 1920), pp. 35–36; quoted in William L. Langer, "The Next Assignment," *American Historical Review, 63* (1958), 290. Langer's article is an able statement of the case for bringing the insights of modern psychology to the task of historical interpretation.

75. A conspicuous example is Frederick Morgan Davenport, *Primitive Traits in Religious Revivals; a Study in Mental and Social Evolution* (New York, 1917), a work which shows no understanding whatsoever of the nature of religious experience, in spite of which it continues to be cited by "social historians" who should know better.

not being offered by the standing churches. Their withdrawal in search of fulfillment, as far as it was motivated by nonreligious factors, was due to their differing personality traits and psychological needs as much as to their geographical location or cultural situation. Such variations in personal religious propensities are often enough to explain (if not justify) religious differentiation entirely apart from social or economic differences. The highly individualized, emotional faith of the Separates was what William James would have called "the religion of the sick soul," or, to use a less invidious term, that of the "twice-born."[76] It was inevitable under the circumstances that people of this inclination not only should experience the kind of conversion they did in the Great Awakening, but also should gravitate together in the formation of exclusive groups where their experiences would be accepted and understood as a normal Christian response.

Decline of the Congregational Separates

Notwithstanding the fact that by the time of the second generation of Separates a disciplined, self-conscious denomination was emerging, legal standing and permanence were achieved by relatively few of their churches. Some five factors contributed to the decline of the Strict Congregationalists: persecution by the standing order, disintegration due to lawless elements, removal to the frontier, reunion with the regular churches, and conversion to Baptist sentiments. Each of these will be discussed briefly.

Persecution by the standing order. Frequent reference has been made to the determination of the establishment to suppress the Separates.[77] One of the first moves was to clear all political offices of New Light sympathizers, which made it extremely difficult for the Separates to obtain a hearing for their petitions and appeals. Their political disabilities extended to the disallowing of marriages and baptisms performed by their ministers, on the ground that a qualified civil officer was required for these acts, and on occasion Separate pastors were

---

76. *The Varieties of Religious Experience* (London, 1902), pp. 127–29. James' bipolar typology in religious psychology has proved as durable as that of Troeltsch in religious sociology. Carl G. Jung has been most influential, enlarging upon James' distinction between "healthy-minded" and "sick-soul" religion under the rubrics of the extrovert and the introvert—two inclusive types in which the basic psychological functions of thinking, feeling, sensation, and intuition are regarded as moving either outward or inward with respect to the subject. See *Psychological Types; or, the Psychology of Individuation*, trans. H. Godwin Baynes (New York, 1933).

77. See especially pp. 59–64.

jailed for joining in marriage their own church members. Sons of Separates were expelled from the established colleges, and the effort of
the Separates to erect their own institution of learning was promptly
squelched by legislative action. But while every civil right was cur-
tailed as far as possible, every legal due was extorted as rigorously
as possible. Because of the all-embracing pattern of the established
church, every resident within a given parish was taxed for the support
of the standing church. Anglicans, Quakers, and Baptists might claim
the benefit of the Act of Toleration; but it was specifically decreed that
no Presbyterian or Congregationalist should be exempted from supporting the established churches. But the Separates had conscientious
objections to supporting the "false" worship, and most of them contributed freely for their own minister and meetinghouse. Therefore the
chief controversy between them and the standing order centered on the
ecclesiastical tax.

It was a very unequal struggle. In Massachusetts, Boston followed a
voluntaristic system as required by the charter of 1691, but in the other
towns it was a matter of *cujus regio, ejus religio.* The region and religion both generally belonged to the Congregationalists, of course,
and it was entirely up to the local officials how far to coerce the Separates to bear their share of supporting the parish church. Sturbridge
seems to have been one of the most severe towns. A contemporary
testimony tells of the heartless distraining of goods from poor people
who would not or could not pay their rates:

> They stripped the shelves of pewter, of such as had it; and of
> others that had not they took away skillets, kettles, pots and warm-
> ing pans. Others they deprived of the means they got their bread
> with, viz., workmen's tools, and spinning-wheels. They drove away
> geese and swine from the doors of some others; from some that
> had cows; from some that had but one they took that away. They
> took a yoke of oxen from one. Some they thrust into prison, where
> they had a long and tedious imprisonment.[78]

The Separates protested so vehemently at these unjust proceedings
that the town called a meeting at the Congregational church on March
18, 1752, to hear their grievances. Moses Marcy, a venerable and original settler, moderated. The Separates sat on one side, their opponents
on the other. No agreement was reached because, in true uncompro-
mising fashion, the Separates would accept only complete restitution

78. Henry Fisk, "The Testimony of a People Inhabiting the Wilderness," quoted
in Backus, *History of New England,* 2, 94–95.

of the value of goods taken from them since the beginning—which of course the town refused to grant.

In Connecticut, the entire conserving force of the colonial government and all its institutions were rallied against the hapless Separates. When they refused to pay their rates, their goods and chattel were distrained and sold at auction. When goods failed, their bodies were taken:

> Most disgraceful scenes occurred at these seizures of goods and persons. The maddened Separates resisted with tongue and fist, refused to walk or ride to the prison, and held by main force on horseback would often be carried there, "crying and screaming till the blood ran out of their mouths." [79]

In Windham County, where separatism was most rampant, a new story had to be added to the jailhouse; and when it proved insufficient, a new jail was ordered constructed in 1753.

At Norwich the Separates and their sympathizers came to outnumber the regular Congregationalists, and they voted in town meeting to withhold the minister's salary altogether. Upon complaint of the church to the General Assembly, a special act was passed for the support of pastor Benjamin Lord. When the Separates refused to pay, their goods were confiscated, and as many as forty were imprisoned in a single year. The mother of Isaac Backus, in a frequently quoted letter to her son, told how the collector came to her home on a dark, rainy winter night, when she was ill and wrapped in blankets by the fire, and carried her to an unheated prison where she languished with several other Separates for many days.[80] While they were incarcerated, one of them addressed a letter to the reverend pastor for whose salary they were delinquent:

> Norwich Goale, November ye I Day, 1752.
> Mr. Lord, Sir, I take this opertunity to present you with these fu lines which I should have thout you would have Pervented By visiting us. . . . But being informed you Refuse to come I shall take Liberty to tell you that I judge it moast un scriptral and unreasonable that I am imprisoned thus by you. Ye lay heavy Burdens and Refuse to touch them with one of your fingers. You say it is the Athority; Simeon and Levi are brethren; instruments of cruelty are in their habitations. Genesis, xlix. 5–7.

79. Larned, *History of Windham County, 1*, 479. The quoted clause is from Trumbull, *Complete History of Connecticut, 2*, 234.

80. Backus, *History of New England, 2*, 98–99. The letter is dated Nov. 4, 1752.

Pray Sir Read the 3 Chapter of Mikes Provesy and may the Lord mack the aplycatyon. Consider also that our Lord Jesus hath toald us that his Kingdom is not of this world, also that he that taketh the sword shall perish by the sword. I could wish you a Deliverance from Mistacal Babelon and from her merchandize. my soul looks to and longs to see hir Receive the cup of the Lord's vengens and that all his Plages may come upon hir In one Day and God's children may come out of hir and that the Kingdom may be given to the saints of the moast high. these lines with oure cause I Leave with God who will I trust Defend it, and so subscribe myself a Prisoner of hope.

CHARLS HILL [81]

What impression such protests made, if any, is unknown. The persecution continued unabated. Thomas Marsh, who was jailed the day before his intended ordination at Mansfield, was confined for six months with less freedom than a cellmate who, though a murderer, had visiting privileges throughout the town. Deacon John Avery of Preston was imprisoned until his church rates should be paid.

Alexander Miller and a group of Separates from Voluntown were confined in Windham prison for ten weeks, during which time their destitute families suffered greatly. From their cell they addressed a petition to the General Assembly, disclaiming any intention to contemn lawful authority or disturb any standing church; their only desire was to serve God according to the dictates of their own consciences, which forbade them to support the religious establishment. Because of this they had suffered untold loss:

Poor men's estates taken away and sold for less than a quarter of their value, and no overplus returned, as hath been the case of your Honor's poor informers; yea, poor men's cows taken when they had but one for the support of their families, and the children crying for milk and could get none, because the collector had taken their cow for minister's rates. Neither have they stopped here, though we have never resisted them, but when our goods could no longer suffice we were taken from our families and cast into prison, where some of us have lain above two months, far distant from our families, who are in very difficult circumstances. Yea! and here we must unavoidably lie the remainder of our days unless we consent to such methods for which we can see no warrant in God's Word. No! surely it never came into his mind, neither hath he commanded that it should be so, that the Gospel of Peace

81. Printed in Denison, *Notes on the Baptists in Norwich*, p. 29.

should be so maintained; he hath told his ministers how they shall have their maintenance, but not a word of imprisoning men for refusing to maintain them, surely the best things corrupted form the worst.[82]

No notice was taken of this pathetic appeal.

Ebenezer Frothingham noted several instances of persecution besides his own case. There was "young deacon Drake of Windsor, now in Hartford prison, for the ministers rates and building their meetinghouse altho' he is a baptist . . . yet notwithstanding he has made this mistake, he is accounted a harmless, godly man; and he has plead the privilege of a baptist, through all the courts, and been at great expence, without relief, till at last the assembly has given him a mark in his hand; and notwithstanding this, they have thrust him to prison for former rates, with several aggravations." [83] These illustrations could be multiplied many times. Backus commented dourly that not only had the Old Guard misapplied the parable of the tares to justify their corrupt churches, they had turned it back on those who sought to erect pure churches: "Yea, while they were for having the tares grow in the church, they would not let the children of God grow peaceably in the world, but took up and imprisoned many of them." [84]

In spite of the unevenness of the battle, the Separates struggled doggedly on, convinced that right was on their side. In 1748 Solomon Paine and Matthew Smith collected the signatures of 330 persons in eastern Connecticut on a petition to be presented to the General Assembly. They affirmed their loyalty as subjects of king and colony, asserted liberty of conscience as the inalienable right of every man, called attention to the Act of Toleration, which had been abridged by the persecuting tactics of Connecticut, and pleaded with the legislators to "enact universal Liberty, by repealing all those Ecclesiastical Laws that are or may be executed, to the debaring of any of this Colony of the Liberty granted by God, and tolerated by our King; or forbid the Execution of said Laws." [85] Although Paine was permitted to read the petition before the Assembly, the plea was rejected. The first concerted attempt on the part of the Massachusetts Separates was

82. Quoted in Larned, *History of Windham County,* 1, 479. The appeal is dated May 13, 1752.

83. *A Key to Unlock the Door,* p. 183. The meaning of the "mark in the hand" is not clear. It is probably figurative (cf. Rev. 13:16); if literal, it is the only instance of branding dissenters in Connecticut I have discovered.

84. *Abridged History,* p. 164. Let no one accuse the Separates of ulterior economic motives for dissent. Surely it would have been cheaper to pay the tax.

85. Printed in Solomon Paine, *A Short View of the Difference,* pp. 8–11.

equally unsuccessful. Representatives from the churches met at Attle-borough on May 24, 1749, and drafted a petition to the General Court. To obtain signatures on the document, Isaac Backus traveled the length of Cape Cod and visited nearly all the Separate churches in southeastern Massachusetts. The petition was presented to the Court in Boston in June 1749, but because of the opposition of the towns and the universal prejudice against the Separates, no favorable action was taken.

In October 1751 the Preston Separate Church again addressed the Connecticut Assembly in a petition signed by thirty-three of their members.[86] It was dismissed peremptorily by the legislators. On January 17, 1753, the Preston church moved for a union of all the Separate churches in an effort to free themselves from taxation for the established churches. Against this background the first general meeting of the Separate churches in Connecticut was held at Norwich on March 21, 1753. Said Paul Parke, who was undoubtedly the moving spirit:

> The Convocation of *Churches* was attend: by most of the *Churches* and were very wonderfully all of one Mind: viz that it was there Deuty to send first to our General Assembly: and if not heard to sent to England the *Churches* Chose as overseers: to Prepare a Memorial according to what was Purposed to lay before the assembly next May: the over seers: Were Solomon Paine, Ebenezer Froathingham, Jedediah Hide, Ellexander Miller and Paul Parke.[87]

The resulting petition was signed by the representatives of more than twenty Separate churches. The General Assembly accorded them the same contemptuous refusal as before, and they turned their attention to carrying their appeal before King George himself.

The general conferences of the next three years were nearly all on this subject. On June 19, 1754, a memorial was drafted; and on September 26, Solomon Paine and Frothingham were chosen to bear it to England. This mission was thwarted by Paine's death a few months later, and nothing was done until 1756. On April 15 of that year the matter was reopened at a conference in Norwich, and Bliss Willoughby and Moses Morse were selected as agents to carry a petition to England.[88]

86. Printed in Blake, *The Separates*, pp. 118–21.
87. Records of the Preston Separate Church.
88. Willoughby was pastor of the Newent Separate Church; upon returning from England, he migrated to Vermont and later became a Baptist. Morse, a physician, had come from Newbury, Massachusetts, in 1743 and joined the North Preston Congregational Church. On August 8, 1749, he united with the Preston Separate Church.

Headed "To The King's Most Excellent Majesty, in Council," the petition purports to come from "Loyal and Dutiful Subjects to your Majesty, who Detest and Abhor all the Romish Superstition, and are for the most part Heads of family and Freemen of the Corporation, Containing in Number About one Thousand, all of the Age of Twenty-one years and upward Who Constantly Attend the Publick Worship of Almighty God and Have provided Themselves with Ministers in their Respective Churches, and Convenient Meeting Houses for Public Worship, All which They maintain without Being Burdensome or Chargeable to Others." They summarize the principles of strict congregationalism and the ground of their separation from the standing churches of the colony. They make it clear that they have a "Profound Veneration For the Governors and Rulers God Hath set over us and Rejoice to Be our part in the Support Thereof, and we pray For no Indulgence in Idleness, Immorality, or any Thing That Affects the State." Their deprivation of religious privilege and persecution for dissent are recounted as indisputable violations of the Act of Toleration and the colonial charter itself. The petitioners state that it is very "unreasonable And Inconsistent with Equity and Justice" that those who are dissenters themselves should persecute other dissenters and deny them the benefits of the Toleration Act. They point out how often and unsuccessfully they have applied to the colonial government for relief, and conclude with several specific requests:

> That, No man Hereafter Be, by Force and Virtue of the Laws of Said Colony, Hindered to worship God Almighty with Those who worship According as he understands the word of God, Provided the same be not Injurious Nor Dangerous as AforeSaid. (2) That, None of such worshippers Be Hinderd by Said Laws to Build or Repair Meeting Houses For, or Depradations, For not giving Their Attendance at the Parish Meeting House Established, Nor be Liable to Fines (&) Exactions By Said Laws. (3) That no man Hereafter Be Compelled to make or yeald to any such Taxes For the Maintainance of Said Established Ministers or Meeting Houses, or Any such Charges, and, That no Freeman in any such manner be Destrained or Imprisoned. . . . That, in the Things Aforesaid, All your People May Have Liberty to serve God Almighty and your Majesty According to His Word & the Laws and Statutes of your Realm, as They Tender the Glory of God, The Honour of your Majesty, And The Prosperity of This Kingdom.[89]

89. The petition is printed (for the first and only time) in Denison, *Notes on the Baptists in Norwich*, pp. 32–36.

Morse and Willoughby first exhibited the memorial to the English Committee for Dissenters, which was amazed at the revelations therein and feared that its presentation to the king would endanger the charter of the colony. The agents therefore returned home, and the chairman of the Dissenters' Committee, Dr. Benjamin Avery, wrote a sharp letter of reproof to the Connecticut officials. Governor Fitch, by way of answer, attempted to excuse his conduct by recounting the vagaries of the Separates, to which Avery replied that "civil penalties were not the appropriate remedy for spiritual disorders." [90] Though this last-ditch effort of the Separates was never consummated, it probably had a sobering effect on the colonial government and led to a lightening of persecuting pressures.

South Killingly was the first Separate church to obtain tax relief, which it did in 1755. Ratepaying was abolished in Plainfield in 1768. The Killingly Convention in 1781 noted that toleration had greatly increased, and in 1784 the laws of Connecticut were revised to omit any reference to the Saybrook Platform and its enforcement by civil power. The relaxation, however, came too late to save the Separates. The standing order practically won its war of extermination, and in many of the survivors spiritual fervor had been dissipated in a litigious struggle with the tax collector. The few churches which remained were neither vigorous nor vital, and even the Killingly *Declaration* proved to be a futile effort to fan new flames from dying embers. Hardly any lived to see the full religious liberty to which they had borne such important witness.

Disintegration due to lawless elements. The kind of preaching which does too much to inflame the passions and too little to enlighten the understanding produces powerful but often temporary impressions. This explains to some extent the transient loyalties of some who were attracted to the Separates by other than religious motives and it also explains why the process of disintegration set in early. One of the causes of failure was the inclusion of many inflammatory and revolutionary elements. "The Separate movement swept through the lowest stratum of society, in a day of comparative ignorance and imperfect civilization, taking in not only the ignorant, fanatical and visionary, cranks of every variety, but the sore-heads, the grumbletonians; all who for any cause were brought into opposition to constituted authorities." [91] It was from this element that antinomianism, chiliasm, and

90. Larned, *History of Windham County, 1,* 483.

91. Larned, *Historic Gleanings in Windham County,* pp. 38–39. Cranks and grumbletonians, it should be noted, are not necessarily lower class socially.

perfectionism appeared to disgrace and disintegrate some of the Separate churches. Backus cites several examples of these demoralizing influences. At Easton, Massachusetts, some of the Separates forsook their lawful wives and husbands to take others, "and they got so far as to declare themselves to be perfect and immortal, or that the resurrection was past already, as some did in the apostolic age." [92] Shadrach Ireland, a Separate preacher from Charlestown, Massachusetts, seems to have been among this number, for later (1753) he appeared at the town of Harvard and professed to have experienced such a change in both body and mind as to become perfect and immortal. The conduct of Ireland and his followers was so scandalous that to escape prosecution they went underground. Building a large house, they continued their meetings in secret:

> Ireland forbade them to marry, or to lodge with each other, if they were married, and he had left a wife and children in Charlestown; yet he took another woman, and lodged with her in Harvard all his remaining days. And when he was suddenly seized with death, he said, "I am going, but don't bury me; for the time is short; God is coming to take the church." Therefore he was put into a large box filled up with lime, and laid in the cellar, where it continued from September, 1778, to July, 1779, when the body scented so much that it was carried out in the night and buried in a corn-field.[93]

The remaining Separates here eventually succumbed to Shakerism.

At Windham's first parish some of the Separates declared that they had passed the first resurrection and were perfect and immortal, and one of them even declared that he was Christ. Near Attleborough some advanced the opinion that if a saint found that he (or she) had not been married to the person whom God made for him, he had a right to take his true mate as soon as he perceived who it was.

> Hereupon an only child of a rich father, not living comfortably with her husband, ventured to reject him, and to lodge with another man. Some brethren of Attleborough hearing of it, went to labor with her father, and others, to turn them from this delusion; but he said he did not believe there was any harm in it, for they lay with the Bible between them. But to his sorrow and shame his

92. *History of New England, 2,* 446.
93. Ibid., p. 462.

daughter proved to be with child by her new companion, and
her husband obtained a legal divorce from her.[94]

At Canterbury a married man with two children declared that it had
been revealed to him that his family would perish and that a certain
other woman would become his wife. The church called him to account for harboring a notion that implied murder, and finally excommunicated him on September 27, 1749. A few months later his wife
and children were poisoned, and he married the other woman. Backus
says that though the facts were widely known, the pair was acquitted
in court; the church, however, expelled all who defended them on
ground of perjury.[95] Such instances make it plain that disciplining
the "mixed multitude" was a tremendous task.

While the core of committed Christians among the Separates was
moving toward maturity, the radical fringe was bringing the movement
into disrepute. Some churches succumbed to the disintegrating forces
generated by the lawless elements and dissolved, leaving their former
members as liabilities on society. Such persons often became more irreligious than before, and impervious to any new appeal. In 1815 a
Vermont writer observed that large numbers of former Separates had
fallen away and become completely inured to churchly influences,
while many of their children likewise were entirely outside the reach
of religion. "Having imbibed early prejudices against religious order
and a regular ministry, [they] have grown up in a spirit of discontent,
and have been rendered turbulent and refractory members of ecclesiastical society, and not unfrequently have they been found enlisted in
the ranks of error and infidelity." [96] This appraisal coming from the
frontier at the close of the second generation of Separates is extremely
significant. It is painfully apparent that many of the Separate churches
suffered a catastrophe similar to that of Eliphalet Wright, who is said
to have died "from the effects of leading a fractious heifer." [97]

Removal to the frontier. The third factor in the decline of the Separates is their removal from the fetters of ecclesiastical conservatism
to the freedom of the frontier. This phenomenon has been described
already,[98] and it is necessary only to mention it here. Frequently one
reads in a local history that "the Separate church in this community

94. Ibid., pp. 88–89.
95. Ibid., p. 89.
96. "Memoir of the Rev. Joseph Marshall," *Adviser,* 7, 204.
97. *History of the Congregational Church in South Killingly* (Danielson, Conn.,
1896), p. 4. Wright was pastor of this Separate church 1765–84.
98. See above, p. 107.

died out after a few years," but sometimes closer investigation reveals that most of the members had emigrated to some distant frontier to make a fresh start. In such cases the Separates who remained sought fellowship with a neighboring Separate church, gradually drifted back into their original communion, or fell by the wayside entirely. Most of the churches established by the Separates on the frontier became in time regular Congregational or Baptist churches. There was no need in their new surroundings to perpetuate themselves in separatism, especially since their ecclesiastical neighbors usually had similar origins. Thus removal to the frontier contributed to the decline of the Separates in the older areas, while self-conscious separatism died quickly in the newer regions. But this by no means implies the demise of New Light revivalism in either sector, though that tradition began to be carried more by the Separate Baptists than by the Strict Congregationalists.

Reunion with the regular churches. Two things made the return of the Separates to the standing churches increasingly easy: changes in the regular Congregationalists and moderating viewpoints among the Separates. As to the first factor, the most important change was the gradual abandonment of the Halfway Covenant. Evangelical leaders in the establishment opposed it with growing success. Taking their cue from Jonathan Edwards, these men eventually coalesced as a definable party whose position became known as "New Divinity." Its leaders were Joseph Bellamy, Samuel Hopkins, and Jonathan Edwards, Jr. Where Edwardseans were dominant (mainly western Massachusetts and the Connecticut Valley), few churches adhered to the Halfway practice after 1784. One must add quickly, however, that although this presumably made the return of the Separates easier, it did not constitute a clear vindication of their most cherished principle, regenerate church membership. The basic thrust of the Halfway Covenant was toward an identification of religion with morality, and it is doubtful that this presupposition was discarded in every church which dispensed formally with halfway membership. "The Half-Way Covenant was more easily deserted because visible sainthood was more readily allowed. . . . As full membership became less difficult, half membership became less necessary." [99] At all events, it was quietly laid aside, to the gratification of such Separates as lived to see it.

Another major change in the standing churches in Connecticut was the weakening of the authoritarian consociational system and the abrogation of legislation to enforce the Saybrook Platform. These changes came about as a result of the changed political climate. New Lights

99. Gaustad, p. 107.

gained control in Connecticut during the fifties; and although they had little sympathy with separatism per se, they accelerated the transition to a situation in which the Separates' petitions for freedom from oppressive taxation were finally heard and heeded. In Massachusetts, the new constitution of 1780 provided for minority worship in each town, though it added the insufferable restriction that dissenters should pay their ecclesiastical rates to the established church and then sue them back for the support of their own worship. The temper of the times favored a larger liberty, which operated to reopen the channels of communication between the remaining Separates and their erstwhile persecutors. In many parishes the regular minister freely relinquished the rate system of support and depended on voluntary contributions. Some of these high-principled men nearly starved; but they persisted as a matter of conviction, and this paved the way for improved relations with the dissenting groups. As the main matters of contention between the Separates and the standing order began to disappear, there was little to justify their continued independent existence.

On the other hand, reunion was facilitated by the moderation of the Separates themselves. This was demonstrated in the attitude of the Killingly Convention of 1781, which obviously wished to establish a basis for fellowship if not union with the standing churches. Having recognized with gratitude that "the Lord hath inclined many of the established Ministers, and Churches, to adopt the same Principles, and Practice in Reformation, that first influenced us," the delegates went on to say:

> As their is a Number of Churches in this State, that we have before mentioned, that are called Standing Churches, that are disintangled from the Law established Constitution; and make the Christian Profession as above said, and practice accordingly; with all such Churches we could freely hold Communion although they may differ from us in some Things respecting Church Discipline, that are of lesser Moment.[100]

There were three ways in which the restoration of fellowship was effected. The most common of these was simply that when a Separate church dispersed, its members returned as individuals to the churches from which they had withdrawn. Some persons did this even before the Separate church formally disbanded. Usually they were welcomed back with no further penance than a request to be received. This hap-

100. *An Historical Narrative and Declaration,* pp. 20–21, 36.

pened at New London shortly after the infamous bonfire of 1743. The Chelmsford Separates nearly all returned to the parish church by 1772. Those at Sturbridge who did not become Baptists soon re-entered their former communion. At most places where the New Lights seceded only temporarily and formed no Separate church, the dissidents were soon restored to their original fellowship. The Old Light separation from the Second Church in Boston ended in 1785 with the death of Samuel Mather, whose dying request was that his followers rejoin their brethren at the Old North. The conservative faction at Plymouth likewise returned to the First Church in 1783.

Another way in which merger was accomplished was through the calling of a mutual pastor under whom both churches agreed to unite. This happened at Plainfield, where both Separates and regulars were enfeebled by their lengthy struggle over church taxes. In February 1769 both groups agreed to call John Fuller, a Separate preacher who now submitted to regular ordination.[101] The reunited church enjoyed his ministrations until his death in October 1777. The same thing happened at North Stonington. The regular and Separate churches were on such friendly terms that they erected a common meetinghouse in 1816. In 1824 they were both pastorless and agreed to call Joseph Ayer to minister to both groups. Complete union was consummated on March 15, 1827. This happy solution, however, occurred in relatively few instances.

A third method of reunion came about when a Separate church achieved permanent standing and was received into the fellowship of the regular churches. This happened in several places. The church formed under Ebenezer Frothingham still exists as the South Congregational Church in Middletown, and its reception into the ranks of the regulars dates from its reorganization in 1816. The present United Church in New Haven traces its history back through several schisms and mergers to the Separate church formed in 1742, and its "regularity" may be said to date from its incorporation as a legal ecclesiastical society in 1759. The Church of Christ in Yale University, which originated in one sense as a Separate church, is still in existence. The Second Congregational (Plymouth) Church in Milford, which sought with little success to secure New Side Presbyterian preachers from the Middle Colonies during the early days of its existence, became a permanent church. Its Presbyterianism vanished after it obtained legal standing from the legislature in 1770. The Separate church at South Killingly, formed in a remote corner of a sparsely settled parish, never

101. See above, p. 77.

met the persecution suffered by other Separates; its members were never excommunicated by the established church and they were the first to gain tax exemption (1755). In 1799 its pastor, Israel Day, was accepted into the Windham County Ministerial Association, and the church from then on was numbered with the Congregational churches of Connecticut. The Beneficent Church in Providence, Rhode Island, has an unbroken history back to the separation from the First Congregational Church in 1743. The Separates at Newburyport, under Jonathan Parsons, cleared themselves from taxation to the standing order by denominating themselves Presbyterians, and became the first permanent church of that order in Massachusetts. At Chebacco, where John Cleaveland ministered, there was a somewhat different result: the Separate church outstripped the regular; Cleaveland was accepted by all but the most reactionary Old Lights; and in 1774 the few remaining members of the original church united with the Separate church, which then became the regular parish body. At Exeter, New Hampshire, the Separate church achieved a permanent existence. However, after a very complicated later history, it was reorganized in 1813 with little relation to the original constitution.[102] Many of the churches organized by Separates on the frontier, such as that at Bennington, Vermont, became permanent churches also. This list does not pretend to be complete, but it shows that the Separate movement did not dissolve without leaving a trace in the organized life of the Congregational churches of New England.

Conversion to Baptist sentiments. There were very few Separate churches that did not have to write, not once but many times, the notation that a certain member had defected to the Baptists.[103] It has been impossible to tell the story of the Separate movement thus far without frequent reference to this fact. The rise and spread of Baptist sentiments among the Separates is perhaps the chief cause of their decline as a self-contained entity among the religious groups of eighteenth-century New England. Some Separate churches were converted bodily into Baptist churches. Many of the Separate churches practiced mixed communion for a time, after which the rebaptized members withdrew to organize a strict-communion Baptist church. A steady stream of individual converts went from Separate to Baptist ranks. New Light Congregationalists in the regular churches, especially in frontier regions, became Baptist in great numbers. And because few

102. See J. T. Perry, *First Church in Exeter*, pp. 98–100.
103. Occasionally a defection to the Shakers occurred, the only sizable one being at Enfield, Connecticut. Surprisingly few drifted off to the Quakers.

of the Baptist churches formed before the Great Awakening cooperated in the revival, some of them divided in much the same manner as the Congregational churches whose leaders opposed the Awakening. Thus there arose a vigorous, fast-growing body of Separate Baptist churches quite dissimilar to the older Baptists in New England. It was indeed through this newly risen group that the more permanent fruits of the Great Awakening were borne off by the Baptists. Because the Separate Baptists are important—not only to complete the story of separatism in the eighteenth century but also to show their large influence on American Baptist life—these developments will be expanded in the subsequent chapters.

6. CONVERSION OF THE SEPARATES TO BAPTIST SENTIMENTS

"Gone to the Baptists" is a frequent entry in the record books of the Separate churches beside the names of former members who had adopted the principle of believer's, as opposed to infant's, baptism. Few Separate consciences escaped turmoil over this point, and as a result their churches earned the epithet "nurseries of baptists." The problem they faced was identical to that of the early English separatists a century before: having come out from the standing order, they could hardly fail to sense a vague uneasiness, which is best attributed to the fact that they stood in an unstable "halfway house" between churchly and fully dissenting positions. Many were not prepared to yield their pedobaptist traditions and assume a thoroughly sectarian stance without a struggle, and the baptismal controversy raged just as fiercely among them as it had among their English forebears. This chapter will review the reasons for the rise of Baptist sentiments among the Separates, recount the spiritual pilgrimage of an outstanding Separate Baptist, and describe the formation and spread of Separate Baptist churches.

THE RISE OF BAPTIST BELIEFS

The logic of the pure church ideal. One effect of discussions about the Halfway Covenant from its inception in 1657 was to revive concern as to the importance of baptism and its relation to membership in the visible church. That question became much more urgent when converts of the Great Awakening attacked the Halfway Covenant as an evil compromise with the world whose effect was to dilute the purity of the churches. In professing to return to the pure church ideal, the Separates almost inevitably came to the conclusion that if churches were to be composed only of the regenerate, the rite of admission should be restricted to confessed believers. The baptism of infants, whether of believing parents or not, appeared to deny the strict standard of church membership and to undo the work of reformation in one generation. If this practice were not repudiated, the unregenerate were not explicitly excluded from the church and the basic presuppositions of a worldly religious establishment were still retained. The gravitation of many Separates to the practice of believer's baptism, therefore, was a logical termination of their quest for the true church in all its purity.[1] It would have been strange if such a development had not taken place.

Jonathan Edwards, who provided the classic articulation of the pure church ideal in the eighteenth century, betrays the dilemma which confronts every conservative reformer. After stating his case in *An Humble Inquiry*,[2] Edwards essays to answer several objections, among which is the protest that if genuine faith is to be required for the Lord's Supper, it also ought to be required for baptism. "For parents [says the objector], cannot convey to their children a right to this sacrament, by virtue of any qualification *lower* than those requisite in order to their own right."[3] By way of an answer, Edwards admits that children lack the one thing needful for salvation, i.e. faith in Christ, and that therefore baptism can do their souls no good.[4] But he argues that by Christ's own institution, the divine blessing attends the baptism of believers' children; parents, however, must encourage their children to press on to personal faith and not remain content with merely the external badge of it. Here he involves himself in a contradiction by asking, "What is the *name* good for, without the *thing*?" It apparently never occurs to him that the acceptance of the badge might more logically follow, rather than precede, the thing it purports to signify. Edwards avers that if the church insists on experimental religion on the part of the parents as the indispensable prerequisite for having their children baptized, all parents will be stirred up to submit themselves to Christ for the sake of their children. This is a curious blindness to history, and one wonders how such a perceptive thinker could advance an argument which immediately preceding generations had proved fallacious. He does suspect that "the way of baptizing the children of such as never make any proper profession of godliness, is an expedient orig-

1. James Fulton Maclear makes this analysis with respect to the sixteenth-century English situation in "The Birth of the Free Church Tradition," *Church History*, 26 (1957), 99–131.
2. See above, pp. 160–61.
3. *Works*, 1, 184. One must not think the objector is an antipedobaptist, however. He is horrified by the thought that if Edwards' doctrine is allowed, with the result that children logically must remain unbaptized, the land will be filled with multitudes who, because they lack the "badge" of Christianity, will revert to heathenism.
4. Note the absence of a doctrine of baptismal regeneration, always an important fact facilitating conversion to Baptist beliefs.

inally invented for that very end, to give ease to ancestors with respect to their posterity." [5] He seems not to recall that the children of the first American Puritans received the very sort of baptism for which he argues. He places upon parents the responsibility for religiously educating their children; he observes that the children of irreligious parents will grow up to be irreligious "whether baptized or not"; he affirms that persons who have received "the sacred badge of Christianity" but who live in wickedness are hardened in "habitual contempt of sacred things." [6] But he does not press on to the obvious conclusion that on his own presuppositions the root of the errors which he opposes lies in the very practice of infant baptism itself! The dilemma is thrown in sharpest relief by his concluding observation: "To give that which is holy to those who are profane [and when he is not arguing from the premise of family and national solidarity signified to the Jews by circumcision, he classes all who lack personal faith as profane] is not the way to make them better, but worse." [7]

All of the Separates agreed with Edwards at the point of insisting on experimental faith as a term of communion in the visible church, differing only on the manner by which real saints might be known and admitted to fellowship. Those who adopted Baptist views, however, regarded his position on baptism as groundless sophistry, and determined that if the fruits of the new reformation were to be preserved, it must be done by a strict adherence to the concept of the gathered church. Isaac Backus wrote that the great tragedy of the whole Awakening had been that many of its converts flocked into churches "very much blended with the world," and did not see that infant baptism was the root of the evil which had deadened them in the first place. But when "some of us were convinced of this, and acted accordingly," they saw that their only course of consistency was to adopt the principle of believer's baptism. [8] He stated in a number of places that he dissented from the pedobaptist scheme "because it tends to destroy that *distinction* between the church and the world." [9] This is simply to say that the only way to guard against the dilution of the churches which had led to such vapidity in the past was to admit by baptism only convinced believers. The logic of the pure church ideal was inescapably on the side of believer's baptism.

5. *Works, 1,* 187.
6. Ibid.
7. Ibid., p. 188.
8. *A Reply to a Piece Wrote Last Year, by Mr. Israel Holly* (Newport, 1772), p. 28.
9. *The Bond-Woman and the Free,* p. 56.

The requirements of thorough biblicism. The early English Baptists, it will be recalled, answered the covenantal argument of the pedo-baptists with injunction and example drawn from the Scriptures. The same biblicistic principle operated to give the Separate Baptists their strongest assurance. They pointed out repeatedly that the apostles of New Testament times baptized no one without a credible profession of faith, and if there were occasions of "household baptisms" (as pedo-baptists frequently insisted), these did not necessarily include children. "What! did you never see a household without an infant in it?" [10] Backus went a step further and turned even the covenant argument to the advantage of the Baptists. He pointed to God's promise in Hebrews 8:9, "I will make a new covenant, not according to the covenant I made with their fathers," which new covenant is marked by the fact that *all* shall know Him, from the least to the greatest. That is to say, the new covenant is the covenant of grace which is entered by personal faith—regeneration rather than natural generation. The chief argument revolves around the point of divine institution and express biblical command, which things seemed to be lacking in the case of infant baptism. "You say," Backus accuses the baby-baptizers, " 'The baptized child of a true believer is, *by God's appointment* and the parent's act, brought under the bond and seal of the covenant.' This is all the question between us; only prove that it is *God's appointment*, and I will give up the dispute in a minute." [11] The all-important thing for the Separate Baptists was the positive command of Scripture, which they felt to be lacking in the crucial case of baptizing infants.

It is not true that the Separate Baptists forsook the centrality of inner experience, which was the chief determinant of New Light acts and attitudes, to quibble over an outward ceremony.[12] Rather, they contended that whatever ceremonies were allowed in the church ought to be truly expressive of inward realities. To the eye of the biblically oriented Baptist, nothing pictured the essentials of the gospel better than the immersion of a new believer in water. The imagery of burial and resurrection recalled vividly the redemptive work of Christ, who died for sin, was buried, and rose triumphant over death. It depicted the experience of the Christian by showing that he was dead to sin and raised to walk in newness of life with Christ.[13] And it portrayed the eschatological hope of the Christian in bodily resurrection and life

10. Backus, *Reply to a Piece Wrote Last Year*, p. 19.
11. Ibid., p. 17.
12. This charge is made by Armstrong, "Religious Enthusiasm and Separatism in Colonial New England," *Harvard Theological Review*, 38 (1945), 138.
13. Cf. Rom. 6:3–11.

beyond the grave. Thus when a Separate, who already believed in these things fervently, came to feel that God had appointed believer's baptism not only to preserve the purity of the church but to portray the very heart of the gospel, he was often seized with a conviction that permanently overrode his pedobaptist heritage.[14]

The way such minds worked was revealed in a letter from a recent convert in the Boston *Weekly Post-Boy*, February 21, 1743:

> Sir, I am one of the many in this Land, who in this Time of general Awakening and Enquiry, are unable to reconcile the Practice of Infant-Baptism with the Doctrine of the new Birth, that has of late been preached up with such great Power and remarkable Success. . . .
>
> If the Baptism of Infants, don't avail to the Pardon of the Guilt of their original Sin, nor to the Renovation of their corrupt Nature, but such Infants remain under the condemning Sentence of the Law of God, and subject to the corrupt Desires of the Flesh and of the Mind, equally with others, that have not been baptis'd, and must be Converted, born again or regenerated, in order to their Salvation, and must make a public Declaration of it, in order to their Admission to Church Privileges and the Table of the Lord, —what Benefit or Advantage is it to them to be baptized, seeing they remain in the very same natural State of Sin and Guilt with other children, till they are afterwards effectually called, and are really born again? —And if it be no Advantage to them to be baptised, because, it alters not their Condition from what it is by Nature; how can it be thought a Divine institution, seeing God doth nothing in vain? —And if it be not a Divine Institution, why is it practiced among us, seeing we profess to make the Scriptures the Rule of our Faith and Worship? [15]

There were, of course, many Separates who strenuously resisted such a conclusion; the controversy sparked by wholesale defections to Bap-

14. The word "permanently" should be stressed. Depositions of the earliest Separates reveal doubts regarding infant baptism, but an irreversible movement into Baptist ranks did not begin until after 1749. Frothingham said he knew of eight Separate preachers, besides a number of "private Christians," who had been rebaptized and later retracted it. Backus tells of several Baptists who "were frightened and turned back" (*The Bond-Woman and the Free*, p. 49).

15. Printed in Backus, *Letter to Lord*, p. 55; also in Gaustad, *Great Awakening in New England*, p. 122. The latter suggests that the writer may not have been "a puzzled New Light" but a "propaganda-wise Baptist." In either case, the force

tist principles will receive more complete treatment in the next chapter. Here it is observed only that an uneasy conscience regarding infant baptism was part of the separatist ferment almost from the very beginning.

Economic motives. There are always cynics who argue that the conversion of Separates to Baptists was prompted not by lofty ideals of church purity or strict obedience to biblical mandates but by selfish considerations. Simply put, the Baptists were permitted to claim the Act of Toleration, the Separates were not; *ergo,* many of them were "dipped to wash away their taxes." [16]

This argument needs examination. Some pedobaptist Separates did accuse their former brethren of turning Baptist from purely economic motives. Solomon Paine, by far the most bitter antagonist of Baptists in the whole New Light camp, lashed out at them in a published word of "advice":

> O ye tolerated *Baptists,* even such of you as have not only set up a Constitution contrary to Christ's, by making your own Traditions Terms of Communion; forbiding to bring little Children, and offer them up to Christ; and having Believers and their Houses baptized, as a Sign of their Faith, and answer of a good Conscience toward God; and binding the Adult to be plunged, and thereby denying Communion with such as Christ owns; but you also have seen the Thief and consented [i.e. accepted exemption], and have Part with the Whore of *Babylon,* in such a Way as to save your Money, and leave the People of God under stronger Bonds, to suffer Affliction, and a greater Temptation to hearken to your proselyting Spirit, promising them Liberty, while yourselves are the Servants of Corruption, spreading a Net for the Feet of the Simple, you say, *I have paid my Vows,* i.e., been into the Water, and stolen Water is sweet: Come and you may save your Rates, *&c.* . . . To you I write! Hear ye the Word of the Lord which ranks you in the Catalogue of the Beasts Followers; you have his Mark in your Hand, or else you would not be suffered to buy, &c. [17]

---

of the argument is the same. Notice again the absence of belief in baptismal regeneration as the vulnerable point in the pedobaptist argument.

16. This charge is repeated frequently by Jacob C. Meyer, *Church and State in Massachusetts from 1740 to 1833* (Cleveland, 1930). Estimates of its real truth seem so colored by personal prejudice as to be practically worthless.

17. *A Short View of the Difference,* pp. 66–67. The "Mark" here is clearly

The extremely bitter tone of this almost incoherent raillery brands it as a gross exaggeration prompted more by vituperative malice than dispassionate regard for truth. There is much doubt that Baptists were as tolerated as Paine thought. In many localities, especially in Connecticut, legal pressures were applied indiscriminately to "baptists," "anabaptists," "separates," and "new-lights" of all descriptions.[18] In Massachusetts, where the older Baptists had won a modicum of privilege before the law (hardly enough to attract adherents on that account, however), the Exemption Act, which had been on the books since 1728, was revised in 1752 to exclude as far as possible the Separate Baptists. This law allowed the difference between Separate and regular Baptists to be decided by the local authorities, who in most cases were inclined to exercise their powers broadly rather than leniently.[19] The net result was indiscriminate taxation of most Baptists regardless of the pretense to toleration represented by the formal statute.[20]

Where Baptists were exempt, however, the Separates who united with them were naturally suspected of having base motives. On the other hand, appearing to flee from persecution might deter overly conscientious Separates from becoming Baptists even though deeper reasons were impelling them to do so. Such was Isaac Backus. In an unpublished fragment concerning the rise of Baptist sentiments in his Separate church at Middleborough, Massachusetts, he wrote:

> Mr. Hinds signed covenant with us on March 8, 1748, in which month a precinct tax was voted for which some of us were imprisoned the next year, and suffering on such accounts looked very threatening; in the midst of which he and one member more [Deacon Jonathan Woods] brought the baptist principles into our church on Aug. 7, 1749, and urged us to receive them as the way God had opened to escape such sufferings. [A subtle argument indeed!] This raised great fears in my mind that their principles

figurative, referring to Baptists having qualified themselves under the Act of Toleration. This may shed some light on Frothingham's remark above (p. 197).

18. Witness the case of Deacon Drake of Windsor (p. 197), where there were no known Baptists at the time of his accusation. Daniel Marshall, later a Separate Baptist preacher in the South, was called a "baptist" when he withdrew from the standing church at Windsor, though he did not become a Baptist until several years later.

19. See, e.g., Chaffin, *History of Easton*, pp. 180–83. Sturbridge, as noted before, was especially severe (see above, p. 194).

20. The struggle for religious liberty as it involved the Separate Baptists will be discussed in the next chapter.

were wrong, which held me in long suspence and caused much of the changeableness for which he now would reproach me.[21]

It was two years before Backus submitted to believer's baptism, and five more before he organized a Baptist church; at the latter time, moreover, only four persons signed covenant with him and his wife. Whatever degree of toleration the Middleborough authorities granted, it apparently was slight incentive for these Separates to turn Baptist.

Another consideration in evaluating the extent of economic motives in the conversion of Separates to Baptists is that this was not the only —perhaps not even the surest—course to exemption from ecclesiastical taxation. Quakers had at least as much toleration, and offered enough doctrinal similarity (belief in "inner light") to make transition easy. Indeed, it is surprising that more Separates did not become Quakers; apparently few did. Other Separates turned Presbyterian and stated quite frankly that their chief motive in doing so was to secure tax relief; this happened at Newburyport and Easton, Massachusetts, while the Separates at Milford, Connecticut, tried the same thing with less success. Finally, in most places the Separates who remained Strict Congregationalists were under no more disabilities than those who became Baptists.

It is of course impossible at this distance to assess precisely the extent to which economic motives figured in the movement from Separate to Baptist ranks, but it does not appear that sweeping assertions as to the primacy of this factor are justified. There is better ground for believing that the charge of covetousness was leveled more accurately against those who bent all their force to prevent the rise of religious pluralism and to preserve the tax roll intact in order to lighten the load on their own pocketbooks—and who pleaded conscience in so doing.[22]

An Outstanding Convert: Isaac Backus

The most outstanding illustration as well as the best documented case of a Baptist convert is the man whose name has appeared frequently in these pages already, Isaac Backus (1724–1806). His career

21. Quoted in Thomas Buford Maston, "The Ethical and Social Attitudes of Isaac Backus" (dissertation, Yale University, 1939), pp. 38–39. The man referred to here is Ebenezer Hinds, who served as pastor of the Second Baptist Church in Middleborough 1758–1812.

22. Backus makes this charge in *The Testimony of the Two Witnesses, Explained and Improved* (Providence, 1789), p. 29.

well typifies how the revivalistic piety of the Separates gradually infiltrated Baptist ranks.

Ministry as a Separate preacher. The revival came to Backus' home town of Norwich in 1741 through the preaching of Eleazar Wheelock, Benjamin Pomeroy, James Davenport, and others. Meetings were characterized by the same type of preaching and emotional response that marked the impact of the Great Awakening elsewhere. Backus was among those affected, although he is careful to state that he was not transported with emotion and ecstasy like some of those around him. His conversion in 1741 was comparatively quiet, though in the familiar pattern of the revival movement of the time.[23]

With the other new converts in Norwich, Backus hesitated to join the standing church because pastor Benjamin Lord, in spite of his cooperation in the revival, continued to sanction the Halfway Covenant and to hold Stoddardean views of the Lord's Supper. Eleven months after his conversion, however, wishing to "enjoy the precious ordinance of the supper," and finding no other way to secure that privilege, Backus joined the Norwich church, "concluding to bear those things as a burden and to hope for a reformation." [24] Such hopes proved illusory, and after two years the restive New Lights began to think of establishing private worship for mutual edification. Their reasons were substantially the same as those given by dissatisfied converts everywhere, and after a lengthy labor with them, the church excommunicated them on November 10, 1745. They organized a Separate church at Bean Hill, and selected Jedediah Hyde, one of their number, as pastor.[25]

In the new freedom with which laymen were allowed to express their religious sentiments, Backus soon reached the conviction that he had an internal call from God to preach the gospel.

> Being at a certain house where a number of the saints were met, the command, "pray ye the Lord of the harvest that He will send forth laborers into his harvest," was read and spoken upon. A conviction seized my mind that God had given me abilities which his

23. See Hovey, *Memoir of Isaac Backus*, p. 39. Another account of Backus' experience in his own words is in his *History of New England*, 2, 106–18. Maston, "Ethical and Social Attitudes of Backus," has carefully researched all the materials, but his emphasis lies in another direction from that in view here. I have relied more largely upon Hovey, who also has compared all the pertinent references from Backus' diary and several other unpublished manuscripts.

24. Hovey, p. 42.

25. See above, pp. 83–84.

church had a right to the use of, and which I could not withhold with a clear conscience. Soon after, a spirit of prayer for divine teaching was given me in a remarkable manner, and eternal things were brought into a near view, with a clear sight of the truth and harmony of the Holy Scriptures; also these words were impressed on my mind: "Son of man, eat this roll." Never did I more sensibly eat natural food than did my soul feast upon the solid truths of God's Word.[26]

After appropriately humble demurrings, Backus announced to the church two days later (September 28, 1746) that he was ready to answer God's call. This was received with approval by the church, and Backus concluded his account of the experience by saying, "And as I was then free from all worldly engagements, I devoted my whole time to that great work." [27] The fact that he had only a common-school education was no hindrance—it may even have been an advantage.

Plunging immediately into the work of itinerant evangelism, Backus spent fourteen months of untiring labor in the towns of eastern Connecticut, Rhode Island, and southeastern Massachusetts. For reasons that are not entirely clear, he seems to have escaped being molested by the authorities, despite the stringent proscriptions of such activity. In December 1747, while visiting in Providence, he was urged to accompany the Separate pastor Joseph Snow on a preaching mission to Titicut, a new parish between Middleborough and Bridgewater in which revival sentiments were still strong. He went, and soon discovered a hunger for "gospel food" that was translated speedily into a call to settle in the place as permanent preacher:

I was led to discover in this place a large field all white to the harvest. Other men had labored here in years past, and the Lord had wrought wonders by them, but now my soul was constrained by divine light, love and peace to enter into their labors. My heart was so drawn forth towards God and in love to this people, that I felt myself willing to impart unto them not only the Gospel but my own soul also. Thus the Lord bound me to this people ere I was aware of it and before I knew any of them personally.[28]

This was the place at which he was to spend the rest of his life, a ministry of fifty-eight years. Titicut precinct had been granted parish

26. Ibid., pp. 60–61.
27. Ibid., p. 62.
28. Ibid., p. 67.

privileges by the General Court in 1743, but no church had been formed because of the tension between its two neighbors. The Middleborough church under Peter Thacher (died 1744, succeeded by Sylvanus Conant) was revivalistic, the Bridgewater church under John Shaw antirevivalistic; and both feared that if a new church were formed, it might call the wrong kind of minister. The majority of the inhabitants of Titicut, however, were converts of the Great Awakening (Tennent had passed through in 1741) and were anxious to have a New Light preacher. They had previously heard such men as Eliab Byram, Silas Brett, John Wadsworth, Solomon Reed, and Nathaniel Shepard; and this explains the alacrity with which they received Snow and Backus. When the young evangelist from Norwich announced his willingness to remain, they would be restrained no longer and proposed to form a church without the approval of the neighboring ministers and without regular dismissions from their respective churches. At their request Backus drew some articles of faith and a covenant, which were signed by sixteen persons on February 16, 1748. He was ordained their pastor on April 13, with the help of representatives from Separate churches at Providence, Attleborough, Canterbury, and Norwich. At that time the church had thirty-four members.

Acceptance of Baptist sentiments. The introduction of Baptist beliefs into the Titicut Separate Church by Ebenezer Hinds and Jonathan Woods on August 7, 1749, has been mentioned.[29] In spite of their inability to convince the pastor, they continued to propagate their beliefs zealously; and Backus chose not to interfere. He did, however, begin a fitful search for light which only compounded his perplexity:

> On Saturday night, August 26th, while crying to God for help and direction, he found there were many things very dear to him which yet he could freely give up into the hands of God, but that in this case he felt a sensible pulling back. At length this conclusion suddenly came into his mind: namely, *the Baptist principles are certainly right, because nature fights so against them.* The next day, he felt a secret hurrying on to preach upon this subject; which he did in the afternoon, taking for his text, Romans 6:4, and maintaining that none have any right to baptism except believers, and that immersion seems to be the only correct mode.[30]

He regretted this hasty act almost immediately, and spent the next several days in doubt and darkness. After confessing publicly that he

29. See above, p. 214.
30. Ibid., pp. 84–85. It should be added that Backus later renounced the contrary-to-nature argument. See his *History of New England, 2,* 119.

probably had been mistaken, he left for a three-week visit to his old home in Norwich. In his absence Ebenezer Moulton, a Baptist elder from South Brimfield, came to Titicut and immersed nine of his church members along with one other person.

The first Sunday after his return, September 26, Backus retracted the Baptist sentiments he had preached a month earlier. Though his immersed members were offended and withdrew to worship by themselves, he declared himself "willing to venture into eternity" on the practice of infant baptism. This also was too rash a conclusion, no sooner uttered than regretted. The vexing question returned: "Where, and in what relation to the church of God do those stand who have been baptized and yet are not believers?" [31] Then began an extended period of agonizing prayer and intense study, of which he said later, "No man, who has not experienced the like, can form a proper idea of the distress I endured for two years." [32] The work of his church, anxiously awaiting the outcome of his spiritual struggles, came almost to a standstill. After months of painstaking examination of every biblical passage bearing on the covenants and of every argument advanced to justify the baptizing of infants, Backus communicated to the church his conviction that there was no scriptural warrant for that practice. This was July 26, 1751. The predominant sentiment in his church was opposed to his conclusion, and he prayed that he might die rather than be a stumbling block to others. After spending another day in prayer and fasting, he was satisfied that his duty lay before him. He sent for Elder Benjamin Pierce of Warwick, Rhode Island; and on August 22 was immersed with six fellow church members on profession of faith in Christ.

Formation of a Baptist church. There were now seventeen immersed Baptists in Titicut, but no church was formed until five years later. It is clear that Backus did not have in mind the forming of a Baptist church at the time he finally decided what his personal course must be. He sought to minimize the disturbance his act caused in the church by refusing to raise the issue of baptismal qualifications for communion; and though he himself could not conscientiously sprinkle the infants of his members, he tried to keep peace by arranging for a neighboring minister to do it. But continuing dissension over his stand led to the calling of a peace council on October 2, the first of many which were to meet before the problem was finally resolved—if permanent schism may be called a resolution.

This first council soon turned from hearing Backus' tale of travail

31. Hovey, p. 87.
32. Ibid., p. 90.

to inquire into the state of the church. They found it in utter confusion, and recommended that the members who chose to travel on together in church estate renew their covenant. Sixteen persons consented, and the rest were censured. Backus, who was already under censure for permitting confusion to reign in the church and failing to discipline the "scandalous walkers," could not join with them and so was left under censure. He retired to Norwich until November 8, at which time the church declared its willingness to restore him to fellowship and the pastoral office. This meant adopting a *via media*. Two reactionary brethren, Samuel Alden and Robert Washburn, would not accept a minister who refused to baptize infants, and assumed a position to the right; the Baptist members who agitated for immersion as a term of communion made up a very vocal left. The church admonished and suspended both groups of extremists. This led to council after council, and was undoubtedly the major catalyst in bringing the issues of believer's baptism and communion between Baptists and pedobaptists to a head among all the Separate churches. That story is reserved for the next chapter.

In the meantime, the church tried for five years to live in peace on the mixed-communion plan:

> If any member of the church desired to have his children baptized, he had full permission to call in a minister from abroad to perform the act; and if any member who had been sprinkled in infancy wished to be baptized, full permission was granted Mr. Backus to administer this rite. Moreover, it was agreed, that no one should introduce any conversation which would lead to remarks on the subjects or mode of baptism.[33]

This compromise, however, soon broke down in actual practice. Whenever an infant was sprinkled, the Baptists made their displeasure unpleasantly obvious; and whenever a believer was immersed, the pedobaptists boycotted the ceremony and called it taking the name of the Trinity in vain. The disagreement seethed in semisilence for many months before it came to an open issue. The sorely tried pastor was forced into another extended season of soul-searching and study. He reviewed the arguments for mixed communion, the chief one of which was that God had communion with all sincere believers regardless of how or when (or even if) baptized, and that a Christian breaks the rule of charity by refusing to commune with a fellow Christian. Backus came to believe that there are some things in which men cannot imi-

33. Ibid., p. 114.

tate God, and that Christians had no right to break one rule in order to
unite in another. Said he:

> Baptism and the Lord's Supper, appear to be ordinances of Christ
> of equal weight, and the one to be placed before the other; and
> therefore, after many cries for divine direction and much search-
> ing of the Scriptures, I was constrained to give in that we ought
> not to receive any to the Lord's table who have not been baptized
> according to the gospel rule. I was brought to see that we had
> made Christians our rule, instead of the Word of God; for his
> Word requires a credible confession of saving faith, in order to
> baptism; and if we come to the Holy Supper with any who were
> only sprinkled in infancy, we commune with unbaptized persons,
> which Pedobaptists themselves do not profess to do.[34]

He agreed that union and communion of the believer with the Lord
are the foundation for the fellowship of the saints, but questioned
whether this is all that is necessary to constitute a visible church. This
was indeed the heart of the question. "There are things not essential
to salvation which are necessary in the visible building [of the church].
For instance, *those who hold the church to be national cannot build
with those who hold it to be congregational.*"[35] He saw that the practice of infant baptism was the foundation of a national religious establishment, a territorial church which tended to become little different
from the total culture.

By 1756 Backus was ready to follow his conscience in forming a
strict-communion Baptist church. On January 16 he and his wife, with
four others who had gathered in their home for the purpose, entered
into covenant with one another and affixed their names to a confession
of faith which Backus had drawn. He was formally installed as their
pastor on June 23, by which time they had received at least four more
members. This was "the first Baptist church between Boston and
Rehoboth, a distance of almost fifty miles, and between Bellingham
and the end of Cape Cod, a distance of more than one hundred
miles."[36] In later years Backus summarized his long pilgrimage by
saying:

> After renewing grace was granted, I was such a dull scholar in
> Christ's school, that I was thirty-two years in learning a lesson

34. Ibid., p. 116.
35. Ibid. Italics mine.
36. Ibid., p. 119.

of only six words, namely "one Lord, one faith, one baptism." It
took ten years to get clear of the custom of putting baptism before
faith, and near five more to learn not to contradict the same in
practice; after which, above seventeen trying years rolled over us,
before we could refrain from an implicit acknowledgement of
more than "one Lord" in religious affairs.[37]

The last lesson refers to Backus' decision to press for complete religious
liberty rather than accept the secondary status implied by toleration.
That story also is reserved for the next chapter.

Zeal in the Baptist cause. His long indecision over, Backus was free
to devote his energies to advancing the cause of the faith he had won
through arduous wrestling. Having put his hand to the plow, he
not only never looked back but pushed straight on down the furrow.
The story of the next several years is one of vigorous local ministry,
far-ranging evangelistic tours, ready response to requests for aid from
sister churches old and new, and indefatigable zeal in seeking new
converts. During the eleven years after he led in the organization of
the First Baptist Church in Middleborough, he traveled 14,691 miles,
preached 2,412 sermons, and baptized 62 persons.[38] From this time forward he was also busily engaged in writing, and a recent student of
Backus' life asserts that his influence through the written word was
possibly greater than in any other way.[39] He was certainly one of the
most prolific writers of the period, and claimed that he wrote more
than any other Baptist.[40] One of his most important works, and an in-
valuable source of information for religious developments in eighteenth-century New England, is *A History of New-England with Particular Reference to the Denomination of Christians Called Baptists.*[41]
George Bancroft called Backus "one of the most exact of our New
England historians," whose work is marked by "ingenuousness, clear

37. Ibid., p. 118. It is sometimes assumed that the Titicut Separate Church became Baptist in a body or that the pedobaptist remnant dispersed. This is not true.
After the Baptists withdrew, the original church called Solomon Reed, who served
as pastor from 1756 until his death in 1785. Reed was a graduate of Harvard
(1739), a close associate of Whitefield, and had been pastor of a New Light
church at Framingham 1746–56. See S. Hopkins Emery, *The History of the
Church of North Middleborough, Massachusetts* (Middleborough, 1876), pp. 1–36.
38. Hovey, p. 130.
39. Maston, p. 40.
40. *History of New England*, 2, 427.
41. Originally published in 3 vols. Boston, 1777, 1784, 1796. I have used consistently the Weston edition of 1871 as more accurate, more readily available, and
most helpfully annotated.

discernment, and determined accuracy." [42] Of the other writings, Maston said:

> Fully as voluminous as his history and probably more influential in his age were his numerous [thirty-seven in all] pamphlets. They touched on a wide variety of subjects but practically all of them dealt with some current theological or political problem and most of them were in propagation or defense of some truth or position held by Baptists. . . . The tracts by Backus, in spite of the financial and transportation difficulties of his age, were circulated rather widely. [They found their way into many libraries in England and America.] They, with his books, won him many friends and opened avenues of service. [43]

There was, of course, much opposition to his published sentiments—a fact not at all surprising when it is considered that most of them dealt with controversial subjects. Some of the most vicious criticism came from within his own Baptist ranks. He was aware of the strictures, recorded them patiently, and published his pamphlets anyhow.

Much of his writing was a polemic against pedobaptism, partly as self-defense and partly as witness to what he believed was truth. There were three main points which he made again and again in various ways: (1) Infant baptism falsely supposes that the New Testament church is grafted onto the Old Testament Israel with no distinction between the old covenant, based on the family and the nation, and the new covenant, based on individual personal response in faith. (2) Infant baptism leads naturally to a territorial church which becomes so intermingled with society in general ("the world") that it loses its distinctive character as a fellowship of the redeemed. (3) Infant baptism is cruel to children because it engenders a false sense of security and thus endangers their opportunity to realize their sinful condition and need for personal faith in Christ. In breaking with both the standing churches and the pedobaptist Separates, Backus simply followed New Light theology and Strict Congregational ecclesiology to their logical conclusions.

Beyond his preaching and writing ministry, Backus' third major contribution came from his persistent and productive efforts in behalf of religious liberty. Some of the events in this struggle will be recounted in the next chapter, but here it should be noted that Backus

42. Quoted in George E. Horr, "The Baptists," *The Religious History of New England*, King's Chapel Lectures (Boston, 1917), p. 157.
43. "Ethical and Social Attitudes of Backus," pp. 43–44.

went further to develop a rational theory of the rights of conscience than perhaps any of his contemporaries. For this he drew heavily on John Locke, who was popular with the colonists for other aspects of his political theory. Backus was especially fond of citing Locke's *Letter on Toleration*. Maston has stated, however, that Backus' basic ideas on civil and ecclesiastical governments and the relation between them were formulated early, before he had had much contact with Locke's writings.[44]

The whole theology of the revival party, moreover, was framed in such a way as to heighten the sense of individual responsibility before God; and such responsibility is meaningless without freedom to respond according to the promptings of conscience. This is why Maston could conclude his illuminating study with the assertion that "Backus brought together the theology and ethical theory of the 'New Divinity,' the ecclesiastical polity of the congregationalism of the Baptists and the political philosophy of John Locke and welded them into a more or less consistent system; at least consistent enough to live by." [45] He did live by it, and along with his confrère John Leland struck many a "blow at the root" which eventually toppled the ecclesiastical establishment in New England. He was, it can be said without exaggeration, "the most outstanding Baptist of his day." [46]

THE ORGANIZATION OF SEPARATE BAPTIST CHURCHES

There were four main ways in which Separate Baptist churches, such as the one under Isaac Backus at Middleborough, were formed: the en bloc conversion of entire Separate congregations, the division of mixed-communion churches, individual converts to Baptist principles, and schisms in some of the older Baptist churches. These will be considered individually and illustrations of each will be given.

Conversion of entire Separate churches. The story may begin with the New Lights at Sturbridge, Massachusetts. The Separate church formed here on November 10, 1747, was under the leadership of John Blunt, one of their own number whom they ordained on September 28, 1748. Partial records of the church appear in the journal of Henry Fisk, who served as clerk of the church and whose testimony as to the persecutions of this "People inhabiting the Wilderness" has already been noted.[47] Under the date of May 16, 1749, he wrote:

44. Ibid., p. 239.
45. Ibid., p. 240.
46. Ibid., p. 233.
47. See above, p. 194.

About this time the trial concerning baptism came up. Now the voice is, *'Take heed how ye build;* for every man's work shall be tried, of what sort it is; for the day shall try it.' The day is come that shall burn as an oven. Now the daughter of Zion is called to arise and thresh. The Lord made her horn iron and her hoof brass. Infant sprinkling, which we called baptism, went away like the chaff of the summer threshing-floor.[48]

The instrument of threshing in this case was Ebenezer Moulton, the ubiquitous Baptist evangelist from South Brimfield.[49] He came to Sturbridge in June and immersed thirteen members of the Separate church, including its pastor and deacon; "and in a little time after, all their officers, and the main body of the church, were baptized, even above threescore persons." [50] Blunt soon reverted to pedobaptism and left the church in 1753, when it was in the throes of a severe trial because of oppression by the authorities.[51] The church endured, however, and was estimated to have about forty families in 1760. Its pastors after Blunt were William Ewing 1768–75, Jordan Dodge 1784–88, and Zenas Lockwood Leonard 1796–1832. The church, later known as the Fiskdale Baptist Church, practiced open communion until 1782, when it was received into the Warren Baptist Association.

The Separate Baptist church in Attleborough has a similar history. The Separate church there was formed by seventy-four persons on January 20, 1747, and Nathaniel Shepard ordained as their pastor on the same day. He died in 1752 and the church remained pastorless a number of years. In 1767 they called Abraham Bloss, formerly of Sturbridge and most recently pastor of a mixed-communion church of Separates and Baptists at Upton, Massachusetts 1751–65. At his coming the Attleborough church voted to change its constitution from Strict Congregational to open-communion Baptist. Bloss died after two

48. Quoted in Backus, *History of New England,* 2, 94 n.
49. A Baptist church, the first in Hampshire County, was organized at South Brimfield in 1736. Moulton was ordained there Nov. 4, 1741, by Jeremiah Condy of Boston, John Callender of Newport, Benjamin Marsh of Sutton, and Samuel Maxwell of Swansea. He ranged from Connecticut to Nova Scotia, immersing New Lights and organizing Baptist churches wherever he could; and returned to South Brimfield a few years before his death in 1783. He has been pointed out (chap. 3, n. 28) as the link connecting many Separate preachers with the regularly ordained Puritan ministers: Boston Congregationalists acted in ordaining both Condy and Callender; Moulton acted in ordaining Thomas Denison, who in turn helped ordain most of the Separate preachers in eastern Connecticut.
50. Backus, *History of New England,* 2, 94.
51. See above, p. 103.

years, and the ten remaining members voted to affiliate with the Separate Baptist church at nearby Bellingham under Noah Alden. The latter was a strict-communion group, and soon the Attleborough church voted to adopt that plan also. Alden preached quarterly at Attleborough until Job Seamans, a product of Backus' church who had lately returned from an evangelistic mission in New Brunswick, became pastor in 1772. The church united with the Warren Association in 1771 and quickly took its place in the common life of New England Baptists. In 1787 Seamans moved to New London, New Hampshire, where he preached until his death in 1830 at the age of eighty-two.

The Baptist church at Montville, Connecticut, is a result of Separate activity in the north parish of New London during the ministry of the Rev. David Jewett 1739–83. Although pronounced unconverted by James Davenport, he had experienced an awakening of evangelistic zeal in 1741 and had promoted the revival in his parish with vigor. After the passage of the restrictive legislation of 1742, however, he chose to remain with the law; and the cooling of his ardor gave rise to a separation on the part of those whose zeal would not be restrained. The Separate church here was organized in 1747 under the leadership of Dyer Hyde. He remained only a short time, and was succeeded on May 17, 1750, by Joshua Morse, under whom the Separates declared themselves an open-communion Baptist church. After some years, Morse adopted the principle of strict communion and led the church to do likewise. It seems that he influenced other churches in the vicinity to do the same thing, insomuch that he is probably responsible for furnishing the initial impulse for the formation in 1772 of the Stonington Baptist Association, a fellowship of strict-communion churches.[52]

Morse's colorful career is of more than ordinary interest. He was born of Baptist parents in South Kingston, Rhode Island, in 1726. Hearing George Whitefield during the evangelist's first visit to New England, he was converted and became an ardent New Light. The years of his young manhood were spent as a lay exhorter in southwestern Rhode Island and southeastern Connecticut. His ministry apparently was characterized by a reckless zeal that invited the most virulent sort of opposition, for he seems to have suffered more than most of his brethren in the Separate or Baptist ministry:

> During a season of revival in North Stonington, he was arrested and "sentenced to pay a fine of twenty shillings, or receive ten lashes at the whipping-post." He was spared only through the compassion of the executioner, who was moved to pay the fine

52. See below, pp. 264–66.

rather than inflict the blows upon a Christian man. "At another time, while preaching, two men rushed in, and with violent blows brought him to the floor." . . . On another occasion, as he was preaching, a clergyman came in, put his hand upon his mouth, and commanded a man who accompanied him to strike him. . . . At another time, while engaged in prayer, he was knocked down, dragged by the hair down a flight of steps into the street, and was there beaten in the most inhuman manner. A gash on his face was laid open so deep that he carried the scar to his grave.[53]

After settling in Montville in 1750, Morse continued his itinerant ministry. An especially interesting story concerns his founding the Separate Baptist Church at Stratfield (now Bridgeport). Here, it will be recalled, a switch of pastoral leadership in the Congregational church had provoked both an Old Light and then a New Light defection.[54] One night in 1751 a woman dreamed of a young preacher who rode up to her house on horseback; and as she was telling the dream to a friend, the preacher suddenly appeared before them in person. It was Joshua Morse. Greatly impressed, the two women immediately gathered together a group to hear his sermon. One of the converts was Captain John Sherwood, long a prominent member of the standing church, who was baptized with a number of others on the second Sunday in October. These entered into covenant together as a Baptist church; and in 1757 Sherwood was ordained as their pastor, serving until his death in 1779.[55] Meanwhile, Morse spent most of 1753–55 in evangelistic labors in the vicinity of Fishkill, New York, apparently without a dismission from his Montville charge. He left permanently in 1779, however, and moved to Sandisfield, in western Massachusetts. Here he organized a Baptist church composed of New Lights who had settled in the area, and served as their pastor until his death in 1795. His youngest son, Asahel Morse, became pastor of the Separate Baptist church in Suffield, Connecticut, and was the author of the clause on religious liberty in the Bill of Rights of the Connecticut Constitution framed in 1818.[56]

53. Denison, *Westerly and Its Witnesses*, p. 90.
54. See above, pp. 111–12.
55. Orcutt, *History of Bridgeport*, p. 85; Lucy S. Curtiss, *Two Hundred Fifty Years* (Bridgeport, 1945), p. 37.
56. M. L. Greene, *Religious Liberty in Connecticut*, p. 487. The Montville Baptist Church languished for several years after Morse's departure, and was reorganized in 1788 by the Rev. Reuben Palmer. He carried on a fruitful ministry until his death in 1822, by which time the church was large and vigorous. See Henry A. Baker, *History of Montville, Connecticut* (Hartford, 1896), pp. 666–67.

One further illustration of the formation of a Separate Baptist church by the total conversion of a group of Separates deserves to be cited. This one occurred at West Woodstock, Connecticut, where the separation was late and the shift to Baptist principles rapid. The movement dates not from the Great Awakening proper but from the spurt of revival in 1763–64.[57] On December 9 of the former year, Noah Alden, then pastor of the Separate Baptist church at Stafford, Connecticut, 1754–66, passed through the community and preached a sermon which struck conviction into the leader of a group of frivolous young people. This young man, Biel Ledoyt, spoke to his merrymaking friends about his experience with such earnestness and power that they, too, came under the sway of strong religious feelings. He appointed a public meeting in a schoolhouse, to which many of his former acquaintances came to mock and remained to pray. They stood "like men amazed" while Ledoyt spoke to a crowded auditory with such convincing force that some forty young people were converted. The scenes of the forties were repeated:

> Meetings were now attended two or three times a week. Convictions increased greatly. Parents were surprised to see their giddy children distressed for their souls. Some old professors, who had thought themselves Christians, now began to see that their building was upon the sand, and cried "God be merciful to us sinners!" and at the first there were hardly any that dared to say a word against the work. Frolicking, which had been practised, came to a stop. The Bible, and other good books, that had never been regarded, were now much in use. Our groves rang with the bitter outcries of the distressed youth. God was soon merciful to some of them, and delivered them from their distresses, and their sorrow was turned into joy, and their mouths filled with praise to their Redeemer, and they were then calling upon all to praise the Lord with them, and they recommended him to others, and this increased their distress.[58]

As before, the revival provoked opposition from those who frowned upon enthusiasm, which resulted in the withdrawing of the new converts from the unsympathetic church. By the fall of 1764 they had loosely organized as a Separate church, enjoying the edifying exhortations of various of their own number, with Ledoyt as leader. Inasmuch as this revival owed its origin to an avowed Baptist, it is not surprising

57. See above, p. 185.
58. Ledoyt, letter to Backus, printed in Backus, *History of New England, 2,* 552.

that several of the converts sought immersion at the first opportunity. In February 1766 fifteen of these persons organized as a Baptist church and were soon joined by others. They continued to rely on the voluntary ministrations of whoever felt the promptings of the Spirit, but more and more it was evident that the hand of the Lord was upon Biel Ledoyt. He was ordained May 26, 1768. Ezra Stiles estimated that this congregation was "near a third part of the Parish; beside some others from neighboring Parishes in To[lland] and Union. His congregation sd. to be near as big as Mr. Williams." [59] After many unsuccessful attempts to suppress the new church, assault its pastor, and amerce its members, the Old Lights were advised by Governor Trumbull in March 1771 to apply the provisions of the Toleration Act to these Baptists and cease further oppression. This done, "the Woodstock Baptist Church increased in numbers and influence, united with the Warren Baptist Association, and gained a respectable standing among its sister churches." [60] It soon had branches at Pomfret and Killingly, which were constituted as independent churches in 1776. Ledoyt went in 1790 to Newport, New Hampshire, where he organized a church and served as its pastor until 1804. Then he returned to his old charge at Woodstock and ministered until his death in 1813.

Division of mixed-communion churches. The problems arising from the attempt of Baptists and pedobaptists to remain in one church have been mentioned frequently, and the whole communion controversy will be examined closely in the next chapter. It is not at all difficult to see how, in the religious understanding of the times, tensions would increase until both parties felt justified in going their separate ways. This is what happened under Isaac Backus at Middleborough. Three other illustrations will show how Separate Baptist churches resulted from the withdrawal or excommunication of the Baptist party from the Separate church to which it belonged.

59. *Itineraries of Ezra Stiles*, p. 267. Stephen Williams was the regular Congregational pastor in West Woodstock.

60. Larned, *History of Windham County*, 2, 103. Miss Larned incorrectly implies that opposition ceased forever. In 1780 the Woodstock church wrote to the Warren Association: "We are much affected with the long confinement of our brethren in Worcester goal . . . nor can we expect to fare better ourselves very long, notwithstanding our endeavoring to answer the unjust law of the ruling party, by giving certificates to the members of our society, which have been carried to the parish clerk; yet a considerable number of them are rated to the standing ministry, and soon expect to be distressed on that account. Our oppressors are deaf to all reasoning upon the subject, and are determined to prosecute their design, let the consequence be what it may" (Backus, *History of New England, 2,* 524).

The Separate activity on Cape Cod led to the formation of several Baptist churches. Its main center was in the south parish of Harwich, where a widespread revival had occurred under Elisha Paine in 1744. The Separate church was constituted on February 23, 1749, and Joshua Nickerson ordained pastor with the help of Isaac Backus, John Paine from Rehoboth, and Nathaniel Shepard from Attleborough. Fifty members subscribed the covenant on that day, and special note was made of the fact that "this church admitted to communion all Christians whether they had been sprinkled in infancy, or been baptized by immersion." [61] In 1751 a second Separate church was organized in the west part of the town, and Richard Chase of Yarmouth was ordained pastor on December 11 by Backus, Paine, and William Carpenter of Norton. This church also accepted both forms of baptism, but soon the pastor and most of the church adopted decidedly Baptist sentiments and neglected infant baptism. The pedobaptist members called for a council, which convened on December 20, 1752. "After a full hearing the council censured the pastor, and that portion of the church who held with him, and advised the aggrieved members to withdraw from 'the pastor and church as disorderly walkers.'" [62] The Baptist faction summoned another council, which met August 23, 1753, and revoked the censure. Plainly enough, both votes followed a strict party line because of the composure of the respective councils. The day after the second (Baptist) council, Backus baptized Pastor Chase and his sympathizers.

Mixed communion continued to cause friction. In 1757 the Baptists of both the Harwich Separate churches withdrew and united to form a strict-communion church. Chase was ordained their pastor on September 29 by Backus and Richard Round, Baptist pastor from Rehoboth. This was the first Baptist church in Barnstable County and soon it included members from Barnstable, Yarmouth, Chatham, Eastham, and Truro. In 1771 sixteen members of this church living in Hyannis were dismissed to form an independent church. Joshua Nickerson's Separate church was so depleted by defections to the Baptists that he became discouraged and removed in 1772 to Tamworth, New Hampshire, where he died in 1791. Nathaniel Ewer, pastor of the Separate church in Barnstable, had much the same experience; he moved to Newmarket, New Hampshire, in 1773 and preached there until 1797. In the meantime, the Baptist church at Harwich was scandalized by

61. Josiah Paine, *History of Harwich*, p. 364. It is not clear whether this action was taken at the organization of the church or shortly thereafter.
62. Ibid., p. 367.

its pastor's lapse into intemperance. He was deposed by advice of a council in January 1777. Deacon Seth Clarke succeeded him, and the church united with the Warren Association the same year. This marks the entrance of the Separate Baptist churches on the Cape into the fellowship of the regular Baptists.

Another Separate (perhaps New Light would be a more accurate designation in this case) church which apparently pursued the plan of mixed communion from the outset was the one organized by James Rodgers at South Kingston, Rhode Island, in the fall of 1750. He remained as pastor for some twenty years, after which he removed to New York and left his church to divide into three parts. One branch remained in the old meetinghouse at Weight Corner under the leadership of Elliott Locke 1794–1805. It continued to follow the mixed-communion plan and was a member for a while of the Groton Union Conference.[63] It dissolved soon after Locke's death. Another branch moved to Richmond, designated itself as the First Baptist Church of that town, adopted strict communion, and united with the Stonington Association in 1776. Its pastors were Benjamin Barber, Jr., and Phineas Palmer; it seems to have disbanded shortly after the latter's death in 1818. (Another Baptist church at Richmond enjoyed a brief existence under Charles Boss 1781–89.) The sole survivor of the Rodgers church was the First Baptist Church of South Kingston. After meeting in private homes for a while, it reorganized in 1781 and ordained Dr. Benjamin Weight, a physician, who served the church from 1781 to 1811. This church was a member of the Stonington Association 1782–1836, the Warren Association 1836–60, and the Narragansett Association after 1860.

The Separate church at Westerly, formed in 1750,[64] was mixed communion from the start. Stephen Babcock was ordained pastor by David Sprague, a Baptist, and by Solomon Paine, a pedobaptist. This was the first time the two groups joined in an ecclesiastical action of this nature. Backus states that Babcock was a Baptist at the time of his ordination, and Stiles says he was not; actually it is not known when he was immersed. Although the church received members sprinkled in infancy, its articles of faith define baptism as "Dipping the subject all over in the water." [65] The communion issue was raised by deacon Simeon Brown, who lived across the line in North Stonington (as did

63. This was an association of mixed-communion churches, not all of which were of separatist origin, organized in 1786. See below, p. 266.
64. See above, pp. 90–92.
65. Denison, *Westerly and Its Witnesses,* p. 101.

several other members). He had had no baptism beyond sprinkling as an infant, but became increasingly agitated over the baptismal question after the general conference on that subject at his home in 1754.[66] In the next decade he fell out with his pastor over the "divine testimony" as evidence in disciplinary cases, and withdrew along with several sympathizers in 1764. After brief consideration of the baptismal question, they submitted to immersion at the hands of Wait Palmer, pastor of the First Baptist Church of North Stonington, and organized the Second Baptist Church of that town. Following strict communion from the start, this body became a charter member of the Stonington Association in 1772. Brown was ordained in March 1765 and served the church until his death in 1815.

Individual converts to Baptist principles. Most of the Separate churches which remained pedobaptist nevertheless lost members who one by one became persuaded of Baptist sentiments and found their way into nearby Baptist churches. Perhaps the best way to illustrate this process is to follow one particular church through its travail with those of its members who accepted believer's baptism. The church chosen for this purpose is the Preston Separate Church, which lost fewer than a dozen members to the Baptists in its seventy years of existence; yet its well-documented experience with these few demonstrates what went on in varying proportions in numerous other churches of its kind.

The first appearance of trouble because of Baptist opinions, as far as the records go, was on May 27, 1752:

> This Church Meet May the 27 AD 1752 to Treate with Br Samuel Palmer about Baptism, after Some labour he told us Plainly that Infant Baptism was not of God: at which we were Greived and desired him to take it up againe and not speak against what we knew to be of God: But he did not Suitable Pains being taken: we found it to be against the Interests of Christ's Kindom: We having Cleare Evidence against his declarations: from God's word and the Present testimony of the holy Ghosts. We admonished him in the name of the Lord.[67]

That the body of the church clearly believed infant baptism "to be of God" is indicated further by the fact that the vast majority of the 362

66. See below, pp. 262–63.
67. This and the following quotations from Records of the Preston Separate Church, under dates as noted.

infants sprinkled by Pastor Paul Parke are entered in the records as "_____ felt called of God to give up his [her] child to baptism." Nevertheless, on November 15, 1752, it was reported that "Sistor Zerviah Lamb had said that Infant Baptism or Sprinkling was nothing but a tradition of Men and Came from the whore of Babilon: and that our Pastor was Not Baptized: and that she Never wood Commune with us any More." The church, being grieved, appointed a meeting to consider her case, and invited the Groton Separate Church, "because she lived there and had Signed there Church Covenant." They voted to admonish her. In the meantime, the church continued to labor with Samuel Palmer. Being unwilling to confess any wrong, he was finally excommunicated on August 27, "because he is gon out from us and we look upon our selves Cleare of our Charge Concerning him."

Samuel Clarke was one of the members who fell out with the Preston church over its reception of John Blunt after the latter's inconstancy with respect to baptism at Sturbridge.[68] When Clarke finally confessed that he had been wrong in acting "Contrary to the Principles of Catholick Communion," he still refused to return to the church because now "his Principles and ourn was so Conterary in Respect of Baptism he coold not Consistantly walk with us." In July 1754 he and his wife withdrew entirely from communion. The next April the church was still laboring with them, and cited them to a disciplinary inquiry:

> They held so strictly to what they Cald Belevers Baptism viz: that Baptism was Not Baptism if done before faith and that no Religious Covenant obligation is any obligation or ought to be looked upon [as] binding: if mad before Convertion and faith: which Principles the *Church* looked upon [as] corrupt: whereupon they viz Clark & his wife said they could not walk with us: they seemed honnest and Conciencious But the *Church* ajudged they were gon out frome us and were not of us &c.

This was not all. On July 23, 1755, one for whose salvation they had travailed in prayer and who had rejoiced their hearts often with his inspired exhortations revealed that he was infected with the Baptist heresy:

> This *Church* meet by apointment to Convers with Br Daniel Whipple [69] and he declared his satisfaction with the *Church*: Escept about Baptism and that because said *Church* held and

68. See above, pp. 103, 225.
69. See above, p. 125.

> Practised Infant Baptism he could not Commune with the *Church* and desired to be dismist from It: But the *Church* did not give him an answer Now.

Loathe to excommunicate so beloved a brother, the church deferred action. Whipple's wife soon announced similar sentiments. The church discussed the problem on August 13 and 15, but still took no action. Eventually the Whipples withdrew without formal dismission.

By 1757 ten individuals had either withdrawn in this fashion or been excommunicated for Baptist beliefs. The church considered this to be such a serious inroad upon their fellowship that on January 26 they drew up a formal "Testimony of the Church upon the Withdrawal of Sundry Baptist Brethren." This so fully reveals the way in which most of the pedobaptist Separates regarded such behavior that it is copied in full from the church records:

> To the Baptist Bretheren and sistors that have gon out from our Communion Namely: Daniel Whipple; Samll Clarke; Samll Palmer; Jemimah Clarke; Abigale Clark alias Bennet; Eunice Whipple; Freelove Pettis; Bridgit Gates; Anna Branch: Whereas you and Each of you Joyned in Covenant with this *Church* to walk with us in the Practice of Gods worship and ordinances according to the Laws of Gods house: and did for some time so walk with us to our mutual Edifycation and Comfort—Untill upon farther Proof and tryal it appeared that while you Strictly held to the Baptist Principles of Baptism and we to Infant or household Baptism, that our Principles on the Score of Baptism were so Contrary one to the other: that it led us into Sundry jars and Diffeculties: which occationed Breaches of Charity and intorupted our harmonious sweet Gospill travil: and occationed the Admonition of Some of our Baptist Bretheren viz Br. Samll Clarke & his wife and Br. Samll Palmer although said Palmer was not Practically a Baptist ondly held to the Principle: and the Rest of you are withdrawn from our Communion Some of which desired to be dismised from us as Regularly as they Could And it is surely a lamentation, and shall be for a lamentation, that, Christians who are so well agreed and have Com into so near and sweet a union in the life and Power of Religion: who have such access to the throne of Grace together: who hope to spend one Eternity together in the Praises of God and our ondly Redeemer: and yet should be found so unhapily divided here in there Judgments about baptism: that they must seperate Contend and Rent asun-

der: but however lamentable it is may our *Church* say: We have occation [to] mourn the loos of Excellent ones with whome we had took sweet Councill and had sat with in heavenly Places Rejoycing together in the Love of God: for we Cant but think you are misled while you differ so much from us about Baptism as to occation your withdraw: which we Pray you to Concyder: And as far as Posible avoide all occasions of offence and Division — — — But now Bretheren and Sistors: inasmuch as you are gon out from us as afore said we Cannot Give you felloship: nor Dare we bid you God Speed: (as to the Cause of your Going:) yet in as much as you Plead Concience: And we wood by No means Pretend to Govern any mans Concience for God and his word ondly are Lord of the Concience: therefore we leave you to Stand or fall to your own Mastor: — — — — And we look upon our Selves Discharged from our Special watch over you: and the Visable Covenant Relation Desolved Between us and you.

This resolution seemed to clear the atmosphere, and after its adoption there was little more trouble with Baptist sentiment in the Preston church. In 1789 Mrs. Elizabeth Stanton desired a letter of dismission to join the Baptists. After some discussion this was granted; it was the first such instance. The last defection recorded was on August 19, 1800, when Cyrus Gates and his wife were admonished for having been "rebaptized by Diping by a baptist Elder."

One cannot help remarking again upon the gentle temper of the Preston church in dealing with these members who it was convinced were absolutely wrong. Perhaps this is the most atypical aspect of this illustration; certainly the contest was a great deal more bitter in many other Separate churches. Possibly the Preston Separates' moderation helped to keep the departures at a minimum. Nevertheless, two important things are obvious. One is that not all the patience and persuasion at their command could prevent the incursion of Baptist beliefs into their ranks. This is something which, in the nature of the case, simply could not be avoided. The other thing is that the convinced Baptists persistently refused to account the baptismal question a matter of indifference, and once Baptist opinions had made their inroads they upset the unstable equilibrium between churchly and fully dissenting positions. There were forces generated by separatism that ineluctably carried the more consistent dissenters all the way to a thoroughly sectarian stance. The Separates who did not press on to the logical end of their position by adopting believer's baptism, if they adhered to Christian faith at all, usually returned to the establishment. It is more than interesting that the Preston Separates, who struggled so valiantly to live in their halfway house, reunited with the regular Congregationalists just when Connecticut voted disestablishment. After unrestricted religious liberty was enacted, making a state church impossible, pedobaptists—even strict congregational ones—could remain in their more churchly tradition without being too conscious of tension, while Baptists could take advantage of the new freedom to press the claims of their individualistic gospel.

New Light separations from older Baptist churches. Few of the twenty-five Baptist churches in existence at the time of the Great Awakening participated in the revival. There were three reasons for this: they were suspicious of anything sponsored by pedobaptists, all but six had a long-standing aversion to Calvinism, and their tenuous existence everywhere but in Boston and Rhode Island had made them largely isolationist in outlook. They were constitutionally unable to sympathize with or profit from the Awakening. It was impossible, however, that the revival should pass them by entirely. Backus, in speaking of "that glorious work of divine grace," said:

> A measure of it was granted to the Baptists in Boston, Leicester, Brimfield, Newport, Groton, and Wallingford; but as the work was begun and carried on almost wholly by Paedobaptists, from which denomination their fathers had suffered much, most of the Baptists were prejudiced against the work, and against the Calvinian doctrine by which it was promoted.[70]

Wallingford (organized 1739) was where Joseph Bellamy and Philemon Robbins preached by invitation to the Baptists, to the great dismay of the Congregational clergy of Connecticut. Groton (organized 1705) was the home of Valentine Wightman, founder of the first Baptist church in Connecticut and, though a quiet man, one of the most hearty sponsors of the revival in his area; he was instrumental in forming the New Light Baptist church at North Stonington in 1743 under Wait Palmer.[71] At Newport the Second Baptist Church (organ-

70. *History of New England,* 2, 41.
71. This church deserves larger mention, although it does not fit any of the categories of the present discussion. It was formed directly as a Baptist church by Separates from the standing churches of Stonington and North Stonington. Wait Palmer, who had been refused a license to preach by the New London Ministerial Association, was one of the first members and was ordained their "watchman" the same year. Palmer itinerated widely and in 1751 baptized at Tolland the celebrated Shubal Stearns, who later carried the Separate Baptist fire into the South.

ized 1656) shared in the revival to the extent of receiving forty-eight new members between March and August in 1741. South Brimfield (organized 1736) was the home of the intrepid evangelist and baptizer, Ebenezer Moulton, whose work has been mentioned already.[72] The First Baptist Church at Leicester,[73] under Dr. Thomas Green 1738–73, was one of the few Calvinistic Baptist churches in New England at the time; the Congregational church in the town was strongly revivalistic, and the two shared alike in the fruits of the Awakening.

By the eighteenth century the First Baptist Church in Boston, founded by Thomas Gould in 1665, had risen far above the status of a disinherited sect. After the Mathers had accorded fraternal recognition by participating in the ordination services for Elisha Callender in 1718, both church and pastor enjoyed social elevation and widened influence. In 1737 it erected a new meetinghouse and had branches at more than a dozen towns. On the eve of the Great Awakening it was at a peak of its prosperity. But Callender died on March 31, 1738, and was followed by a man of totally different temperament. There was little difference between Jeremiah Condy and the typical eastern Congregational minister of his time except that he had been immersed by the affable and urbane Callender in 1730, four years after graduating from Harvard. He preached briefly in Newport during 1731, but there his main interest seemed to be in the Literary and Philosophical Society which he helped to found. After spending the next several years in England, he returned to Boston to find the Baptists seeking a pastor and was called immediately. His ordination was performed on February 14, 1739, by the Congregational ministers of Boston, the only Baptist present being John Callender (nephew of Elisha) from the First Baptist Church in Newport.

Condy was not the type of man who could lead the church to profit, even in a modest way, from the religious fervor of the times. His doctrinal sentiments were called Arminian, and his phlegmatic disposition was more like that of Charles Chauncy than of George Whitefield. While many of the surrounding churches were expanding their services and multiplying their membership, the Boston Baptists were retrenching. The customary Wednesday lecture was abandoned when on

---

In 1764, shortly after the church refused him a stated salary, Palmer claimed to have an "internal dismission" from them; and after much controversy he was deposed by a council on Jan. 9, 1766. The church continued, and became the First Baptist Church of North Stonington.

72. See above, p. 225.

73. A branch of the Sutton Baptist Church (organized 1735) until 1738.

October 31, 1742, "the Brethren taking into Consideration the very thin appearance at the Lecture, voted that the Lecture be dropped." [74] In the meantime, however, some of the members had become filled with the spirit of the revival around them and began a controversy with the church and pastor that reads exactly like those in nearly a hundred Congregational churches across the land.

The first note of discord was injected on February 1, 1742, when Elizabeth Pitson [75] wrote a letter of complaint which the church judged an insult and admonished her to retract. She, however,

> justifyed her Letter, and behaved with a great deal of arrogance & haughtiness; insomuch that Several of the Brethren expressed their wonder & resentment, and gave her admonition and caution. —Upon the whole, No Vote was passed respecting her & her Conduct, but the Church seemed disposed to wait to see whether time would not cure her false Zeal, bitterness, and high Spirit.[76]

On September 29 four disaffected members (James Bound, John Dabney, Thomas Boucher, and John Proctor) presented to Condy a letter complaining that he and the church had departed from the original faith of the founders, and that his preaching was "so inter-mixed with Arminianism" that it was "like the high Arminian clergy." They asserted that the church had always been strictly Calvinistic and would never "by any means, as we can prove, suffer a Free Willer, or Arminian, if they knew a person so to be, to join with the church." [77] The church chose to suppress the letter and to deal privately with its authors. Bound was cited later for absenting himself from worship, and was judged "very obstinate." Ruth Bound informed a committee that called on her that she had been much impressed by the text, "Come out from among them and be ye Separate," and that "she was not one of us, that the Church had no *business* with her, and [she]

74. Records of the First Baptist Church of Boston (microfilm copy, Yale University Library), Oct. 31, 1742.

75. The spelling of this name is uncertain due to mutilation of the records.

76. Records of the First Baptist Church of Boston, March 3, 1742.

77. Quoted in Nathan E. Wood, *The History of the First Baptist Church of Boston* (Philadelphia, 1899), pp. 240–41. The letter is not in the records, which say simply that the church voted not to read it. (Part of it is printed in Backus, *History of New England*, 2, 421.) Its rather extreme charges stretch the truth somewhat. The church was reputed to be Calvinistic; but its Confession of Faith, adopted in 1665 and never altered, is completely silent on the distinguishing points of Calvinism. (It does not even specify the mode of baptism!)

declined coming before them." John Proctor appeared "very stiff, and among other things which he said, asserted that they were all a parcel of Arminians." [78] All the church's labor proving in vain, the dissidents were finally suspended from communion.

The Separates met at the home of James Bound on July 27, 1743, and organized themselves into an independent Baptist church, apparently with no outside assistance or encouragement. Ephraim Bound, son of James, was called to be their pastor, but surprisingly his ordination was sought from other Baptist ministers rather than at the hands of the congregation. This presented something of a problem: few of the existing Baptist churches were willing to recognize the schismatics, nor did the latter hold fellowship with many of the former; and no Separate Baptist church had been formed as yet. Finally, in September 1743, it was arranged that Valentine Wightman, Thomas Green, and Ebenezer Moulton should perform the ceremony. "The said elders," say the new church's records, "we apprehend to be sound, clear, and zealously affected to the doctrines of free and sovereign grace, and absolutely averse to the Pelagian and Arminian tenets." [79] To accommodate the distant ministers, especially the aged Wightman, the Boston brethren traveled to Warwick, Rhode Island, for the services.

For two years they met at James Bound's house, then moved in June 1745 to the building where Proctor taught school. In March 1746 they entered a new meetinghouse built in what later became Baldwin Place, a block from the building of the First Church. John Proctor gave the ground on the condition that the church would adhere to the Second London Confession.[80] The new church received books and communion ware from Dr. John Gill, a leading Calvinistic Baptist minister in England. Frequent additions brought the membership to forty by the end of the first year and to 120 within five years. When Ephraim Bound died in 1765, the church was twice the size of the First Baptist Church, many of whose members openly preferred to worship with the Separates. For a while the New Lights "called themselves the First Baptist Church of Boston, because they claimed that the old church had so

78. Records of the First Baptist Church of Boston, Nov. 23 and Dec. 20, 1742.
79. Quoted in "History of the Second Baptist Church," *Christian Watchman,* ed. E. Thresher, *17* (April 15, 1836), 62. This is rather amusing: Condy had acted at Moulton's ordination. But of course the latter had redeemed himself from this taint by his zeal in the revival.
80. A Calvinistic confession drafted in 1677 along Westminster lines. The Philadelphia Baptist Association followed it closely.

far departed from Baptist doctrine as held by the founders as to have
lost right to the name." [81] This claim was never made good, and the
church soon became known as the Second Baptist, later Warren Ave-
nue. Although the new church soon took its place among the regular
Baptists of New England, uniting with the Warren Association in 1772,
it differed little in its origin and early character from the Separate Baptists who were converted from Congregationalism.[82]

The Baptists of Rhode Island were more suspicious of the revival
than those in any other area. John Callender of the First Church in
Newport denounced Whitefield as "a second George Fox." Nevertheless, they were not exempt from New Light influences. Just before
the visit of Whitefield, the Second Church in Newport was agitated by
the rise of a Calvinistic party led by Timothy Packom and Daniel
Greene. Their zeal probably accounts for the revival in this church,
and when they withdrew to form their own church under Packom in
1742, it is likely that most of the new converts followed them. Although in the background there were hints of a personal quarrel with
Pastor Nicholas Eyres, the ostensible cause of the schism was entirely
doctrinal.[83] Divisions such as this one erupted in several other churches,
much to the dismay of the older Baptists of Rhode Island. At the General Meeting in 1749, the assembled brethren considered "the sad dis-
sensions and divisions which seem to be carrying on in several churches;
more especially at South Kingstown, North Kingstown, Warwick,
Greenwich, &c." [84] They had been quite provoked with Valentine
Wightman for acting in the ordination of Ephraim Bound at Warwick

81. Wood, *History of First Baptist Church Boston*, p. 242. When the First
Church sent brethren to inquire why Cornelius Thompson had been absent from
worship in June 1748, he said "he went to hear Ephraim Bound and was much
edifyed by his Exhortations; and when asked how he could dispense with the
Covenant he had entered into with the Church he answered, that he thought those
he worshipped with and we were the same Church!" (Records of the First Baptist
Church of Boston, June 22, 1748).

82. The celebrated Samuel Stillman preached at the Second Baptist Church
during 1765, then answered a call to First Baptist, where he remained until his
death in 1807. Thomas Baldwin came to the Second Church in 1790 and served
until 1825. Both these men were warmhearted evangelicals under whom Boston
Baptists forgot their previous rancor and entered into the work of the new century.

83. See Greene's letter to Eyres, dated July 2, 1745, in Backus, *History of New
England*, 2, 104.

84. Minutes of the Rhode Island General Meeting, quoted ibid., p. 506. All
these churches are discussed below except that at Greenwich. It was organized in
1743 by Daniel Fisk, who was dismissed for adopting Calvinistic sentiments in
1752.

a few years before, and now they were even more upset because Separate preachers from Connecticut and Massachusetts were evangelizing in Rhode Island and drawing off the converts into mixed-communion New Light churches.

The way in which Calvinistic doctrine and New Light revivalism infiltrated the General Baptist churches of Rhode Island is illustrated by the career of David Sprague, whose early ministry antedates the Great Awakening by several years. A native of Hingham, Massachusetts, he moved as a young man to Scituate, Rhode Island, where he was converted and joined the Six-Principle church under Samuel Fiske. Recognized as a man of considerable gifts, he was invited to preach. At first he feared to undertake such great work, but soon a passage of Scripture came to his mind and he delivered a sermon. His first discourse was well received, but after a second sermon he was told, "If you go on in this way, you will be as bad an *electioner* as any of the Presbyterians." Such criticism, he testified later, "turned him back into their general [i.e. Arminian] way of preaching for a number of years." [85] In 1737 he moved to North Kingston, where he was ordained assistant to the aged Richard Sweet. Then Whitefield came, and Sprague was caught up in the revival movement. His return to Calvinistic sentiments resulted in his dismission from the church. This failed to silence him, and his continued preaching in the area resulted in divisions in the churches of North and South Kingston. In 1749 he attended the ordination of a New Light preacher at Coventry, where he "got such an acquaintance with some Separate elders, as to invite them to come and preach in the Narragansett country." [86] Soon several New Lights had been drawn off from the General Baptist churches in western Rhode Island, and in the summer of 1750 Sprague organized them into a church at Exeter. They adopted a predestinarian confession of faith.[87]

Exeter was a mixed-communion church and entered immediately into sisterly relations with the church formed on similar principles by Stephen Babcock at Westerly the same year. (Sprague joined with Solomon Paine of Canterbury in ordaining Babcock.) A general conference between Separates and Baptists, held at Exeter in 1753, af-

85. Quoted ibid., p. 508.
86. Ibid., p. 105.
87. Simon Smith on Feb. 13, 1753, gave land for the meetinghouse, deeding it to "David Sprague, Elder, and Joseph Rogers and Philip Jinkins Deacons and theire successors in said office, and to the Church of Christ in Exeter . . . for the use of said Church and their successors in Said Principles and none else." See Willet H. Arnold, "Historical Sketch of the Baptist Church in Exeter," *Narraganset Historical Register,* 2 (July 1883), 2–3.

firmed communion between the two groups.[88] Sprague was scribe of this meeting; but his sentiments underwent a change soon afterward, and the reluctance of his church to follow him into strict communion led to his departure in 1754. He preached for a time at New London (Waterford Baptist Church), then went to Block Island. When he returned to Exeter in 1766, his old church had called as pastor his son Solomon, a prominent physician and an able preacher, and was on the point of becoming a strict-communion body.[89] He died there in 1777, having lived to witness the church he founded come fully into accord with his own cherished convictions. It soon united with the Stonington Association, and Backus noted in 1796 that it had "experienced greater blessings since they gave up mixed communion than they ever did before." [90]

About 1741 another New Light Baptist church was formed in the west part of Warwick by Benjamin Pierce, the same man who ten years later baptized Isaac Backus. This church increased so rapidly that in 1751 Peter Werden was ordained colleague pastor. Werden was another convert of the Great Awakening, of whom John Leland said, "When he first began to preach, he was too much of a New-light, and too strongly attached to the doctrine of salvation by sovereign grace, to be generally received among the old Baptist churches in Rhode Island, which had been formed partly upon the Armenian [sic] plan." [91] Werden won a hearing for himself, however, by an impassioned prayer for the conversion of a condemned criminal who was standing on the gallows. Though he never retracted his Calvinistic sentiments, he ministered at Warwick until 1757, then moved to Coventry. Here a New Light Baptist church had been formed in 1748 under Samuel Drowne, who had reverted to pedobaptism and removed to Portsmouth, New Hampshire. Werden preached to this church for thirteen years, and in 1770 emigrated to Cheshire, Massachusetts, where he formed the First Baptist Church and preached until his death in 1808. At West Coventry was another New Light Baptist church formed under Caleb Nichols; he removed in 1788 to Pownal,

88. See below, pp. 261–62.
89. Solomon Sprague, though not ordained until 1769, preached at Exeter from 1763 until his death in 1794. He served as moderator of the Stonington Association in 1776 and preached the annual sermon in 1781.
90. *History of New England*, 2, 509–10.
91. "A Biographical Sketch of the Life and Character of the Rev. Peter Werden," *Writings of John Leland*, p. 319.

Vermont, and the church declined. Many of these churches were scattered during the Revolution, their members emigrating to newer lands and becoming an important means of transplanting Separate Baptists to the frontier.

On the Frontier

It is not generally recognized that most of the Baptist churches organized on the fringes of settled New England in the latter half of the eighteenth century (and some even beyond the turn of the century) have the character of Separate Baptist churches. This is not to say that they all originated in exactly the same way as the churches described in the more settled territories. But almost without exception the Baptist churches in the newer areas were formed by and of converts from Congregationalism who were, if not outright Separates, at least strong New Lights who had moved out to the frontier. The usual claim is that the major missionary impulse among New England Baptists came from the Particular Baptists of the Middle Colonies, who sent James Manning to found Rhode Island College in 1764 and organize the Warren Association in 1767,[92] and Hezekiah Smith to evangelize the northern territories.[93] And because the latter was so highly successful in establishing new churches in northeastern Massachusetts and New Hampshire, it is claimed that these churches were all constituted on the same plan as the churches of the Philadelphia Association. This interpretation overlooks the fact that most of the members of these churches were New Light Congregationalists converted to Baptist sentiments (this was true even of Smith's own church at Haverhill), that their pastors in many cases were far-ranging evangelists from Separate Baptist churches farther south, and that their growth for more than half a century was due to a steady stream of converts from these

92. James Manning (1738–91) graduated at the College of New Jersey (later Princeton) in 1762 and was the founder and first president of Rhode Island College (later Brown) 1764–91. These matters are discussed at length in the next chapter.

93. Hezekiah Smith (1737–1805) was a classmate of Manning's. He was ordained at Charleston, South Carolina, in 1763, accompanied Manning to Rhode Island in 1764, preached throughout New England, and became pastor of the Haverhill, Massachusetts, Baptist Church which he organized in 1765 and served until his death. He was both a fellow of Rhode Island College and a far-ranging evangelist, and withal an extremely important figure in the spread of Baptist principles in New England. See Reuben Aldridge Guild, *Chaplain Smith and the Baptists* (Philadelphia, 1885).

same sources. It is probable that the new churches in frontier areas, even those which owe their initial impulse to such men as Hezekiah Smith, should be considered as Separate Baptist churches, at least until increasing rapprochement with the regular Baptists made that name passé. To substantiate this thesis, developments in each of three frontier areas will be treated briefly, and illustrations given of how New Light Baptists found on the frontier their most fruitful field for expansion.

The northeastern frontier. This area includes New Hampshire east of the Merrimac River and all of Maine. The first Baptist church in this sector was at Newtown, New Hampshire, which had been settled largely by Separates. It was the first church in the town, organized in 1755. Walter Powers, one of the original members, was ordained as pastor in June of that year. In 1761 friction arose over procedures in church discipline, and a four-day council moderated by Isaac Backus censured the pastor but failed to effect a reconciliation between him and the church. He left shortly thereafter, and Samuel Hovey succeeded him. Hovey had been a separatist at Mendon, Massachusetts, where he was ordained on May 31, 1749. He seems to have become a Baptist about 1758. The dates of his service at Newton are uncertain. The church seems to have declined or died during the Revolution, and was reorganized in 1796 by John Peak, a New Light Baptist evangelist born in Walpole, Massachusetts, and ordained at Windsor, Vermont. During the several visits of Hezekiah Smith to Newtown, he records that he always had a full congregation in Elder Hovey's meetinghouse.[94]

In 1764 Ebenezer Jones, quondam pastor of the Third Baptist Church (Separate) of Middleborough, Massachusetts, preached through southeastern New Hampshire. One of the converts at Stratham was a young man named Eliphalet Smith, who six years later was ordained pastor of a New Light church in Deerfield (then part of Nottingham). In May 1770 while he was preaching on John 14:15, "If ye love me, keep my commandments," the command to "believe and be baptized" was impressed with peculiar force upon his mind. He led his congregation in searching the Scriptures for some positive command to baptize infants; failing to find any, they all came to regard themselves as unbaptized. They wrote to President James Manning of Rhode Island College

94. Backus errs in saying the Newtown church dissolved after Powers' departure and the remaining members worshiped at Haverhill (*History of New England, 2*, 535). Smith's journal indicates that Hovey was still at the head of a vigorous church in 1770 (Guild, *Chaplain Smith*, p. 138).

to come and immerse them, but because of the distance he referred their request to Hezekiah Smith at Haverhill. The latter's diary for the occasion reads as follows:

> Wed., June 13. Went to Deerfield, and preached from Acts 11:28: "Who when he came and had seen the grace of God, was glad, and exhorted them all, that with purpose of heart they would cleave unto the Lord." After the sermon I examined the Rev. Eliphalet Smith and a number of his hearers for baptism. — Thurs., 14. I preached in Mr. Smith's meeting house in Deerfield, from Col. 2:11, 12. After sermon I baptized fourteen persons . . . who the same day were embodied into a Baptist Church. A good day it was indeed.[95]

This church, however, continued to embrace pedobaptist members. Around 1790 Eliphalet Smith went to Fayette, Maine, where by 1792 he had formed another New Light Baptist church on the open-communion plan. Soon afterward he was visited by Isaac Case, a Separate Baptist evangelist from Middleborough, who persuaded him to adopt strict communion.[96] Smith served here six years.

Within a week after the Deerfield church was formed, Hezekiah Smith baptized twenty-four more persons in nearby Epping, Brentwood, and Stratham. Among these was Dr. Samuel Shepard, in whose mind Baptist principles had lodged earlier in a most interesting manner. The story begins in 1720, when a young Baptist woman from Rehoboth married a resident of Stratham and came to live in the wilderness on the Piscataqua River. Rachel Scammon was then the only Baptist in that country, and though she witnessed to her faith for forty years, she convinced only one person, another woman who traveled the fifty-five miles to Boston for baptism at the hands of Ephraim Bound. Mrs. Scammon was so fired with zeal that she herself went to Boston to arrange for the reprinting of a popular English work on baptism.[97] To her delight, she discovered that the printer had

95. Quoted in Guild, *Chaplain Smith*, pp. 135–36.

96. Case was from Backus' church; his work in Maine is discussed below. His argument for strict communion was naive but effective: "If a person should come to your house and you should invite him to walk in, but he should object to coming in at the door, would you take down one side of your house to accommodate him?" Pastor Smith and his immersed friends were persuaded that believer's baptism was the only proper way to church membership. (Joshua Millet, *A History of the Baptists in Maine*, Portland, 1845, p. 132.)

97. This was John Norcott, *Baptism Discovered Plainly and Faithfully, According to the Word of God. Wherein Is Set Forth the Glorious Pattern of Our Blessed*

110 copies in stock, all of which she purchased and distributed near her home to settlers old and new. This work bore an immense amount of fruit, although she did not live to see it. Dr. Shepard chanced upon a copy of the book in the home of one of his patients, and upon reading it was convinced of its truth, though he did nothing about it immediately. When Hezekiah Smith came to his neighborhood, these arguments returned to him with renewed force and he persuaded several of his associates to join him in seeking immersion from Smith. Soon afterward Baptist churches were formed in Stratham, Brentwood, and Nottingham; and Shepard was ordained to the pastoral care of them on September 25, 1771. The Brentwood Church, as the whole was named, grew rapidly and established branches at nearly a dozen places within a fifteen-mile radius. At one time it numbered approximately one thousand members. David Benedict wrote of this sprawling parish in 1813:

> They are mostly supplied with preachers, and all of them enjoy the privileges, and exercise, in some measure, the power of distinct churches. Brentwood is their Jerusalem, to which they frequently repair. Here, like a bishop, in the midst of his diocese, resides the venerable elder, who is considered as the pastor of this extensive flock, and who, in his active days, spent much of his time in visiting among them, and whose popularity has probably been the means of collecting this extensive and unwieldy body, this church of churches, whose affairs must certainly be managed with peculiar inconvenience.[98]

The churches in this cluster are rarely referred to as Separate Baptists, yet it must be insisted that all of them were formed in the first instance out of Congregational New Lights. The people at Brentwood, for example, had worshiped at the Exeter Congregational Church until the visit of Whitefield made them wish to be free from the lifeless preaching of John Odlin. They became an independent parish in 1742, and though enjoying legal status were popularly known as Separates.

Saviour, Jesus Christ, the Pattern of All Believers in Their Subjection to Baptism (London, 1670). This work went through many editions and was widely distributed.

98. *History of the Baptist Denomination* (1st ed. Boston, 1813), *1*, 320–21. Benedict names only six branches, but authors closer to the situation list the following: Canterbury, Chicester, Epping, Hampstead, Hawke, Lee, Loudon, Meredith, Salisbury, Southampton, "and others" (William Hurlin, O. C. Sargent, and W. W. Wakeman, *The Baptists of New Hampshire*, Manchester, N.H., 1902, p. 11).

This is the church that in 1768 issued a call to Joseph Marshall, pastor of the Separate church at Canterbury, Connecticut.[99] New Light characteristics were still prominent when the conversion to Baptist sentiments began; in fact, it may be that their conversion was possible only because the Baptist missionary among them was a staunch Calvinist and an ardent revivalist.

An interesting sidelight of Hezekiah Smith's experience in these parts concerns the fact that he did not make Baptists out of quite all the New Lights who heard him. Nathaniel Ewer, who had left the Barnstable Separate Church sadly depleted by virtue of wholesale defections to the Baptists, was now at Newmarket, New Hampshire. On June 18, 1770, Smith visited there:

> Went to New Market, and preached in Mr. Ewers' meeting house, from Ezk. 36:26, after which I had a conference with their Church about some of their members who wanted to be baptized; but the Church as a Church would not give me any leave to baptize their members.[100]

He remained over the next day, when Isaac Backus was present and preached, then went to Stratham to meet with his customary success. On Thursday, June 21, he "went home, after having baptized 38 persons within seven days and preached seven sermons." [101] Convinced that these New Lights were a fruitful field for Baptist doctrines, he returned often. At Exeter on October 9, 1770, he preached an outdoor sermon from Mark 16:16, then baptized a half-dozen people, among whom was Joseph Sanborn, a New Light Congregational preacher from Epping. "It was judged," Smith recorded, "that 2000 people were at the water side to see the ordinance administered, it being the first time that it was ever administered in that place." [102] On December 24, 1771, he preached in the new Baptist meetinghouse at Brentwood and after the sermon baptized Stephen Sleeper, a deacon of the Separate church of that town, and seven others.[103] Repeated evangelistic tours of this area resulted in similar victories.

Baptist work at Berwick, Maine, began in much the same way. The initial impulse came when Joshua Emery separated from the First Congregational Church and persuaded a dozen others, including

99. See above, pp. 103–05, 145–46.
100. Quoted in Guild, *Chaplain Smith*, p. 137.
101. Ibid.
102. Ibid., p. 145.
103. Ibid., p. 151.

deacon John Knight, to do likewise. They sent for Hezekiah Smith in 1767; he came and baptized them, and the next year assisted them in forming a church on June 28. Emery served as "teacher," though he was never ordained. The separatist and Baptist ferment continued to work in the Congregational church; and the next year Abraham Lord and his wife Elizabeth became uneasy with the pastor, Matthew Merriam, because he manifested "a spirit of opposition against the spirit of God in the church, in keeping out some preachers, and depriving the members of hearing, and improving their gifts." [104] The church voted these reasons insufficient to excuse Lord for absenting himself from worship, and placed him under censure. Upon this, his wife wrote to the church telling them that she had considered the principles of the Baptists, thought them correct, and desired a letter of dismission to unite with them. Pastor Merriam answered her in a letter "long as a sermon," denying her request. Isaac Backus, always sensitive to what he felt was an abridgment of the rights of conscience, learned of the case and was so incensed that he intervened in behalf of the Lords. He wrote a spirited letter to the church, justifying the Baptist body in Berwick as a regularly constituted church owned by its sister churches and faithful in its conduct of divine worship, and rebuked the Congregationalists for their unjust reproaches on the Baptists and for their interference with the Lords' convictions. He traveled to Berwick in 1769 and baptized Mr. and Mrs. Lord himself, then published with appropriate comments the documents of the whole controversy.

Some members of the Berwick Baptist Church lived in Madbury, New Hampshire, where there had been a Separate church under Samuel Hyde since 1758. Hyde was originally from Canterbury, Connecticut; his father Jonathan was pastor of the Separate church in Brookline, Massachusetts, and one or both of them had preached to the Separates at Chelmsford. He published a pamphlet in 1770 in which he reprehended Baptists as bitterly as the standing churches, but was unable to prevent the defection of his members to the growing Baptist movement in his neighborhood.[105] The Madbury Baptists

---

104. Lord's letter to the church, quoted in Backus, *A Seasonable Plea for Liberty of Conscience* (Boston, 1770), p. 15. Lord also accused the pastor of baptizing children of persons "of various characters"—probably Halfway members.

105. I have not located this pamphlet. Ezra Stiles reported on it thus: "He holds Sinners unregenerate not to be exhorted to duties in order [to] Salvation— Sandiman's Notion of Faith—Universal Vote in Church Acts, no dissenting voice —Laying on of hands at Baptism—no Deacons in present state of Churches—

were set off independent of the Berwick church in 1776. William Hooper was ordained their pastor on August 14, and served until around the end of the century. Perhaps his most noteworthy act was performed immediately after his ordination when he baptized the Separate from Newcastle, Benjamin Randall, later to become the founder of the Freewill Baptists.

One of the group baptized with Randall was Nathaniel Lord, whose work as an itinerant evangelist linked the previously described movements with New Light Baptist churches farther north and east. His base of operations was the Baptist church at Wells, Maine, which he gathered in 1780 against the violent opposition of the Congregational pastor, Moses Hemmenway. On a preaching tour in 1782 Lord came to Potterstown (now Bowdoin), where he was approached by James Potter, a New Light Congregationalist who had been studying the question of baptism in the New Testament. Potter's journal says that all he knew of Baptists at the time was that they were a fanatical sect.

> I then spake to him [Lord], and informed him that I heard he was a Baptist. He said he was. I desired him not to tell one word of what he held to, because they say I am a Baptist—and I will relate to you what I believe. I did so, concerning the faith and order of the primitive church of Christ, as I received it from the Scriptures. He said if I believed what I had told him, I was a Baptist, for I had told everything the Baptists believe and hold.[106]

Potter was forty-eight years old, a prosperous farmer, and a man of influence in the community. His conversion made a deep impression on the people there, and many of his friends were won to his views. He preached at Litchfield, Brunswick, Bowdoin, Pownalborough, and other places with notable response, finally settling as pastor of the church organized at Brunswick (East Harpswell) on January 19, 1785.

The forming of a Baptist church at Bowdoin was left to Job

Community of Goods—no gathering by Church Covt—nor assent to Articles of Faith or Covt at admissions—every church chuse & ordain two or more Elders, &c. . . . He has written some things very sensibly. This with the Writings of *Backus* & [Israel] *Holly*, might be shewn as a specimen of the Abilities of the Illiterate Men of New England even in Writing as well as the Things of Religion. These productions would be considerable even for University Men" (*Literary Diary of Ezra Stiles, 1*, 68).

106. "Narrative of the Experience, Travels and Labours of Elder James Potter," p. 17; quoted in Henry S. Burrage, *History of the Baptists in Maine* (Portland, 1904), p. 63.

Macomber, a former member of Isaac Backus' church at Middle-borough. He had been converted in 1772, began to preach two years later, served as a chaplain in the Revolutionary War, and came after-ward to Maine with a horde of new settlers.[107] In January 1783 he wrote to his former pastor of the unparalleled evangelistic opportunity in the new district. Backus read the letter to Isaac Case, who was so impressed that he purposed to leave immediately for Maine, upon which the Middleborough church ordained him as preacher to that destitute district. Although only twenty-two years old, Case had al-ready preached in Massachusetts and Vermont. He now joined Ma-comber and they went to Harpswell, where they gained a hearing in the Congregational church of the Rev. Samuel Eaton. As a result of their labors a revival swept the whole region around what is now Brunswick. The records of the Congregational church in Harpswell show that in May 1784 the pastor was advised, "provided he sees his way clear, to baptize by immersion those who conscientiously desire it, provided they give satisfaction to the church of their faith in Christ and live holy lives." [108] As elsewhere, mixed communion proved un-satisfactory and, as was noted above, the Baptist members soon with-drew to form their own church under James Potter. Macomber organ-ized the Bowdoin Baptist Church, also in May 1784, and remained as its pastor until his death in 1821.

Case meanwhile preached on up to Thomaston, where he found only one Baptist and a few other "pious souls." Soon, however, he was crowded with eager listeners.

> In less than three weeks a powerful work of grace was in prog-ress. The first baptism was on Feb. 26 [1784], when fifteen per-sons were baptized; on March 12, sixteen others followed. In April, twenty-five were baptized, and May 23, six others.[109]

Case organized the church on May 27 and settled down as its pastor. One of his converts was Elisha Snow, the town's leading citizen, a lumberman, miller, shipbuilder, and merchant. Case married his daughter Joanna the next year. Snow became an effective evangelist himself, being ordained in 1788 as an itinerant minister.

Illustrations might be multiplied to show that most of the new

107. Massachusetts, which still governed Maine, had offered one hundred acres to any settler who would clear sixteen. Many returning soldiers claimed these free lands, and the district filled up rapidly after the Revolution.
108. Quoted in Burrage, p. 70 n.
109. Ibid., p. 73.

Baptist churches in this section were an outgrowth of the Separate Baptist witness more than of any other stream of Baptist influence. Paris, Maine, was settled by a group from the Third (Separate) Baptist Church of Middleborough, Massachusetts, about 1780. They experienced a revival under James Potter in 1790 and formed a church with the aid of Elisha Snow on November 18, 1791. Fayette's first preacher was Eliphalet Smith, the New Light Congregationalist converted to Baptist views by independent study of the Scriptures and baptized by Hezekiah Smith. Livermore was transformed by the influence of a sole New Light upon Elisha Williams (son of the Rev. Eliphalet Williams of East Hartford, Connecticut), who turned from his duties as schoolmaster in the frontier town to become a Baptist preacher. Baptist work in Greene stems from a private prayer meeting begun by Lemuel Cummings, a Separate from Charlestown, Massachusetts, who was baptized after hearing James Potter and who led in the formation of a Baptist church in 1793. Even in Portland, a relatively cultured town at the end of the century, a group of evangelicals became dissatisfied with the Arminian preaching of the Rev. Dr. Samuel Deane, withdrew to establish private worship, invited Isaac Case to preach to them, and subsequently formed a Baptist church on July 24, 1801, thus repeating a pattern of fifty years' standing.[110] By this time, of course, the name "Separate Baptist" had fallen into disuse. But it is clear that these churches stood in the same tradition and partook of the same characteristics as the earlier ones of that name. In the eighties they began to gravitate together into associations and to articulate a self-conscious denominational structure that made them an integral part of the common life of New England Baptists. Indeed, they almost *became* the denomination, and the transforming effect of the overwhelming numbers of New Light Baptists on the older Baptist life will be considered in detail later.

The northwestern frontier. Many of the Baptist churches in western New Hampshire and Vermont have even more clearly Separate origins. Bennington, in the southwest corner of the latter state, was a center of Separate life from the start, and the first Baptist church in Vermont was formed in nearby Shaftsbury by Separates who had become Baptists. The leader in this work was Bliss Willoughby, former pastor of the Newent (Connecticut) Separate Church and one of the Separate agents to England in 1756. While abroad or shortly after returning, he imbibed Baptist opinions, and removed to Vermont about 1764. The Shaftsbury church was organized in August 1768, and

110. Cf. Caleb Blood, *A Discourse* (Portland, 1811), p. 22.

though it had no settled pastor for twelve years, Willoughby and John Millington were permitted to "improve" their ministerial gifts. Within fifteen years, four Baptist churches had been organized at Shaftsbury. In 1772 one was gathered at Pownal, a few miles south of Bennington. This church was served briefly by Benjamin Gardner 1772–74 and Francis Bennett 1782–87, both from Rhode Island. Afterward Caleb Nichols, a New Light Baptist from Coventry, Rhode Island, became pastor and remained until his death in 1804.

The other main area of Separate Baptist activity on the northwestern frontier is the Connecticut River Valley. Much of this territory was settled by people from eastern Connecticut, and a good proportion of them were religious radicals. In 1768 Ebenezer Mack and a large group of his Separate Baptist congregation from East Lyme moved to Marlow, New Hampshire. Caleb Blood, from the Separate Baptist church at Charlton (West Leicester), Massachusetts, became pastor here in 1777 and wrote about the spiritual destitution of the region to the Warren Association, which in 1779 sent two evangelists on a mission up the Valley. The missionaries it selected for this purpose were both Separate Baptists: Biel Ledoyt of West Woodstock, Connecticut, and Job Seamans of Attleborough, Massachusetts. They preached up both sides of the Connecticut River as far as Woodstock, Vermont, a little below Eleazar Wheelock's new school at Hanover, New Hampshire, and from their labors came several new Baptist churches. A church organized in 1778 at Croydon, New Hampshire, united in 1790 with a group of Baptists in Newport and called Ledoyt to return as their pastor. He remained fourteen years. New London, New Hampshire, formed a church in 1788 and persuaded Seamans to come as pastor; he remained until his death in 1830. The Rhode Island element was strong here also, as these place names suggest. Westmoreland, New Hampshire, was settled in 1771 by a group from Isaac Backus' church in Middleborough. A church was organized shortly afterward, and Ebenezer Bailey ordained its pastor on November 30, 1773. Farther up the river, Lebanon was settled by New Light Congregationalists under the Rev. Isaiah Potter, but soon afterward, in June 1771, a Baptist church was formed here under Jedediah Hibbard. The Baptist church formed in Canaan in 1783 introduces a link back to the Separate Baptists of the older territories: its pastor from 1783 to 1790 was the celebrated Thomas Baldwin, who was born in Bozrah, Connecticut, in 1753, brought by his family to Canaan in 1769, converted by Baptist evangelists in 1780, and baptized by Elisha Ransom of Woodstock in 1781. In 1790 he went to the Second

Baptist Church of Boston for a fruitful ministry which lasted until his death in 1825.

West of the Connecticut River, Chester may be taken as an example of Separate Baptist activity. In 1786 fifteen persons, none of whom was a Baptist, wrote to Aaron Leland (a distant relative of John) who had been ordained recently at Noah Alden's Separate Baptist church in Bellingham, requesting him to come and preach to them. Leland journeyed immediately to Chester.

> But when he arrived, he found it so much uncultivated, both in a natural and moral point of view, and the prospect so unpromising, that he was unwilling to think of tarrying with them long. But after being here a short time, he felt a powerful application to his mind of this passage, "The Lord hath much people in this city." This scripture afforded him much comfort then, and he has had the happiness since of seeing it abundantly verified.[111]

After a brief return to Bellingham, Leland agreed to settle at Chester, and in three years a church of ten members was organized. For ten years it grew very slowly, but in 1799 a powerful revival produced a large in-gathering. The whole area was affected, and soon the Chester church embraced members in several surrounding communities. On August 31, 1803, four churches were set off from the original body—Andover, Grafton, Wethersfield, and Cavendish—and the mother church was still left with some seventy-odd members. In the large degree of liberty which prevailed in Vermont, the Separates and Baptists were not averse to taking part in public affairs, and Aaron Leland became an outstanding example of the minister-politician. For nine years he represented the town of Chester in the state legislature, and for four of these he was Speaker of the House; in 1803 he was appointed Judge of the County Court, in which office he remained a number of years, and from 1822 to 1824 he served as Lieutenant Governor of the state. From time to time friends remonstrated with him for neglecting his spiritual duties, and he affably agreed; but his church continued to prosper, and he remained its pastor until 1832.

Wallingford, unlike Chester, was settled by people of predominantly Baptist sentiments, and the church organized there in 1780 claims to be the oldest Baptist church in the state with a continuous history. Elisha Rich, from the Separate Baptist church in Chelmsford, Massa-

111. Benedict, 1st ed., *1*, 344.

chusetts, was its first preacher, although he soon withdrew because the church refused to accept the constitution he proposed. Henry Green was settled in 1787 and remained for twenty years. In 1793 he was recognized unanimously by people of all persuasions as the "minister of the town," although he was supported by a modified form of voluntary contributions.

At Poultney, on the western edge of the state, there was a situation similar in some respects to the relationships between Separates and Baptists in former years. It will be recalled that among the Strict Congregationalists of Bennington there appeared a group of extreme separatists led by Ithamar Hibbard.[112] After some years of friction, this group moved to Poultney in about 1780. Either there were several Baptists already there or else the Hibbard company included some of that inclination. At all events, the church organized in 1782 was a mixed-communion church. As usually happened elsewhere, this became an abundant source of tension, and after twenty years of trial the plan was abandoned. A strict-communion Baptist church was organized in 1802 and Clark Kendrick became its pastor. As elsewhere, these later churches could not be called properly "Separate Baptist." But by following out the tradition which produced them, one discovers the real extent and spread of revivalistic Baptists who emerged from the New Light ferment of the Great Awakening.

The western frontier. This area takes in western Massachusetts and the Hudson River Valley. As before observed, it offered many attractions to religious radicals from the east. The church at Sandisfield, Massachusetts, gathered by Joshua Morse from New London, Connecticut, in 1779 and served by him until his death in 1795, was for a time one of the largest Baptist churches in the state. After the Revolution, Berkshire County quickly filled up with New Lights, and although they tried for a while to keep out Baptist sentiments, a second Baptist church was formed in Sandisfield in November 1787. Benjamin Baldwin was ordained its pastor on June 9, 1790. The Pittsfield Baptist church was transplanted from Stonington, Connecticut, by Valentine Rathbun, who moved with a group of Separate Baptists in 1772. By 1780 it was a sizable church, but in that year a number of its members defected to the Shakers; among them was the pastor himself, though he returned in three months and "published a discourse against their abominations" which went through five editions the first year.[113] He remained with this church until 1798.

112. See above, p. 109.
113. Backus, *History of New England*, 2, 474.

The major center of Separate Baptist activity in western Massachusetts, however, was at Cheshire, in the northwest corner. It began to be settled soon after 1750, mainly by New Lights from Providence and Coventry in Rhode Island and Rehoboth and Swansea in Massachusetts. The first Baptist church here was organized in 1769, and Peter Werden [114] was pastor from 1770 to 1808. Benedict says, "From his first settling in Cheshire until he was 70 years old, he was a father to the Baptist churches in Berkshire county and its environs, and in some sense apostle to them all." [115] At the time of his death Werden was eighty years old and had been in the ministry longer than any Baptist preacher then living. A second Baptist church, formed in the west part of Cheshire in 1771, split over the doctrine of laying on hands in 1789, and John Leland became pastor of the "no hands" faction in 1792. This last group merged with the First Baptist Church in 1834, seven years before Leland's death.[116]

The future of Baptist work in Berlin, New York, was assured when young Justus Hull's parents moved their family there from Redding, Connecticut, in the sixties. A powerful revival radiating from Elder Clark Rogers' Baptist church in Hancock, Massachusetts (organized 1772, near Pittsfield), brought him under the sway of New Light religion in 1773 or 1774.[117] Within five years he felt an inspired urge to share his faith with his family and friends, and soon he was preaching far and wide.[118] In 1783 a Baptist church was gathered in Berlin,

114. See above, p. 242.

115. *History of the Baptist Denomination*, 1st ed., 2, 403.

116. Next to Isaac Backus, John Leland (1754–1841) was probably the most important Separate Baptist of the age. He does not appear more prominently in this study because his early ministry was spent in Virginia 1775–91; and his influence in New England toward republicanism, disestablishment, and anti-ecclesiasticism falls in the nineteenth century. A sketch of his life is prefixed to *Writings of John Leland*. See also L. H. Butterfield, "Elder John Leland, Jeffersonian Itinerant," *Proceedings of the American Antiquarian Society*, new ser. 62 (1952), 155–242; and Byron Cecil Lambert, "The Rise of the Anti-Mission Baptists: Sources and Leaders, 1800–1840 (A Study in Religious Individualism)" (dissertation, University of Chicago, 1957).

117. Hull's account of his conversion, which reads like that of the most exuberant convert from the halcyon days of the Great Awakening, is in Stephen Wright, *History of the Shaftsbury Baptist Association* (Troy, N.Y., 1853), pp. 317–19.

118. He visited his birthplace often and the people of that area long recalled his fervency in the pulpit. When a college-bred minister would read an elaborate discourse, some old-timer might remark, "Brother Hull would take off his coat and beat that" (D. Hamilton Hurd, ed., *History of Fairfield County, Connecticut*, Philadelphia, 1881, p. 211).

largely through his efforts, and he was ordained pastor in 1785 by a council including Joshua Morse from Sandisfield and Valentine Rathbun from Pittsfield. Revivals were frequent and the church attained a membership of over six hundred. During his ministry of forty-eight years, independent churches were set off at Williamstown in Massachusetts, and at Petersburg, Grafton, and Sandlake in New York. When Hull died in 1833, John Leland eulogized him in highest terms, saying "he had been acquainted with about eleven hundred baptist ministers, and he thought Elder Hull possessed the most of the christian and ministerial graces of any one he ever met with." [119]

The Separate church organized at Canaan, New York, in 1770 by Jacob Drake from Windsor, Connecticut, has already been described.[120] Eight years after its formation it became Baptist in a body. It grew rapidly, both numerically and geographically.

> Mr. Drake traveled and preached abundantly with great success, insomuch that his church, in ten years from its beginning [as Baptist], amounted to between five and six hundred members. They were spread over a great extent of country, not only in the neighboring towns, but branches were scattered at many miles distant, on both sides of the Hudson River; for wherever Mr. Drake baptized any disciples, he gave them fellowship as members of his flock.[121]

Besides Drake, there were seven other preachers and four ruling elders who administered the ordinances to care for this vast flock. In time, however, the wisdom of setting off the branches as independent churches became evident. In 1781 a church was set off in West Stockbridge. In 1789 five more: Great Barrington and Egremont (one church at first which divided in 1792), in Massachusetts; and Warren, Coeymans, Duanesburg, and Rensselaerville, in New York. New Concord was set off in 1791. A glance at Map II [122] will show how wide a territory was covered by Drake's work. In 1792 he removed to Wyoming, Pennsylvania, and repeated the same process along the Susquehanna River.

Farther down the Hudson Valley several Baptist churches sprang up whose constituency was drawn largely from New England New

119. Quoted in Benedict, 2d ed., 1848, p. 550.
120. See above, p. 110.
121. Benedict, 2d ed., p. 551. The whole account is from John Leland.
122. Below, at p. 257. Data regarding Separate Baptist churches not discussed in the text may be found in the Appendix.

MAP II. LOCATION of the SEPARATE BAPTISTS

- • Separate Baptist Church Organized. Separate Church if any, may or may not continue.
- ■ Separate Church Becomes Baptist in a Body.
- ▲ Some Separates Become Baptist but Organize No Baptist Church. May worship with a neighboring Baptist Church.

Lights who had settled there. A Separate church organized at Philips-town in 1751 divided over the baptismal question in 1753, and Simon Dakin was ordained by the Baptist faction as their pastor. This church was received into the Philadelphia Baptist Association in 1770 and three years later moved to Northeast, New York. For a time it in-cluded members living at Amenia, before a Baptist church was organ-ized there. Amenia's exhorter was Elijah Wood from Norwich, Connecticut, formerly a Separate deacon at Bennington, Vermont; he became a Baptist and in 1790 was ordained pastor of a newly organized Baptist church. James Manning of Rhode Island preached the sermon.[123] Benjamin Miller (regular Baptist pastor at Scotch Plains, New Jersey) and William Marsh (Separate Baptist pastor at Roxbury, New Jersey) came from the Philadelphia Association in 1757 and organized a church at Beekman's (later Pawling's) Precinct. Samuel Waldo became pastor the next year, and the church entered the fellowship of the Philadelphia Association. It later became the Baptist church in Dover and grew so large that it divided into two parts in 1794. In 1788 the Philadelphia Association had dismissed this church so that it might unite with the Shaftsbury Association, and during the next year the Philadelphia Association did the same thing for Northeast (which had been on its records as "Oblong Church").

Far out in the Mohawk River Valley, Whitesborough was planted by a colony from Middletown, Connecticut. Stephen Parsons, pastor of the Westfield branch of the Middletown Separate Church, which became Baptist in a body in 1795, visited friends here in 1796 and immersed five members of the Whitesborough church. They formed a Baptist church and called him as pastor; he accepted and moved his family from Middletown the next year. Whitesborough became a radiating point of Baptist influence in western New York.

If the geographical and chronological scope of this study were ex-tended, such stories might be multiplied many times. Although the Separate Baptists were assimilated quickly into the common life of the denomination, as indicated by their reception into fraternal re-lations in the regular associations, it must be repeated that the origin of these churches is not due to missionary activity on the part of the older Baptists nearly so much as to spontaneous growth out of the Separate New Lights of the Great Awakening.

123. Amenia was formerly called "Nine Partners." Separates had been active here since 1750 (above, pp. 109–10). Baptist congregations appeared 1764–73 and 1780–86, and organized an enduring church in 1790. Elijah Wood (1745–1810) preached at times to all these groups and served the Amenia Baptist Church 1790–1810.

7. ASSIMILATION OF THE SEPARATES INTO THE BAPTIST DENOMINATION

The conversion of the Separates to Baptist sentiments began around 1749, their assimilation into the common life of the Baptist denomination some two decades later. Their withdrawal from the Strict Congregationalists, their struggle for religious rights before the civil government, and their rapprochement with the regular Baptists involve a number of interesting developments.

Break with the Congregational Separates

Problems of mixed communion. The friction arising from attempts of Baptists and pedobaptists to "build together" in the visible church has been observed frequently. That such efforts were made from the very beginning is indicated by the first confession to issue from the Separates. The Mansfield Separate Church declared in 1745: "Tho' most of us agree in the Article of Infant-Baptism, yet a Difference in that Particular doth not break the spiritual Communion of Saints; therefore it is no just Bar to our Covenanting and Partaking of the Ordinances together wherein we are agreed." [1] This represents not the crystallizing of a settled conviction but simply a concession to those whose consciences, for reasons discussed in the previous chapter, were already somewhat troubled over the baptizing of infants. There are many other indications of the early rise of Baptist beliefs, but no question regarding separate communion occurred until the decade of the fifties.

In a few cases where some members of a Separate church had received believer's baptism, Baptists and pedobaptists traveled together in a fair degree of harmony. Perhaps the most noteworthy example of a mixed-communion church in which there was a minimum of friction was at Providence. When Joseph Snow was elected pastor in 1746, it was agreed that "the mode and subjects of Baptism should be indifferent and no Bar of Communion—that the Pastor to baptize Infants

1. Quoted in *The Result of a Council of the Consociated Churches of the County of Windham*, p. 8. The ministers cried in horror that this has opened the door to let "Anabaptistical" errors into the church.

258

&c by Sprinkling and those who desired it by plunging." [2] The historian of the church says:

> Baptism by immersion was frequently practised by Father Snow; and the Providence River, then much wider and purer than now, witnessed many such scenes on either bank, from the shore in front of the First Baptist Meeting-house to that on or near the site of the present City Hall. Many of the early members, and some in later times, were thus baptized. At the same time infant baptism was carefully attended to, though not strictly enjoined. [3]

How many submitted to "plunging" is shown by Stiles' comment that "the Majority of the Church being Baptists, will chuse a Baptist for their next Minister after Mr. Snows Death, and so that church will terminate Baptist." [4] This prediction proved false, although at one time the church membership was said to be about two-thirds Baptist. In the ensuing general controversies Snow always sided with the pedobaptists, but the church remained on friendly terms with the Providence Baptists nevertheless. James Manning and Hezekiah Smith, along with other Baptist preachers, were welcome in his pulpit, and the commencement exercises of Rhode Island College were held in his commodious meetinghouse until 1775 when the new building of the First Baptist Church was ready.

The harmony between Baptists and pedobaptists in Providence was far from usual among the Separates. More typical were churches which tried unsuccessfully to practice mixed communion and ended by dividing in the manner described in the previous chapter. The reasons for this are fairly obvious. Strict biblicism argues not only for believer's baptism but for church fellowship only among those so baptized. That is to say, the baptismal issue could not be regarded with indifference by biblical literalists. Most Christians, including pedobaptists, insist that some form of baptism is prerequisite to church fellowship and to participation in the Lord's Supper; and if infant baptism is counted a nullity, strict communion becomes the only course for a convinced Baptist. Isaac Backus called mixed communion "practical lying":

> Though the communion of all real saints together appeared to be of great importance, yet many found by degrees that it could

2. *Literary Diary of Ezra Stiles, 1,* 275.
3. Vose, *History of the Beneficent Church,* p. 103.
4. *Literary Diary of Ezra Stiles, 1,* 278.

not be done in that way; for they saw that if they came to the Lord's supper with any who were only sprinkled in their infancy, it practically said they were baptized, when they believed in their consciences that they were not. And practical lying is a great sin.[5]

Other arguments were advanced for strict communion. Baptism was instituted before the Lord's Supper, which is presumptive evidence of its primacy in the obedience of the Christian. The order of commands in the Great Commission (Matthew 18:18–20) reinforced the same conviction. Apostolic practice placed baptism before the breaking of bread (Acts 2:41–47). Some argued also from the differing significance of the two ordinances: baptism marked the beginning of the Christian life and the Lord's Supper the nourishment of it. When the proponents of these views were accused of breaking fellowship with their "unbaptized" brethren, they replied that the way to Christian union was to adhere strictly to the commands of Christ and the practice of the apostles, not to deny them, and that those who departed from the plain sense of the New Testament were in fact the schismatics. All these arguments rested on the same foundations as those for believer's baptism, namely the logic of the pure church ideal and the requirements of thorough biblicism. If they seem naive in the twentieth century, it must be remembered that the Separate Baptists were the strictest biblical literalists of their age, and that a great deal of their strength with the masses came from insisting on complete adherence to the plainest sense of the Word of God. Considering the milieu in which the Separates lived, it is not surprising that they divided over this issue.

The parting of the ways. The course of the division is documented by a series of conferences and councils which eventually involved most of the Separate churches in southern New England. These meetings were precipitated not only by growing numbers of defections to the Baptists everywhere but by the conversion of Isaac Backus, whose influence reached far beyond the confines of his own parish. For this reason, it is best to approach the story through the strife reverberating from the Middleborough Separate Church. The confusion here after Backus was immersed in August 1751 became so distressing that a council was called on October 2 to inquire into their broken and divided condition.[6] Only sixteen members renewed covenant on this

5. *Abridged History,* pp. 177–78.
6. See above, pp. 219–20.

occasion, and these were advised to labor with the others until they were either restored to fellowship or cut off by discipline. Backus was not one of the sixteen, nor was he received back until November 8. When he returned to the church, Samuel Alden and Robert Washburn declared that they could not receive a pastor who refused to baptize infants even though he permitted another minister to do so. Another council meeting on May 27, 1752, failed to resolve the dispute, and the church, in accord with the advice of the first council, excluded the two recusants. Alden and Washburn called an ex parte council which met on November 1, 1752; it justified them and censured Backus and all who had acted against them. It is very interesting that the first and third councils (thirteen months apart), whose decisions were exactly opposite, were both led by Solomon Paine of Canterbury and Thomas Stevens of Plainfield. Their change of view with regard to Backus and the whole communion controversy indicates the rapid deterioration of fraternal relations between Baptists and pedobaptists while both parties were still nominally in the same camp.

The Baptist party was alarmed by the apparent effort of the pedobaptists to make the adoption of believer's baptism a censurable offense. Backus convened a group of open-communion Baptists (as he himself was at the time) and more moderate pedobaptists at Middleborough on January 31, 1753. The following decision was a result of this meeting:

> We find a peculiar difficulty subsisting among them [Backus' church] which affects the whole number of the Separate churches; therefore we refuse to give our opinions of judgments until the number of the faithful, by their messengers, meet together in a general assembly, to settle points of communion . . . at Exeter, R.I. . . . on the 23d of May next.[7]

A copy of this decision was sent to all the Separate churches in the land. Representatives from twenty-seven churches met in David Sprague's meetinghouse at Exeter on the appointed day. Stephen Babcock and Sprague, both open-communion Baptists, served as moderator and scribe respectively. Solomon Paine and Thomas Stevens, in what seems to have been a deliberate act of boycott, sent letters to excuse themselves. One of the participants testified that open communion won unanimous consent:

7. Quoted in Hovey, *Memoir of Isaac Backus*, p. 108.

The Enquiry in the first Days conference was as to our Agreemt in the Doctrines of the Gospl. & experiml. standg in Christ. Unanimously agreed.

The 2d Days conference was respectg Term of Comun, upon which two Votes passed—1. That if any one who had been bapd by sprinkg or in Infancy, & belonged to a Congl church, & was hopefully a gracious person—yet scruples arisg. as to the mode & Subjt or both, & desires Bapm by plungg—& went to a Bapt Eldr—& was so bapd, & returned to his own Church—whether he sh'd be received to comun or censured. —2. If a Bapt should have scruples, & manifest his Belief of Inft Baptm—& go to a Congl Church & get his childn baptized, & return to his own Church, whether Church would receive or censure him? —Voted unanimously not to censure, but to receive in both cases;—this is open Comunion.

Then the Modr. declared that they, i.e. all the Churches of this Body, were one Church. —& henceforth the Words *dip* & *sprinkle* sh'd cease, & the word *baptize* only be used—And as a Test[imon]y of the mutual Comunion Elder David Sprague, a Bapt. (who was to have the Comun next Sabbath) desired Elder Peck a Congl & paed., to stay and administer the L'ds supper with his Church: but Mr Peck was obliged to return home. The Door however was open for pastoral & Church Comun in all Ordinances & Office Acts.[8]

The week following this meeting had been designated by the Separate church at North Stonington for the ordination of Oliver Prentice as their pastor.[9] Solomon Paine and Stephen Babcock were invited to participate in the ceremonies, but because of the former's refusal to accept the compromise proposed at the Exeter conference, Babcock declined to act with him. He gave his reasons frankly to the church, adding that Paine had abused the Baptists in general and Backus in particular. Paine took offense because Babcock had aired his grievances publicly before coming directly to him, and "commenced a labor with Elder Babcock" that eventually led to a call for another general conference.

The resulting meeting at the house of Simeon Brown (a deacon in Babcock's church at Westerly) in North Stonington on May 29,

8. "Account of a Conference in 1752 [1753], which [Ezra Stiles] wrote down after being told orally by Elder Samuel Peck of Rehoboth on August 7, 1772," *Proceedings of the Massachusetts Historical Society*, 8 (1864–65), 221–22.

9. Prentice succeeded Matthew Smith and served 1753–55.

1754, was the largest convention of Separates ever held. "Elders and brethren from forty churches then met, viz., from twenty-four in Connecticut, eight in the Massachusetts, seven in Rhode Island, and one on Long Island." [10] Baptist and pedobaptist delegates were about evenly divided. After three days of wrangling, Elisha Paine, who was considerably more astute than his bullish brother, called the assembly to face frankly that they were divided by irreconcilable principles. In lawyerlike fashion he declared:

> A holds out his principles. 1. He declares he will administer baptism to none but adult believers. 2. That he will go to any church, and baptize all persons that were baptized in infancy, if they will declare they were dissatisfied with their infant baptism. B holds out his principles, and declares that he will administer baptism to all adult believers and their infant seed, and that he doth it in the name of the Trinity, in obedience of a divine precept. Now the question is, Be these two persons agreed in their principles? or will there be any essential difference between their practice, if they practice according to their professed principles? . . . My dear brother, if you can reconcile the above principles, in the essential parts thereof, you will remove all the grounds of bars and disputes. . . . Either B sins in making infants the subjects of baptism, or A in cutting them off.[11]

The crux of the whole matter was not whether the immersion of believers should be considered valid baptism, but whether the sprinkling of infants could be counted as baptism at all. Mixed communion might succeed only so long as the Baptists did not explicitly repudiate infant baptism by declaring it a nullity, but to do this would involve a denial of their basic principle. The conference broke up with Solomon Paine declaring in behalf of the pedobaptists that "tho' they could yet commune with saints who did *not see* light for infant baptism; yet they did withdraw the hand of fellowship from all such as professed *to see* that there was no warrant for bringing infants to that ordinance." [12]

10. Backus, *History of New England, 2,* 113. The Long Island church was the one at Bridgehampton under Elisha Paine.
11. Quoted ibid., p. 114.
12. Backus, *A Fish Caught in His Own Net,* p. 118. The final position of the pedobaptist Separates was stated at Killingly in 1781: "And as to our Baptist Brethren, we are free to hold occasional Communion, with such as are regular

Backus (and his biographer after him) tried hard to fasten the blame for breaking fellowship on Solomon Paine and those who shared his stubbornness. This is fatuous. The truth of the matter is that the pedobaptists saw more clearly and quickly than the Baptists that there must be a parting of the ways. The Stonington conference of May 1754 marks the decisive breach. Later that year (September) Stephen Babcock convened a rump council of Baptists and moderate Separates which declared again for open communion, "because we dare not shut out such as Christ evidently receives." [13] But two years later Backus acknowledged the futility of proceeding further along that path and formed a strict-communion Baptist church, while others sooner or later did the same. At the end of the century he confessed that they had drawn a mistaken conclusion from manifestly good premises. He had learned from experience, he said, "that the holding of internal union [i.e. Christian fellowship] as the rule of church communion, naturally leads to the censuring of brethren of both denominations, if they refuse to act according to that rule, which is making our affection to creatures the standard instead of the revealed will of God." [14] This did not deny that pedobaptists are Christians, or that there can be Christian fellowship across denominational lines, but it did preclude "building together" with them in the visible church.

Independent organization. While the pedobaptist Separates were moving toward what would become in 1781 the Strict Congregational Convention of Connecticut,[15] the Separate Baptists were gravitating into two associations, one formed on the principle of strict, the other of mixed, communion. The strict-communion body came to be known as the Stonington Baptist Association, the initial impulse for which was probably furnished by Joshua Morse. He had adopted the strict principle shortly after settling in Montville, Connecticut, in 1750, and this was likely the reason for his being excommunicated by a council of Separate ministers early in 1752.[16] A few years later, pastor Ebenezer Mack of the East Lyme Separate Church declared for strict communion. A council in which Morse participated justified Mack in a significant decision which marks the first movement to-

---

Churches, and make the Christian Profession as above said; *and acknowledge us to be Baptized Churches,* and own the Morality of the Ten Commands of the Decalogue" (*An Historical Narrative and Declaration,* p. 21; italics mine). But this, of course, was just the rub.

13. Quoted in Hovey, p. 113.
14. *History of New England,* 2, 119.
15. See above, p. 173.
16. See above, pp. 169–70, 226.

ward an organization of strict Baptist churches. Mack moved to Marlow, New Hampshire, in 1768, and Morse ministered to the East Lyme church as often as possible. On one of his visits in 1771 he proposed that it and his church should "enter into a sisterly relation."

> The brethren requested him to state what his Articles were. He replied, "*That none be admitted to membership but real believers, and nothing be practiced for baptism, but immersion.*" His first proposition was unanimously adopted, and the second, by a large majority.[17]

Morse's second article, though not explicitly antipedobaptist, obviously implied in this context the repudiation of infant baptism. In spite of the "large majority" which agreed to this point, the lack of unanimity prevented the consummation of the proposed relation. (The East Lyme church remained on the open-communion plan until 1795.) The next year (1772), however, Morse succeeded in bringing together in an informal "conference" a group of messengers from Separate Baptist churches which had adopted strict communion. This marks the beginning of the Stonington Baptist Association, although it did not take this name until 1781. Morse was elected as the first moderator.

The Association's concern for doctrinal unanimity is reflected in an action of the second year (1773):

> Voted that it is not the duty of any of the churches of this Association to covenant and build with persons or churches that hold sprinkling to be baptism; and therefore *not to commune* with those we can not build with (unite in church relation), to the grief of any of the churches.
>
> Adopted English Baptist *Articles of Faith* [the strongly Calvinistic Second London Confession, 1677], so called, as our articles, believing them in the main to be agreeable with the Scriptures of Truth. Request that each respective church adopt the same, or any shorter creed if a church chooses, if not inconsistent with above.[18]

17. *Historical Sketch of the New London Baptist Association, from Its Organization in 1817, to 1850. Together with a History of the Churches of Which It Is Composed* (Boston, 1851), p. 41. Complete doctrinal accord was presumed necessary for connectional relations.

18. *Minutes of the Stonington Union Baptist Association*, 1866. The name was changed in 1817. Minutes for 1866 furnish a résumé of important actions of earlier years.

The actions of subsequent years are concerned primarily with receiving new member churches as one by one they purged themselves of pedobaptist members (or immersed them) and followed strict communion. For example, by 1782 the Baptist churches at Groton, East Lyme, and Waterford communed only occasionally with pedobaptists but were denied admission to the Association on that account. In 1785 the First Baptist Church of Saybrook was admitted, it having "purged itself of mixed communion." [19] The rapprochement of Separate Baptists and regular Baptists, already indicated by this time in the membership of other associations, was furthered when the Stonington Association entered into correspondence with these groups: the Shaftsbury Association in 1781, the Warren in 1782, the Philadelphia in 1784, the Danbury in 1790, the New York in 1793, the Charleston (South Carolina) and the Bowdoinham in 1794, and so on. In 1784 it began to assume denominational missionary functions by appointing supplies for destitute churches. At the end of the century it was a vigorous body that had taken its place in the life of New England Baptists.

Mixed-communion churches, likewise feeling a need for fraternal connection, formed in 1786 the Groton Union Conference. It covered the same territory as the Stonington Association, and embraced not only the mixed-communion churches of separatist origin but also a few of the older Baptist churches of eastern Connecticut and Rhode Island, many of which were still Arminian. This body reached a peak of strength about 1805, when it had twenty churches with some twenty-five hundred members, but it gradually saw that it would have to come to terms with the Stonington Association sooner or later.

A committee appointed to explore their similarities and differences met in 1791, but the time was not ripe for action then. In 1815 negotiations were begun in earnest, and by 1817 a merger was consummated. At that time the Stonington body numbered twenty-four churches with 3,215 members, and was the more vigorous spiritually. After the merger, there were still two associations, but the division was according to geographical lines and not doctrinal sentiment or practice in regard to communion. The churches west of the Thames River formed the New London Association, those east of the river the Stonington Union Association. Both new bodies unanimously adoped the constitution of the old Stonington Association. This represents the triumph of Calvinism and strict communion among churches which owed their origin to many heterogeneous sources—a triumph

19. Ibid.

won mainly because of the energy and zeal with which the Separate Baptists sought their destiny.

CONFLICT WITH THE STANDING ORDER

Disabilities before the law. The reluctance of the Congregational establishment in New England to allow even minimum rights to dissenters is well known. The English Act of Toleration (1689) was intended to apply also in the colonies, but the dominant party in church and state allowed its application only to themselves until finally they were forced to grant it to others. In Massachusetts the royal charter of 1691 required liberty of conscience in Boston, but other towns still enforced parish privileges for the Congregational church. An exemption act for Episcopalians was passed in 1727, one for Baptists and Quakers the next year. It provided that none of those who conscientiously dissented from the established churches

> shall have their polls taxed towards the support of such minister or ministers, nor shall their bodies be at any time taken in execution, to satisfy any such ministerial rate or tax, assessed upon their estates or faculty; provided, that such persons do usually attend the meetings of their respective societies, assembling upon the Lord's day for the worship of God, and that they live within five miles of the place of such meeting.[20]

This, it will be observed, not only places severe restrictions on the persons who may be excused from the obligations of majority party members, but it provides exemption only from personal, not property, taxes for religious purposes. Rather importantly, it outlaws corporal punishment for nonpayment of the tax. The next year a supplementary act was passed exempting the estates of dissenters from the ministerial rates. It became the responsibility of the county clerk to make a list of dissenters so that they might not be assessed, but no penalty was attached for nonperformance of this duty. Few clerks troubled themselves to do it, and consequently, most dissenters were assessed anyway. In actual practice this law afforded very little relief.

The Exemption Act of 1728 was renewed in essentially the same form in 1734, 1740, and 1747, and it indicates the measure of toleration accorded dissenters during the decade of the Great Awakening. Massachusetts, unlike Connecticut, never enacted any specific laws against the disorders of the revival, but each parish church went as far as it could to collect rates from all New Lights who separated

20. Quoted in Backus, *History of New England, 1,* 517.

from its worship. When the movement of Separates into Baptist ranks assumed large proportions, however, the General Court moved to define more closely the conditions of exemption for Baptists. In 1753 Moses Marcy, representative from Sturbridge, led the enactment of the following measure:

> That no person, for the future, should be esteemed to be an Anabaptist, but those whose names are contained in the lists taken by the assessors, or such as shall produce a certificate, under the hands of the minister and of two principal members of such church, setting forth that they conscientiously believe such person or persons to be of their persuasion. . . . That no *minister* nor the *members* of any Anabaptist church, as aforesaid, shall be esteemed qualified to give such certificates, as aforesaid, other than such as shall have obtained *from three other churches,* commonly called Anabaptists, in this or the neighboring Provinces, a certificate from *each respectively,* that they esteem such church to be one of their denomination, and that they *conscientiously believe them to be Anabaptists.*[21]

The act was highly offensive for a number of reasons, but its main force lay in the provision that no church was qualified to issue certificates to its members until its minister and constituency had obtained, from previously existing and regularly certified Baptist churches, an affidavit stating that it was duly recognized as a Baptist church. The pinch of this clause came when the newly formed Separate Baptist churches, not yet in fellowship with the older Baptist churches, found it almost impossible to obtain the required vouchers. It betrays the feeling of the authorities that the Separates not only were seeking to evade responsibility but were such a receptacle for scandalous and disorderly persons that not even self-respecting "Anabaptists" would own them.

This act, renewed in 1757 and lasting until 1770, is the one of which Backus said, "no tongue nor pen can fully describe the evils that were practiced under it." [22] Town officials, moreover, were willing to see that the requirements of the law were not met easily, and they continued to amerce the Baptists in their midst wherever possible, distraining goods in lieu of unpaid taxes and even imprisoning some in open defiance of the law. It is impossible to read the records of suf-

21. Quoted in Hovey, pp. 170–71. For Marcy's part in oppressing dissenters, see above, p. 194.
22. *History of New England,* 2, 141.

fering and loss on the part of the Separate Baptists and believe that pecuniary considerations motivated their profession of Baptist principles to any great extent.

In Connecticut the legal disabilities of dissenters were, if anything, more severe. The toleration clause of the Saybrook legislation (1708) was intended primarily for Anglicans, to prevent possible interference from England. A formal exemption act of 1729 released Baptists from contributing to the support of the standing ministry or maintenance of the parish meetinghouses whenever they produced a certificate that they supported and worshiped regularly in a society of their own. When the New Light schism began in the Congregational churches, the benefits of toleration were denied to those who styled themselves Congregationalists or Presbyterians.[23] In the excitement of those days, the distinction between Baptists and separatists tended to become blurred. "The Connecticut authorities, when imbued with the persecuting spirit, did not always stop to distinguish between the legally exempt Baptist dissenters and the unexempted Separatists."[24] When Separates began to move into Baptist ranks, what difference there had been in the past was practically forgotten. The repressive legislation was omitted from the revision of Connecticut laws in 1750, but this was primarily to protect the record against complaints to England—the spirit of oppression continued unchanged. Here and there local leniency mitigated the pressure of persecution, but no general relief was obtained until disestablishment was won in 1818.

The struggle for religious liberty. In view of the circumstances, it is not surprising that the Separate Baptists led the fight for rights of conscience in New England. Their background as the most radical of the despised and illegal Separates exposed them to the most severe religious persecution in the eighteenth century, preparing them to give effective testimony to the evils of ecclesiastical establishment and oppression. They furnished the largest part of the agitation which won eventual freedom of religion, and the chief role in the long and bitter struggle was carried by Isaac Backus. It may be recalled that he was the one who traveled the length of Cape Cod and visited every Separate church in southeastern Massachusetts to obtain signatures on the petition for legal status presented to the General Court in 1749 (see above, p. 198). Later, as the agent of the Warren Baptist Association, he stood for thirty years in the forefront of the battle waged by Baptists for universal religious liberty.

23. See above, pp. 63–64.
24. M. L. Greene, *Religious Liberty in Connecticut*, pp. 275–76.

Nothing better illustrates the spirit of the Separate Baptists in pro-
testing against abridgment of the rights of conscience than the "Memorial and Remonstrance," which was drawn in reaction against the
harsh law of 1753 and presented to the Massachusetts General Court
in May the next year.[25] Its author was John Proctor, the Boston school-
teacher who was one of the original members of the Second Baptist
Church there; the other signers were Thomas Green of Leicester,
Ebenezer Moulton of South Brimfield, and six others, three of whom
were members of the Boston Second Church. These men called themselves "a Committee appointed in behalf of several Societies of the
people called Baptists." They first reviewed the Toleration Act and
claimed its extension to all who dissented from the Established Church
of England, however denominated, and on this ground "insist upon
and claim their privileges by birthright." They argued that in con-
travention of this right and notwithstanding the royal indulgence,
the Baptists of Massachusetts had been forced "with a high hand
and by compulsion" to support a religious establishment which they
could not in conscience attend. The memorialists submitted a long
list of grievances due to distraint of goods and imprisonment for
ministerial taxes in numerous towns outside Boston, and also a list
of the many efforts they had made to secure redress. On top of all
these frustrations came the new law, giving cause not only for added
complaint but for downright alarm. The remonstrants reminded the
Court that their legislative power is "amenable to a much higher
tribunal at home," and that the new act is surely "repugnant to the
laws of England and . . . [has] usurped an illegal power over all
the religious Societies of the people in the said act called Anabaptists, throughout this his Majesty's Province." One cannot mistake
here the willingness of the writers to play on the fear with which the
colonial government regarded a possibility of interference by the
crown.

The petition continued by roundly denouncing the unreasonable
requirements of the act:

> [It subjects] each and every Anabaptist Church in the Province
> in a very unreasonable and unheard of manner to a new sort
> of Spiritual Court, consisting at least of three other Anabaptist
> Churches, as the acts call them, to give each of them a certificate
> respectively,—and for what? —why, truly that an Anabaptist

25. Printed in David B. Ford, *New England's Struggles for Religious Liberty*
(Philadelphia, 1896), pp. 151–66.

Church is truly an Anabaptist Church, so that, indeed, it is necessary by this act the four Anabaptist churches must be co-operating together in this jumbled decision. But may it please your Excellency and Honors, when is it possible for the poor Anabaptists to find in this or the neighboring Provinces, or indeed *in all the world,* the first three authenticated Anabaptist Ministers and Churches to certify and authenticate the first three? Over and above the obvious absurdities in this unreasonable act, the severity thereof is remarkable in exposing of our said brethren to the loss of so much time, and the considerable charge and expense which necessarily must arise in journeyings to and fro in this Province and the neighboring Provinces in pursuit of such chimerical certificates utterly impossible to be obtained.

With rising spirit the remonstrants declared their determination at all costs never to submit to the obnoxious act, because "the people commonly called Anabaptists in this Province are, and ought to be, by the said Royal Charter, in all points of a religious nature, equally as independent and free from all spiritual subordination" as any other religious group in the colony. They vigorously denied that the numerical superiority of any one denomination gave it a right to "oppress, afflict, or unjustly subordinate the less or more feeble Denominations of his Majesty's Protestant subjects of this Province in matters of religion and conscience." Therefore, they concluded, the unjust act had to be repealed, and all persons "that have at any time within the space of five years last past had their bodies imprisoned for ministerial rates, or their estates, goods and chattels distrained therefor, may be honestly refunded their just damages." This was the only course that they felt would demonstrate the provincial government to be "honourable, upright, and impartial." [26]

Backus says that the memorial "stated matters so plainly, that a motion was made by some to take the signers of it into custody; but Governor Shirley, newly returned from Europe, convinced them of the impolicy of such a step; and then they appointed a committee to

26. While resting ostensibly on the Act of Toleration, this petition is moving plainly in the direction of claiming religious freedom as a natural right. The Separates and Separate Baptists increasingly decried "toleration" as an arrogant and presumptuous concession of what in the nature of the case was inalienable. Such an argument bears the mark of the Enlightenment and stands in contrast to the more theologically oriented plea of Roger Williams that "soul liberty" was necessary in order for the individual to seek and follow the revealed will of God.

confer in a friendly way with the Baptists; and matters were shifted along, until the [French and Indian] war came on, and their design for [sending an appeal to] England was dropped." [27] Not until 1770 were the worst features of the odious act repealed. In the certificate law of that year, the words "Anabaptist Church" were changed to "Antipedobaptist Congregation," which seems to indicate that the authorities had given up trying to distinguish between regular and Separate Baptists. But annual certificates were still required to be given to the county clerk on behalf of those who desired exemption, although local parishes were empowered to abate the Baptists' rates without certificates if they so desired. It was still a far cry from complete religious liberty, and not until two full generations later was that privilege finally gained in Massachusetts. The primary agency of the Baptists in pressing the struggle from this point on, however, was the Warren Association, in which Separate and regular Baptists became merged organizationally. The rest of the story belongs to the history of the Baptists generally and not specifically to that of the Separate Baptists.[28]

Rapprochement with the Regular Baptists [29]

In the 1760s three distinct strands of Baptist life mingled in New England. Many of the Separate Baptist churches were beginning to achieve a measure of stability, and their rapid growth and vigorous

27. *History of New England*, 2, 140.

28. Even in the acts of the Warren Association, some thought they saw the dominant influence of the Separates. When Backus headed a delegation of New England Baptists to the Continental Congress at Philadelphia in 1774 to add the argument for religious liberty to the general movement toward independence, Samuel Adams sought to represent that *regular* Baptists were well pacified. "More than once he insinuated that complaints came from *enthusiasts* only, who 'made it a merit to suffer persecution' " (Joseph Martin Dawson, *Baptists and the American Republic*, Nashville, 1956, p. 71). This was hardly the whole truth. It was the Separates who were multiplying so rapidly and thereby creating the largest part of the problem, but after 1770 the standing order generally recognized that it faced a united enemy to establishment.

29. I have nowhere used "regular" as a proper adjective, as it sometimes is applied to Calvinistic Baptists in the colonial South. Whether it stands before "Baptist" or "Congregationalist," it means simply the older churches which antedated the rise of the Separates. "General" and "Particular" Baptists are differentiated by their view of the atonement; i.e. they are Arminian and Calvinistic respectively. The Generals were usually Six-Principle, regarding laying on of hands as an ordinance and usually a term of communion. The Separates were also Calvinistic, but see below, pp. 285–87.

life soon transformed almost the entire denomination. The coming of new and powerful influences from the Particular Baptists of the Middle Colonies, who were already well structured denominationally in the Philadelphia Association,[30] brought a sense of order and direction that assured the future integrity of the previously inchoate body of Baptists in New England. The older General Baptists were perhaps the least virile of the three, and those which were not swept along in the new tides of evangelical influence were largely left to stagnate. The interaction of these three types of Baptist life became an important part of the story of the Separate Baptists. Their relation to the General Baptists was primarily a matter of doctrinal conflict, which eventually resulted in a victory for the evangelical Calvinism of the Separates. Their relation to the Particular Baptists helped them to resolve the issues of education and ecclesiastical connectionalism. It was the Separates' doctrinal agreement with the Particulars, and the Particulars' willingness to cooperate with the Separates, that made possible the ultimate absorption of the Separates into the ongoing life of American Baptists.

Doctrinal conflict with the General Baptists. The inroads of Calvinism and New Light revivalism on the older General Baptist churches were discussed in the previous chapter.[31] When the Separate Baptists emerged as a fairly well-defined group, it was evident that there were radical differences between them and those who had stood clear of (or backed off from) the entire revival movement. Nothing indicates the transformation of the doctrinal character of New England Baptists better than Backus' amazing statement that the movement of which he was practically the heart and soul stood in the tradition not of John Smyth and Roger Williams (though he revered those men highly), but of John Robinson and the purest of the Pilgrims!

> In general, their faith and practice come the nearest to that of the first planters of New England, of any churches now in the land, excepting in the single article of sprinkling infants. In particular, they believe:

30. Formed in 1707 with five churches, this body embraced in the next half-century nearly thirty churches located from Virginia to upstate New York, and its missionaries ranged from Carolina to Nova Scotia. The provincial name of this body should not obscure the fact that it was national in scope and carried on all the missionary and disciplinary functions of an actual denomination. To New England it contributed the leadership for two extremely important enterprises: Rhode Island College and the Warren Association.

31. See above, pp. 240–42.

1. That God set Adam as the public head of all mankind; so that when he revolted from heaven, and seized upon the earth as his own, all the human race fell in him, and all bear his earthly image, until they are born again.

2. That in infinite mercy the eternal Father gave a certain number of the children of men to his beloved Son, before the world was, to redeem and save; and that he, by his obedience and sufferings, has procured eternal redemption for them.

3. That by the influence of the Holy Spirit, these persons individually, as they come into existence, are effectually called in time, and savingly renewed in the spirit of their minds.

4. That their justification before God, is wholly by the perfect righteousness of Jesus Christ, received by faith.

5. That every such soul will be kept by the power of God, through faith, unto eternal salvation.

6. That, according to God's institution, regenerate souls are the only materials for particular Christian churches.

7. That the right way of building such churches is by giving a personal, verbal account to the church of what God has done for their souls, to the satisfaction of the church.

8. That the whole power of calling, ordaining, and deposing officers, is in each particular church; although it is ordinarily proper and expedient to call in the advice and assistance of sister churches upon many such occasions.

9. That the whole power of governing and disciplining their members is in each particular church; though advice and counsel from others, in some cases, is becoming and even necessary.

10. That the government of the church should be wholly by the laws of Christ, enforced in his name, and not at all by the secular arm.

11. That gospel ministers ought to be supported by his laws and influence, and not by tax and compulsion enforced by the civil power.

12. That ministers ought to preach, and not read their sermons, at least in ordinary times, that being evidently the apostolic practice; and the contrary enables men to impose upon people, by reading the works of others, and is attended with other evils.

13. That free liberty ought to be allowed for every saint to improve his gifts according to the gospel; and that the church should encourage and recommend such as are qualified for the gospel ministry.

14. That officers, when chosen and ordained, have no arbitrary, lordly, or imposing power; but are to rule and minister with the consent of the brethren, who ought not to be called *The laity*, but to be treated as men and brethren in Christ.[32]

Here are the five points of Reformed doctrine, the classical sectarian [33] view of the church, and the crucial points of the New Light reformation, all in one brief credo attributed not to Separates or Separate Baptists but to *Baptists per se*. The Separates wrought a doctrinal revolution among the Baptists of New England, overwhelming by sheer force of numbers and unflagging zeal the older General Baptists. The future clearly belonged to the Calvinistic Baptists, largely because of the influence of the rapidly multiplying Separates who soon overran the whole region.[34]

Relation to Rhode Island College. The establishment of a Baptist collegiate institution was proposed first in 1762 by Morgan Edwards, pastor of the First Baptist Church of Philadelphia. After some discussion the Philadelphia Association decided to seek location of the school in Rhode Island, because the predominance of Baptists there and the freedom they enjoyed made it most likely that a favorable charter could be obtained. The man selected to go to Rhode Island and confer with leading Baptists on the steps necessary to secure a charter was James Manning (1738–91), who had been converted by Gilbert Tennent in 1748 and baptized by Benjamin Miller soon afterward. He had graduated from the College of New Jersey, second in the class of 1762, and had preached at Scotch Plains, New Jersey, and at Charleston, South Carolina. In July 1763 he visited Newport and met with several men of influence who were immediately favorable to the idea of a college in their colony. In 1764 the Rhode Island Assembly granted a charter.[35] Manning opened the college at Warren in

32. *History of New England*, 2, 231–33. The articles are run into a single paragraph in the original.

33. Here, as everywhere, this term has sociological significance only, with no pejorative connotations.

34. There was room for New Light Baptists in the ranks of the Arminians also, as indicated by the rise of the Freewill Baptists. But the historian of that movement admits that even on the frontier, where they flourished most, they grew only one-third as fast as the Calvinistic groups (Baxter, *History of Freewill Baptists*, p. 34).

35. The fairest and most accurate account of the charter negotiations is in Walter C. Bronson, *The History of Brown University, 1764–1914* (Providence, 1914), pp. 13–27.

1766, and on September 7, 1769, it held its first commencement, granting bachelors' degrees to seven men.

Not all Baptists in New England welcomed this auspicious enterprise, nor is their suspicion surprising. Backus wrote that as late as 1755, "there were but two Baptist ministers, in all New England, who had what is called a liberal education; and they were not clear in the doctrines of grace." [36] When well-trained and able men came from the highly organized Philadelphia Association to promote a collegiate institution under the Baptist name, many of the uneducated preachers were extremely hostile. What Ezra Stiles wrote of Nathan Young of Smithfield probably typifies their attitude, "Eld Young is Illiterate— don't like the College—says when the old Ministers die off he foresees a new Succession of Scholar Ministers: —that it has got so far already as scarcely to do for a common Illiterate Minister to preach in the baptist meeting at providence." [37]

Undoubtedly many Separate Baptists shared some of this feeling, but in spite of their inherited prejudice toward a learned ministry, it was they who led the acceptance of the college. Isaac Backus was elected in 1765 as one of the first trustees, and was for a time also a trustee of the Education Fund set up by the Warren Association in 1791 to aid pious young men in preparing for the ministry. To be sure, some of his associates criticized his part in those affairs. Thomas Green wrote to Ebenezer Hinds:

> E[lder] Backus's concern in the College, with the views he undertook it, appears to me to be plausible enough; yet I cannot see how he, acting faithfully, upon his own declared principles, can long keep his standing as a member of that body the chief of whose principles and views differing so widely from his. —Perhaps he is to have the great blessing of being cast out for the truth's sake, and so leave a testimony behind him.[38]

But he served faithfully for thirty-four years. Whatever fears he may have had at the first were allayed by Manning's conduct of the school, and his own sentiments were doubtless echoed by the president at the commencement of 1769:

> Should the christian ministry with any of you become an object, reflect on the absurdity of intruding into it while strangers to ex-

---

36. Letter to John Gill, quoted in Hovey, p. 153. The two men referred to were Jeremiah Condy of Boston and Edward Upham of Newport, both Arminians.

37. *Literary Diary of Ezra Stiles, 1,* 49.

38. Letter dated Sept. 1, 1766, quoted in Maston, "Ethical and Social Attitudes of Backus," p. 39.

perimental religion. See that yourselves have been taught of God, before you attempt to teach godliness to others. To place in the professional chairs of our universities the most illiterate of mankind, would be an absurdity by far less glaring, than to call an unconverted man to exercise the ministerial function. This is to expose our holy religion to the scoffs of infidels, and to furnish to their hands the most deadly weapons. I omit to insist on the account such must render in the great tremendous day! [39]

That the college won the confidence of other Separates is indicated by the fact that one of its first graduates, Charles Thompson, was ordained to the pastoral care of the church at Warren (the early home of the school) by Noah Alden of Bellingham and Ebenezer Hinds of Middleborough Second Church—both Separate Baptists. And perhaps the final proof of Backus' own cordiality was his acceptance of an honorary master's degree in 1797.

Problems of denominational organization. An even more difficult hurdle for the Separate Baptists was presented by the question of ecclesiastical connections. This became crucial in 1766 when Manning proposed an association of churches. The acute interest of the Philadelphia Association in this affair is unmistakable. When that body met on October 14, 1766, they voted "to write to the Association to be held at Warren, the Tuesday before the second Sunday in [next] September; and Rev. John Gano, Samuel Jones, and Morgan Edwards, appointed to meet them as delegates from us." [40] The missive they drafted points unmistakably to a larger goal of denominational organization:

A long course of experience and observation has taught us to have the highest sense of the advantages which accrue from associations; nor indeed does the nature or thing speak of any other language. For as particular members are collected together and united in one body, which we call *a particular church*, to answer those ends and purposes which could not be accomplished by any single member, so a collection and *union of churches* into one associational body, may easily be conceived capable of answering those still greater purposes, which any particular church could not be equal to. And by the same reason, a *union of associations*

39. Quoted in Hovey, p. 318.
40. *Minutes of the Philadelphia Baptist Association*, ed. A. D. Gillette (Philadelphia, 1851), p. 97. That a definite date was set so far in advance indicates that Manning had laid careful plans. His own church at Warren voted to participate on August 28, 1766.

will still increase the body in weight and strength, and make it good, that *a threefold cord* is not easily broken. . . . From considering the divided state of our Baptist churches in your quarter, we foresee that difficulties may arise, such as may call for the exercise of the greatest tenderness and moderation, that if haply, through the blessing of God on your endeavors, those lesser differences may subside, and a more general union commence.[41]

The Philadelphia Association, in spite of its strong desire for "a more general union," was obviously aware of the difficulties the associational idea would encounter in New England.

Among the heterogeneous Baptists of that quarter were three strong prejudices which operated against Manning's proposal. One was fear of authoritarian ecclesiastical organization. The only interchurch relations they had known beside their own occasional councils and fraternal yearly meetings were the synods and consociations supported by the civil power and exerting more or less coercive power over the churches. Assemblies convened by clerical or magisterial authority had to them what Roger Williams had called "a most sowre and uncomely deformed looke of a meare human invention." [42] The Second Church in Coventry voiced this fear in a letter to the newly formed association:

We have considered the plan on which the Association aforesaid have formed themselves for the year past, and have searched for the authority referred to in Acts [1]5 to support such Association; and we are not convinced that that chapter, or any other sentence in the Bible, supports a classical government over the church or churches of Christ. And as that plan appears to be full of that design, we think it our duty to express our grief and disapprobation of such a plan, which we conclude will, if countenanced, overthrow the independence of the churches of Christ, so far as that is allowed to operate.[43]

Another fear was associated with the prejudice toward a learned ministry. Since the president of the new college was the prime mover in the forming of the association, it was easy to transfer suspicion of one to distrust of the other. Manning did nothing to disarm this prejudice, announcing rather that one aim in uniting the churches in an

41. Printed as Appendix D in Hovey, pp. 342–44; italics mine.

42. Quoted in Samuel Lunt Caldwell, *A Discourse Preached in Warren* (Providence, 1867), p. 11.

43. Quoted from unpublished records of the Warren Association, 1768, ibid., p. 14.

association was to promote the cause of the college. On the other hand, the gradual acceptance of the one helped to allay fears regarding the other, and vice versa. The third obstacle was doctrinal. The promoters of the new organizational venture were strongly Calvinistic, and this was enough to prejudice the General, or Six-Principle, Baptists against them from the start. At the same time, however, the fact that doctrinal concord was so important to church fellowship in that day enabled Manning to win the cooperation of the Separate Baptists, who were also Calvinistic, and thus make the association eventually a success. What finally convinced the latter of the usefulness of an association whose powers were carefully defined and limited was the advantage it would give them in making a concerted attack on the oppressiveness of the standing order. Manning played heavily on this motive, and this is probably one intention of the "threefold cord, not easily broken" mentioned in the letter from the Philadelphia Association.

At all events, delegates from eleven churches—eight of which had New Light or Separate origins—met at Warren on the appointed day, September 8, 1767.[44] Isaac Backus was elected clerk, and recorded the first minute:

> Whereas there hath of late years been a great increase of Baptist churches in New England, which yet have not such an acquaintance with each other and orderly union together as ought to be, it has been thought by many that a general meeting or association might be a likely means to remove this evil and to promote the general good of the churches. Therefore a number of elders, being occasionally together last year, did appoint a meeting at Warren in Rhode Island colony, on September 8, 1767; and sent an invitation to others of their brethren to meet them there, to confer upon these affairs. Accordingly, a considerable number of elders and brethren met at the time and place appointed; and elder John Gano, from New York, opened the meeting with a suitable sermon from Acts 15:9.[45]

Only four churches entered into the organization at the first meeting: Warren, Haverhill, Bellingham, and Middleborough Second. Backus re-

44. These were Warren, Cumberland (Rhode Island), Rehoboth, Attleborough, Norton, Bellingham, Middleborough First and Second, Boston First and Second, and Haverhill.

45. Quoted in Hovey, p. 155. Gano, pastor of First Baptist Church, New York City, represented the Philadelphia Association. It was to his sermon using Acts 15 to support the associational idea that the Coventry Second Church had objected.

corded in his diary the events of the day, and added, "I did not see my way clear to join now, if ever I do." [46] The reason for his hesitation and that of others was fear that the Association would assert too much authority over the churches, a prime cause of their separation from the standing order. This is especially interesting, because the initial plan proposed by Manning was identical with that of the Philadelphia Association, which had already carefully defined its powers in this regard. A handwritten note on one copy of *The Sentiments and Plan of the Warren Association* (1769) says that the issue of this first meeting was "Adopting the sentiments and platform of the western [Philadelphia] association; and thereon forming churches themselves into a like body to be known by the name of the Warren Association." [47] This seems to have been too much for most of the Separate Baptists.

The usefulness of an association whose prerogatives were adequately guarded, however, was too patent to ignore. On September 19, 1768, Backus wrote to Manning that some modification might permit greater cooperation: "I leave it to your candid consideration whether it would not be best to have a new plan drawn." [48] Manning heeded his advice, and the revised plan made it quite explicit that the association might not violate "the independency and power of particular churches, because it pretends to be no other than an *Advisory council,* utterly disclaiming superiority, jurisdiction, coercive right, and infallibility." It provided further that "All matters [are] to be determined in this Association by the suffrage of the messengers, except what are determinable by Scripture—such matters are never put to the decision of votes." To ensure that scripturally determinable matters would be determined properly, the association was to consist "of men knowing and judicious, particularly in the Scripture." The Philadelphia (or Second London) Confession of Faith was adopted, presumably for substance of doctrine, and the leading points of its Calvinism given special emphasis; the article regarding laying on of hands, which had been added at Philadelphia in 1742, was omitted. A correspondence was to be maintained with the Philadelphia Association by exchange of annual letters and fraternal messengers.[49] The year after this revised plan was approved, the First Church in Middleborough united with the Association. Backus wrote in a manuscript history of the organization:

46. *History of New England, 2,* 409 n.
47. This copy is in the archives of the American Baptist Historical Society, Rochester, New York.
48. Quoted in Maston, p. 59.
49. *The Sentiments and Plan of the Warren Association* (Germantown, Pa., 1769).

They waited until they could be satisfied that this Association did not assume any jurisdiction over the churches, before they joined. And now they joined upon the express condition that no complaint should ever be received by the Association against any particular church that was not of the Association, nor from any censured member of our churches.[50]

Backus himself never missed a meeting of the Association from its formation in 1767 to 1796, when the enfeeblements of age began to curtail his activities.

In a few years it was evident that the Warren Association not only had allayed the suspicions of the Separate Baptists who were overly cautious toward all denominational connectionalism, but also had become a real source of strength and help to the churches. The rising confidence is shown by the increase of member churches: in 1768 First Church Boston (now under the evangelical leadership of Samuel Stillman), and the churches in Sutton, Leicester, and Ware were received; in 1769, Sturbridge, Enfield, Wilbraham, and Montague; in 1770, First and Third Middleborough; and in 1772, Second Boston. Very few churches in Rhode Island joined because they were still predominantly Arminian, and the utilitarian motive of associating against the encroachments of a standing order had no relevance in that colony where separation of church and state had always prevailed. (Even the First Baptist Church of Providence, of which Manning became pastor when the college moved there in 1770, did not unite until 1782; First Church Newport joined four years later.) In Connecticut the Stonington Association, which originated in 1772 and began correspondence with the Warren in 1782, was providing a means of mutual aid and encouragement for the Separate Baptists of that colony. This left the Warren Association to serve primarily the Baptists of Massachusetts, and increasingly the Separates of that province found a congenial fellowship in its fold. Here they added their weight in the struggle for religious liberty, even furnishing the man who did more in that cause than any other. Here also they supplied evangelistic zeal and preachers to answer the frequent calls from the frontier, and thus they became a prime factor in maintaining the Baptist witness in the rapidly filling lands beyond. Within the framework of the Warren Association and others formed soon afterward on the same model, the Separate Baptists were brought into the main stream of Baptist life in America, and through interassociational exchanges

50. Quoted in *History of New England*, 2, 409 n.

they were assimilated more and more into the larger life of the denomination.[51]

CONTINUING INFLUENCE OF THE SEPARATE BAPTISTS

Although the name "Separate Baptist" became passé before the end of the eighteenth century, the churches with Separate and New Light origins continued to exert a powerful influence within the Baptist denomination. There are at least three areas in which their influence was crucial: evangelism, theology, and ecclesiology.

Evangelistic zeal. One of the amazing aspects of the story of the Separate Baptists is that they bore off the largest fruit of the Great Awakening to a denomination that had remained largely aloof from that sweeping movement. But the revivalistic tradition, and the evangelistic zeal that keeps it alive, came to prevail among Baptists chiefly through the direct influence of the Separates. From the time of Isaac Backus until now, no history of Baptists in America could be written without giving a large place to the part played by revivals in the growth and spread of the denomination. This is true of the town as well as of the frontier, and there are few communities which have not known with some regularity the Baptist revival. In the period covered by this study there were repeated revivals, especially in southeastern Massachusetts, north central Connecticut, and on every section of the frontier. Such activity, reinforced by a steady stream of converts from Congregationalism, resulted in a remarkable proliferation of Baptist churches. An example is the First Baptist Church of Middleborough, organized in 1756 as the first in Plymouth County:

> The first year after its organization it dismissed a few members to help form the Second Baptist Church in Middleborough, afterwards the First Baptist Church in Lakeville, or the Beech Woods Church. In 1761, it dismissed a larger number to help form the Third Baptist Church in Middleborough, now the Rock Church, which in turn in 1788 gave birth to the First Marshfield Church. From the three Middleborough churches was formed, in 1828, the Middleborough Central Baptist Church, and, in 1839, the Baptist Church in Raynham. In 1833, the parent church dismissed six-

51. Other associations in New England were formed with large numbers of Separate or New Light Baptist churches as follows: New Hampshire, 1776; Shaftsbury, 1781; Woodstock, 1783; Bowdoinham, 1787; Vermont, 1787; and other later ones, many of which represent subdivisions of these. By 1804 there were thirteen, embracing 312 churches with 23,638 members (Backus, *Abridged History*, p. 237).

teen members to form the [reorganized] Baptist Church in West
Bridgewater. In 1843, the Baptist Church in Halifax was formed
chiefly from the Middleborough Central Church. Isaac Backus
baptized one John Tripp, who had been a Congregationalist
minister, and he, in 1791, gathered the Baptist Church in Carver.
And in one of Backus' many missionary tours he preached for
some time in a town in New Hampshire; a revival occurred, and
he formed a church there. All these churches, and still others
through them, may point to this and say, as the apostolic churches
said of Jerusalem, "She is the mother of us all." [52]

Such a summary says nothing of the number of congregations gathered by the sons of these churches who went in all directions to preach
and baptize. In 1804 Backus wrote that New England had 312 Baptist
churches; many of these were small, but they took this only as further
incentive to bring others into the fold. Nor did the lack of trained
ministers handicap them. Ezra Stiles commented caustically, "Wherever they find a Bunch of ten or a dozen baptist Families they form
a Chh & ordain a Brother an Elder." [53] It might be added that if a
community had not even this many Baptists, an itinerant evangelist
would soon come along and remedy that!

The history of the Separate Baptists, moreover, had taught them
that it could be quite profitable to fish in Congregational waters. Upon
entering a town where there was no church of his order, the Baptist
evangelist would go to the Congregational meetinghouse just as me-
thodically as St. Paul on his missionary journeys went to the synagogue
of the Jews. Usually his efforts would be attended by the same results
that Paul had—revival or riot, sometimes both—and the issue would
be a new Baptist church. It is not too much to say that the same factors which operated in the first instance to turn many of the Strict
Congregationalists into Baptists continued to influence pedobaptists,
particularly in the newer regions.[54]

The publication after 1790 of "annual" statistics measuring the
growth of Baptists fired Noah Worcester, already warm from a baptismal controversy with Thomas Baldwin, to write *Impartial Inquiries, Re-*

52. David Weston, *The Baptist Movement of a Hundred Years Ago* (Boston,
1868), p. 20.

53. *Literary Diary of Ezra Stiles, 3,* 148.

54. A striking instance occurred in Daniel Merrill's Congregational church at
Sedgwick, Maine, in 1805. See *Massachusetts Missionary Magazine, 1* (May 1805),
125–26, for an eye-witness account. Others are noted briefly in Mary Ellen Chase,
Jonathan Fisher: Maine Parson, 1768–1847 (New York, 1948), pp. 95–102.

specting the Progress of the Baptist Denomination.[55] The whole drift of his argument shows that the Baptists who were registering the phenomenal gains had the character of Separates, or New Lights. They might not have been called by this name at such a late date, but they had infused the denomination as a whole with their distinguishing traits so that the marks are unmistakable. There are the earnest zeal inherited from the Great Awakening, the animosity toward established religion, the holy whine which inflamed the passions of uncritical listeners, the insistence on conscious conversion as prerequisite to baptism and church membership, the belief in immediate inspiration, the wide use of lay preachers, and the thorough biblicism of their sermons —all in the same tenor as of thirty and forty years before. Said Worcester:

> Many people are so ignorant, as to be more charmed with sound than sense. And to them, the want of knowledge in a teacher, or of instruction in his discourses, may easily be made up, and overbalanced, by great zeal, an affecting tone of voice, and a perpetual motion of the tongue. If a speaker can keep his tongue running, in an unremitting manner, during the time of exercise; and can quote, memoriter, a large number of texts from within the covers of the Bible, it matters not, to many of his hearers, whether he speaks *sense* or *nonsense;* or whether his quoting scripture be *pertinent* or *impertinent.* And when such persons hear a speaker, who has had but little advantage for education, preach in such a manner, and this too without forethought or study, as he may profess, and we may believe, they think he is most certainly called of God, that he is wonderfully assisted, and speaks as the Spirit gives him utterance. Ergo, he must be a good man, and his sentiments are doubtless right.[56]

Perhaps this is only another instance of the contempt felt by the aristocratic conservative as he watched his congregation forsake his correct niceties to seek more spiritual food from the lips of some New Light exhorter. But it describes a pattern that persisted well into the nineteenth century and followed the frontier to remain alive long after it was a memory in the land of its birth. Evangelistic zeal bequeathed by the Separate Baptists became a long-lived heritage of the denomination for whose growth they were so vital.

Evangelical Calvinism. It has been stressed that the Separate Bap-

55. Worcester, Massachusetts, 1794.
56. Ibid., pp. 19–20.

tists, in contradistinction to most of the older New England Baptists, staunchly upheld the doctrine of sovereign grace. It must be emphasized, however, that their revivalism guarded them from the stultifying effects of rigid predestinarianism. Theirs was an evangelical Calvinism, and not so extreme as that of the Baptists of the Middle Colonies. As an illustration of the latter, one may look at the Philadelphia Association's decision in 1752 that a person denying unconditional election, original sin, and final perseverance should not be retained in full communion.[57] With their general position the Separates doubtless would have agreed, especially Backus and most of the first generation of Separate Baptists. But in practice the urgency with which Baptist evangelists pressed for immediate commitment to Christ, pleading for an inward experience of heartfelt religion rather than a clear understanding of some doctrinal system, greatly modified their original Calvinism. The prevailing attitude by the end of the century was that of John Leland, who dismissed doctrinal controversy in order to make way for experimental faith. He said:

> I conclude that the *eternal purposes* of God, and the *freedom of the human will*, are both truths; and it is a matter of fact, that the preaching that has been most blessed of God, and most profitable to men, is *the doctrine of sovereign grace in the salvation of souls, mixed with a little of what is called Arminianism*. These two propositions can be tolerably well reconciled together, but the modern misfortune is, that men often spend too much time in explaining away one or the other, or in fixing the lock-link to join the others together; and by such means, have but little time in a sermon to insist on those two great things which God blesses.[58]

This is virtually to say that whatever makes for good preaching is *ipso facto* right doctrine. Creeds and systems, in fact, were things for which the Separate Baptists had little use. Their attitude on this point also is best expressed by Leland. A confession of faith, he declared, may be useful to convince an oppressive government that dissenters are not seditious; but in a free state, "where the only punishment inflicted on the enthusiastical is pity," no confession is needed. A rigid

---

57. *Minutes of the Philadelphia Baptist Association*, pp. 68–69.
58. "Letter of Valediction on Leaving Virginia, in 1791," *Writings of John Leland*, p. 172. The date of this piece marks Leland's return to New England, shortly after which he assumed the pastorate of a Separate Baptist church at Cheshire, Massachusetts. The quoted sentiments became typical of Baptists in that whole section.

creed, he declared, was but a "Virgin Mary between the souls of men and the scriptures." [59]

Leland was writing against the background of the merger of Separate and Regular Baptists in Virginia, which had been consummated in 1787 on the basis of the Philadelphia Confession of Faith. The Separates received it only "as containing the great essential doctrines of the gospel, yet, not in so strict a sense, that *all* are obliged to believe everything therein contained." [60] A similar agreement probably prevailed at the forming of the Warren Association (although the records do not say so explicitly), and in both cases utilitarian considerations were strong enough to make both groups willing to compromise in order to unite. Sometimes the differences between the Philadelphia and the Warren associations are so subtle that they are overlooked, and because of the dominance of James Manning, Hezekiah Smith, and the delegates from Philadelphia, it is assumed that the New England body was a replica of the older group. But the presence of the Separate Baptists and their insistence on modifying the initial proposal of Manning lead one to suspect that the divergences so clearly discernible in John Leland were present in incipient form at the very beginning. [61]

This general tendency continued to work until it had modified significantly the strict Calvinism professed by the first generation of Separates, and it culminated in the New Hampshire Confession of Faith (1833). This document, the work of a committee appointed by the Baptist Convention of New Hampshire, declares that "all mankind are sinners, not by constraint but by choice"; and that "nothing prevents the salvation of the greatest sinner on earth except his own voluntary refusal to submit to the Lord Jesus Christ." Election is defined as

> the gracious purpose of God, according to which he regenerates, sanctifies, and saves sinners; that being perfectly consistent with the free agency of man, it comprehends all the means in connection with the end; that it is a most glorious display of God's sovereign goodness, being infinitely wise, holy, and unchangeable; that . . . it encourages the use of means in the highest degree;

59. "The Virginia Chronicle," ibid., p. 114 n.

60. Ibid., p. 114.

61. Leland, incidentally, was baptized and licensed to preach at Noah Alden's Separate Baptist church in Bellingham, which was a charter member of the Warren Association.

that it is ascertained by its effects in all who believe the gospel . . . and that to ascertain it with regard to ourselves, demands and deserves our utmost diligence.

The perseverance of the saints is "the grand mark which distinguishes them from mere professors," and "such only are real believers as endure unto the end." [62] It is clear that this confession has proceeded from an originally Calvinistic source, but it is equally plain that its Calvinism has become greatly attenuated. One writer remarks, "It is doubtful if it ought to be called Calvinistic, since it is non-committal on every point of difference between the Calvinistic and Arminian systems." [63]

Perhaps it is not amiss to repeat that there was one group of New Light Baptists with separatist origins that discarded the Calvinistic background entirely. Benjamin Randall, a separatist from the Congregational church at Newcastle, New Hampshire, baptized by William Hooper at Madbury in 1776, was "preaching up" his religious experiences when some other Baptist ministers asked why he did not preach up election as he should. He replied, "Because I do not believe it"; and then began to study the question in the New Testament, which confirmed him in his Arminianism. Out of the ensuing collision with Calvinistic Baptists, other preachers sided with him and the Freewill movement (a name attached by their enemies and ultimately accepted by them) was born. According to a recent historian, it was theologically quite meager, with emphasis on the Christian life rather than on doctrine or creed. It had three cardinal tenets:

The first was that the sinner, once converted, might, and often did, fall from the state of grace. The second was that the salvation offered by Christ is for all men, and the third was that man has the power of choice in either refusing or accepting what is offered to him.[64]

Freewill Baptists were strongest in northern New England, but even here they declined in influence as other Baptists became less strict in their Calvinism due to the moderations stemming from the revivalistic Separates. The movement also had some appeal to the remaining Ar-

62. W. J. McGlothlin, *Baptist Confessions of Faith* (Philadelphia, 1911), pp. 302–05.
63. Ibid., p. 299.
64. Baxter, p. 57.

minian churches in Rhode Island, which after 1790 tended to become loosely associated with the Freewillers.[65]

Local church ecclesiology. All separatism is perforce based on a sectarian doctrine of the church which exalts local independency and autonomy at the expense of acknowledging the larger fellowship of catholic Christianity. The beginnings of Congregationalism in England are marked by this characteristic; but in New England a much more churchly tradition developed, so that local independency had been subjected to the structures of interchurch connections supported by clerical and magisterial authority. Massachusetts' Cambridge Platform was not strongly democratic, and the Strict Congregationalists who made it their shibboleth were always careful to excise its undemocratic aspects. Connecticut, whose Saybrook Platform readily lent itself to a semipresbyterian interpretation, enforced an even larger measure of ecclesiastical control. Of this the Strict Congregationalists would have no part. And yet they retained a very strong belief in the universal church as embracing all believers on earth and becoming visible as Christians gathered in local congregations by confession of faith and mutual covenant. The Killingly *Declaration* defines the church in general as the whole body of the elect in heaven and on earth, while the visible catholic church is the whole company of professing believers on earth.[66]

The Windham County Ministerial Association criticized the Separates for having "set up as absolute an Independency as ever was heard of in the Church." [67] This was before they heard of the Separate Baptists. The latter went all the way to a completely atomistic view by denying categorically that there was any such visible catholic church in the sense of all professing believers on earth. "Christ has instituted none but particular churches." [68] These are entirely self-sufficient and have no necessary or essential connection with any

65. I am inclined to minimize the "democratizing effect" of frontier life in the rise of Arminianism. Baxter shows that Calvinistic Baptists grew three times faster than Freewills or Methodists, while regular Congregational growth was far from negligible. He cites specific figures and concludes that "enough growth occurred among Calvinistic groups to belie the thesis that the Arminians far outstripped the Calvinists on the frontier because the preaching of 'whosoever will' harmonized more readily with the frontier social order" (ibid., p. 34).

66. *An Historical Narrative and Declaration,* pp. 25–26. They deny, of course, a "Political Catholic Church."

67. *The Result of a Council of the Consociated Churches of the County of Windham,* p. 17.

68. Backus, *A Discourse, Concerning the Materials, the Manner of Building, and Power of Organizing of the Church of Christ* (Boston, 1773), p. 145.

other particular church. Such a view is the ultimate end of the individualism which was implicit in Puritanism from the start, fostered by revivalism and the emphasis on personal conversion, and quite in keeping with the spirit of the post-Revolutionary republican age. One sees this quite clearly in a piece by the "Jeffersonian Itinerant," entitled *The Government of Christ a Christocracy* (1804). Here Leland says:

> The saints on earth are Christ's subjects, forming his kingdom below. When Christ went to heaven, and left his house below, he gave authority to his servants, and to every man his work; and as far as church government on earth is the government of Christ, it is of democratical genius. Church government is congregational, not parochial, diocesan, nor national. Each congregated church disclaims the power of Popes, kings, bishops, parliaments, kirks, or presbyteries, and claims the right and power to govern itself according to the laws of Christ. And it must be confessed, that the spirit and rule by which the subjects of Christ's kingdom are to live one among another, greatly resemble the genius of a republic. . . . By a Christocracy, I mean nothing more than a government of which Christ is law-giver, king, and judge, and yet so arranged, that each congregational church is a complete republic of itself, not to be controlled by civil government or hierarchy. . . . [Churches are] little republics which form the empire of Christ.[69]

By "the empire of Christ" Leland meant roughly what the New Testament calls the "kingdom of Christ"—not, in his view, to be equated with a visible catholic church in any sense. With him the individual local congregation is not a component part of a larger whole (as with the Strict Congregationalists) but a microcosm of Christ's entire spiritual kingdom. As such it is entirely self-contained and self-sufficient, having full freedom to order its own affairs under no other authority than the Lordship of Christ, and under no necessary obligation to any other ecclesiastical body. This is a radical individualism which makes even the church itself of secondary importance. The fundamental relationship is between Christ and the individual, and since salvation is prior to church membership, the church is important only as a fact after salvation.

69. *Writings of John Leland*, pp. 275–78. Elsewhere Leland referred to the church as "a voluntary association for religious purposes" (*The Connecticut Dissenter's Strong-Box*, New London, 1802, p. 38).

Where, then, was any ground or motive for interchurch relations? Only in the force of purely pragmatic considerations. The Separate Baptists entered into the Warren Association, as has been seen, only after its powers had been carefully delimited and when they were convinced that it would prove a powerful tool with which to free the Baptists from the grip of their ecclesiastical oppressors.

> The early experience of Backus suggested to him that synods and councils were the instruments through which the will of the state was executed; as such they were to be denounced, opposed and, if possible, dissolved. In the instance of the Warren Association, however, the opposite seemed to be true. Here was a council through which the domination and control of the state could be frustrated; and as such, clearly it should be supported, strengthened, and used. In short, this association could properly be used to lengthen the arm of the local congregation, but never to shorten it; to add to its power and not to take away.[70]

Leland's part in the General Association of Virginia was on the same basis. Although deploring the supposed necessity of basing the Separate-Regular merger on a creed, he confessed that

> a union seemed so necessary and desirable, that those who were somewhat scrupulous of a confession of faith, other than the Bible, were willing to sacrifice their peculiarities, and those who were strenuous for the confession of faith, agreed to a partial reception of it. "United we stand, divided we fall," overcame, at that time, all objections.[71]

There appears to have been little concern with searching for a theological basis for organic relationships between churches.

To see how far the Separate Baptist ecclesiology prevailed, one must review the kind of thinking with which these churches collided when they joined the Warren Association with men who were oriented toward Philadelphia. There is no need to go further than the "Essay on the Power and Duty of an Association," [72] prepared by Benjamin Griffith at the instruction of the Philadelphia Association in 1749 "to prevent the contempt with which some are ready to treat such an as-

70. Edwin Scott Gaustad, "The Backus-Leland Tradition," *Baptist Concepts of the Church*, ed. Winthrop Still Hudson (Philadelphia, 1959), pp. 124–25.

71. "The Virginia Chronicle," *Writings of John Leland*, p. 114.

72. Printed in *Minutes of the Philadelphia Baptist Association*, pp. 61–63. The following quotations are all from this source.

sembly, and also to prevent any future generation from claiming more power than they ought—lording it over the churches." The essay begins by admitting that "an Association is not a superior judicature, having such superior power over the churches concerned; but that each particular church hath a complete power and authority from Jesus Christ to administer all gospel ordinances . . . to receive in and cast out, and also to try and ordain their own officers, and to exercise every part of gospel discipline and church government, independent of any other church or assembly whatever." But such independent churches, if they agree in doctrine and practice, "may and ought, for their mutual strength, counsel, and other valuable advantages, by their voluntary and free consent, to enter into an agreement and confederation." When they confederated, the churches themselves were to be the constituents, and the assembly of their delegates should be not superior but subservient to the churches.

Yet the power of an association was considerable:

> For if the agreement of several distinct churches, in sound doctrine and regular practice, be the first motive, ground, and foundation or basis of their confederation, then it must naturally follow, that a defection in doctrine or practice in any church, in such confederation, or any party in any such church, is ground sufficient for an Association to withdraw from such a church or party so deviating or making defection, and to exclude such from them in some formal manner, and to advertise all the churches in confederation thereof, in order that every church in confederation may withdraw from such in all acts of church communion, to the end they may be ashamed, and that all the churches may discountenance such, and bear testimony against the defection.

Griffith was careful to say that this is not excommunication but withdrawing fellowship. "In the capacity of a congregational church, dealing with her own members, an Association, then, of the delegates of associated churches, may exclude and withdraw from defective and unsound or disorderly churches or persons, in manner abovesaid."

So far, perhaps, few Separate Baptists would have quarreled with Philadelphia's position. But next, after pointing to Acts 15 as a biblical instance of churches associating together to deliberate on matters of common concern, Griffith declared that the ecclesiastical councils of "after ages" harmonized with this practice. When a matter "grew too big for a particular church peaceably to determine," a council was called. "In such cases all the churches were looked upon as one church, and all the bishops as universal, because of the unity of the faith and conformity of practice which ought to be in the churches of Christ though in all other cases, the several distinct churches acted independent of each other." He quotes approvingly from Cyprian to support this point, commenting that "the bishops were so united in one body, that if any one of the body broached any heresy, or began to waste and tear the flock of Christ, all the rest came immediately to its rescue . . . [and] disowned the faulty [person or church], and advertised all the churches of the same." This would sound to Separate ears suspiciously like an attempt to erect a Baptist catholicism, and some would begin to fear that Philadelphia had affinities with Canterbury and Rome! Griffith pressed directly on to his conclusion, a conviction that had been implemented many times in the actions of the Philadelphia Association, namely that *unity is based on complete accord in doctrine and practice.* To preserve its status, therefore, the association must maintain close vigilance over the faith and order of its members.

> An Association of the delegates of confederate churches may doctrinally declare any person or party in a church who are defective in principles or disorderly in practice, to be censurable, when the affair comes under their cognizance, and without exceeding the bounds of their power and duty, to advise the church that such belong unto, how to deal with such, according to the rule of gospel discipline; and also to strengthen such a church, and assist her, if need be, by sending able men of their own number [uninvited?] to help the church in executing the power vested in her by the ordinance of Jesus Christ, and to stand by her, and to defend her against the insults of such offending persons or parties.

If this were interpreted strictly, it would make every member of every associated church amenable to theological policing by the association.

In the light of this asserted power, one can understand the hesitancy of the Separates to join the Warren Association until they had forced a revision of the original (Philadelphia) plan. The independency and power of particular churches were safeguarded when the Association agreed to be "no other than an *Advisory council,* utterly disclaiming superiority, jurisdiction, coercive right, and infallibility." [73] The associations which the Separates dominated in the frontier areas, mostly formed on the same basic plan, also expressed this concern. Here, as in the case of theology, there are minor divergences at the beginning

73. *Sentiments and Plan of the Warren Association.*

which later move farther and farther away from the original position. The universal-church philosophy of Philadelphia was actualized briefly in a General Convention formed in 1814; however, because of strong forces pulling toward atomistic diffusion, this body soon became little more than a foreign mission society embracing only those interested enough to contribute to its purpose. Individuals interested in other missionary and benevolent enterprises formed distinct societies for each cause. Meanwhile the Baptists of Separate background followed a radical form of local church ecclesiology which barely recognized provincial associations for fraternal and local missionary purposes, and they resisted with all their might the movement toward "a more general union."

If the New Hampshire Confession of Faith, in comparison to that of Philadelphia, reveals significant modifications of Calvinism,[74] it is even more striking for its changes concerning the doctrine of the church. The Philadelphia (Second London) Confession retains the idea of the universal church from its parent formulary, the Westminster Confession, and in its lengthy Article xxvi spells out in detail the early Particular Baptists' concern to realize the ideal qualities of the universal church in their local congregations. In extreme contrast is the brief statement of the New Hampshire Confession, "Of a Gospel Church":

[We believe] That a visible Church of Christ is a congregation of baptized believers, associated by covenant in the faith and fellowship of the Gospel; observing the ordinances of Christ; governed by his laws; and exercising the gifts, rights, and privileges invested in them by his word; that its only proper officers are Bishops or Pastors, and Deacons, whose qualifications, claims, and duties are defined in the Epistles to Timothy and Titus.[75]

This is all—and in view of what has been said about the predominance of Separates in the region which produced this confession, one cannot escape the conclusion that it has been decisively influenced by their atomistic doctrine of the church.

The tremendous later influence of the New Hampshire Confession of Faith carried Separate Baptist thinking far beyond its original environs. The document was mainly the work of J. Newton Brown, the only one of the initial committee to complete the task of formulating a confession. He later became editorial secretary of the American Baptist

74. See above, pp. 286–87.
75. McGlothlin, *Baptist Confessions of Faith*, pp. 305–06.

Publication Society, in which position he took the liberty of printing the confession (with two additional articles, "Repentance and Faith" and "Sanctification") in *The Baptist Church Manual*. The little book had wide circulation in several editions, and many parts of it—including the New Hampshire Confession—were copied in similar manuals. One of the most influential of the latter works was that compiled by. J. M. Pendleton in 1867 for use among the Landmark Baptists.[76] Thus the confession enjoyed wide popularity not only in the Northeast and Middle West, but also in the Southwest through the influence of the Landmarkers. The continued jealousy for local church autonomy and the thinly veiled suspicion of "ecclesiasticism" in denominational organization among some Baptists is an outgrowth of this influence which stems from the Separates.

In these three significant ways, and perhaps in countless others that are more subtle, the Separate Baptists continued to spin out their heritage in such fashion as to transform the denomination into which they had moved with such startling rapidity and numbers. By way of summing up, it may be said that they bequeathed to Baptists the revivalistic tradition, in which the prophetic individualism of the early Puritans was fully (and perhaps permanently) institutionalized. In and after the Revolutionary era they were able to realize their ideals of liberty and freedom, while the rise of republicanism encouraged their pioneering spirit of independent self-sufficiency. They were thus the religious harbingers of the "Age of the Common Man." Their chief task was to prepare individuals for eternity, and they pursued it with vigor. Every other concern, at least in the realm of religion, was subordinated to the primacy of the evangelistic imperative. This wrought significant changes in their doctrinal stance, as well as bound them to an emasculated doctrine of the church.

Their concentration on "this one thing" was at once the secret of their greatest strength—the harvesting of converts and the planting of churches—and of their greatest weakness—the refusal to work out the full implications of personal religious experience in the context of the total Christian tradition and its larger social concerns. This para-

76. Pendleton's *Manual* has gone through countless editions and is still available. The Landmark movement, of which Pendleton (along with J. R. Graves and A. C. Dayton) was a leader, carried local church ecclesiology to an extreme height, claiming that only particular Baptist churches were true churches and had unbroken succession back to the time of Christ. Cf. Robert G. Torbet, "Landmarkism," *Baptist Concepts of the Church*, pp. 170–95, and the other literature there cited.

dox and its ambiguous value are well stated by Gaustad at the close of his essay on the two men who did more to fashion the Separate Baptist ethos than any others. Asking, "Can the churches ever become the Church?" he answers:

> If it took Backus thirty-two years to understand "one Lord, one faith, one baptism," perhaps he ran out of time before understanding "that ye may all be one." The plain fact is that there was too much uneasy suspicion, there were too many bitter memories, and too many legitimate fears to permit either man at this period of our national development hopefully to view the prospects of concerted Christian effort. Let the Christian be free and his slavery to Christ will be complete; let the congregation have "such a gospel freedom that it may know where every particular gift is" and the glory of God will be served. This was the faith of Backus and Leland, as it was in political terms, the faith of an entire party of earnest patriots. That this faith proved too sanguine is now recognized. But we should be ready to recognize that this same faith forged freedoms which may be dearer than denominational life itself.[77]

What is now necessary is that the numerous progeny of the Separates address themselves seriously to the responsible use of those freedoms. The world has yet to see a truly redemptive society using its Christian liberty to forge the positive unities that give form to the kingdom of God among men.

77. "The Backus-Leland Tradition," *Baptist Concepts of the Church*, p. 134.

EPILOGUE

The most phenomenal story of Separate Baptist expansion was written not in New England but in the South. The foregoing pages are largely a prologue to the amazing spread of the Separates in the South, which resulted from the work of two ardent evangelists from Connecticut, Shubal Stearns (1706–71) and Daniel Marshall (1706–84). Stearns was born in Boston, converted in Connecticut during Whitefield's second visit (1745), and baptized at Tolland by Wait Palmer on May 20, 1751. The day of his baptism was also the date of his ordination as a missionary preacher to New England, in which capacity he evangelized widely for three years. In July 1754 he left the Separate Baptists at Tolland in the care of Noah Alden of Stafford, whom he had baptized recently, and followed an inner voice directing him to the South. Marshall was a native of Windsor, Connecticut. He also was converted in 1745, and separated soon afterward from the standing church which he had served twenty years as deacon. In 1747 he married Martha Stearns, Shubal's sister. Five years later he followed an impulse to do missionary work among the Mohawk Indians at the head of the Susquehanna River, where he labored for eighteen months before he too went south. Joining his brother-in-law at Opekon in northwestern Virginia (near what is now Winchester) in 1754, Marshall was immersed, and with Stearns he took up the tremendous task of evangelizing the rapidly filling southern frontier.

They settled first at Cacapon, about thirty miles from Opekon, but results here did not equal their expectations. Stearns heard that in a hundred-mile tract of North Carolina's piedmont section there was no preaching of any kind and "the people were so eager to hear, that they would come forty miles each way, when they could have opportunity to hear a sermon." [1] Again, the inner voice translated spiritual need into a divine summons. In November 1755 Stearns led a company of fifteen (mostly his family and Marshall's) to Sandy Creek in Guilford (now Randolph) County, North Carolina, where they immediately constituted themselves into a church. Morgan Edwards, a Baptist historian who visited this area in 1772, wrote in his notebook:

1. Stearns' letter to friends in Connecticut, dated June 13, 1755, quoted in Backus, *Abridged History*, p. 228.

Soon after the neighbourhood was alarmed and the Spirit of God listed to blow as a mighty rushing wind in so much that in three years time they had increased to three churches, consisting of upwards of 900 communicants, viz: Sandy Creek, Abot's Creek, Deep River. . . . [Sandy Creek] is a mother church, nay a grand mother, and a great grand mother. All the separate baptists sprang hence: not only eastward towards the sea, but westward towards the great river Mississippi, but northward to Virginia and southward to South Carolina and Georgia. The word went forth from this sion, and great was the company of them who published it, in so much that her converts were as drops of morning dew.[2]

When Edwards later worked his notes into fuller form, he recorded that the Sandy Creek Church, "in 17 years, is become mother, grandmother, and great Grandmother to 42 churches, from which sprang 125 ministers, many of which are ordained and support the sacred character as well as any sett of clergy in America."[3] This amazing growth is due directly to the lively perpetuation of the revivalistic patterns inaugurated in the Great Awakening, and is almost a repetition of the work of Whitefield himself in the Carolina back country. Stearns' soul, said Backus, "was fired with zeal to carry light into these dark parts";[4] and he did so in the most ebullient manner of the New Light evangelists. Others imitated him, and Morgan Edwards intimated that a few even exceeded him. The year before Edwards wrote, the far-ranging Marshall had settled at Kiokee, in northeastern Georgia, where he gathered the first Baptist church in that colony; and it became the progenitor of numerous others.[5] From the Potomac to the Savannah, their churches continued to multiply at a phenomenal rate. When settlers began to press through the mountain passes to the West, the Separates made up a fair proportion of the vanguard and soon were planting churches in Kentucky and Tennessee. Newman, rarely given to exaggeration, says that the progress of the Separate

2. "Tour of Morgan Edwards of Pennsylvania to the American Baptists in North Carolina in 1772–73," printed in George Washington Paschal, *History of North Carolina Baptists* (Raleigh, N.C., 1930), 1, 227.
3. Morgan Edwards, "Materials toward a History of the Baptists in North Carolina," *North Carolina Historical Review*, 7 (1930), 385.
4. *Abridged History*, p. 228.
5. The historic church is still in existence at Appling. See James Donovan Mosteller, *A History of the Kiokee Baptist Church in Georgia* (Ann Arbor, Mich., 1952).

Baptist movement in the South "was almost unexampled in Baptist history." [6]

As in New England, the Separates were regarded with suspicion by the Regular Baptists.[7] The earliest Baptist churches in the South had been formed by General Baptists from England in the early years of the eighteenth century, and by the fifth decade they were in a generally moribund condition. A few years before Stearns' company arrived, representatives of the Philadelphia Association had "reformed" a number of these churches by reconstituting them on the Particular Baptist plan, with a Calvinistic confession of faith and high standards of church membership. The Separates objected to the creedal rigor of the Regulars, while the latter were more than a little chary of the unrestrained enthusiasm of the Separates. The Regulars, however, had been influenced by the Great Awakening in the Middle Colonies, and this evangelical penetration enabled them to see a genuine spiritual dynamic in the zeal of the Separates—a dynamic with which they might do well to associate themselves. On their part, the Separates agreed with the substance of doctrine in the Philadelphia Confession and were drawn into union by common Baptist convictions and by the urgent necessity to join forces in the struggle to disestablish the Church of England. A formal union was consummated in Virginia in 1787, by which it was agreed that the former party names should be "buried in oblivion; and that; from henceforth, we shall be known by the name of the *United Baptist Churches of Christ, in Virginia.*" [8] In North Carolina the two groups coalesced more informally, as the Kehukee Association (organized 1769) began to receive both Regular and Separate churches. Union was even more natural and rapid in South Carolina and Georgia, and the last important merger occurred in the West when the Elkhorn and South Kentucky associations came together in 1801.

But though the name of the Separates was buried, their influence was not. They put their characteristic stamp on much of southern Baptist life and thought, just as they had done in New England. They helped to modify the rigid Calvinism of the Philadelphia Confession in a way that left room for the intense revivalism which they continued to foster. They resisted the centripetal forces toward a more closely

6. Albert Henry Newman, *A History of the Baptist Churches in the United States* (New York, 1894), p. 296.

7. "Regular" is here a proper adjective. See above, p. 272, n. 29.

8. Semple, *History of Baptists in Virginia*, p. 75.

compacted denominationalism which radiated from Philadelphia.[9] They made important contributions in the struggle for religious liberty by reinforcing the rising tide of democratic individualism in politics. The overwhelming number of their converts soon filled the back country with churches; and their untutored pastor-evangelists furnished the prototype of the Baptist "farmer-preacher," the institution that proved so significant in the numerical growth and westward expansion of the denomination. All of this makes a fascinating sequel to the story of the rise and spread of the Separates in New England. When the record of New England separatism has been written, "the half hath not been told."

9. The opposite has been affirmed by some Southern Baptist historians on the ground that the Sandy Creek Association (organized 1758) carried ecclesiastical authority to a rather extreme height. It is true that Stearns himself tended in such a direction, but it is an obvious fact that his backwoods converts rebelled against an authoritarian system and broke apart his "diocese" the year before his death (1771). The ecclesiological views which the Separates bequeathed to Southern Baptists are represented not in Shubal Stearns but in John Leland, and the eventual triumph of a centralizing ecclesiology in the South is due not to Separate Baptist influence but to continued agitation by Philadelphia-oriented leaders in the East.

APPENDIX

On the following pages are charted all the Separate and Separate Baptist churches located in this study. No pretense to completeness is made: there may have been other temporary separations, or Separate churches in remote areas, that escaped detection. On the other hand, it is possible that a more strict interpretation of what constitutes a Separate or Separate Baptist church would forbid the listing of a few churches which appear in the chart. For example, the church at Southold, Long Island, was clearly a regular Congregational church both before and after the pastorate of James Davenport, but under his leadership it seems natural to consider it a Separate church. In the same class is the church at Durham, New Hampshire, and probably those at Athol and West Medway, Massachusetts.

The lines of differentiation are even more vague in the frontier sections. Most of these towns were settled by restive radicals whose religious disposition, if any, was clearly New Light or separatist. In some cases they were transplanted colonies from Separate or Separate Baptist churches in older regions. In other cases they were formed by and of persons of New Light background. Because of the difficulties in determining exactly where to draw the line between a regular and a Separate church, only the more outstanding and representative ones have been included in the chart and plotted on the maps, pages 115 and 257. Where a church established branches or set off independent bodies, these have been assumed to have the same character as the mother church.

On the chart, towns have been located in the states to which they presently belong, although during the period under study they may have been in another colony; this is particularly true of those on the Massachusetts-Connecticut border. The date of separation is the time of the first large defection from the standing church, and is usually also the date of organization for the Separate church, if any. An asterisk indicates an Old Light separation. Where a Separate church was not organized until several years later, this has been noted. The names of the pastors, both Separate and Baptist, with dates of service where these could be ascertained, are given only for the first years of the church's life and do not include later pastors in the cases of the longer-lived churches. The "Baptist Date" column gives the organization date for the Baptist church in the place indicated. The "Comments" of necessity are brief.

Town or Parish	Sepn Date	Separate Pastor(s)	Bapt Date	Baptist Pastor(s)	Comments
CONNECTICUT					
Ashford	1743		1743	Thomas Denison 1743–44 Thomas Ustick 1774–76	Denison returned to pedobaptism. Church died, and was reorganized 1774. A second Baptist church was formed 1780.
Bloomfield (5th parish Windsor)	1760		1786	Ashbel Gillet	
Bozrah (5th parish Norwich)	1745			Peter Rogers 1790–94	Separate church apparently never completed its organization.
Brooklyn (2d parish Pomfret)	1742				Temporary separation, no church organized.
Canterbury	1744	Solomon Paine 1746–54 Joseph Marshall 1759–68		Benjamin Herrington ca. 1750 Ebenezer Lyon 1770s	Too few Baptists to organize a church. Separate church died 1831.
Colchester	1743	Jabez Jones 1751–?	(1743) 1784	Abel Palmer 1784–?	Baptists present from the first. Baptist church fully organized by Palmer 1784.
Coventry (South parish)					Temporary separation.
East Hampton			1784	William Welsh ?–1824	Joined by Haddam Separates 1792. Church died 1824.
Enfield	before 1751	Names unknown Nathaniel Collins, Jr. 1762–87	before 1785	Joseph Meacham Christopher Miner George Atwell	Separate church gained legal status 1770. Shared pastor with Baptists after 1795, merged ca. 1806. Became Adventist 1842.

302

Location	Date	Minister(s)	Notes
Essex (2d parish Saybrook)	1811		Separates never completed church organization. Baptist church organized 1811.
Farmington	ca. 1750		Said by Benedict to have Separate origins.
Franklin (2d parish Norwich)	1746	Thomas Denison 1746–59	Meetinghouse controversy in 1730s preceded disputes over revival.
Goshen (3rd parish Lebanon)			Temporary separation.
Granby	1790		Set off from Suffield Baptist Church.
Greenwich, West	1747	John Stephens 1747–?	"Horseneck Church." Joined Philadelphia Baptist Association 1747.
Guilford	1729	Edmund Ward 1729–34 Joseph Lamb 1735–41 James Sproat 1743–68	Became 4th parish 1733. Antedated the Great Awakening, but issues were the same. Sproat, a New Light, followed Gilbert Tennent at Philadelphia's Second Presbyterian Church.
Haddam	1750	Charles Smith 1785?–1800	Included Separates from East Haddam. Church not organized till 1785. Baptists went to East Haddam till 1822.
Haddam, East	1822	Simon Shailer	
Hadlyme	1792	Simeon Dickinson	Separates went to Haddam, and most of them had become Baptists by 1792.
Hampton (Canada parish Windham)	1775	Christopher Miner ca. 1760 William Grow 1776–83 Peter Rogers 1794–?	Had 30 families in 1769, including several Baptists. Grow dismissed for immorality, went to Vermont. Rogers came from Bozrah.

Town or Parish	Sepn Date	Separate Pastor(s)	Bapt Date	Baptist Pastor(s)	Comments
Hartford, South (2d parish Hartford)	1743		1789		Separates went to Wethersfield. Baptists went to Suffield till they organized their own church in 1789.
Kensington	1747	Nathan Cole (lay leader)			Went to Middletown Separate Church.
Killingly, South (3d parish)	1746	Samuel Wadsworth 1747–62; Thomas Denison 1763–65; Eliphalet Wright 1765–84; Israel Day 1785–1826	1776	George Robinson 1776–85	Separate church legalized 1770 and became regular Congregational church 1799. Still exists. A Six-Principle Baptist church organized in 1752 died.
			1803	(2d Baptist Church)	The Second Baptist Church had been a branch of the Woodstock Baptist Church.
Ledyard (North Groton)	1750	Nathaniel Brown, Jr. 1751–55; Park Allyn 1755–65?			Andrew Croswell, regular Congregational pastor 1736–48, became Separate. Allyn was dismissed for immorality. Methodists took over Separate meetinghouse 1803.
Lyme (1st parish = Old Lyme)	1746	John Fuller 1746–59			Separation followed the dismissal of Jonathan Parsons in 1745. Baptists went to East Lyme.
Lyme, East (2d parish)	1749	Ebenezer Mack 1749–52	1752	Ebenezer Mack 1752–68; Jason Lee 1771–1810	Church became Baptist en bloc, held open communion till 1795. Member of Groton Union Conference in 1786, joined Stonington Association 1800.
Lyme, North (3d parish)	1755	Daniel Miner 1755–99			"Grassy Hill Church." Baptists went to East Lyme.

304

Location	Year	Pastors	Notes
Mansfield	1745	John Hovey 1746–75 Thomas Marsh 1746–?	First Separate church to organize, ordain a pastor, and draft a confession of faith. Many moved to Wantage, New Jersey, after 1751.
Middletown	1747	Ebenezer Frothingham 1747–88 Stephen Parsons 1788–95	1795 — Stephen Parsons 1795–97 Joshua Bradley Josiah Graves Organized at Wethersfield, moved to Middletown 1754. Divided 1788 and Westfield branch became Baptist. Middletown group became regular Congregational church and still exists.
Milford	1743	Samuel Finley (temporary supply) Job Prudden 1747–74	Remained under the Presbytery of New Brunswick till 1750. Gained full legal status 1760. Now known as Plymouth Congregational Church.
Montville (North New London)	1747	Dyer Hyde 1747–50	1750 — Joshua Morse 1750–79 Reuben Palmer 1788–1822 Baptist church died after 1779, reorganized 1788.
Newent (3d parish Norwich, Lisbon)	1746	Jeremiah Tracy, Jr. 1746–53 Bliss Willoughby 1753–56	(Baptists went to Preston-Canterbury Baptist Church, organized 1786) Most of Separate church moved to Bennington, Vermont, 1761. Remainder went to Scotland Separate Church, reunited with the standing church, or became Baptists.
New Fairfield	1764	James Taylor 1764–68	Taylor had been regular pastor since 1758. Dismissed for opposing the Saybrook Platform, he became leader of the Separate church.
New Haven	1742	Various supplies Samuel Bird 1751–68 Jonathan Edwards, Jr. 1769–95	Known as White Haven Church. Gained legal status 1759. Split 1769, reunited 1796. Now known as United Congregational Church.

Town or Parish	Sepn Date	Separate Pastor(s)	Bapt Date	Baptist Pastor(s)	Comments
New Haven (Yale College)	1757	Naphtali Daggett 1757–80			Established partly to remove students from controversies in the First Church. Led by the professor of divinity. Still exists.
New London	1742	Timothy Allen 1742–44	1748	Noah Hammond 1748–65	Hammond went to Coram, Long Island, and organized a Baptist church of which he was pastor till his death in 1774. Baptists of New London merged with the Waterford Baptist Church under Nathan Howard.
New Milford	1747* 1753	Elihu Marsh Robert Campbell 1772–84 Barnabas Lathrop 1791–93			First Church reorganized 1810 and Separate church disbanded two years later. Some Separates went to form a Baptist church at Northville in 1814.
Norwich (1st parish = Bean Hill)	1745	Jedediah Hyde 1747–57 John Fuller 1759–69	1766	Gamaliel Reynolds 1766–76 John Sterry 1800–	Most Separates who had not become Baptists became Universalists. Baptist church not fully organized till 1800.
Plainfield	1746	Thomas Stevens 1746–55 Alexander Miller 1758–69 John Fuller 1769–77	1792	Nathaniel Cole	Separates had a majority in this town. United with Voluntown Separates under Miller 1758, and reunited with the regular Congregational church under Fuller 1769.

306

* An asterisk beside the Separation date denotes an Old Light separation.

Place	Date	Minister	Date	Notes
Preston (Separate church in 2d parish, Griswold, included some from 1st parish)	1747	Paul Parke 1747–1802 Amos Reed 1786–1825 Thomas Goddard 1786	1786 1786	Reed led the Preston-Canterbury Baptist Church on the west side of the parish. Goddard ministered on the east side of North Preston.
Preston Long Society	1752	Jonathan Storey 1752–65		Disbanded 1765. Members went to other Separate churches nearby.
Prospect (West Cheshire)	1770	Benjamin Beach 1770–98?		Separates formed the first church in the town. Later united with the regular Congregational church formed in 1798.
Salisbury	1741	Jonathan Lee 1744–88		Town settled by New Lights and church organized on the Cambridge Platform. Had legal status but practically a Separate church.
Saybrook	1744	(Joshua Morse 1750–76) Eliphalet Lester 1776–96	1744	Baptists present since 1729, organized New Light church 1744. Supplied by Morse from Montville till 1776.
Scotland (3d parish Windham)	1746	John Palmer 1746–1807		"Brunswick Church." Gained legal status 1774, disbanded 1813.
Somers	1751	Joseph Marshall 1751–57? Samuel Ely 1769–74		Most Separates returned to the regular church after 1774. Marshall went to Canterbury. Ely went to Massachusetts and later led Shay's Rebellion.
Southington	1751?	John Merriman 1739–84	1751	Baptists moved here from Wallingford, where they had organized a church in 1739. Separates joined with them till 1775, then moved to Prospect.

Town or Parish	Sepn Date	Separate Pastor(s)	Bapt Date	Baptist Pastor(s)	Comments
Stafford		Noah Alden	1754	Noah Alden 1754–66	Alden was baptized by Shubal Stearns. Served as pastor at First Baptist Church Bellingham, Massachusetts, from 1766 till his death in 1797.
Stonington			1772	Valentine Rathbun 1772	Most of this church emigrated to Pittsfield, Massachusetts, 1772.
Stonington, North (2d parish Stonington)	1743	Matthew Smith 1746–49 Oliver Prentice 1753–55 Nathan Avery 1759–80 Christopher Avery 1786–1819	1743	Wait Palmer 1743–66 Eleazar Brown 1770–95	Both Separate and Baptist churches became permanent. The Separate church absorbed the regular Congregational church in 1827.
			1765	Simeon Brown 1765–1818	The Second Baptist Church was formed by a strict-communion group from the Babcock church in Westerly.
Stratfield (Bridgeport)	1748* 1751		1751	John Sherwood 1757–79 Benjamin Coles	Old Lights formed St. John's Episcopal Church. New Light Baptist church organized by Joshua Morse from Montville.
Suffield (in Massachusetts)	1747	Joseph Hastings 1750–63 Israel Holly 1763–75	1763	Joseph Hastings 1763–75 John Hastings 1775–1811	Hastings was baptized in 1752 and organized the Baptist church in 1763. Holly returned to the standing order. A second Baptist church was formed in 1804.
Thompson			1750	Wightman Jacobs 1750–70 John Martin 1773	Became a Six-Principle Baptist church and disbanded 1770. Reorganized 1773, and joined the Stonington Association 1785.

Location	Year	Minister	Year	Minister	Notes
Tolland	1745	Shubal Stearns? 1745–51	1751	Shubal Stearns 1751–54	Stearns went to the South and the church merged with the Stafford Separates, who became Baptists in 1754.
Torrington	1785	Lemuel Haynes 1785–91			Haynes, a Negro, split the church by preaching New Light doctrines. It reunited when he left.
Voluntown	ca. 1745	Alexander Miller 1751–69			United with the Plainfield Separate Church in 1758. Miller remained pastor of the combined group.
Wallingford	1758	Simon Waterman 1761–87	1739	John Merriman 1739–84	Baptists moved to Southington 1751. Separates formed the "Wells Society," and secured legal recognition from political New Lights then controlling the colonial legislature.
Waterford (Nahantic)	1742	Timothy Allen (New London)	1748	Nathan Howard 1748–77 Zadoc Darrow 1769–1827	Separates from First Church New London. Baptists joined by New London Separate Baptists 1765. Darrow served as assistant pastor till 1777.
Watertown (Northbury)	1742*				Old Lights seized the meetinghouse and established Episcopal worship.
Wethersfield	1747 1782	Ebenezer Frothingham 1747–88	1784		Many Separates moved to New York, the remainder to Middletown. The later separation (1782) soon became Baptist.
Windham (1st parish)	1747	Elihu Marsh 1747–?			Marsh became a Baptist and moved away. Church then disbanded.
Windsor (1st parish)	1747		1786?	Eliakim Marshall 1786–91	Temporary separation. Included Daniel Marshall, who later became a Separate Baptist evangelist in the South.
Woodstock, West	1764	Biel Ledoyt	1766	Biel Ledoyt 1766–90 1804–13	A second Baptist church was organized ca. 1790, and Amos Wells was pastor till 1819.

Town or Parish	Sepn Date	Separate Pastor(s)	Bapt Date	Baptist Pastor(s)	Comments
MAINE					
Berwick	ca. 1760	Joshua Emery	1768	Joshua Emery 1768–?	Included Baptists at Madbury, New Hampshire, till 1776.
Bowdoin			1784	Job Macomber 1784–1821	Macomber was from Backus' church in Middleborough, Massachusetts.
Cornish			1792	Nathan Jewett	Set off from the Sanford Baptist Church.
Dunston	1744	Richard Elvins 1744–76			Elvins was from the Separate group at Salem, Massachusetts.
Fayette			1792	Eliphalet Smith 1792–98	Isaac Case helped organize the church on a strict-communion basis.
Gorham	1758	Ebenezer Townsend 1759–62	1768		Pedobaptist Separates reunited with the regular Congregational church in 1764.
Greene			1793	Lemuel Cummings	Cummings was from Charlestown, Massachusetts.
Harpswell (East Brunswick)			1785	James Potter 1785–?	The regular Congregational church voted to immerse those desiring it in 1784.
Leeds	1795		1800		Separates were first Methodist then Baptist.
Livermore			1793	Elisha Williams	Williams, the son of the regular Congregational minister at Hartford, became a New Light Baptist in a frontier revival in Maine.
Lyman			1782		
Nobleborough			1768	Ebenezer Stearns 1768–?	Stearns had been pastor of the Separate Baptist church at Easton, Massachusetts.
Paris			1791		Formed by a colony from the Third Baptist Church of Middleborough, Massachusetts.

Town	Date	Minister	Date	Minister	Remarks
Portland			1801	Benjamin Titcomb	
Sanford			1772	Peletiah Tingley 1772–82	The first church in the town, New Light and Calvinistic. Tingley later became a Freewill Baptist.
Sedgwick	1793	**Daniel Merrill 1793–1805**	1805	Daniel Merrill 1805–?	The whole Congregational Church was baptized en bloc.
Shapleigh			1781		A charter member of the York Association, which was organized 1785.
Thomastown			1784	Isaac Case 1784–?	A charter member of the Bowdoinham Association, which was organized 1787.
Wells			1780	Nathaniel Lord 1780–?	A second Baptist church was organized in 1804.
Woolwich			1800		All members of this church had separated from the Congregational church.
Yarmouth, North			1797	Benjamin Titcomb	Baptists had been here since 1780.

311

MASSACHUSETTS

Town	Date	Minister	Date	Minister	Remarks
Abingdon	1745				Temporary separation promoted by John Cotton of Halifax, Massachusetts.
Athol	1750	James Humphrey 1750–82			Returned to the fellowship of regular Congregational churches 1830, became Unitarian 1851.
Attleborough	1747	Nathaniel Shepard 1747–52	1767	Abraham Bloss 1767–69 Job Seamans 1772–87	Separate church became Baptist en bloc. A second Baptist church was organized ca. 1760 and disbanded 1802; its pastors were Elihu Daggett 1765–69, and Elisha Carpenter.
Barnstable	1750	Nathaniel Ewer 1750–60			Included members from Yarmouth and Hyannis (South Barnstable). Ewer left this church to go to Newmarket, New Hampshire. After 1771 Baptists went to Hyannis.

Town or Parish	Sepn Date	Separate Pastor(s)	Bapt Date	Baptist Pastor(s)	Comments
Boston	1742	John Cleaveland 1745–47 Andrew Croswell 1748–85			Eleventh Congregational Church, included Separates from most of the regular churches of Boston. Disbanded at Croswell's death in 1785. A few individuals became Baptists.
Boston, 2d Congregational Church (Old North)	1741*	Samuel Mather 1741–85			Tenth Congregational Church, Old Light. Returned to the Second Church after Mather's death in 1785.
Boston, 1st Baptist Church	1743		1743	Ephraim Bound 1743–65	Became Second Baptist Church, then Warren Avenue.
Bradford					Met with Separates at Rowley.
Bridgewater, West	1749		1785	George Robinson 1785–98 Valentine Rathbun 1800–12	Baptists met with First Baptist Church Middleborough till organized their own church in 1785.
Brookline	1751?	Jonathan Hyde 1751–87			Separates who became Baptists went to Newton.
Byfield	1744?				Temporary separation.
Cambridge			1751	Nathaniel Draper 1751–53	Dispersed between 1784 and 1817.
Carver, South	1771		1791	John Tripp 1791–99	Tripp a New Light Congregationalist minister before his baptism at the hands of Backus.
Charlestown					Probably no church was organized, though several Separates here by 1749.

Town	Sep. org.	Separate pastor	Baptist org.	Baptist pastor(s)	Notes
Chatham	before 1749				Separates belonged at Harwich. Most had become Baptists by 1757.
Chelmsford	1743	Samuel (?) Hyde 1743–58?	1771	Elisha Rich 1771–78	Separates went to Concord till 1743. Hyde went to Madbury, New Hampshire.
Cheshire			1769 / 1771	Peter Werden 1770–1808; Nathan Mason 1771–88; John Leland 1792–1841	Town settled by New Lights. Werden came from Rhode Island. Second Baptist Church under Mason split over laying on of hands 1788, reunited under Leland 1834.
Concord	1741*				Temporary withdrawal of Old Lights—the first schism on record caused by revivalism in the Great Awakening.
Dunstable	1747	Samuel Bird 1747–51			Bird later became pastor of the Separate church in New Haven, Connecticut.
Eastham					Separates went to Harwich Separate Church.
Easton	1752	Solomon Prentice 1752–54	1762	Ebenezer Stearns 1762–66; Eseck Carr 1766–94	Prentice, a radical New Light, was pastor of the regular Congregational church. He led a separation, became a Presbyterian, and was dismissed. His church disbanded 1762. The Baptist church was unstable and disappeared ca. 1794.
Egremont	1789				Set off from the Separate Baptist church at Canaan, New York.
Framingham	1746	Solomon Reed 1747–56	1762?	Charles Train 1811–?	Separate church died 1757. Baptists were not fully organized till 1811.

Town or Parish	Sepn Date	Separate Pastor(s)	Bapt Date	Baptist Pastor(s)	Comments
Freetown	1747	Silas Brett 1747–75	1775	Abner Lewis 1776–84	No regular Congregational church here. Separate Baptists came from the Third Church Middleborough and had no clear connection with the Freetown Separates.
Georgetown (2d parish Rowley)	1754	Eliphaz Chapman 1770–72	1781		Baptists were a branch of the Haverhill Baptist Church till 1785.
Grafton	1743* 1751	Ebenezer Wadsworth 1751–67	1767	Elhanan Winchester 1773–77	Old Lights returned to the regular church when Prentice left to go to Easton. Baptists became Universalists in 1788, reorganized in 1800.
Granville			1790		Set off from the Suffield Baptist Church.
Great Barrington			1792		Set off from the Egremont Baptist Church.
Hardwick	ca. 1749				Moved to Bennington, Vermont, in 1761.
Harvard	1753	Shadrach Ireland 1753–78	1776	Isaiah Parker 1776–98	Separate church became Shaker. Parker became a Universalist in 1798.
Harwich	1749	Joshua Nickerson 1749–72 Richard Chase 1751–57	1757	Richard Chase 1757–77 Seth Clarke 1777–?	Two Separate churches organized, the second by dismission from the first. The second became Baptist en bloc and united with the Warren Association.
Haverhill			1765	Hezekiah Smith 1765–1806	There had been an earlier temporary separation from the Congregational church. From these New Lights the Baptist church was formed.
Hopkinton	1744				Temporary separation.
Hyannis (South Barnstable)			1771	Enoch Eldredge 1771–94 Barnabas Bates	Before 1771 the Separates went to Barnstable and the Baptists to Harwich.

314

					Notes
Ipswich (1st parish)	1747*	John Walley 1747–64			Granted legal status as South Parish. Old Light.
Ipswich (2d parish, Chebacco = Essex)	1746	John Cleaveland 1747–99			Separates were designated as the fourth parish until 1774, when the original church (second) rejoined them.
Leicester, West (Charlton)	(no church organized)		1762	Nathaniel Green 1763–91	This was the second Baptist church in Leicester, and was organized by Separates. The First Baptist Church, formed in 1738, cooperated in the revival.
Medfield	(no church organized)		1776		Some Baptists present since 1734.
Medway, West	1750	David Thurston 1752–69			Thurston had graduated from Princeton in 1751.
Mendon	1749	Samuel Hovey 1749–58	1758?	Samuel Hovey 1758–?	Hovey went to Newtown, New Hampshire.
Middleborough, North (Titicut parish)	parish 1743 church 1748	Isaac Backus 1748–56 Solomon Reed 1756–85	1756	Isaac Backus 1756–1804	The Separate church continued as the North Middleborough Congregational Church. The Baptist church continued as the First Baptist Church of Middleborough.
Middleborough (Lakeville)	1751	James Mead 1751–56	1757	Ebenezer Hinds 1758–1812	This was the Second Baptist Church of Middleborough, later First Baptist Church of Lakeville.
Middleborough, South (Rock)			1761	Ebenezer Jones 1761–63 Asa Hunt 1771–89 Samuel Nelson	Third Baptist Church of Middleborough, later First Baptist Church of Rock. Organized by members dismissed from the Second Baptist Church. Sent several colonies to form other churches.

315

Town or Parish	Sepn Date	Separate Pastor(s)	Bapt Date	Baptist Pastor(s)	Comments
Millbury (2d parish Sutton)	1747	James Wellman 1747–60 Ebenezer Chaplin 1764–92			Separated from the First Congregational Church of Sutton. Gained legal status as First Congregational Church of Millbury.
Newbury (3d parish = Newburyport)	1743	Joseph Adams 1743–45 Jonathan Parsons 1746–76			Became Presbyterian in 1748, the first permanent church of this order in Massachusetts. Acquired full legal status in 1780.
Newton	1753?	Nathan Ward 1753–58	1780	Caleb Blood 1780–87 Joseph Grafton	Ward went to Plymouth, New Hampshire. Separates joined with Brookline Separate Church under Jonathan Hyde.
Norton	1747	William Carpenter 1748–61	1761	William Carpenter 1761–68 William Nelson 1769–86	Separate church became Baptist en bloc, merged with Taunton Baptist Church under Nelson in 1769.
Pittsfield			1771	Valentine Rathbun 1772–98	Church constituted by a colony from Stonington, Connecticut.
Plymouth	1744°	Thomas Frink 1744–48 Jacob Bacon 1749–76			Old Lights formed Third Congregational Church. Disbanded 1783 and returned to the First Church. Frink left to go to Barre, Massachusetts.
Raynham					Temporary separation. Some were immersed in 1749, and probably united with First Baptist Church Middleborough.

Rehoboth	1748	Richard Round 1743–68	There were several Baptist churches here. Strongest New Light body was Second Baptist under Round, which received several members from the Separate church; it merged with the First Baptist Church in 1749.
Rockport (5th parish Gloucester)	1751		
Royalstone		John Paine 1748–51 Samuel Peck 1751–88	
	1768	Wightman Jacobs 1768–86	New Light church with Separate pastor (brother to John), though it always had legal status. Pastor and church moved from Thompson, Connecticut.
Russell	ca. 1800		Set off from Suffield Baptist Church.
Salem	1742	Ebenezer Cleaveland 1751–1805	"Tabernacle Church." Included some Baptists. Later merged with the Third Congregational Church.
		Richard Elvins 1742–44 ——— Leavitt	
Sandisfield	1779	Joshua Morse 1779–95	Formed by a colony from Montville, Connecticut. A second Baptist church was organized in 1787.
Southwick	ca. 1790		Set off from the Suffield Baptist Church.
Stockbridge, West	1781		Set off from the Separate Baptist Church at Canaan, New York.
Sturbridge	1747	John Blunt 1749–52 William Ewing 1752–75 Jordan Dodge	Separate church became Baptist en bloc, though Blunt returned to pedobaptism. Ewing was not ordained till 1768. This became the Fiskdale Baptist Church.
	1749	John Blunt 1747–49	
Sunderland	1749		Moved to Bennington, Vermont, in 1761.

317

Town or Parish	Sepn Date	Separate Pastor(s)	Bapt Date	Baptist Pastor(s)	Comments
Sutton	1747	Ezekiel Cole 1751–91	1765	Jeremiah Barstow 1768–72 Elisha Ransom 1773?–79 Ebenezer Lamson	The Baptist church organized in 1735 died and a Separate Baptist body was formed in 1765. Barstow was dismissed for Arminianism, and the church suffered a large Universalist defection under Lamson ca. 1794. The remnant became the First Baptist Church.
Upton		(no church organized)	1751	Abraham Bloss 1751–65	Bloss went to Attleborough in 1767. The church died and was reorganized in 1787.
Westfield	1748	Jedediah Dewey 1748–63	1784	Adam Hamilton	Separates moved to Bennington, Vermont, in 1763 and Dewey became pastor of a newly-organized Separate church there. The Baptist church was set off from the Suffield, Connecticut, Baptist Church.
Williamstown			ca. 1790		Set off from the Baptist church in Berlin, New York.
Woburn	1746	Josiah Cotton 1747–56			Reunited with the regular church in 1756.
Wrentham	1747?	Elihu Daggett 1747–?	1769	William Williams 1773–1823	Daggett became a Baptist and went to the South Attleborough Baptist Church. Williams had graduated from the College of Rhode Island with the first class in 1769.
Yarmouth	ca. 1747		1757		Separates and Baptists worshiped at Barnstable and Harwich.
MIDDLE COLONIES					
Roxbury, New Jersey	1750		1753	Henry Crosley 1753–58	Settled by a colony of Separates from eastern Connecticut.

Town	Date	Minister	Date	Minister	Notes
Wantage, New Jersey	1751	William Marsh 1756–58	1756	William Marsh 1756–63 / Nicholas Cox	Formerly Newtown. Settled by a colony of Separates from Mansfield, Connecticut. (Off Map)
Wyoming, Pennsylvania			1792	Jacob Drake	Drake was from Canaan, New York. He organized several Separate Baptist churches in the Wyoming area. (Off Map)
New Hampshire					
Brentwood	1742		1771	Samuel Shepard 1771–1815	Separates mostly from Exeter. Many had been baptized by Hezekiah Smith. Brentwood Church had many branches which eventually became independent churches.
Canaan			1781	Thomas Baldwin 1781–90	Baldwin afterward became pastor of the Second Baptist Church in Boston.
Croydon			1778		Merged with Newport Baptist Church 1790.
Deerfield			1770	Eliphalet Smith 1770–76	Entire Congregational church baptized by Hezekiah Smith.
Durham	1742	Nicholas Gilman, Jr. 1742–48			Regular Congregational church became fanatically New Light.
Epping	1741		1772	Joseph Sanborn?	Separates were from Exeter. Baptists at first a branch of the Brentwood church.
Exeter	1744	Daniel Rogers 1748–85	1800		Separate church gained legal standing 1755. Later its constituency changed and it eventually became Unitarian.
Gilmanton			1772	Walter Powers 1776–?	Powers was from Newtown, New Hampshire.

Town or Parish	Sepn Date	Separate Pastor(s)	Bapt Date	Baptist Pastor(s)	Comments
Grafton			1785	Oliver Williams 1785–90	Formed by a colony from Rehoboth and Swansea, Massachusetts.
Hampstead			1771?		A branch of the Brentwood church.
Lebanon			1771	Jedediah Hibbard 1784–90	Hibbard moved to Cornish, New Hampshire, and the church dispersed.
Lee			1771?		A branch of the Brentwood church.
Madbury	1758	Samuel Hyde 1758–70	1768	William Hooper 1776–ca. 1800	Baptists belonged at Berwick, Maine, till 1776.
Marlow			1768	Ebenezer Mack 1768–? Caleb Blood 1778–79	Formed by a colony from East Lyme, Connecticut. Church not fully organized till 1777. Blood came from West Leicester, Massachusetts.
Newcastle	1775	(Benjamin Randall)	1776	Benjamin Randall	Randall became an Arminian and founded the Freewill Baptist movement.
New London			1788	Job Seamans 1788–1830	Seamans came from Attleborough, Massachusetts.
Newmarket	1773?	Nathaniel Ewer 1773–97			Ewer came from Barnstable, Massachusetts. This church was not very susceptible to Baptist tenets.
Newport			1790	Biel Ledoyt 1790–1804	Ledoyt came from West Woodstock, Connecticut, and returned there in 1804.
Newtown			1755	Walter Powers 1755–61 Samuel Hovey 1764–70 or later	Powers went to Gilmanton, New Hampshire. Hovey came from Mendon, Massachusetts.
Nottingham			1771		A branch of the Brentwood church.

Town					Notes
Plymouth	1764	Nathan Ward 1765–88			Ward came from Newton, Massachusetts, where he had been leader of the Separate church.
Portsmouth	1757	——— Walton 1757–60 Samuel Drowne 1761–70	1780	Nicholas Folsom 1782	Separates organized the "Independent Congregational Church." Drowne was a former Baptist from Rhode Island. Most of the Separates were Baptists by 1826.
Richmond			1770	Matturin Ballou 1770–90	Ballou came from Rhode Island. (He was the father of Hosea Ballou, the early Universalist leader.)
Salisbury			1771?		A branch of the Brentwood church.
Stratham	1747	Joseph Adams 1747–85	1770	Samuel Shepard	Separates merged with the regular Congregational church in 1756 and Adams became pastor of the combined body. Baptists here were a branch of the Brentwood church.
Weare			1768?	Peletiah Tingley 1768–72	Tingley, later a Freewill Baptist, went to Sanford, Maine.
Westmoreland			1771	Ebenezer Bailey 1773–1800	Formed by a colony from the First Baptist Church of Middleborough, Massachusetts.
NEW YORK					
Amenia	1750?	Abraham Paine 1750–? (Elijah Wood)	1790	(Elijah Wood) 1790–1810	Located in the "Great Nine Partners," or "Oblong," Wood had been a Separate deacon in Bennington, Vermont (see p. 257).
Berlin			1783	Justus Hull 1785–1833	Set off several branches which became independent churches.
Berne				Philip Jenkins 1796?–1811	Jenkins came from Exeter and North Kingston, Rhode Island.
Bridgehampton (Long Island)	1749	Elisha Paine 1752–75			Became the Second Presbyterian Church. Now extinct.

Town or Parish	Sepn Date	Separate Pastor(s)	Bapt Date	Baptist Pastor(s)	Comments
Canaan	1770	Jacob Drake 1770–78	1778	Jacob Drake 1778–92	Drake came from Windsor, Connecticut, organized several Separate Baptist churches here, then moved to Wyoming, Pennsylvania, and did the same thing.
Coeymans			1789		Set off from Canaan church.
Coram (Long Island)			1765	Noah Hammond 1765–74	Hammond was a Separate Baptist from New London, Connecticut.
Cortland			before 1769	John Lawrence	Merged with the Philipstown Baptist Church sometime after 1773.
Dover			1757	Samuel Waldo 1758–93	Organized at Pawling, New York. Divided to form a second church in 1794.
Duanesburg			1789		Set off from Canaan church.
Fishkill	1745	——— Halstead 1745–?	1782	James Philips 1782–93	Baptist church organized by men from the Philadelphia Association, but did not join this body.
Grafton					A branch of the Berlin Baptist Church.
New Concord			1791		Set off from Canaan church.
Northeast			1753	Simon Dakin 1753–1803	Organized at Philipstown, moved to Northeast in 1773. Joined Philadelphia Association in 1770.
Petersburg					A branch of the Berlin Baptist Church.
Philipstown	1751	Simon Dakin 1751–53	1753	Simon Dakin 1753–73	Dakin's group went to Northeast. Philipstown later merged with Cortland church.
Rensselaerville			1787		Set off from Canaan church.
Sandlake					A branch of the Berlin Baptist Church.
Stanford			1759	Comer Bullock 1759–1812	Formed by a colony from Swansea, Massachusetts.

Location	Date	Pastor	Notes
Southold (Long Island)	1741	James Davenport 1738–48	A regular Congregational church, led during the Great Awakening by a fanatical New Light pastor.
Warren	1789		Set off from Canaan church.
Whitesborough	1796	Stephen Parsons 1796–?	Formed by a colony from the Separate Baptist Church at Middletown, Connecticut. Became a mother of churches.

RHODE ISLAND

Location	Date	Pastor	Notes
Charlestown	1750	Samuel Niles 1750–90? James Simon 1752–?	A mixed-communion Indian church which had separated from the Congregational church at Westerly. Divided over contending pastors in 1752.
Coventry	1749	Samuel Drowne 1749–57? Peter Werden 1757–70	This was the Second Baptist Church (the First was Six-Principle). Drowne came from the Providence Separate Church, returned to pedobaptism, and went to Portsmouth, New Hampshire. Werden went to Cheshire, Massachusetts.
Coventry, West	1773	Caleb Nichols 1773–88	Nichols moved to Pownal, Vermont, and the church disbanded.
Exeter	1750	David Sprague 1750–54 Solomon Sprague 1763–94	Members were drawn from several of the older Baptist churches. Followed mixed-communion plan until 1769.
Glocester	1742	Thomas Knowlton 1742–62	Second Baptist Church. Knowlton came from the Providence Separate Church.
Greenwich, West	1750	Elisha Green 1775–97	Church not fully organized till 1773.

323

Town or Parish	Sepn Date	Separate Pastor(s)	Bapt Date	Baptist Pastor(s)	Comments
Newport, 2d Baptist Church			1742	Timothy Packom 1742–?	A Calvinistic secession from the Second Church, which was Six-Principle.
North Kingstown			1764	Philip Jenkins 1764–96?	Formed by dismission from Exeter Separate Baptist Church. Followed open-communion plan.
Providence	1743	Joseph Snow, Jr. 1746–93			Included some Baptists. Achieved permanent standing as Beneficent Congregational Church.
Richmond			1774	Benjamin Barber, Jr. 1792–96 Phineas Palmer ?–1818	A branch of the South Kingston church. Moved to Richmond, Rhode Island, 1788, and died ca. 1818.
Richmondtown			1781	Charles Boss 1781–89	A branch of the South Kingston church. Joined the Stonington Association as the Second Baptist Church of Richmond.
South Kingstown	1750	James Rodgers 1750–70 Elliott Locke 1794–1805	1781	Benjamin Weight 1781–1811	Original Separate church became three Separate Baptist churches. Its sole survivor is the First Baptist Church of South Kingston.
Warwick			1741	Benjamin Pierce 1741–51 or later Peter Werden 1751–57	Church organized by converted revivalists from the Six-Principle churches at Warwick and East Greenwich. Pierce was the one who baptized Isaac Backus. Werden went to Coventry, Rhode Island, then to Cheshire, Massachusetts.

Town	Year	Minister(s)	Remarks
Westerly	1742	Joseph Park 1742–77	Park's church, though New Light, was regular. It suffered two separations: the Indian church at Charlestown, and the First Baptist Church of Westerly. The latter included members from Stonington, and spawned two other Baptist churches in 1765 and 1790.
	1750	Stephen Babcock 1750–75, Oliver Babcock 1775–84	
VERMONT			
Andover	1803		Set off from Chester church.
Bennington	1762	Jedediah Dewey 1763–78, David Avery 1780–83, Job Swift 1786–1801	Town settled by Separates, who formed the first church in Vermont. Baptists went to Shaftsbury, organized a church in 1768. Blood's church moved to Shaftsbury in 1788 and became the Fourth Baptist Church there.
	1783	Caleb Blood 1788–1807	
Cavendish	1800		Set off from Chester church.
Chester	1789	Aaron Leland 1786–1832	The first church in the town. Set off four others by 1803.
Grafton	1803?		Set off from Chester church.
Poultney	1782	Ithamar Hibbard 1782–1802	Settled by Separates from Bennington. Included some Baptists and practiced mixed communion till 1802.
	1802	Clark Kendrick 1802–?	
Pownal	1772	Benjamin Gardner 1772–74, Francis Bennet 1782–87, Caleb Nichols 1788–1804	Organized by Separate Baptists from Shaftsbury. Nichols came from West Coventry, Rhode Island.

Town or Parish	Sepn Date	Separate Pastor(s)	Bapt Date	Baptist Pastor(s)	Comments
Shaftsbury			1768	Bliss Willoughby 1768–82 John Millington 1782–87 Cyprian Downer	Organized by Separate Baptists from Bennington. Second Baptist Church formed 1789, Third (Six-Principle) 1782. The Fourth Baptist Church, organized at Bennington 1783 and moved here 1788, was the only permanent one.
Wallingford			1780	Elisha Rich 1780–? Henry Green 1787–1807	Rich was a Separate Baptist from Chelmsford, Massachusetts. This was the only church in town till 1792.
Wethersfield			1803?		Set off from Chester church.
Woodstock			1780	Elisha Ransom 1781–?	

Summary of Map Plottings

	1	2	3	4	5	6
Connecticut	12	42	13	8	27	3
Maine	1	2	0	1	19	0
Massachusetts	17	33	7	6	36	5
Middle Colonies	0	1	0	0	3	0
New Hampshire	2	8	1	2	22	0
New York	0	6	0	2	19	0
Rhode Island	0	4	2	0	10	0
Vermont	0	2	0	0	13	0
TOTALS	32	98	23	19	149	8

Code for Above Table

1 — Temporary separation, no church organized.

2 — Separate New Light church organized.

3 — Some Separates, with or without organized Separate church, become Baptist but organize no Baptist church; may worship with a neighboring Baptist church.

4 — Separate or New Light church becomes Baptist en bloc.

5 — Separate or New Light Baptist church organized; Separate church, if any, may or may not continue.

6 — Old Light separation; may or may not form separate church (usually Episcopalian).

Numbers 1, 2, and 6 plotted on Map 1, "The Extent of Separatism," opposite p. 114.

Numbers 3, 4, and 5 plotted on Map 2, "Location of the Separate Baptists," opposite p. 256.

SOURCES

Older unpublished materials concerning separatism in eighteenth-century New England are not plentiful. Apart from the records of individual Congregational churches, few of which tell much of the story, the sources are scattered and incomplete.[1] The best single collection of documents is the Canterbury Separate Papers, three large volumes of correspondence and miscellaneous materials at the Connecticut Historical Society. These concern not only the Canterbury church but many of the ideas and events in the Strict Congregational fellowship of which it was a part. At the same place is the fascinating "Spiritual Travels of Nathan Cole," the autobiography of a Separate layman. Not many of the record books of Separate churches are extant. One of the best preserved and most informative is that of the Preston Separate Church (1747–1817), which is at the New London County Historical Society. A collection of materials concerning the Sturbridge separation is at the Congregational Library in Boston; these have been reported on recently in Ola E. Winslow, *Meetinghouse Hill* (New York, 1952). The Backus papers at Andover-Newton Theological School are a mine of information, and form the staple of Maston's work (see below).

Of the unpublished historical studies, the most useful were two dissertations. Thomas B. Maston, "The Ethical and Social Attitudes of Isaac Backus" (Yale, 1939), represents the fruit of thorough research into all the Backus materials and includes a full bibliography. Byron C. Lambert, "The Rise of the Anti-Mission Baptists: Sources and Leaders, 1800–1840" (Chicago, 1957), is a superb study in its own right and was helpful here because of its penetrating analysis of John Leland. A most perceptive paper by Lawrence Jones, a Yale graduate student, "James Davenport: Prodigal of the Great Awakening," was also useful.

PRIMARY SOURCES

This group of materials includes not only publications from the period under study but also edited collections of contemporary materials and historical works by authors near enough to the period to speak with some degree

1. The bibliography in Emil Oberholzer, *Delinquent Saints* (New York, 1956), reports on the records of nearly every Congregational church in Massachusetts dating from colonial times. For other data on church records see the various mimeographed volumes by the Historical Records Survey, e.g. *Inventory of the Church Archives of Connecticut* (Hartford, 1942).

of personal observation. It is a selected listing of only the most useful works consulted in this study. Attention should be called to the primary sources listed as "a step toward a complete bibliography of the Great Awakening" in Gaustad, *The Great Awakening in New England* (New York, 1957). Among contemporary works, Thomas Prince, *Christian History* (2 vols. Boston, 1744–45), is the most broadly informative. The theologian and sympathetic interpreter of the revival was Jonathan Edwards; see especially his *Faithful Narrative* (1737), *Distinguishing Marks* (1741), and *Thoughts on the Revival* (1742). Edwards' *Humble Inquiry* (1749) explicates his doctrine of the church and is of special importance here. Attacks on the revival and its disorders were led by Charles Chauncy, from whom *Seasonable Thoughts* (Boston, 1743) is the most comprehensive indictment.

Of the works describing the rise and spread of separatism, a few may be singled out for special emphasis. Isaac Backus is unquestionably the most important in-group writer for both Separates and Separate Baptists. His *History of New England* is a treasure of information, though much of it is poorly accessible because of inadequate indexing. (Ralph Chandler Drisko, "A New Index of Backus," *Colgate-Rochester Bulletin*, V [1933], 253–75, is no better than the one supplied by David Weston in the 1871 edition; and an adequate index of this work is still a desideratum.) Other works by Backus of special usefulness in this study are *A Discourse, A Fish Caught, A Letter to Lord,* and *A Short Description* (see list below for full titles). From the pedobaptist Separates, the most important works having more than local significance are Frothingham, *Articles of Faith and Practice*, a doctrinal exposition and practical apology; and *A Key to Unlock the Door*, a strong plea for religious liberty. Solomon Paine, *A Short View* (1752) is an early manifesto, while the *Historical Narrative and Declaration* of the Killingly Convention (1781) states the mature convictions of the Strict Congregationalists in a brief work of inestimable value. (The copy used is in the Rhode Island Historical Society.) Among the out-group writers whose polemical works give much information regarding the Separates are Devotion, *Answer of the Pastor;* Fish, *The Church of Christ;* and the two "official" publications of the Windham County ministers. The strongest attack on enthusiasm and separatism is Robert Ross (the Connecticut Chauncy!), *A Plain Address*.

AVERY, DAVID, *A Narrative of the Rise and Progress of the Difficulties which Have Issued in a Separation between the Minister and People of Bennington, 1783*, Bennington, Haswell and Russell, 1783.

BACKUS, ISAAC, *All True Ministers of the Gospel, Are Called into That Work by the Special Influences of the Holy Spirit. A Discourse Shewing the Nature and Necessity of an Internal Call to Preach the Everlasting Gospel. . . . To Which is Added Some Short Account of the Experiences and Dying Testimony of Mr. Nathanael Shepherd*, Boston, Fowle, 1754.

———— *Church History of New England, from 1620 to 1804*, Philadelphia, Baptist Tract Depository, 1839. Usually referred to as *Abridged History*.

BACKUS, ISAAC, *A Discourse, concerning the Materials, the Manner of Building, and Power of Organizing of the Church of Christ; with the true Difference and Exact Limits between Civil and Ecclesiastical Government; and also What Are, and What Are Not Just Reasons for Separation* . . . , Boston, John Boyles, 1773.

———— *The Doctrine of Sovereign Grace Opened and Vindicated: and also the Consistency and Duty of Declaring Divine Sovereignty, and Mens Impotency, while yet We Address Their Consciences with the Warnings of Truth, and Calls of the Gospel,* Providence, John Carter, 1771.

———— *A Fish Caught in His Own Net. An Examination of Nine Sermons* . . . *by Mr. Joseph Fish of Stonington* . . . , Boston, Edes and Gill, 1768.

———— "An Historical Account of Middleborough, in the County of Plymouth," *Collections of the Massachusetts Historical Society,* Ser. 1, 3 (1794), 148–53.

———— *A History of New England. With Particular Reference to the Denomination of Christians Called Baptists;* 2d ed. with notes by David Weston, 2 vols. Newton, Mass., Backus Historical Society, 1871. First published in 3 vols. 1777, 1784, 1796.

———— *The Infinite Importance of the Obedience of Faith* . . . , 2d ed. Boston, Samuel Hall, 1791.

———— *A Letter to a Gentleman in the Massachusetts General Assembly, Concerning Taxes to Support Religious Worship. From a Countryman,* n.p., 1771.

———— *A Letter to the Reverend Mr. Lord, of Norwich; Occasioned by Some Harsh Things which He Has Lately Published against Those Who Have Dissented from His Sentiments about the Ministry, the Church, and Baptism,* Providence, William Goddard, 1764.

———— *The Liberal Support of Gospel Ministers, Opened and Inculcated,* Boston, Samuel Hall, 1790.

———— *A Reply to a Piece Wrote Last Year, by Mr. Israel Holly, Pastor of a [Separate] Church in Suffield; entitled "The New-Testament Interpretation of the Old, Relative to Infant Baptism"* . . . , Newport, Solomon Southwick, 1772.

———— *A Seasonable Plea for Liberty of Conscience, against Some Late Oppressive Proceedings; Particularly in the Town of Berwick, in the County of York [Maine],* Boston, Philip Freeman, 1770.

———— *A Short Description of the Difference between the Bond-Woman and the Free, as They Are the Two Covenants.* . . . *[with] an Answer to Mr. Frothingham's Late Letter, Concerning Baptism,* Boston, Edes and Gill, 1770.

———— *The Sovereign Decrees of God, Set in a Scriptural Light* . . . , Boston, Kneeland, 1773.

———— *The Testimony of the Two Witnesses, Explained and Improved,* Providence, Bennet Wheeler, 1786.

———— *True Faith Will Produce Good Works. A Discourse, wherein Are Opened the Nature of Faith, and Its Powerful Influence on the Heart and Life; together with the Contrary Nature and Effects of Unbelief: and Answers to Various Objections* . . . , Boston, Kneeland, 1767.

Barnstable Association, *The Declaration of Ministers in Barnstable County, Relating to the Late Practice of Itinerant Preaching*, Boston, Rogers and Fowle, 1745.

BARTLET, MOSES, *False and Seducing Teachers to Be Expected in the Gospel-State, and Latter Days of the Church. And Many Shall Be Deceived by Them; with Some Marks of False Teachers, and the Danger of Following Them* . . . , New London, John Green, 1757.

BECKWITH, GEORGE, *Second Letter on the Subject of Lay-Ordination, Occasioned by Exceptions Taken on My First Letter on That Subject, in a Pamphlet, Entitled, A Word in Zion's Behalf . . . by Israel Holly, who Stiles Himself Pastor of a Congregational Church, in Suffield*, New London, T. Green, 1766.

BEEMAN, ANNA, *Three Letters to a Lady [Who Is] in Opposition to the Baptist Plan*, Norwich, John Trumbull, 1794.

BLOOD, CALEB, *A Discourse, Delivered July 11, 1811, at the Opening of the New Meeting-House, Belonging to the First Baptist Church and Society in Portland [Maine]*, Portland, J. M'Kown, 1811.

BUELL, SAMUEL, *A Faithful Narrative of the Remarkable Revival of Religion, in the Congregation of Easthampton, on Long-Island, in the Year of Our Lord, 1764* . . . , 2d ed. Sag Harbor, Alden Spooner, 1808.

Canterbury Congregational Church, *Records of the Congregational Church in Canterbury Connecticut 1711–1844*, ed. Albert C. Bates, Hartford, Connecticut Historical Society and the Society of Mayflower Descendants in the State of Connecticut, 1932. It includes records of the Canterbury Separate Church.

A Caveat against Unreasonable and Unscriptural Separations. In a Letter Sent from a Minister to Some of His Brethren, Boston, 1748.

CHAUNCY, CHARLES, *Enthusiasm Described and Caution'd against. A Sermon Preach'd at the Old Brick Meeting-House in Boston, the Lord's Day after the Commencement, 1742. With a Letter to the Reverend Mr. James Davenport*, Boston, J. Draper, 1742.

———— *The Late Religious Commotions in New-England Considered. An Answer to the Reverend Mr. Jonathan Edwards's Sermon, Entitled, The Distinguishing Marks of a Work of the Spirit of God. . . . By a Lover of Truth and Peace*, Boston, Green, Bushell, and Allen, 1743.

———— *A Letter from a Gentleman in Boston to Mr. George Wishart* . . . *Concerning the State of Religion in New-England*, Edinburgh, 1742.

———— *Seasonable Thoughts on the State of Religion in New England, a Treatise in Five Parts* . . . , Boston, Rogers and Fowle, 1743.

CLEAVELAND, JOHN, *The Chebacco Narrative Rescu'd from the Charge of Falshood and Partiality. In a Reply to the Answer Printed by Order of the*

Second Church in Ipswich . . . by a Friend of Truth, Boston, Kneeland and Green, 1738 [1748].

CLEAVELAND, JOHN, *A Plain Narrative of the Proceedings which Caused the Separation of a Number of Aggrieved Brethren from the Second Church in Ipswich: or a Relation of the Cause which Produced the Effects that Are Exhibited in the Reverend Mr. Pickering's Late Print, Intitled, A Bad Omen to the Churches*, Boston, Kneeland and Green, 1747.

———— *A Short and Plain Narrative of the Late Work of God's Spirit at Chebacco in Ipswich, in the Years 1763 and 1764 . . .* , Boston, Z. Fowle, 1767.

COLMAN, BENJAMIN, *A Letter from the Reverend Dr. Colman of Boston, to the Reverend Mr. Williams of Lebanon, upon Reading the Confession and Retractations of the Reverend Mr. James Davenport*, Boston, Rogers and Fowle, 1744.

Connecticut Colony, *Public Records of the Colony of Connecticut*, ed. Charles J. Hoadly, Hartford, Case, Lockwood and Brainard, 1874.

Connecticut General Association, *Records of the General Association of the Colony of Connecticut*, Hartford, Case, Lockwood and Brainard, 1888.

COTTON, JOHN, *Seasonable Warning to These Churches. A Narrative of the Transactions at Middleboro, in the County of Plymouth, in the Settling of a Minister in the Room of the Reverend Mr. Peter Thacher, Deceas'd . . .* , Boston, Kneeland and Green, 1746.

CROSWELL, ANDREW, *A Narrative of the Founding and Settling the New-Gathered Congregational Church in Boston with the Opposition of the South Church to the Minister, His Defence of Himself before the Council, and Expostulatory Letter to That Church Afterwards*, Boston, Rogers and Fowle, 1749.

———— *A Reply to the Declaration of a Number of the Associated Ministers in Boston and Charlestown, with Regard to the Reverend Mr. James Davenport and His Conduct*, Boston, Rogers and Fowle, 1742.

DAVENPORT, JAMES, *Confession and Retractations*, Boston, Kneeland and Green, 1744.

DEVOTION, EBENEZER, *An Answer of the Pastor and Brethren of the Third Church in Windham, to Twelve Articles, Exhibited by Several of Its Separating Members, as Reasons of Their Separation: Shewing that Said Members Have Unhappily Mistook the Occasion of Their Separation*, New London, T. Green, 1747.

EDWARDS, JONATHAN, *The Works of President Edwards*, 4 vols. New York, Robert Carter and Bros., 1881. The Worcester edition, with only minor variations.

———— *Selections from the Unpublished Writings of Jonathan Edwards, of America*, ed. Alexander B. Grosart, Privately printed in Edinburgh, 1865.

EDWARDS, MORGAN, "Materials for a History of the Baptists in Rhode Island [1771]," *Collections of the Rhode Island Historical Society*, 6 (1867), 302–70.

Exeter, New Hampshire, Association, *The Result of a Council of Ten Churches; Conven'd at Exeter, Jan. 31, 1743*, Boston, B. Green, 1744.

FERRIS, DAVID, *Memoirs of the Life of David Ferris, an Approved Minister of the Society of Friends . . . Written by Himself*, Philadelphia, Merrihew and Thompson, 1855.

FISH, JOSEPH, *The Church of Christ a Firm and Durable House. Shown in a Number of Sermons on Matth. XVI. 18. . . . the Substance of Which Was Delivered at Stonington, Anno Domini, 1765*, New London, Timothy Green, 1767.

——— *The Examiner Examined. Remarks on a Piece Wrote by Mr. Isaac Backus, of Middleborough; Printed in 1768. (Called, "An Examination of Nine Sermons . . .") Wherein Those Sermons Are Vindicated, from the Exceptions Taken against Them by Mr. Backus—Many of His Errors Confuted, and His Mistakes Corrected*, New London, Timothy Green, 1771.

FLETCHER, REUBEN, *The Lamentable State of New-England: Being an Account of the Beginning, or Original of the Separates in New-England, and Their Progress, with Their Errors and Faults. Also, an Account of the Beginning, or Original of the Standing Churches in New-England, and Their Progress, with Their Errors and Faults*, Boston, printed for the author, 1771.

Franklin Congregational Church, *Records of the Congregational Church, Franklin, Connecticut, 1718–1860*, Hartford, Society of Mayflower Descendants in the State of Connecticut and the Society of the Founders of Norwich, Connecticut, 1938.

FROTHINGHAM, EBENEZER, *The Articles of Faith and Practice, with the Covenant, That Is Confessed by the Separate Churches of Christ in General in This Land. With a Discourse, Treating upon the Great Privileges of the Church of Jesus Christ*, Newport, 1750.

——— *A Key to Unlock the Door, That Leads in, to Take a Fair View of the Religious Constitution, Established by Law, in the Colony of Connecticut . . .*, n.p., 1767.

GREENLEAF, JONATHAN, *Sketches of the Ecclesiastical History of the State of Maine from the Earliest Settlement to the Present Time*, Portsmouth, Harrison Gray, 1821.

HEMPSTEAD, JOSHUA, *Diary of Joshua Hempstead of New London, Connecticut . . .*, New London, New London County Historical Society, 1901.

Ipswich Second Congregational Church (Chebacco), *The Pretended Plain Narrative Convicted of Fraud and Partiality. Or, a Letter from the Second Church in Ipswich, to Their Separated Brethren, in Defence of Their Deceased Pastor and Themselves, against the Injurious Charges of the Said Separated Brethren, in a Late Print of Theirs . . .*, Boston, Kneeland and Green, 1748.

Killingly Convention of Strict Congregational Churches, *An Historical Nar-*

rative, and Declaration. Showing the Cause and Rise of the Strict Congre-gational Churches, in the State of Connecticut; and Their Present Views, Respecting Several Interesting Matters of a Religious Nature. Also, a Pro-fession of Their Faith; and Several Heads of Agreement, Respecting Church Discipline, Agreed upon by a Number of Strict Congregational Churches, Convened by Delegation at Killingly. September 19, 1781. To Which Is Added, an Address to the Several Churches: and a Letter upon the Sub-ject of Ordination, Providence, Bennett Wheeler, 1781.

LELAND, JOHN, *The Writings of the Late Elder John Leland, Including Some Events in His Life, Written by Himself, with Additional Sketches, &c.*, ed. Louise F. Greene, New York, G. W. Wood, 1845.

McGLOTHLIN, W. J., *Baptist Confessions of Faith*, Philadelphia, American Baptist Publication Society, 1911.

"Memoir of the Rev. Joseph Marshall," *The Adviser; or Vermont Evangelical Magazine*, 7 (1815), 193–207.

Middleborough First Congregational Church, *Book of the First Church of Christ, in Middleborough, Plymouth County, Massachusetts . . .* , Bos-ton, C. C. P. Moody, 1852.

New Haven Association, *The Declaration of the Association of the County of New-Haven in Connecticut, Conven'd at New-Haven, Feb. 19. 1744,5. Concerning the Reverend Mr. George Whitefield, His Conduct, and the State of Religion at This Day*, Boston, T. Fleet, 1745.

NILES, SAMUEL, *Tristitiae Ecclesiarum, or, a Brief and Sorrowful Account of the Present State of the Churches in New-England . . .* , Boston, J. Dra-per, 1745.

ODLIN, JOHN and WOODBRIDGE, *An Account of the Remonstrances of the Church in Exeter [New Hampshire], and of a Number of Neighboring Ministers, Against the Installment (So Term'd) of Mr. Daniel Rogers, over a Number of Separatists Belonging to Said Church . . .* , Boston, Bushell and Green, 1748.

PAINE, SOLOMON, *A Short View of the Difference between the Church of Christ, and the Established Churches in the Colony of Connecticut, in Their Foundation and Practice, with Their Ends: Being Discovered by the Word of God and Certain Laws of Said Colony, Called Ecclesiastical. With a Word of Warning to Several Ranks of Professors; and Likewise of Comfort to the Ministers and Members of the Church of Christ*, Newport, James Franklin, 1752.

PARSONS, JONATHAN, *A Needful Caution in a Critical Day. Or, The Christian Urged to Strict Watchfulness, that the Contrary Part May Have No Evil Thing to Say of Him. A Discourse Delivered at Lyme February 4th, 1741, 2*, n.p., n.d. [1742].

PERRY, WILLIAM STEVENS, ed., *Historical Collections Relating to the Amer-ican Colonial Church [Episcopal]*, 3, Hartford, the Church Press, 1873.

Philadelphia Baptist Association, *Minutes of the Philadelphia Baptist Asso-ciation, from A.D. 1707 to A.D. 1807 . . .* , ed. A. D. Gillette, Philadel-phia, American Baptist Publication Society, 1851.

PICKERING, THEOPHILUS, *A Bad Omen to the Churches of New-England: in the Instance of Mr. John Cleaveland's Ordination so Termed, over a Separation in Chebacco-Parish in Ipswich . . .* , Boston, Rogers and Fowle, 1747.

PRINCE, THOMAS, JR., *The Christian History, Containing Accounts of the Revival and Propagation of Religion in Great-Britain & America. For the Years 1743 and 1744*, 2 vols. Boston, Kneeland and Green, 1744, 1745.

ROBBINS, PHILEMON, *A Plain Narrative of the Proceedings of the Reverend Association and Consociation of New Haven County, Against the Reverend Mr. Robbins of Branford, since the Year 1741 . . .* , Boston, Kneeland and Green, 1747.

RODGERS, JOHN, "A Brief View of the State of Religious Liberty in the Colony of New York, Read before the Reverend General Convention of Delegates from the Consociated Churches of Connecticut, and the Synod of New York and Philadelphia, Met at Stamford Sept. the 1st. 1773," *Collections of the Massachusetts Historical Society*, Ser. 2, 1 (1814), 140–55.

ROOTS, PETER PHILANTHROPOS, *A Letter to the First Congregational Paedobaptist Church at Rutland in Vermont*, Hartford, Hudson and Goodwin, 1794.

ROSS, ROBERT, *A Plain Address to the Quakers, Moravians, Separatists, Separate-Baptists, Rogerenes, and Other Enthusiasts; on Immediate Impulses and Revelations, &c.*, New Haven, Parker and Company, 1762.

STILES, EZRA, "Account of a [Separate] Conference in 1752 [1753], which he wrote down after being told orally by Elder Samuel Peck of Rehoboth on August 7, 1772," *Proceedings of the Massachusetts Historical Society*, 8 (1864–65), 220–23.

—— *Extracts from the Itineraries and Other Miscellanies of Ezra Stiles, D.D., LL.D., 1755–1794, with a Selection from His Correspondence*, ed. Franklin Bowditch Dexter, New Haven, Yale University Press, 1916.

—— *The Literary Diary of Ezra Stiles, D.D., LL.D.*, ed. Franklin Bowditch Dexter, 3 vols. New York, Charles Scribner's Sons, 1901.

STILES, ISAAC, *A Looking-Glass for Changlings. A Seasonable Caveat against Meddling with Them that Are Given to Change . . .* , New London, T. Green, 1743.

—— *A Prospect of the City of Jerusalem, in It's Spiritual Building, Beauty and Glory. Shewed in a Sermon Preach'd at Hartford in His Majesty's Colony of Connecticut, May 13th, 1742, Being the Anniversary Day for Electing the Honourable the Governour, the Deputy-Governour, and the Worshipful Assistants There*, New London, T. Green, 1742.

Stonington Baptist Association, *Minutes*. Historical résumé in published minutes for 1866.

TENNENT, GILBERT, *The Danger of an Unconverted Ministry, Considered in a Sermon on Mark VI. 34*, Boston, Rogers and Fowle, 1742.

—— *The Examiner Examined, or Gilbert Tennent Harmonious. In Answer to a Pamphlet Entitled, The Examiner, or Gilbert against Tennent . . . an Essay to Vindicate the Late Glorious Work of God's Power and Grace in These Lands, from the Unreasonable Cavils and Exceptions of Said Pamphlet, and Others of Like Nature . . .* , Philadelphia, William Bradford, 1743.

The Testimony and Advice of an Assembly of Pastors of Churches in New-England, at a Meeting in Boston July 7. 1743. Occasion'd by the Late Happy Revival of Religion in Many Parts of the Land. To Which Are Added, Attestations Contain'd in Letters from a Number of Their Brethren Who Were Providentially Hinder'd from Giving Their Presence, Boston, Kneeland and Green, 1743.

The Testimony of a Number of New England Ministers Met at Boston Sept. 25. 1745. Professing the Ancient Faith of These Churches; Inviting Others Who Hold It, to Unite in Professing and Maintaining the Same; Reciting and Recommending an Excellent Act Concerning Preaching Lately Made by the General Assembly of the Church of Scotland, Boston, Kneeland and Green, 1745.

The Testimony of the Pastors of the Churches in the Province of Massachusetts-Bay in New-England, at Their Annual Convention in Boston, May 25. 1743. Against Several Errors in Doctrine, and Disorders in Practice, Which Have of Late Obtained in Various Parts of the Land; as Drawn up by a Committee Chosen by the Said Pastors, Read and Accepted Paragraph by Paragraph, and Voted to be Sign'd by the Moderator in Their Name, and Printed, Boston, Rogers and Fowle, 1743.

Todd, Jonathan, *A Defence of the Doings of the Reverend Consocation and Association of New Haven County, Respecting Mr. Philemon Robbins of Branford . . .* , n.p., 1748.

Townsend, Jonathan, *A Caveat against Strife, especially among Christian Brethren: A Sermon Preached at Medfield, Nov. the 13th. 1748,* Boston, n.p., 1749.

Trumbull, Benjamin, *A Complete History of Connecticut, Civil and Ecclesiastical,* 2 vols. New Haven, Maltby, Goldsmith, 1818.

———— "Extracts of Letters to Rev. Thomas Prince Containing Historical Notices of Sundry Towns [in Connecticut]," *Collections of the Connecticut Historical Society,* 3 (1895), 271–320.

Wadsworth, Daniel, *Diary of Rev. Daniel Wadsworth,* ed. George Leon Walker, Hartford, Case, Lockwood and Brainard, 1894.

Walker, Williston, *The Creeds and Platforms of Congregationalism,* New York, Charles Scribner's Sons, 1893.

Warren Baptist Association, *A Compendium of the Minutes of the Warren Baptist Association, from Its Formation, in 1767, to the Year 1825, Inclusive,* n.p., n.d.

———— *The Sentiments and Plan of the Warren Association,* Germantown, Christopher Sower, 1769.

Whitefield, George, *A Continuation of the Reverend Mr. Whitefield's Journal, from a Few Days after His Return to Georgia to His Arrival at Falmouth, on the 11th of March, 1741. Containing an Account of the Work of God at Georgia, Rhode-Island, New-England, New-York, Pennsylvania and South-Carolina. The Seventh Journal,* 2d ed. London, W. Strahan, 1744.

WILLIAMS, SOLOMON, *The More Excellent Way, or, The Ordinary Renewing and Sanctifying Graces of the Holy Spirit, More Excellent than All Extraordinary Gifts that Can Be Coveted or Obtained by Men,* New London, T. Green, 1742.

—————— *The Sad Tendency of Divisions and Contentions in Churches, to Bring on Their Ruin and Desolation . . . ,* Newport, James Franklin, 1750.

WILLIAMS, SOLOMON, and ELEAZAR WHEELOCK, *Two Letters from the Reverend Mr. Williams & Wheelock of Lebanon, to the Rev. Mr. Davenport, Which Were the Principal Means of His Late Conviction and Retractation. With a Letter from Mr. Davenport, Desiring Their Publication, for the Good of Others. And His Explanation of Some Passages in His Late Confession,* Boston, Kneeland and Green, 1744.

Windham County Association, *A Letter from the Associated Ministers of the County of Windham, to the People in the Several Societies in Said County,* Boston, J. Draper, 1745.

—————— *The Result of a Council of the Consociated Churches of the County of Windham: Relating to the Principles and Practices of the Several Bodies of People in Said County, Who Have Separated from the Communion of the Churches in This Land, and Set up an Uninstituted Worship among Themselves,* Boston, J. Draper, 1747.

WORCESTER, NOAH, *Impartial Inquiries, Respecting the Progress of the Baptist Denomination,* Worcester, Leonard Worcester, 1794.

WRIGHT, ELIPHALET, *The Difference between Those Called Standing Churches and Those Called Strict Congregationalists Illustrated . . . together with a Short Account of the Sentiments of Strict Congregational Churches, so Far as It Respects Gathering Churches and Church Government,* Norwich, John Trumbull, 1775 [1778].

Yale College, *Documentary History of Yale University under the Original Charter of the Collegiate School of Connecticut, 1701–1745,* ed. Franklin Bowditch Dexter, New Haven, Yale University Press, 1916.

—————— *Judgment of the Rector and Tutors of Yale-College, Concerning Two of the Students Who Were Expelled; together with the Reasons of It,* New London, T. Green, 1745.

LOCAL HISTORIES

As pointed out in the Preface, the nature of this study required large dependence on local histories. The uncritical and generally eulogistic nature of such works makes it necessary to emphasize that my use of them was limited chiefly to quotations from ecclesiastical and civil records that are not easily accessible otherwise. There are, however, a number of local histories which deserve special mention for their thoroughness and perceptiveness. By far the most useful is Larned, *History of Windham County*, which is a comprehensive study of the region where separatism was strongest. Also it devotes a hundred pages exclusively to the Separates. This part of Miss Larned's work is on a par with the monograph on the Separates by Blake, listed in the next section. Among the town histories, the more substantial works are Allen, *History of Enfield* (3 vols., with all extant records of the town and its churches); Chaffin, *History of Easton;* Denison, *Westerly and Its Witnesses;* Jennings, *Memorials of a Century* (includes a church history of Bennington, Vermont); and Waters, *Ipswich*, Vol. 2. Denison, *Notes on Baptists in Norwich*, is valuable for preserving a number of fugitive materials relevant to separatism which otherwise would have been lost.

Among the most useful church histories are Blake, *Later History of First Church, New London;* J. T. Perry, *First Church in Exeter [New Hampshire];* and G. L. Walker, *History of the First Church in Hartford.* Historical studies of individual Separate churches are few. The most eminent Separate church in Connecticut is described in Mitchell, *History of the United Church in New Haven.* The story of the college church is told with deftness and insight in Gabriel, *Religion and Learning at Yale.* The Beneficent Church in Providence is the main subject of Vose, *Sketches of Congregationalism in Rhode Island.* An historical address by Amos A. Browning on the Preston Separate Church is in the *Bi-Centennial Celebration of the First Congregational Church in Preston, Connecticut.* Means, *Sketch of the Strict Congregational Church in Enfield*, was a doctoral dissertation; though a competent study of undeniable value, its brevity attests the limitations faced by the investigator of the Separate societies, many of which were more evanescent than that at Enfield.

ALLEN, FRANCIS OLCOTT, *The History of Enfield, Connecticut. Compiled from All the Public Records of the Town Known to Exist, Covering from the Beginning to 1850*, 3 vols. Lancaster, Pa., Wickersham Printing Co., 1900.

ARNOLD, WILLET H., "Historical Sketch of the Baptist Church in Exeter [Rhode Island]," *Narragansett Historical Register*, 2 (July 1883), 1–23.

AVERY, F. D., "Historical Discourse," *The 150th Anniversary of the Organization of the Congregational Church in Columbia, Conn., October 24th, 1866* (Hartford, Case, Lockwood, 1867), pp. 5–27.

AVERY, JOHN, *History of the Town of Ledyard [Connecticut], 1650–1900*, Norwich, Noyes and Davis, 1901.

BAKER, HENRY A., *History of Montville, Connecticut, Formerly the North Parish of New London, from 1640 to 1896*, Hartford, Case, Lockwood and Brainard, 1896.

BISHOP, HENRY F., *Historical Sketch of Lisbon, Conn., from 1786 to 1900*, New York, privately printed, 1903.

BLAKE, S. LEROY, *The Later History of the First Church of Christ, New London, Connecticut*, New London, Day Publishing Co., 1900.

BRONSON, HENRY, *The History of Waterbury, Connecticut*, Waterbury, Bronson Brothers, 1858.

CAULKINS, FRANCES MANWARING, *History of New London, Connecticut*, 2d ed. New London, Author, 1860.

———— *History of Norwich, Connecticut, from Its Settlement in 1660, to January 1845*, Norwich, Thomas Robinson, 1845.

CHAFFIN, WILLIAM L., *History of the Town of Easton, Massachusetts*, Cambridge, England, University Press, 1886.

CLARK, JOSEPH SYLVESTER, *An Historical Sketch of Sturbridge, Mass., from Its Settlement to the Present Time*, Brookfield, E. and L. Merriam, 1838.

COFFIN, JOSHUA, *A Sketch of the History of Newbury, Newburyport, and West Newbury, from 1635 to 1845*, Boston, Samuel G. Drake, 1845.

CURTISS, LUCY S., *Two Hundred Fifty Years. The Story of the United Congregational Church of Bridgeport [Connecticut], 1695–1945*, Bridgeport, 1945.

DAGGETT, JOHN, *A Sketch of the History of Attleborough [Massachusetts] from Its Settlement to the Division*, Boston, Samuel Usher, 1894.

DENISON, FREDERICK, *Notes on the Baptists, and Their Principles, in Norwich, Conn., from the Settlement of the Town to 1850*, Norwich, Manning, 1857.

———— *Westerly and Its Witnesses, for Two Hundred and Fifty Years. 1626–1876*, Providence, J. A. and R. A. Reid, 1878.

DUTTON, SAMUEL W. S., *History of the North Church in New Haven . . . ,* New Haven, A. H. Maltby, 1842.

EMERY, S. HOPKINS, *The History of the Church of North Middleborough, Massachusetts*, Middleborough, Harlow and Thatcher, 1876.

Essex North Association, *Contributions to the Ecclesiastical History of Essex County, Massachusetts*, Boston, Congregational Board of Publication, 1865.

FIELD, DAVID DUDLEY, *Centennial Address, with Historical Sketches of Cromwell, Portland, Chatham, Middle-Haddam, Middletown and Its Parishes*, Middletown, William B. Casey, 1853.

Franklin, Connecticut, Congregational Church, *The Celebration of the One Hundred and Fiftieth Anniversary of the Primitive Organization of the Congregational Church and Society, in Franklin, Connecticut, October 14th, 1868*, New Haven, Tuttle, Morehouse and Taylor, 1869.

GABRIEL, RALPH HENRY, *Religion and Learning at Yale; the Church of Christ in the College and University, 1757–1957*, New Haven, Yale University Press, 1958.

"History of the Second Baptist Church [Boston]," *The Christian Watchman*, ed. E. Thresher, *17* (April 15, 1836), 62.

HUNTINGTON, B., *History of Stamford, Connecticut, from Its Settlement in 1641, to the Present Time, Including Darien*, Stamford, William W. Gillespie, 1868.

HURD, D. HAMILTON, ed., *History of Essex County, Massachusetts, with*

Biographical Sketches of Many of Its Pioneers and Prominent Men, 2 vols. Philadelphia, J. W. Lewis, 1888.

HURD, D. HAMILTON, ed., *History of Fairfield County, Connecticut* . . . , Philadelphia, J. W. Lewis, 1881.

———— *History of Middlesex County, Massachusetts* . . . , 3 vols. Philadelphia, J. W. Lewis, 1890.

———— *History of Plymouth County, Massachusetts* . . . , 2 vols. Philadelphia, J. W. Lewis, 1884.

———— *History of Worcester County, Massachusetts* . . . , 2 vols. Philadelphia, J. W. Lewis, 1889.

JENNINGS, ISAAC, *Memorials of a Century. Embracing a Record of Individuals and Events Chiefly in the Early History of Bennington, Vt. and Its First Church,* Boston, Gould and Lincoln, 1869.

KENNEY, JOEL, "Historical Sketch of the Baptist Church in Sturbridge," *Baptist Memorial and Monthly Record,* 3 (1844), 201–06.

Killingly, South Congregational Church, *History of the Congregational Church in South Killingly, Conn., with a Record of Its Doings at Its 150th Anniversary,* Danielson, Conn., Transcript Print, 1896.

LARNED, ELLEN D., *Historic Gleanings in Windham County, Connecticut,* Providence, Preston and Rounds, 1899.

———— *History of Windham County, Connecticut,* 2 vols. Worcester, Mass., Charles Hamilton, 1874.

MEANS, OLIVER WILLIAM, *A Sketch of the Strict Congregational Church of Enfield, Connecticut,* Hartford, Hartford Seminary Press, 1899.

MITCHELL, MARY HEWITT, *History of the United Church of New Haven,* New Haven, United Church, 1942.

New London Baptist Association, *Historical Sketch of the New London Baptist Association, from Its Organization in 1817, to 1850. Together with a History of the Churches of Which It Is Composed,* Boston, J. Howe, 1851.

ORCUTT, SAMUEL, *A History of the City of Bridgeport, Connecticut,* New Haven, Tuttle, Morehouse and Taylor, 1887.

———— *History of the Towns of New Milford and Bridgewater, Connecticut, 1703–1882,* Hartford, Case, Lockwood and Brainard, 1882.

PAINE, JOSIAH, *A History of Harwich, Barnstable County, Massachusetts 1620–1800. Including the Early History of That Part Now Brewster, with Some Account of Its Indian Inhabitants,* Rutland, Vt., Tuttle Publishing Co., 1937.

PALMER, ALBERT GALLATIN, "Discourse at the 100th Anniversary of the Organization of the First Baptist Church in North Stonington, Connecticut, September 20, 1843," *A Memorial of Albert Gallatin Palmer, D.D.,* ed. Edward T. Hiscox (Philadelphia, American Baptist Publication Society, 1894), pp. 167–205.

PERRY, JOHN TAYLOR, *The First Church in Exeter, New Hampshire,* Exeter, News-Letter Press, 1898.

Preston, Connecticut, Congregational Church, *The Bi-Centennial Celebration of the First Congregational Church of Preston, Connecticut, 1698–1898*, n.p., 1900.

Stiles, Henry R., *The History and Genealogies of Ancient Windsor, Connecticut; Including East Windsor, South Windsor, Bloomfield, Windsor Locks, and Ellington. 1635–1891*, Hartford, Case, Lockwood and Brainard, 1891.

Stonington, North, First Baptist Church, *Papers and Addresses Delivered at the Dedication of a Granite Memorial on the Site of the First [Baptist] Church Edifice September 23, 1934*, Westerly, R.I., Utter, 1936.

Timlow, Heman R., *Ecclesiastical and Other Sketches of Southington, Connecticut*, Hartford, Case, Lockwood and Brainard, 1875.

Trumbull, James Hammond, ed., *The Memorial History of Hartford County, Connecticut, 1633–1884*, 2 vols. Boston, Edward L. Osgood, 1886.

Vose, James Gardiner, *Sketches of Congregationalism in Rhode Island, with Special Reference to the History of the Beneficent Church*, Boston, Silver, Burdett, 1894.

Walker, George Leon, *History of the First Church in Hartford, 1633–1883*, Hartford, Brown and Gross, 1884.

Waters, Thomas Franklin, *Ipswich in the Massachusetts Bay Colony, 2*, Ipswich, Ipswich Historical Society, 1917.

Willson, Edmund B., *A Sermon Preached in Grafton, Sunday, December 27, 1846; Containing Historical Notices of the Congregational Church in Said Town*, Worcester, National Aegis, 1847.

Wood, Nathan E., *The History of the First Baptist Church of Boston (1665–1899)*, Philadelphia, American Baptist Publication Society, 1899.

Special Historical Studies

The Great Awakening is the subject of two monographs. The more recent is Gaustad, *The Great Awakening in New England*. It chronicles the events of the revival at its height but is interpretatively weak, particularly in regard to the religious significance of the movement. It hardly displaces the classic work by Tracy, *The Great Awakening*, which, if for no other reason than preserving a number of the primary documents *in toto*, is still valuable. The only study of separatism per se is Blake, *The Separates;* though a half-century old, this is still a good introduction to the subject. Hovey, *Memoir of Backus,* sheds much light on the Separate movement as well as on the conversion of Separates to Baptists. Like Tracy, it preserves a number of otherwise inaccessible rare documents. G. L. Walker, *Some Aspects of the Religious Life of New England,* is another work of ancient vintage which retains high value because of its unusual sensitivity to the subtle nuances of religious issues.

Of the many historical works by and concerning Baptists, the most useful in this study was Benedict, *General History of the Baptists,* though its massive scope, poor organization, and lack of index make it difficult to use. No other writer has gone more thoroughly into the baptismal controversy; and the first edition of 1813 is close enough to the period to make it almost a primary work, while the revised edition of 1848 is fairly sensitive to New Light and separatist origins of Baptist churches. The work of Newman, *History of Baptist Churches in the U.S.*, has not been superseded. Some of the essays in a new symposium edited by Hudson, *Baptist Concepts of the Church*, help to clarify ecclesiological issues of the eighteenth century.

Two special studies which are still of high value are Mathews, *The Expansion of New England*, for migratory movements to the frontier; and Greene, *The Development of Religious Liberty in Connecticut*, for the effect of Separate and Baptist testimony in behalf of freedom of conscience. General historical works on colonial America are not listed.

ALLEN, ALEXANDER V. G., *Jonathan Edwards*, Boston, Houghton Mifflin, 1890.

ARMSTRONG, MAURICE WHITMAN, "Religious Enthusiasm and Separatism in Colonial New England," *Harvard Theological Review*, 38 (1945), 111–40.

BACON, LEONARD, *Thirteen Historical Discourses, on the Completion of Two Hundred Years, from the Beginning of the First Church in New Haven*, New Haven, Durrie and Peck, 1839.

BAILEY, EDITH ANNA, "Influences toward Radicalism in Connecticut, 1754–1775," *Smith College Studies in History*, 5 (1920), 175–252.

BAXTER, NORMAN ALLEN, *History of the Freewill Baptists*, Rochester, American Baptist Historical Society, 1957.

BENEDICT, DAVID, *A General History of the Baptist Denomination in America, and Other Parts of the World*. 1st ed. 2 vols. Boston, Lincoln and Edmands, 1813. Idem, 2d ed. New York, Lewis Colby, 1848.

BLAKE, S. LEROY, *The Separates, or Strict Congregationalists of New England*, Boston, Pilgrim Press, 1902.

BROADUS, JOHN A., "The American Baptist Ministry of One Hundred Years Ago," *Baptist Quarterly*, 9 (1875), 1–20.

BURRAGE, HENRY S., "The Contest for Religious Liberty in Massachusetts," *Papers of the American Society of Church History*, Ser. 1, 6 (1894), 149–68.

——— *History of the Baptists in Maine*, Portland, Marks Printing House, 1904.

BUTTERFIELD, L. H., "Elder John Leland, Jeffersonian Itinerant," *Proceedings of the American Antiquarian Society*, n.s. 62 (1952), 155–242.

BUZZELL, JOHN, *The Life of Elder Benjamin Randall*, Limerick, Maine, Hobbs, Woodman, 1827.

CALDWELL, SAMUEL LUNT, *A Discourse Preached in Warren at the Completion of the First Century of the Warren Association, September 11, 1867*, Providence, Hammond, Angell, 1867.

CLARK, JOSEPH SYLVESTER, *A Historical Sketch of the Congregational*

Churches in Massachusetts, from 1620 to 1858, Boston, Congregational Board of Publications, 1858.

Contributions to the Ecclesiastical History of Connecticut, New Haven, William L. Kingsley, 1861.

COONS, PAUL WAKEMAN, *The Achievement of Religious Liberty in Connecticut,* New Haven, Yale University Press, 1936.

CROCKER, HENRY, *History of the Baptists in Vermont,* Bellows Falls, Vt., P. H. Gobie Press, 1913.

CUTTING, SEWALL SYLVESTER, *Historical Vindications: A Discourse on the Province and Uses of Baptist History . . . with Appendixes, Containing Historical Notes and Confessions of Faith,* Boston, Gould and Lincoln, 1859.

DARGAN, EDWIN CHARLES, *A History of Preaching,* Grand Rapids, Baker Book House, 1954 reprint. 1st ed., 2 vols., 1905, 1912.

DEXTER, FRANKLIN BOWDITCH, "Thomas Clap and His Writings," *Papers of the New Haven Colony Historical Society,* 5 (1894), 247–74.

DWIGHT, SERENO E., *The Life of President Edwards,* New York, G. and C. and H. Carvill, 1830.

FISHER, GEORGE PARK, *A Discourse, Commemorative of the History of the Church of Christ in Yale College, During the First Century of Its Existence,* New Haven, Thomas H. Pease, 1858.

FORD, DAVID B., *New England's Struggle for Religious Liberty,* Philadelphia, American Baptist Publication Society, 1896.

GAUSTAD, EDWIN SCOTT, *The Great Awakening in New England,* New York, Harper and Brothers, 1957.

GREENE, M. LOUISE, *The Development of Religious Liberty in Connecticut,* Boston, Houghton, Mifflin, 1905.

GREENLEAF, JONATHAN, *Memoir of Rev. Jonathan Parsons, M.A., First Pastor of the Presbyterian Church in Newburyport, Massachusetts,* Boston, T. R. Marvin, 1841.

GUILD, REUBEN ALDRIDGE, *Chaplain Smith and the Baptists; or, The Life, Journals, Letters, and Addresses of the Rev. Hezekiah Smith, D.D., of Haverhill, Massachusetts, 1737–1805,* Philadelphia, American Baptist Publication Society, 1885.

———— *Early History of Brown University, Including the Life, Times, and Correspondence of President Manning, 1756–1791,* Providence, Snow and Farnham, 1897.

HENRY, STUART C., *George Whitefield: Wayfaring Witness,* New York, Abingdon Press, 1957.

HOVEY, ALVAH, *A Memoir of the Life and Times of the Rev. Isaac Backus, A.M.,* Boston, Gould and Lincoln, 1859.

HUDSON, WINTHROP STILL, ed., *Baptist Concepts of the Church,* Philadelphia, Judson Press, 1959.

HURLIN, WILLIAM, O. C. SARGENT, and W. W. WAKEMAN, *The Baptists of*

344 SOURCES

New Hampshire, Manchester, N.H., New Hampshire Baptist Convention, 1902.

KNIGHT, RICHARD, *History of the General or Six-Principle Baptists in Europe and America,* Providence, Smith and Parmenter, 1827.

LEARNED, ROBERT C., "The Baptists in Connecticut," *New Englander, 18* (1860), 595–604.

——— "The Separatists of Eastern Connecticut," *New Englander, 11* (1853), 195–209.

MACLEAR, JAMES FULTON, "The Birth of the Free Church Tradition," *Church History, 26* (1957), 99–131.

MATHEWS, LOIS KIMBALL, *The Expansion of New England,* Boston, Houghton Mifflin, 1909.

MAXSON, CHARLES HARTSHORN, *The Great Awakening in the Middle Colonies,* Chicago, University of Chicago Press, 1920.

McCLURE, DAVID, and ELIJAH PARISH, *Memoirs of the Rev. Eleazar Wheelock, D.D., Founder and President of Dartmouth College and Moor's Charity School; with a Summary History of the College and School. To Which Are Added, Copious Extracts from Dr. Wheelock's Correspondence,* Newburyport, Edward Little, 1811.

MECKLIN, JOHN M., *The Story of American Dissent,* New York, Harcourt, Brace, 1934.

MEYER, JACOB C., *Church and State in Massachusetts from 1740 to 1833,* Cleveland, Western Reserve University Press, 1930.

MILLER, JOHN CHESTER, "Religion, Finance, and Democracy in Massachusetts," *New England Quarterly, 6* (1933), 29–58.

MILLER, PERRY, *Jonathan Edwards,* New York, William Sloane Associates, 1949.

——— *The New England Mind from Colony to Province,* Cambridge, Mass., Harvard University Press, 1953.

——— *The New England Mind: the Seventeenth Century,* New York, Macmillan, 1939.

——— *Orthodoxy in Massachusetts,* Cambridge, Mass., Harvard University Press, 1933.

——— "Solomon Stoddard, 1643–1729," *Harvard Theological Review, 34* (1941), 277–320.

MILLER, SAMUEL, *Life of Jonathan Edwards,* New York, Harper and Brothers, 1839.

MITCHELL, MARY HEWITT, *The Great Awakening and Other Revivals in the Religious Life of Connecticut,* New Haven, Yale University Press, 1934.

MORROW, RISING LAKE, *Connecticut Influences in Western Massachusetts and Vermont,* New Haven, Yale University Press, 1936.

NEWMAN, ALBERT HENRY, *A History of the Baptist Churches in the United States,* American Church History Series, 2, New York, Christian Literature, 1894.

PARKER, EDWIN POND, "The Congregationalist Separates of the Eighteenth Century in Connecticut," *Papers of the New Haven Colony Historical Society, 8* (1914), 151–61.

PURCELL, RICHARD J., *Connecticut in Transition 1775–1818*, Washington, American Historical Association, 1918.

QUINCY, JOSIAH, *The History of Harvard University, 2,* Boston, Crosby, Nichols, Lee, 1860.

SCHAFER, THOMAS A., "Jonathan Edwards' Conception of the Church," *Church History, 24* (1955), 51–66.

SMITH, JOHN E., ed., *A Treatise Concerning the Religious Affections, The Works of Jonathan Edwards, 2,* New Haven, Yale University Press, 1959.

SWEET, WILLIAM WARREN, *Revivalism in America: Its Origin, Growth and Decline,* New York, Charles Scribner's Sons, 1944.

THAYER, LUCIUS HARRISON, *The Religious Conditions of New Hampshire during the Period 1750 to 1800,* n.p., 1800.

THOMAS, ALBERT C., "James Manning and His Brave New World," *Chronicle, 13* (1950), 64–77.

TRACY, JOSEPH, *The Great Awakening. A History of the Revival of Religion in the Time of Edwards and Whitefield,* Boston, Tappan and Dennet, 1842.

TRUE, BENJAMIN OSGOOD, "Increase and Characteristics of Connecticut Baptists," *Celebration of the One Hundredth Anniversary of the First Baptist Church, Meriden, Connecticut* (Meriden, Republican Book Department, 1887), pp. 33–51.

TRUMBULL, JAMES HAMMOND, "Sons of Liberty in 1755," *New Englander, 35* (1876), 299–313.

WALKER, GEORGE LEON, "Jonathan Edwards and the Half-Way Covenant," *New Englander, 43* (1884), 600–14.

—— *Some Aspects of the Religious Life of New England with Special Reference to Congregationalists,* New York, Silver, Burdett, 1897.

WALKER, WILLISTON, *A History of the Congregational Churches in the United States,* American Church History Series, 3, New York, Christian Literature, 1894.

—— "Why Did Not Massachusetts Have a Saybrook Platform?" *Yale Review* (1892), 68–86.

WEBSTER, CLARENCE M., *Town Meeting Country,* New York, Duell, Sloan, and Pearce, 1945.

WEIS, FREDERICK LEWIS, *The Colonial Clergy and the Colonial Churches of New England,* Lancaster, Mass., Society of the Descendants of the Colonial Clergy, 1936.

WESTON, DAVID, *The Baptist Movement of a Hundred Years Ago, and Its Vindication,* Boston, Gould and Lincoln, 1868.

WHITE, EUGENE E., "Decline of the Great Awakening in New England: 1741 to 1746," *New England Quarterly, 24* (1951), 35–52.

WILSON, ARTHUR EDWARD, *Weybosset Bridge in Providence Plantations,*

1700–1790, Being an Account of a Quest for Liberty, with Portraits of Many Saints and Sinners, and a Special Study of the Reverend Joseph Snow, Jun'r, Boston, Pilgrim Press, 1947.

WINSLOW, OLA ELIZABETH, *Meetinghouse Hill, 1630–1783,* New York, Macmillan, 1952.

WRIGHT, STEPHEN, *History of the Shaftsbury Baptist Association, from 1781 to 1853; with Some Account of the Associations Formed from It, and a Tabular View of Their Annual Meetings: to Which Is Added an Appendix, Embracing Sketches of the Most Recent Churches in the Body, with Biographic Sketches of Some of the Older Ministers, and the Statistics of Most of the Churches Ever in the Association, and Their Direct Branches, to the Present Time* . . . , Troy, N.Y., A. G. Johnson, 1853.

ZEICHNER, OSCAR, *Connecticut's Years of Controversy,* Chapel Hill, University of North Carolina Press, 1949.

Abbe, Joshua, 81

Abbott's Creek Separate Baptist Church, 297

Act for Regulating Abuses (Connecticut, *1742*), 23, 59–62, 71, 87, 226, 267–68

Adams, Eliphalet, 58 n., 68

Adams, Joseph, 100, 105, 316, 321

Adams, Samuel (of Stratford), 22

Adventists, 86

Alden, Noah: Separate Baptist pastor at Bellingham, Massachusetts, 226, 253, 286; Separate Baptist pastor at Stafford, Connecticut, 228, 308; preaches at Woodstock, 228; assists at ordination of Charles Thompson, 277; relation to John Leland, 286; baptized by Shubal Stearns, 296

Alden, Samuel, 220, 261

Allen, Ethan, 146

Allen, Timothy, 30, 61, 63, 69–70, 305, 309

Allyn, Park, 304

Amenia, New York, 108, 110, 125, 143, 257

Amherst, Massachusetts, 108

Andover, Vermont, 253

Anglicanism: disapproves revivalism, 30, 100, 111–12; early defection to, 59; exempted from ecclesiastical taxes, 64, 267, 269; students in Yale College, 89; attractive to Old Lights, 111–12; in Middletown, Connecticut, 135; faces disestablishment in the South, 298

Anti-intellectualism. *See* Education and the New Lights

Antinomianism, 32, 48 n., 80, 151–54 passim, 182, 200–02

Apocalypticism, 91, 200–01

Ashford, Connecticut, 76 n., 302

Associational principle. *See* Ecclesiology, of the Regular Baptists

Assurance, doctrine of, 32, 44–45, 138

Athol, Massachusetts, 300

Atonement, doctrine of, 153

Attleborough, Massachusetts, 93–94, 201, 218, 225–26, 279 n.

Atwell, George, 302

Avery, Benjamin, 200

Avery, Christopher, 308

Avery, David, 109, 325

Avery, John, 196

Avery, Nathan, 308

Ayer, Joseph, 205

Babcock, Oliver, 325

Babcock, Stephen: leads separation at Westerly, Rhode Island, 91–92, 241, 325;

Bullock, Comer, 322
Burr, Aaron, 20
Byram, Eliab, 218

Cacapon, Virginia, 296
Callender, Elisha, 76 n., 237
Callender, John, 76 n., 225 n., 239, 240
Cambridge, Massachusetts, 97, 118, 127
Cambridge Platform (1648): on church membership and communion, 1–2, 160; on ordination, 1–2, 9; on support of ministers, 39 n.; adopted at Salisbury, Connecticut (1744), 61, at Canterbury (1743), 71–74, at Westerly, Rhode Island (1745), 90, at Bennington, Vermont (1763), 109; basic polity of the Separates, 148; Separates' exception of magistrate's authority in church affairs, 150; not strongly democratic, 288
Campbell, Robert, 90, 305
Canaan, Connecticut, 146
Canaan, New Hampshire, 252
Canaan, New York, 110, 256
Canterbury, Connecticut, 11, 82, 84, 99, 187; church organized (1711), 115
Canterbury Separate Church: organization and history, 70–75; correspondence with Enfield Separate Church, 85; correspondence with Charlestown, Rhode Island, Separate Church, 91; assists in ordinations at other Separate churches, 94, 218; Elisha Paine's leadership, 118, 121; Joseph Marshall's pastorate, 144–46; confession and covenant, 148–50; on discipline, 164–65, 167; on lay preaching, 174; sacramental occasion, 183–84; social structure, 189–90; antinomianism, 202
Cape Cod: Separate churches, 94–95, 118, 171, 198, 230, 269; Baptist churches, 230–31
Carpenter, William, 170, 230, 316
Carr, Eseck, 313
Carver, Massachusetts, 283
Case, Benajah, 87
Case, Isaac, 245, 250, 251, 311
Caulkins, Hugh, 83
Cavendish, Vermont, 253
Chaplin, Ebenezer, 316
Chapman, Eliphaz, 314
Chandler, Samuel, 181
Charleston (South Carolina) Baptist Association, 266
Charlestown, Massachusetts, 98
Charlestown, Rhode Island, 90–91
Charlton, Massachusetts, 252
Chase, Richard, 95, 230, 314
Chase, Stephen, 106
Chatham, Massachusetts, 94, 118, 230
Chauncy, Charles: severe critic of revivalism, 17, 34, of Tennent, 18 n., of Davenport, 20 n., 63 n., of Whitefield, 30; sermon at Plymouth, 113; compared with Jeremiah Condy, 237
Chebacco, 65, 98–100, 184, 206. See also Ipswich

Drowne, Samuel, 93, 105, 170, 242, 321, 323
Duanesburg, New York, 256
Dunstable, Massachusetts, 88, 118
Dunston, Maine, 108
Durham, New Hampshire, 181–82, 300
Dutartes, 132–33
Dwight, Josiah, 41
Dyer, Calvin, 71–73
Dyer, Eliphalet, 120

Eastham, Massachusetts, 94, 115, 230
Easthampton, Long Island, 11, 184–85
East Lyme, Connecticut, 78, 252, 264, 265, 266
Easton, Massachusetts, 56, 95–97, 201, 215
East Norwich, Connecticut. *See* Preston Long Society
East Windsor, Connecticut, 6, 10
Eaton, Samuel, 250
Ecclesiastical constitution. *See* Church
Ecclesiology: of the Regular Baptists, 277–78, 290–93; of the Separate Baptists, 280–81, 288–90, 299 n. *See also* Church
Economic motives of the Separate Baptists, 197 n., 268–69
Education and the New Lights: efforts to establish a seminary, 62–63; uneducated preachers preferred by frontier settlers, 107, 284; belief in immediate inspiration of the preacher, 175–76; extreme anti-intellectualism disowned, 183; suspicion of Rhode Island College, 276, 278
Edwards, Jonathan, 6, 34, 37 n., 43, 175, 203; revival of *1734–35*, 7; approves itinerancy, 10–12; doctrine of conversion, 13–14, 18, 45–46; on church membership, 160–64, 209–10
Edwards, Jonathan, Jr., 88, 191, 203, 305
Edwards, Morgan, 275, 277, 296–97
Eells, Nathaniel, 32
Eells, Nathaniel, Jr., 22, 90
Egremont, Massachusetts, 256
Eldredge, Enoch, 314
Election, doctrine of, 42–43, 137, 151–54 passim
Elvins, Richard, 107–08, 310, 317
Ely, Samuel, 187 n., 307
Emerson, Joseph, 12
Emery, Joshua, 247, 248, 310
Emotional excess, 17–27, 32, 147, 180–82
Enfield, Connecticut, 85–86, 165–66, 169, 190, 281
Enthusiasm, 19 n., 32, 48 n., 174, 182; defined, 20 n.
Episcopalians. *See* Anglicanism
Epping, New Hampshire, 104, 245, 247
Eschatology, 156, 211
Essex, Massachusetts. *See* Chebacco
Evangelistic zeal of the Separate Baptists, 282–84
Ewer, Nathaniel, 95, 230, 247, 311, 320
Ewing, William, 225, 317

Northville, Connecticut, 90
North Windham, Connecticut, 75, 81
Norton, Massachusetts, 167, 279 n., 316
Norwich Connecticut, 3, 10, 77, 78, 83–85, 124, 185, 190, 195–96, 198, 216–17, 218. *See also,* Bozrah, Franklin, Newent, Preston Long Society
Norwich Plains, Connecticut. *See* Bozrah
Nottingham, New Hampshire, 244, 246
Noyes, Joseph, 22, 61, 86, 87

"Oblong Church," 257, 321
Odlin, John, 104, 246
Odlin, Woodbridge, 104
"Old Light," defined, 33–34
Old Light separations, 111–14
Opekon, Virginia, 296
Ordination of ministers: at large, 9, 32; at Mansfield, 75–76; at Preston, 124; at Canterbury, 144; Separate view of, 150, 168, 173
Owen, John (of Groton, Connecticut), 60
Owen, John (Puritan writer), 65
Oyster Ponds, Long Island, 20

Pack, Samuel, 139
Packom, Timothy, 240, 324
Paine, Abraham, 110, 144, 321
Paine, Elisha: life, 115–23; on judging, 47–48; preaches at Canterbury, 71, 74, at Windham, 76, at Providence, 92, on Cape Cod, 94–95, 230; imprisoned at Windham, 81, at Woodstock, 185; brothers in Separate ministry, 110; on perfection, 152; "Moses" of the Separates, 115, 183; on baptismal controversy, 263; pastor at Bridgehampton, Long Island, 321
Paine, John, 94, 95, 110, 144, 170, 230, 317
Paine, Solomon: preaches at Grafton, Massachusetts, 56; on the causes of separatism, 66; leader in Canterbury separation, 71–75 passim; assists in Separate ordinations, 77, 92, 93, 94, 231, 241; brothers in Separate ministry, 110; attacked by Robert Ross, 132; attends Separate councils, 166, 170, 261–63; efforts for religious liberty in Connecticut, 171, 197, 198; pastor of Canterbury Separate Church, 183, 302; accuses Baptists of selfishness, 213; on baptismal controversy, 261–63; death, 144
Palmer, Abel, 302
Palmer, John, 81, 82, 90, 307
Palmer, Phineas, 231, 324
Palmer, Reuben, 227 n., 305
Palmer, Samuel, 232, 233, 234
Palmer, Wait, 79, 232, 236, 296, 308
Pantheistic tendencies, 151–54 passim
Paris, Maine, 251
Park, Joseph, 90, 325
Parke, Paul: life, 123–26; ordained pastor of the Preston Separate Church, 82, 176; present at Separate councils, 109, 171, 178, 198; assists with Separate ordinations, 110, 144, 168 n.; involved in baptismal controversy, 232–33
Parke, Sarah, 124

145–46, 236 n.; Separate approval of voluntary support for ministers, 129 n., 150, 155
Sutton, Massachusetts, 237 n., 281
Swansea, Massachusetts, 255
Sweet, Richard, 241
Swift, Job, 325

Talcott, Joseph, 23
Tamworth, New Hampshire, 230
Taunton, Massachusetts, 111
Taxes, ecclesiastical. *See* Coercive measures against New Lights
Taylor, James, 305
Taylor, Nathaniel, 89
Tennent, Gilbert, 21, 27 n., 68, 92, 93, 218, 275; in New England, 10; manner of preaching, 16–17; on unconverted ministers, 49–52
Testimony and Advice (prorevival), 32–33, 55, 58, 70 n., 83
Testimony of the Pastors (antirevival), 32, 55
Thacher, Peter, 218
Thacher, Peter, Jr., 93
Thomaston, Maine, 250
Thompson, Charles, 277
Thompson, Cornelius, 240 n.
Thurston, David, 315
Tingley, Peletiah, 311, 321
Titcomb, Benjamin, 311
Titicut. *See* Middleborough
Todd, Samuel, 61, 112
Toleration: in Connecticut, 143, 229, 269; in Massachusetts, 204, 213–15, 222, 267–69; in Vermont, 109 n. *See also* Religious liberty
Tolland, Connecticut, 229
Toppan, Christopher, 100, 101
Townsend, Ebenezer, 310
Tracy, Jeremiah, Jr., 84, 305
Train, Charles, 313
Trances and visions, 182
Trinity, doctrine of, 120–21, 152
Tripp, John, 283, 312
Trumbull, Jonathan, 229
Truro, Massachusetts, 230
Tucker, John, 101

Unconverted ministers, attacks on, 48–54
Universalists, 84, 158
Upham, Edward, 276 n.
Upton, Massachusetts, 118, 225
Ustick, Thomas, 302
Uxbridge, Massachusetts, 11

Vermont Baptist Association, 282 n.
Visions and trances, 182

ABOUT THE AUTHOR

C. C. Goen is professor of the history of Christianity at Wesley Theological Seminary, Washington, D.C., where he has taught since 1960. He received his Ph.D. (1960) from Yale University. Goen is the author also of *Broken Churches, Broken Nation: Denominational Schisms and the Coming of the Civil War* and editor of *The Great Awakening*, vol. 4, of *The Works of Jonathan Edwards*. He lives in Washington, D.C.